Women-Identified Women

Women–Identified Women

**EDITED BY TRUDY DARTY
AND SANDEE POTTER**

With a Foreword by Judith Schwarz

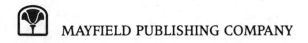 MAYFIELD PUBLISHING COMPANY

Library of Congress Catalog Card Number: 83-062837
International Standard Book Number: 0-87484-573-4

Manufactured in the United States of America
Mayfield Publishing Company
285 Hamilton Avenue
Palo Alto, California 94301

Sponsoring editor: Franklin C. Graham
Manuscript editor: Lorraine Anderson
Managing editor: Pat Herbst
Art director: Nancy Sears
Designer: Paula Schlosser
Cover designer: Nancy Sears
Cover photo: Joan E. Biren (JEB)
Production manager: Cathy Willkie
Compositor: Graphic Typesetting Service
Printer and Binder: Bookcrafters

Trudy Darty and Sandee Potter acknowledge permission of the following writers to quote from copyrighted or previously unpublished material:

Olga Broumas, "Amazon Twins," *Beginning with 0* (New Haven, Conn.: Yale University Press, 1977).

Stephanie Byrd, "I Can Feel It in My Lips," *25 Years of Malcontent* (Boston: Good Gay Poets Press, 1976).

Bernice Goodman, "How to Choose a Nonhomophobic Therapist," copyright by Bernice Goodman.

Judy Grahn, *A Woman Is Talking to Death* (Oakland, Calif.: Diana Press, 1974).

Joan Larkin, "Vagina Sonnet," *Housework* (Brooklyn, N.Y.: Out & Out Books, 1975).

Additional credits appear in the body of the text.

This anthology is lovingly dedicated to Trudy E. Darty. Although she lost her seven-year battle to cancer on May 31, 1983, she achieved her dream of completing work on this book. The tragedy of her death, at age 40, was that she wanted to write so much more.

Contents

Section Two: Oppression   117

Section Three: Culture and Community   231

Foreword

JUDITH SCHWARZ

I assume that you were browsing among the bookstore's many offerings when the cover of *Women-Identified Women* caught your eye. Or perhaps
this book is required reading for a course you are taking in sociology, wom-
en's studies, or American studies. Then again, perhaps a friend whose opinion you trust said to you, "You've got to read this book. It's important." I
will also assume that you have not read beyond these lines, which probably
means you don't know what is in store for you. Well, I am delighted to tell
you that this is not, repeat *not,* your standard dry-as-dust textbookish
anthology on yet another subgroup of the American population.

Let us celebrate this book for what it is: a warm, lively, deeply intelligent and imaginative series of articles about women who choose other
women as their sexual and affectional partners. How a woman breaks out
of the strongly reinforced prevailing heterosexual mode into the world of
the lesbian, how our society attempts to punish her for choosing a life with
women rather than men, and the rich cultural tapestry that lesbians have
woven to tell their stories—all these topics and more are examined by some
of the finest, most provocative scholars and writers now alive. Certainly,
by the time you finish this book, you will find yourself forced to reexamine
many of American society's most cherished beliefs about what a woman
really is and what she really considers important in her life. It is possible,
even probable, that you have already spent a great deal of time pondering
our society's myths and assumptions about women; still, the information
provided in these articles cannot help but challenge your own assumptions
about lesbians in particular and the implications therein for women in
general.

Lesbians are used to being the object of intense academic interest. We
don't like it, but we are certainly used to it after all these years. "Oh, no,"
we groan as we are handed another questionnaire to fill out. "Not *another*
survey!" But for all our grimacing, we still accept the forms (most of the

time), and take them home to fill out. Lesbians have a high rate of returned questionnaires compared to many other groups. We return the forms and answer the questions more often than not for the simple reason that we are just as eager to know about ourselves and each other as the researchers are. Surveys and other research methods can often give us the vital information we greatly need to live our lives in a hostile environment. We cannot learn about lesbian lives from our daily hometown newspapers—we do not find accurate or reliable portrayals there, at any rate. Therefore, we must consciously seek out one of the many lesbian, gay, and feminist periodicals published throughout this country, if we hope to find helpful and more truthful information. Some of the articles in this book were first published in these important journals. Why are we so hungry for information about each other although we are thousands of miles apart and may never meet, and although the differences in our ages may span several generations? Joan Nestle of the Lesbian Herstory Archives says it well:

> We need to know that we are not accidental, that our culture has grown and changed with the currents of time, that we, like others, have a social herstory filled with individual lives, community struggles and customs of language, dress and behavior that when looked at in their entirety form what we call herstory—the story of a people. To live with herstory is to have a memory not just of our own lives but of the lives of others whom we have never met but whose voices and actions we must be connected to. . . . We are able to find patterns both in our oppression and in our responses. We can analyze what went wrong and what went right. We are able to record the birth of new ways and to watch the dying of old ones. Herstory will make all of us feel at one time a part of the community and, at other times, deeply lonely as we watch the changes come. Having a herstory will certainly complicate issues because simplistic positions will seldom do justice to it.[1]

Each and every article within these covers is a window pouring new light upon various aspects of lesbian life, a window chipped courageously out of the solid rock walls of ignorance and fear surrounding lesbians. *Women-Identified Women* gathers together vital information on everything from birth (alternative forms of conception) to death (support groups for lesbians facing life-threatening illnesses). In one very useful book pulled together from vastly scattered sources, college students and nonstudent lesbians alike will now be able to learn more about what it means to be a lesbian in America in the 1980s.

Note

1. Joan Nestle, "Living with Herstory," keynote address for Amazon Autumn's Sixth Annual Lesbian Fall Festival, November 1982.

Preface

"We are everywhere" is a popular slogan that circulates within lesbian and gay communities. It is a slogan that carries a great degree of accuracy since homosexual women and men represent 10 to 20 percent of the American population and can be found, if they wish to be, in virtually every urban, suburban, and rural area of the country. Despite the pervasiveness of the lesbian and gay population, it is a minority group that, until recently, has been almost invisible to most heterosexuals.

Three social movements, originating in the decade of the 1960s, share the responsibility and the credit for the new visibility of lesbians and gays in American society. The social movements are, of course, the women's movement, the gay liberation movement, and the civil rights movement. All three social movements have had their goals articulated by leaders who have spoken out against discrimination and oppression and have reaffirmed the right of equality for every individual. Both the successes and the failures of these three movements have influenced the content of *Women-Identified Women*. Evidence of the successes can be found in Section One, "Identity," as well as Section Three, "Culture and Community." Examples of the failures are cited in Section Two, "Oppression."

The idea and outline for this anthology originated over cups of coffee at our kitchen table in early February 1980. After waiting nearly ten years for someone else to edit an interdisciplinary anthology on lesbians and lesbian culture that could be easily adapted for use in the college classroom, we decided to edit such a book ourselves. We began our self-appointed editorial job by surveying the available literature in both academic and lesbian publications. Predictably, some of the most comprehensive and thought-provoking articles written about lesbians were by lesbians and published in lesbian and feminist journals. This made the material almost completely inaccessible to the college professor who must rely on a university library and a copy machine for assigned classroom readings on lesbians.

Finding that many of the topics that we felt were important to include in the anthology had yet to be addressed in a nonheterosexist manner, we began looking for potential contributors. We used three different search methods. First, we sent a number of personal letters to women who were known for their knowledge in a particular area and who might be interested in writing an original article or granting permission for a specific reprint. Our second method involved sending a "call for papers" to approximately one hundred women's studies departments and programs across the country. Finally, a number of lesbian and gay academic caucuses and lesbian and gay publications cited information about the anthology and our request for papers. The National Gay Task Force was gracious enough to publish our call for papers in their newsletter, *Task Force Report,* which has a national audience of thousands.

The response to our contributor search enabled us to assemble a unique collection of articles, the majority of which are published here for the first time, written by both academics and activists. Interdisciplinary in content, the volume contains the work of sociologists, psychologists, anthropologists, psychotherapists, journalists, poets, and women wishing no other label than lesbian feminist writer. *Women-Identified Women,* then, may serve as a text in courses offered in a variety of departments, such as women's studies, sociology, psychology, social work, and counseling. As the editors of this book, we hope that it will find an audience among both students and nonstudents.

Anthologies by their very nature demand collective effort. We owe debts of gratitude to many people for their help and advice during the three-year odyssey it has taken to produce this collection of articles. The plan for the anthology might never have escaped the confines of our home had it not been for the encouragement of five very special individuals: Judith Schwarz, Judy Reagan, Honor Moore, Marty Levine, and Laud Humphreys. All five unselfishly offered suggestions and information that assisted us in our editorial tasks. We will always remain grateful.

We also wish to give our special thanks to the following: Joan Nestle and Deb Edel for sharing themselves and the resources of the Lesbian Herstory Archives; Alix Dobkin for her exceptional kindness to us and her editorial help in the area of women's music; Diane Langhorst for her unfailing support of this project and for never complaining about Potter's incessant "book" talk; Bonnie Zimmerman, Laud Humphreys, and Pauline Bart for their prepublication reviews of the manuscript; Frank Graham, our sponsoring editor at Mayfield, for his patience, cooperative nature, and editorial assistance; Juanita Swartz and Ginger Usry for cheerfully typing and retyping the manuscript; the James Madison University Library staff for their assistance in a multitude of tasks; and all the anthology's contributors, who have worked so patiently to make this book a reality.

Finally, we wish to thank Cindy, a most extraordinary daughter, for her practical contributions to this work as well as her strong positive emotional support for both of us.

Trudy Darty and Sandee Potter

The Contributors

Trudy Darty, coeditor of this anthology, was a feminist researcher and writer, a lesbian mother, a lifelong social activist and working-class change agent, a social worker, and, for seven years, a cancer patient. She is coauthor with Sandee Potter of "Social Work and the Invisible Minority: An Exploration of Lesbianism," "Challenged Women: The Interaction of Sexism and Sexuality Within the Female Cancer Experience," and "Social Work and the Lesbian Client: A Resource Guide." Reflecting her research interest in lesbian/women's health care issues, she coauthored an article included in this anthology, drawing in part from her own experience with the traditional medical establishment.

Sandee Potter, the other coeditor of this work, is Assistant Professor of Sociology at James Madison University. She received her Ph.D. from Western Michigan University in 1979. In addition to analyzing data gathered from a national survey of women-controlled health clinics, she is currently researching homophobia among mental health professionals. She has been coauthoring articles with Trudy Darty on lesbianism and health care since 1979 and has been a member of the Sociologists' Gay Caucus since its origin in 1974.

Paula Gunn Allen is a Laguna Pueblo/Lebanese American. She received a postdoctoral fellowship in American Indian studies at UCLA (1981–82) and has taught Native American literature at the University of California at Berkeley. Her writing includes five books of poetry, short stories in numerous magazines and anthologies, an edited volume entitled *Studies in American Indian Literature,* and a novel, *The Woman Who Owned the Shadows.*

Ruth Baetz has a master's degree in social work from the University of Washington and is a lesbian feminist counselor. She is the author of *Lesbian Crossroads: Personal Stories of Lesbian Struggles and Triumphs* and currently lives on Vashon Island near Seattle where she listens to the rain and watches the wildflowers grow.

Beth Brant is a Mohawk of the Turtle Clan and a lesbian writer living in Detroit. A woman of the working class, she has had her articles and poems published in *Sinister Wisdom; Common Lives/Lesbian Lives; The Greenfield Review; Native Sun; The Nation Within: An Anthology of Native American Literature,* edited by Ralph Salisbury; and *Songs from Turtle Island: An Anthology of Native American Poetry,* edited by Joseph Bruchac. Recently, Beth edited a special issue of the journal *Sinister Wisdom,* "A Gathering of Spirit," containing the written works of North American Indian women.

Christine Browning is a doctoral candidate in clinical psychology at the University of Maine at Orono. She is currently serving on the steering committee of the Association of Lesbian and Gay Psychologists and is a member of the Association for Women in Psychology. Her research, teaching, and clinical interests include lesbian and gay developmental issues, heterosexual bias against lesbians, and feminist mentoring.

Meredith Gould is Assistant Professor of Sociology at Rutgers University and has been actively involved in the Sociologists' Gay Caucus, Sociologists for Women in Society, and the Society for the Study of Social Problems. She writes on the sociologies of gender, sexuality, and law and is committed to feminism in theory and practice.

Jeannine Gramick is cofounder and codirector of New Ways Ministry, a social justice organization for the reconciliation of lesbians and gay males within the Catholic church. She directed an extensive sociological research project on the coming-out process of lesbians and coordinated the First National Symposium on Homosexuality and the Catholic Church in 1981. A member of the School Sisters of Notre Dame, she has been involved in pastoral work with lesbians and gay males since 1971.

Hilda Hidalgo is Professor of Urban Studies and Social Work at Rutgers University. She has published many articles on different aspects of the Puerto Rican experience in the United States. She is also a community activist and has received national recognition as a leader in the Hispanic community.

Melanie Kaye/Kantrowitz is the author of *We Speak in Code: Poems & Other Writings.* Her poems and writings on feminist and lesbian culture, violence and resistance, and anti-Semitism and Jewish identity are published in *Nice*

Jewish Girls: A Lesbian Anthology, Lesbian Poetry, Fight Back! Feminist Resistance to Male Violence, Calyx, New America, and *Feminary.* She received her Ph.D. from the University of California at Berkeley in 1975. She lives in Maine and teaches part-time in the Adult Degree Program at Vermont College.

Ellen Lewin received her doctorate in anthropology from Stanford University in 1975 and is currently Assistant Professor in Residence in the Medical Anthropology Program at the University of California in San Francisco. In addition to her work about lesbian mothers and on single motherhood in America, she has written on Latin American women immigrants, nursing careers and feminism, and women's health issues.

Sharon Raphael is professor of Sociology and Coordinator of the Graduate Gerontology Program at California State University, Dominguez Hills. She convened the First Conference on Lesbian and Gay Aging in 1981, which was cosponsored by California State University, Dominguez Hills, and the National Association of Lesbian and Gay Gerontologists of which she is a founding member and past national coordinator. Raphael is particularly interested in developing curriculum and promoting research on gay and lesbian aging.

Adrienne Rich is a lesbian feminist poet. Her most recent books of poetry are *The Dream of a Common Language* (1978) and *A Wild Patience Has Taken Me This Far* (1981). She has published two prose books: *Of Woman Born: Motherhood as Experience and Institution* (1976) and *On Lies, Secrets and Silence* (1979). She lives in western Massachusetts where, with the writer Michelle Cliff, she has coedited the lesbian feminist journal *Sinister Wisdom.*

Mina Robinson is an instructor in the Summer Institute of Gerontology at California State University, Dominguez Hills. The anthology article that she coauthored with Sharon Raphael is based on research conducted for her master's thesis, "The Older Lesbian." Robinson has an ongoing interest in research and teaching in the areas of lesbian aging and women and aging. She is in private practice as a feminist gerontologist in the Los Angeles area. Both Robinson and Raphael have been active in the gay and lesbian communities in the Los Angeles area, serving on the boards of directors of numerous institutions in Los Angeles and nationally for the past thirteen years.

Barbara Sang is a clinical psychologist in private practice in New York City. She has been active since 1968 in the gay and women's movements. She is codirector of the Homosexual Community Counseling Center and a member of the Association of Gay Psychologists and the Association for Women in Psychology. Sang was a member of the American Psychological Association's Task Force on the Status of Gay and Lesbian Psychologists. She has taught courses on feminist psychology at New York University and at Sagaris, an institute for the study of feminist political thought, and she has written numerous articles for professional publications on lesbian research and psychotherapy.

Beth Schneider is currently Assistant Professor of Sociology at the University of California at Santa Barbara. Her publications include "Consciousness About Sexual Harassment Among Heterosexual and Lesbian Women Workers" and "The Sexualization of the Workplace." Beth received her Ph.D. from the University of Massachusetts in 1982.

Judith Schwarz is a member of the Lesbian Herstory Archives and the Lesbian Education Foundation, Inc., and she is a cofounder of Washington, D.C.'s Lesbian Heritage. Her research, writing, and teaching interests include self-supporting spinsters and lesbians in the nineteenth and early twentieth centuries, the lives of physically challenged women, and long-term lesbian friendships and relationships. She has recently expanded the information in her book *Radical Feminists of Heterodoxy: Greenwich Village, 1912–1940* into a slide show, which she presents to college classes and community groups.

Ann Allen Shockley was born in Louisville, Kentucky, and was a newspaper reporter, freelance writer, and substitute teacher before becoming an academic librarian. Her short stories have appeared in *Black World, Essence, Freedomways, Liberator, Sinister Wisdom,* and *Azalea* as well as in many anthologies. Among the books that she has written are *Loving Her, The Black and White of It,* and *Say Jesus and Come to Me.*

Betty Steinshouer teaches a course in dyke poetry at Sojourner Truth Women's School of the Washington Area Women's Center in Washington, D.C. She has also edited and directed a production of lesbian poetry entitled "This Is Our Story: We Will Not Give it Up." Her current work in progress includes a one-woman characterization based on the life and writings of Willa Cather, tentatively titled "Mind over Nebraska."

Maida Tilchen has been a producer, publicist, tape collector, and reviewer and writer on women's music; but, most of all, she has been a constant and enthusiastic fan, feeling, as an advertisement once claimed, "the songs we hear form the soundtracks of our lives." For Maida, a lesbian journalist, women's music has been playing either quietly in the background, or thunderously across her emotional silver screen since 1973. Her writings on women's music and other topics have been appearing in Boston's *Gay Community News* since 1977.

Rose Weitz is Associate Professor of Sociology and Director of Women's Studies at Arizona State University. Her current research focuses on the background, role, and problems of lay midwives. She received her Ph.D. from Yale University and has taught at A.S.U. since 1978.

Deborah Goleman Wolf received her Ph.D. in anthropology from the University of California at Berkeley and later did postdoctoral research in medical anthropology at the University of California at San Francisco. She has been doing research in the lesbian community since 1973 and is author of *The Lesbian Community.* She recently completed a book-length manuscript entitled *Growing Older: Lesbians and Gay Men.*

Introduction

My silences had not protected me. Your silence will not protect you. But for every real word spoken, for every attempt I had ever made to speak those truths for which I am still seeking, I had made contact with other women while we examined the words to fit a world in which we all believed, bridging our differences.[1]

AUDRE LORDE

*L*esbians have been an almost invisible segment of American society for much of the twentieth century. Historians have ignored them. For example, when was the last time you read an American history book that informed you that Katherine Lee Bates, the woman who wrote "America the Beautiful," was a lesbian? Or suggested that Eleanor Roosevelt's relationship with Lorena Hickok was anything but platonic? Literary critics have chosen to either neglect the contributions of lesbian writers and poets or have failed to mention that the writers and poets being studied were lesbians (see Steinshouer article). Scholars in the field of women's studies, like academics in many other disciplines, have given only limited attention to lesbianism. As Bonnie Zimmerman has commented, "Most women's studies texts have problems integrating lesbian material into their structure because lesbianism is ghettoized; a lesbian perspective is not presented on the variety of social, cultural, and political issues explored by women's studies."[2] Finally, although sociologists and psychologists have conducted numerous studies concerning lesbians and lesbianism in recent years, their discussions of the research results, in many instances, have contained a strong heterosexist bias. An example of such a study is one by two male sociologists, who concluded that the reason some female strippers are lesbian is that the nature of their occupation discourages a meaningful male-female relationship.[3] By the same token, much of the sociological and psychological research on lesbians has been relegated to the realms of sociology of deviance or abnormal psychology.

Women-identified women, as lesbians are often called,[4] do exist, if until now in silence or as victims of misunderstanding. They are women who choose other women as their sexual and affectional partners, women whose self-concepts are independent of their relationships with men, women whose primary energies and loyalties flow toward other women. The silence that has surrounded them has, as Audre Lorde suggests, not been protective. Silence has served to isolate and separate women-identified women from each other, as well as form their common herstory and culture. Silence has also served, as silence always does, to oppress. One cannot confront or combat what is not spoken or written.

The time has come to end the silence and to affirm lesbian existence. The contributors to this anthology, both academics and activists, possess strong voices that speak knowledgeably to and for the lesbian community. Lesbians are a diverse minority group. Therefore, in an effort to move beyond the stereotyped monolithic perspective frequently presented by educators and the mass media, the articles selected for this collection reflect lesbian diversity.

The organization of the book allows the reader to first consider the psychosocial components of lesbian identity and then the resulting societal oppression with which lesbians must live. It concludes with a section on lesbian culture and community, a culture and community that has developed and flourished without requesting or receiving the approval of the larger society.

Identity

Lesbian identity, like all identities, does not develop in a social vacuum. It is the result of individual interaction within a particular society at a specific point in place and time. Personal identity is scripted by society's socialization processes. In other words, identities are socially bestowed and socially sustained. As sociologist Peter Berger explains: "Every act of social affiliation entails a choice of identity. Conversely every identity requires specific social affiliations for its survival."[5]

Clinical psychologist Christine Browning examines the multiple and complex reasons for society's maintenance of mythical assumptions about lesbians in her article, "Changing Theories of Lesbianism: Challenging the Stereotypes." She reviews the traditional theoretical positions of biology and psychoanalysis, which describe lesbianism as a singular entity manifesting specific features, and then addresses the methodological inadequacies found in the research generated by these theories. Finally, Browning presents two alternative theoretical frameworks, interactionist and feminist, which view lesbianism as a valid and healthy personal choice.

Using a multistage sequential model that spans the time from which a woman first realizes her emotional attraction to other women to self-acknowledgment as a lesbian, sociologist Jeannine Gramick considers in her article, "Developing a Lesbian Identity," how sexual behavioral attachments and committed lesbian relationships impact on the evolution of lesbian identity.

Unlike Gramick's article, which is based on empirical investigation, Ruth Baetz writes about the coming-out process from a more personal perspective. Baetz, a clinical social worker, has titled her paper "The Coming-Out Process: Violence Against Lesbians," and explains that because lesbians are forced to risk violence repeatedly in order to relate intimately with women, there can be tremendous pain and damage in lesbian lives. The fact that the violence is masked, as lesbians mistakenly believe they have power over and can control personal decisions, makes the process especially problematic.

Psychotherapist Barbara Sang discusses a number of themes that frequently emerge in lesbian relationships. Many of her observations relate to the female socialization process and to homosexual oppression. Other relationship issues reflect the development of new ways of relating as a couple so as to accommodate the needs and potentialties of both lesbian partners. In describing lesbian relationships, Sang has intentionally tried to report her observations in the language and style of her own experience as a lesbian psychotherapist.

The fifth article in this section is the first of four that focus on the triple minority status of some lesbians: being female, lesbian, and older, or being female, lesbian, and Native American or Puerto Rican. "The Older Lesbian: Love Relationships and Friendship Patterns" by gerontologists Sharon Raphael and Mina Robinson deals with the subject of intimacy and aging by studying lesbians over the age of fifty. Raphael and Robinson describe the pattern of support and the nature of relationships that exist for the lesbians in their study. Much of the data presented questions popular myths about older lesbians, especially those myths that picture the older lesbian as lonely, isolated, and without anyone to love or care about her in old age.

According to American Indian scholar Paula Gunn Allen, "Lesbian is to the American Indian what Indian is to the American—invisible." Allen's article, "Beloved Women: The Lesbian in American Indian Culture," documents the existence and experiences of Native American lesbians.

Expressing oneself through journal writing is a time-honored women's tradition, a form of recording and communication frequently available when many others are denied. Beth Brant, a lesbian mother whose heritage is a combination of Mohawk and English, uses this format to share portions of her mid-life journey, beginning with her coming out as a lesbian and progressing through her self-affirmation as a woman of color, an American

Indian. In our opinion, Brant's article, "Reclamation: A Lesbian Indian Story," serves as an excellent contemporary extension to Allen's "Beloved Women."

Lesbian activist and psychotherapist Hilda Hidalgo interviewed three hundred Puerto Rican lesbians for her article, "The Puerto Rican Lesbian in the United States." Hidalgo believes that "the Puerto Rican lesbian . . . seems to have accomplished the psychological task of clearly saying to herself, 'I am going to stay within continental U.S. society; I will *incorporate* in the larger society and in the lesbian culture. . . .' " In addition to reporting on her research regarding Puerto Rican lesbians, Hidalgo provides the reader with information on the role of psychotherapy as it relates to lesbian identity and includes psychotherapist Bernice Goodman's guidelines for selecting a nonhomophobic therapist.

Oppression

Lesbians, like members of many other minority groups, have been forced to deal with discrimination and oppression in almost every area of their daily lives. The first article in this section gives an overview of lesbian existence in a heterosexist society while the remaining five articles chronicle lesbian oppression in law, family, health care, and employment.

Adrienne Rich's essay, "Compulsory Heterosexuality and Lesbian Existence," directs attention to the bias of compulsory heterosexuality through which lesbian experience is perceived. Her essay deals extensively with two issues: first, how and why women-identified women have been invalidated and "forced into hiding and disguise"; and second, the almost total neglect of lesbian existence in scholarly feminist literature.

Lesbians share the legal problems of heterosexual women—and then some. Sociologist Meredith Gould's article, "Lesbians and the Law: When Sexism and Heterosexism Meet," discusses some of the legal problems that lesbians must confront. She notes that, while legal victories have some impact, "lesbians have learned that the virulence of negative stereotyping has often rendered the administration of justice quite useless."

On the topic of single-parent families, perhaps least is known about the lesbian mother and her children. In recent years, according to anthropologist Ellen Lewin, this type of family has been brought to the attention of the public through circumstances surrounding contested custody cases. In her paper, "Lesbianism and Motherhood: Implications for Child Custody," Lewin considers some of the assumptions that govern the decisions of the courts in custody cases involving lesbian mothers and compares them with data gathered on lesbian mothers and their families in the San Francisco Bay Area.

Since most adoption agencies do not permit unmarried women to adopt and because most lesbians do not wish to have sexual intercourse with men, many lesbians have felt that their sexual identity precludes them from having children. Deborah Goleman Wolf's article, "Lesbian Childbirth and Woman-Controlled Conception," looks at the growing use of artificial insemination, noninstitutionalized medical practices, and home births among lesbian feminists. As Wolf explains "Though the number of women using these methods is small, it is significant for it makes the choice of motherhood available to women who feel that they are strong enough and temperamentally suited to motherhood without necessarily having to be in a dependent relationship with a man."

Lesbians requesting health care from the patriarchal medical system are faced with numerous difficulties. The source of these problems can be found in the heterosexism and homophobia of the traditional medical establishment. The editors of this volume, lesbian feminist writer Trudy Darty and sociologist Sandee Potter, investigate the oppression experienced by lesbians seeking health care and some of the alternatives offered by women-controlled health clinics in their article, "Lesbians and Contemporary Health Care Systems: Oppression and Opportunity."

"Peril and Promise: Lesbians' Workplace Participation" is sociologist Beth Schneider's paper on sexualization of the workplace. Her survey research project included a sample of over two hundred lesbians employed in a variety of occupations and professions. Specific aspects of working discussed include making friends, finding a partner, coming out, and experiencing sexual harassment.

Culture and Community

Lesbians living in the United States have a national community and a culture of their own. Section Three, Culture and Community, introduces the reader to some of the dimensions of lesbian culture. This section contains five articles dealing with the politicization of the lesbian community, the contributions of literature to lesbian culture, black lesbians and literature, lesbian poetry as a reflection of the variety within the national lesbian community, and the contributions of women's music to lesbian culture.

Sociologist Rose Weitz's paper, "From Accommodation to Rebellion: The Politicization of Lesbianism," traces the development of lesbian group identity from 1956 to 1972. During those years the definitions of lesbianism were transformed. Weitz explains that the existence of a community of similar individuals encouraged the development of more positive definitions of lesbianism. To quote Weitz, "Within that community, individuals could share experiences, discover common troubles, and redefine those personal troubles as social problems. The community provided a network of significant others which helped to maintain the newly established politicized definitions. . . ."

Melanie Kaye/Kantrowitz considers what constitutes a literary classic and then points out which lesbian literary works might be regarded as classics at the beginning of the twenty-first century. "Culture-Making: Lesbian Classics in the Year 2000" provides an interesting commentary on the creation and development of classics as well as presenting the reader with information on a vast array of lesbian literary works.

Ann Allen Shockley attributes the almost total absence of black lesbians in literature to, among other reasons, white female writers not knowing enough about black lesbians to write about them, white women's literature being focused on white women, and black female writers giving top priority to the topic of racism in their writing. Shockley's article, "The Black Lesbian in American Literature: An Overview," provides a perceptive study of the presence, however limited, as well as the absence of the black lesbian in American literature.

"Without Approval: The Lesbian Poetry Tradition," written by Betty Steinshouer, documents the struggle of lesbian poets to be acknowledged and published, as well as chronicling the contribution of lesbian poetry to lesbian culture. Steinshouer's inclusion of poems by three lesbian poets (Pamela Gray, Susanna Sturgis, and Mary Ann Daly) gives the reader the opportunity to experience lesbian poetry in addition to reading about it.

The most commercially successful and, perhaps, the most cohesive component of lesbian community and culture has been women's music. It would, therefore, be an unforgivable oversight to conclude this third section of the anthology without an article on music. Lesbian journalist Maida Tilchen has shared her vast knowledge of women's music in her article, "Lesbians and Women's Music." She begins by presenting some historical information on the origins of women's music, both lesbian and heterosexual, and then goes on to discuss the content of women's music in terms of the lyrics and musical styles.

Women-Identified Women is an incomplete work. There is so much more that needs to be written, that is waiting to be written. It is impossible for this anthology or any anthology to include all the topics on which any one particular individual might wish to read. We have, therefore, included a Selected Bibliography that covers the years 1972 to 1983 and a Selected List of Lesbian Periodicals, compiled by Deborah Edel and Clare Potter.[6]

As editors of this volume, we hope that it serves as a resource as well as a reference for all those seeking information on women-identified women, but most importantly we hope that it breaks the silence. As lesbian poet Audre Lorde has so eloquently stated:

> In the cause of silence, each one of us draws the face of her own fear—fear of contempt, of censure, or some judgment, or recognition, of challenge, of annihilation. But most of all, I think, we fear that very visibility without which we also cannot truly live.[7]

Notes

1. Audre Lorde, *The Cancer Journals* (Argyle, N.Y.: Spinsters Ink, 1980), p. 20.

2. Bonnie Zimmerman, "One Out of Thirty: Lesbianism in Women's Studies Textbooks," in Margaret Cruikshank, ed., *Lesbian Studies: Present and Future* (Old Westbury, N.Y.: Feminist Press, 1982), p. 129. Two other articles that deal with the lack of lesbian visibility in women's studies are Marilyn Frye's "Assignment: NWSA—Bloomington—1980, Speak on 'Lesbian Perspectives on Women's Studies,'" *Sinister Wisdom* 14 (Summer 1980): 3–7; and Marilyn Boxer's review essay, "For and About Women: The Theory and Practice of Women's Studies in the United States," *Signs: Journal of Women in Culture and Society* 7 (Spring 1982): 661–95.

3. Charles McCaghy and James Skipper, "Lesbian Behavior as an Adaptation to the Occupation of Stripping," *Social Problems* (Fall 1969): 262–70. Sandee Potter first encountered this article when she was a graduate student in 1970. Unfortunately, it is still being cited in texts with 1981 copyright dates, like *Social Problems: Role, Institutional, and Social Perspectives* by Ronald W. Smith and Andrea Fontana (New York: Holt, Rinehart & Winston, 1981), as well as in university classrooms. We suspect that it remains popular because it feeds male fantasies.

4. The term *women-identified women* can theoretically apply to heterosexual women as well, but we use it in this anthology to apply exclusively to lesbians.

5. Peter L. Berger, *Invitation to Sociology: A Humanistic Perspective* (Garden City, N.Y.: Anchor Books, 1963), pp. 101–2.

6. Deb Edel is a member of the Lesbian Herstory Archives collective, in New York City, and Clare Potter is a member of the Circle of Lesbian Indexers.

7. Lorde, p. 21.

Section One

Identity

1

Changing Theories of Lesbianism: Challenging the Stereotypes

CHRISTINE BROWNING

*T*hroughout the history of Western civilization, negative attitudes have been expressed toward homosexuality. Multiple and complex reasons can be postulated for society's maintenance of these reactions. These reactions are intricately related to institutions of social control (religious, legal, political, economic, medical, and psychological), which historically have supported a patriarchal social structure that invalidates homosexual lifestyles and defines the context for expression of human sexuality. Deviations from heterosexual lifestyles have been met with societal sanctions in many forms. In the past, for example, both women and men have suffered extreme retribution such as burning, hanging, drowning, and beheading[1] for expressing homosexual preferences. Large numbers of homosexuals during the Nazi regime were placed in concentration camps and identified by pink triangles, just as the Jews were forced to wear yellow stars; an estimated two hundred twenty-five thousand homosexuals died in the concentration camps because of their sexual orientation.[2] Recently, prejudice against lesbians and gay men has taken other forms including employment discrimination, police harassment, court cases involving child custody suits, housing discrimination, rejection by family members and friends upon disclosing one's sexual orientation, violation of due process, limitations regarding freedom of association and speech and equal protection under the law, physical violence, and antigay rhetoric from the streets to the U.S. Senate.

Such negative responses and attitudes endure in spite of a basic shift by the psychiatric and psychological communities from seeing homosexuality as indicative of mental illness to recognizing that lesbians and gay men are not psychopathological by virtue of their sexual orientation.[3] For the most part, attitudes have been slow in changing despite the contributions of organizations that acknowledge and support the basic civil rights of lesbians and gay men and the implementation in school curricula of enlightened educational material regarding homosexuality.

One result of these initiatives has been an increase in the visibility of lesbians and gay men in society. Consequently, stereotypes regarding homosexuals are being challenged and reexamined. How did such stereotypes evolve? What factors have contributed to the acceptance of stereotypes about lesbians? In this article, I will first examine how the traditional theories of lesbianism—the biological and psychoanalytic—have contributed to the creation and maintenance of stereotypes about lesbians. These theoretical perspectives have made an initial assumption that heterosexuality is the "natural" outlet for female sexuality and thus consider lesbianism as a deviation from normality. This article will also address the methodological inadequacies found in the research generated by these theories. Second, I will present two alternative conceptualizations of lesbianism—the feminist and the symbolic interactionist theories—that assume there is nothing inherently deviant, pathological, immoral, destructive, or dysfunctional about lesbianism as a sexual preference or lifestyle.

Biological Theories of Lesbianism

The study of lesbianism from a biological perspective (defined as hormonal imbalance or genetic variation) has been alternately accepted and rejected over the years. Currently, no research evidence unequivocally implicates physiological development with sexual orientation. But this body of literature does reveal how stereotypes about the etiology of lesbianism emerged. In addition, it is crucial to consider the social/political implications of biological theories of lesbianism. For example, if researchers were able to identify specific biological determinants of homosexuality, would it follow that specific treatments (hormonal or surgical) would be developed to "cure" homosexuality? Would a biological explanation create a climate wherein systematic genocide in vitro of fetuses with a homosexual orientation would become a method to eradicate the "homosexual problem," or would society accept homosexuality as a natural biological difference akin to eye color? These are important questions to consider as consequences of this line of research.

The central hypothesis of biological theorists has been that lesbianism originates within the individual and that various biological factors are responsible for its development. Biological research, however, has yielded inconsistent conclusions. For example, sexual inversion (homosexuality) was considered by Krafft-Ebing[4] to be a cerebral anomaly indicative of an inherited diseased condition of the central nervous system. Similarly, Ellis[5] and Hirschfield[6] concluded that lesbians are born with faulty genes, thus suffering from an incurable disease. In support of a genetic theory of lesbianism, Henry and Galbraith[7] reported that lesbians exhibit a degeneration of their sexual organs, physiques, and endocrine systems. Contrary to this finding, Krafft-Ebing concluded that lesbians do not differ in physiology from heterosexual women but differ in their behaviors and patterns of interests. Both Ellis and Krafft-Ebing agreed that lesbians are more likely to display nontraditional aspirations and interests. In addition to genetic predisposition, environmental factors were seen by Ellis as significant in influencing the development of lesbianism. For example, living in sex-segregated environments, seduction by other women, experiencing disappointment in heterosexual love, or engaging in masturbation could all interact with a genetic disposition to produce lesbianism.[8]

These early medical researchers were hindered in their work by a scarcity of knowledge about hormones, sex glands, and neurology. Advancement in the area of hormonal research did not appear until the 1940s when synthetic sex hormones became available, and medical techniques used in determining genetic sex were not available until the 1950s. Hence, earlier researchers based their conclusions on extreme physical characteristics of women labeled lesbian. Most of the lesbians observed were women hospitalized in mental institutions or believed to have mental illnesses. The early works of these researchers contributed to the belief that lesbians are sick, degenerate, and controlled by excessive sexual desires.

Early sex researchers both influenced public opinion and provided the basic hypotheses for later empirical studies. As with earlier studies, the relationship between homosexuality and the distribution of sex hormones has been the subject of many research studies that have yielded inconsistent results.[9] In a review of the literature comparing testosterone levels of male homosexuals and male heterosexuals, Meyer-Bahlburgh[10] concluded that there are no distinguishable differences between the two groups. The few studies examining lesbians also do not provide any evidence for hormonal imbalances. Gartrell, Loriaux, and Chase[11] found higher levels of testosterone in lesbians than in heterosexual women; however, these levels fell within the expected range for healthy women. Griffiths et al.[12] found no difference in testosterone levels between lesbian and heterosexual women. In a review of the literature on sex hormones and lesbians, Meyer-Bahlburgh[13] maintained that based on current empirical evidence, a conclusion as to whether or not there is a neuroendocrine predisposition for sexual orientation was not possible.

Research studies examining hormone levels in women are difficult to conduct due to the effects of the various steroid hormones associated with the menstrual cycle, the influence of contraceptive steroids, and the drastic changes that occur during menopause. Not all researchers have controlled for these factors in their research methodology; hence, it is difficult to draw conclusions across studies.[14] Even if a consistent pattern of hormonal differences were found, it would remain uncertain whether the differences were a precursor or a consequence of sexual orientation. Kreuz, Rose, and Jennings[15] have posited that stress and anxiety alter the level of androgens in humans. It could be argued that the significant amount of societal oppression toward the lesbian might increase her experience of stress, thereby altering her hormone balance.

Research generated by Ehrhardt and Money[16] on the prenatal adrenogenital syndrome is often cited in biological studies on lesbianism. Females who have this syndrome have a genetic defect involving the adrenal gland, causing a hormone to be released that masculinizes the external genitalia but does not interfere with the development of the female reproductive organs. These females typically undergo surgical procedures and cortisone treatment to alleviate this condition.

Prenatal adrenogenital females are typically raised as females and exhibit a heterosexual dating and arousal pattern in spite of the effects of the syndrome, thus disconfirming theories that lesbianism is related to excessive male sex hormones. Furthermore, in childhood these females typically display a preference for cross-sex play, toys, and interests. One might speculate that some of the subjects of early sex research may have exhibited prenatal adrenogenital syndrome, leading to the hypothesis that lesbians have masculinized genitalia and male interest patterns.

In conclusion, the biological causation theory of lesbianism remains highly speculative. But it is important, in order to understand the origins of stereotypes about lesbians, to note several conclusions reached by biological theorists: (1) Lesbians are born homosexual, with an abnormality of either chromosomes, genes, or hormonal balance. (2) This congenital "disease" might cause deformities in physical appearance and attitudes, specifically mannish behaviors, attitudes, and masculinization of genitalia. (3) Certain environmental factors might elicit more homosexual behavior in a genetically predisposed individual. (4) Because lesbians are born homosexual, they are incurable and not in control of their sexual desires, hence "sick" although not necessarily sinful.

Psychoanalytic Theories of Lesbianism

Psychoanalytic theories have probably been the most influential of all hypotheses regarding the etiology of lesbianism.[17] As the fields of psychology and psychiatry developed, various theoretical positions were posited to "explain" lesbianism. Common to all these positions was the belief that lesbianism is wrong not for religious reasons (as had been maintained previously) but rather because it is indicative of mental illness, arrested psychosexual development, or constitutional inferiority.

Among the first to differ from the biological theorists was Freud, who maintained that both heredity and environment are significant factors in the development of lesbianism. Freud did not consider homosexuality to be a neurosis or a disease, nor did he consider the homosexual person to be degenerate. He stressed that homosexuals could only be considered degenerate if they "exhibited a number of serious deviations from normal behavior and if their capacity for survival and 'efficient functioning' was severely impaired."[18] Freud viewed homosexuality as a natural feature of human psychosexual development, a component of the libidinal drives of all women and men. In his essay "Female Sexuality"[19] he posited that every woman is innately bisexual and therefore can experience sexual gratification via many sources (polymorphous perverse). Hence, the search for a sexual object can take one of two paths, leading to a heterosexual or a homosexual choice. A preference by an adult for a homosexual object, however, is due to a "fixation" or arrested psychosexual development.

The development of homosexuality was thought to occur during early childhood. Two factors—parental relationships (interpreted with reference to the Electra complex) and penis envy—were central to Freud's hypothesis of the development of lesbianism. The Electra and penis envy hypotheses, however, have proven to be inadequate in explaining the origins of lesbianism or the development of female sexuality in general. As Marmor[20] concludes, no particular "family constellation" is causative, since weak fathers and dominant mothers are found in the family histories of both lesbian and nonlesbian women. With regard to the penis envy hypothesis, several authors have suggested that penis envy may be best interpreted as a woman's desire for the political, economic, and social power that the penis represents rather than for the acquisition of the male sex organ per se.[21]

An essential feature of normal female sexual development posited by Freud is the transfer of the site of orgasm from the clitoris to the vagina in order to accommodate heterosexual functioning. It was hypothesized that women who do not make this transition are not able to fully adopt a feminine identity; consequently, they remain at a less mature state of sexual development. Contrary to Freud's hypothesis, Kinsey[22] and Masters and Johnson[23] have established that all orgasms are extensions of sensations originating in the clitoris. The "myth of the vaginal orgasm"[24] has had far-reaching implications for female sexual socialization, particularly in defining female sexuality in heterosexual terms. In short, Freudian theory of female sexual development was based on incorrect knowledge of female anatomy and should be judged accordingly.

Another aspect of Freudian theory relevant to female sexuality is "feminine masochism," which was considered by Freud to be a natural expression of "feminine nature."[25] He identified passivity with femininity and masochism with passivity. Bergler[26] maintained that because the lesbian does not engage in heterosexual sadistic/masochistic relationships, she experiences female masochism through unresolved maternal conflict. This conflict is related to the lesbian's presumed inability to separate from her mother's breast; consequently, she seeks infantile gratification of oral needs through her lesbian relationships. Although Bergler viewed this as psychic masochism, Wolff[27] concluded that lesbianism is a natural outgrowth of a child's love for her mother, and suggested that lesbian partners' flexibility in being both subject and object is a positive characteristic distinguishing lesbian from heterosexual relationships.

In agreement with Freud, Wolff posited that everyone is born with a predisposition to bisexuality and recognized the impact of environmental influences in the development of sexual orientation. The lesbian is not neurotic per se, said Wolff, but because she must live a secretive lifestyle, the lesbian might be vulnerable to the development of nervous strain, anxiety, and paranoia.

In contrast, Adler[28] offered a perspective on lesbianism that reflected the position of women in society. He argued that lesbianism is a form of "masculine protest" whereby the lesbian refuses to submit to being a sexual object or in a second-class position relative to men. Thus, Adler thought that the development of a lesbian lifestyle is based on resentment of males rather than on an affirmation of women. He argued that the lesbian adopts a masculine role identity, which interferes with the psychosexual and psychosocial development of the "natural" female role.

The female role has traditionally been defined within the context of marriage and motherhood. Wolfe[29] concluded that lesbianism represents a way for women to avoid these responsibilities. He differentiated between two types of lesbians, "predatory" lesbians (women who are not heterosexually married) and women who have been or are currently married and who are mothers. "Predatory" lesbians were considered by Wolfe to be a potential threat to family life and hence a danger to society. Married women who became lesbians were viewed more compassionately because they had fulfilled their "obligations" as women.

Caprio[30] rejected certain psychoanalytic formulations and regarded narcissism as a primary drive and lesbianism as an extension of autoeroticism (through cooperative masturbation). Lesbianism, argued Caprio, is a symptom of a deep-seated neurosis related to family and environmental influences (such as psychic trauma, frustrations, homosexual seductions in childhood, and excessive use of alcohol). Caprio is considered to have written the most comprehensive account of lesbianism prior to 1954, and his work is still cited today by many psychoanalytically oriented theorists. Methodological problems, however, severely limited the accuracy of his conclusions. He based his information about lesbians on accounts from women who were in prisons or who were prostitutes, autobiographical confessions of lesbians, fictional novels, and case histories of clients with moderate to severe emotional problems. Perhaps the most unique of Caprio's "research techniques" was his use of magazine articles from explosive, confessional-type tabloids such as *My Confessions, Life Romance Magazine, Male Magazine,* and *Coronet Magazine.*[31] Thus, Caprio's conclusions about the lesbian as being intensely jealous and exhibiting sadomasochistic tendencies, strong guilt feelings, and insecurity may well be related to his particular subject and anecdotal sources.

Research generated by psychoanalytic theories of lesbianism must be examined in relation to methodological considerations. There are several research problems inherent in testing psychoanalytic hypotheses: (1) several of the concepts (such as libido, fixation, repression, sublimation, regression) are difficult to operationally define and measure; (2) most early psychoanalytic theorists lacked adequate knowledge regarding complex physiological functioning; (3) theorists did not note under what conditions or when a woman might develop a lesbian identity, or if they did so—suggesting, for example, certain family dynamics that might produce a homosexual child—they were not supported by sufficient evidence; and (4) the theories are based on evidence from nonrepresentative clinical and/or institutionalized populations and thus may be more related to irrelevant subject variables than sexual orientation and should not be generalized to describe nonpatient and noninstitutionalized populations or lesbians.

In summary, the major ideas postulated by psychoanalytic theories are that (1) human sexuality begins with a bisexual disposition, and as a result, all people experience a homoerotic phase of psychosexual development;[32] (2) homosexual tendencies reside in every individual because repression or sublimation of homosexual desires is never totally achieved;[33] (3) psychosexual development may become arrested or fixated due to an overgratification or undergratification of needs;[34] (4) multiple factors (hereditary and environmental components) are related to the development of homosexuality;[35] and (5) because homosexuality is a disease that has neurotic manifestations, it can be treated if the individual is motivated.[36]

Inadequacies of Traditional Theories

There are several important theoretical and methodological inadequacies inherent in the biological and psychoanalytic theories of lesbianism. First, most traditional theories of homosexuality have focused on sexual acts rather than on lesbian identities and lifestyles. This has created a unidimensional perspective, which in turn has contributed to a distorted view that lesbians are a homogeneous population. This has led to overgeneralizations about lesbians and has blurred the significance of individual differences among lesbians.

Second, the biological and psychoanalytic theorists have adopted the premise that the development of sexual orientation is fixed and occurs at an early developmental stage. Many biological theorists have believed sexual orientation to be fixed as a result of prenatal hormone influences that occur during the first three to four months of fetal development. The psychoanalytic theorists have typically been concerned with events during the Oedipal[37] or pre-Oedipal stages of development.[38] As a result, the traditional theories have been unable to adequately explain why women with extensive heterosexual experiences (for example, marriages) adopt a lesbian identity later in life. Similarly, traditional theorists have generally ignored sociocultural variables that may significantly influence the development of sexual orientation.

Third, there has been little differentiation in the literature among the concepts of homosexuality, transvestism, transsexualism, and pederasty. This has weakened the distinction among these concepts, thus limiting the theories' contributions to the understanding of lesbianism. Moreover, a lack of knowledge by researchers regarding the nature and relationship between gender identity, biological sex, gender roles, and sexual orientation has further complicated the contributions of these theories. Similarly, cause-and-effect relationships have been postulated about the etiology of homosexuality and the relationship between a person's gender identity and sex role behaviors, without adequate evidence.

A final criticism regarding the theoretical inadequacy of the traditional theories rests with the influence of biased social mores on their development. The early theorists were influenced by the prevailing religious values, which considered procreation as the only justification for sexual activity. Violators of this norm were considered to be either sick or sinful. In general, the traditional roles of women and men, which restricted both social and sexual behaviors, were accepted without question as part of the destiny of human experience. Hence, deviations from expected behaviors were suspect and led to speculation or investigation about their etiology. Feminist analysis would argue that the social mores of the time represented a patriarchal ideology that posed a significant barrier to the understanding of the full range of human behavior. Consequently, since this paradigm was accepted a priori by traditional theorists, their contributions are limited by this cultural bias.

In addition to the criticisms described earlier, additional methodological inadequacies are found in the research generated by the biological and psychoanalytic theories. First, evidence of several problems regarding the selection of subject samples is found in this body of literature. Nonrepresentative samples (criminals, psychiatric patients, volunteers from homophile organizations) were used, sample sizes were small, and either a lack of adequate control groups were used or control groups poorly matched to homosexual groups were used. Second, many studies used retrospective accounts by subjects and their families. Typically, the use of this technique presents a problem of interpretation, given that a person is likely to interpret past experiences in accordance with his/her present self-perceptions. Similarly, much of the traditional literature represents only psychoanalytic conceptualizations of these retrospective accounts and naturally supports a psychoanalytic interpretation of the etiology of homosexuality.[39] Further, other writers have then based their conclusions on the interpretations by psychiatrists and psychoanalysts of case histories.[40] Last, there is a tendency in the traditional literature to imply causality among events. This is particularly true in reports that examine the relationship between family dynamics and the etiology of homosexuality. In reality, family relationships are a two-way interactive process. Certain family constellations may not cause homosexuality, but rather may be a consequence of the child's effect on the parent.[41]

Beyond the Psychoanalytic Theories

As a consequence of the psychoanalytic theories, homosexuality was deemed to be a psychological disorder. Thus treatments were developed to change homosexual behavior to heterosexual behavior or at least to extinguish homosexual behavior.[42] The methods developed or used to achieve these

goals for lesbians and gay men included castration, vivisection, clitoridectomy, lobotomy, electroshock treatments, pharmacologic and hormonal
injections, and aversion therapies.[43]

Gradually, psychological researchers became more suspicious of the
early information about homosexuals that was gathered from nonrepresentative samples. Consequently, research on noninstitutionalized and nonpatient populations developed. Pioneers in the field, such as Davis,[44] Kinsey,[45] and Hooker,[46] began to accumulate evidence about lesbians and gay
men that contradicted previously held assumptions. Their research found
that most lesbians and gay men were remarkably similar to heterosexuals
with the exception of their sexual preference. Kinsey argued that homosexuality was a normal variation of sexual expression. Furthermore, he
challenged the model of human sexuality that conceived sexuality as a polar
construct with heterosexuality on one end and homosexuality on the other
end and concluded that only a very small percentage of adults could be
categorized as exclusively heterosexual or exclusively homosexual. In fact,
Kinsey found that a majority of individuals sampled had had incidental to
substantial homosexual and heterosexual experiences. Substantiating Kinsey's conclusions were Ford and Beach,[47] who examined homosexual
behavior from a cross-cultural perspective and found that some form of
homosexual behavior occurred in almost all species across all cultures.

To investigate the relationship between homosexuality and psychological functioning, several research studies were conducted using a variety of
assessment techniques (projective and objective personality measures).
Researchers, failing to find any consistent differences between homosexual
and heterosexual subjects, concluded that considering homosexuality as a
clinical entity was not justified on the basis of empirical evidence.[48]

These research conclusions contributed to the momentum of the early
lesbian/gay civil rights movement of the 1960s and 1970s. Lesbian/gay
activities challenged the psychiatric and psychological associations to carefully examine the validity of making homosexuality a diagnostic category.
In 1973, the American Psychiatric Association voted to remove homosexuality from their *Diagnostic and Statistical Manual* as a diagnostic category.
This decision was not fully accepted by all members of the psychiatric community, particularly the psychoanalysts who consider homosexuality as a
perversion of normal psychosexual development. Thus, despite the official
positions of the American Psychiatric and American Psychological Associations, significant numbers of psychiatrists and psychologists continue to
view homosexuality as a pathological condition and are able to lend professional and scientific weight to the powerful social resistance to the legitimization of lesbian/gay lifestyles.[49]

Alternative Theoretical Approaches to Lesbianism

The following theoretical positions are offered as an alternative to traditional biological and psychoanalytic formulations of lesbianism. These positions—the symbolic interactionist and feminist theories—represent the viewpoint that there is nothing inherently deviant, pathological, immoral, destructive, or dysfunctional about lesbianism as a sexual preference. Both perspectives are suited for understanding societal attitudes toward lesbianism because they examine the conditions under which lesbians become labeled deviant by society as a function of societal forces that determine "appropriate" behavior for women and men.

Symbolic Interactionist Account of Lesbianism

According to proponents of symbolic interactionist theory, the development of sexual orientation and sexual identity is an ongoing life process that involves a complex system of interaction between social and personal experiences and their acquired meanings. The interaction theorists do not view lesbian or same-sex sexual behaviors as stemming from abnormal chromosomes, hormonal imbalances, or disturbed family relations. Rather, they focus on the development of sexual orientation as a process during which certain kinds of feelings and situations are interpreted in a certain way.

Symbolic interactionists maintain that people have a varying capacity for sexual experiences, defined and limited by both a personally constructed and a socially constructed idea of sexuality. The interactionists view the development of sexual orientation as a process that emerges through interactive encounters in an intersubjective world. When examining the development of a lesbian identity, interactionists maintain that the lesbian cannot be understood in isolation from the reactions of society, which potentially stigmatize her. Similarly, in the development of a heterosexual identity, the individual experiences positive reinforcement from society to maintain these behaviors and this identity, but only when he/she follows culturally prescribed rules (for example, rapists and child molesters are not rewarded for their expressions of heterosexuality but are censured for breaking roles for heterosexual conduct).

The process of becoming sexual, like all human activities, is considered to be a learned process involving the use of symbolic gestures, language manipulation, and role-taking. Throughout the life span, learning is a two-way experience requiring the internalization and modification of ideas and life experiences. In early stages of development, the individual builds a stable self-concept through assessment of self and others, which facilitates the development of a stable world view. This world view includes a perspective on sexuality. The world view continues to be modified, and new roles and knowledge are acquired. At each stage of development, "what a person becomes—including how he behaves—will depend in large measure on the way he has been and continues to be assessed and defined by others."[50]

Particular stages in the development of a lesbian/gay identity are outlined by Plummer.[51] He suggests that the initial stage is sensitization, the first conscious or semiconscious moments in which a person comes to perceive herself as potentially a lesbian. This involves the general process of constructing new sexual meanings, modifying them, and reconstructing former meanings attached to lesbianism and heterosexuality. The individual may attempt to neutralize her lesbian potential or fortify it. When an attempt is made to neutralize, the individual may engage in same-sex sexual behavior but does not adopt a lesbian identity. This may be seen in cases of sexual behavior that occurs in prisons, sex-segregated environments, or in the context of sexual experimentation in the presence of a male partner. In these cases, most individuals maintain a commitment to heterosexual culture and create reasons to account for their sexual behavior.

If the individual does not seek to avoid a lesbian label, the next developmental stage according to Plummer is signification and disorientation. Signification involves all the actions that lead to a heightened lesbian identity or self-awareness: acquiring knowledge about lesbianism, discovering a peer group, and defining oneself as lesbian. Within the interactionist perspective, self-labeling is as crucial to the formulation of a lesbian identity as labeling by others. Labeling oneself as a lesbian and integrating that identity with other elements of personal identity facilitates the development of a positive lesbian identity.[52]

The difficulty in arriving at a positive, integrated identity is called by Plummer disorientation. This disorientation results from the negative reaction that society and the individual, by the process of socialization, have toward the lesbian label. The negative meanings attached to the lesbian label and the related social meanings of "woman" and gender roles confront the woman as she tries to stabilize her self-concept. The woman may come to view herself as others who accept the stereotypes about lesbians do. Hence, the potential for variation in the personal meaning of lesbianism is consistent with the interactionist perspective of a complex and problematic view of objective sexual reality.

The final phase in the development of a lesbian identity is stabilization. Although interactionists posit that sexual preference is an ongoing life process and not necessarily an end product, they maintain that there is considerable societal pressure to stabilize one's sexual orientation. Whether one is heterosexual or homosexual, there are social support structures that reward individuals who maintain a consistent sexual orientation. Furthermore, Plummer maintains that throughout the series of stages, the individual becomes committed to a particular sexual orientation because it is experienced as pleasurable, which serves as a positive reinforcement.

In summary, symbolic interactionists do not directly focus on causal factors in the development of a lesbian identity but consider sexual orientation as developing in a sequential manner. Critical in the interactionist perspective is that "sexual meanings do not automatically emerge; rather they are mediated through interaction with other social beings."[53] Stable sexuality and attitudes toward sexuality are possible because of the formulation of a world view and stable self-concept through the consistent, predictable interaction of the self with others.

Feminist Perspective on Lesbianism

Feminist writers describe the effect that patriarchal values have on inhibiting the independence of women and the full development of female sexuality. They describe the cultural influence on female-male relationships and offer a social rather than a biological or psychoanalytical view of lesbianism.[54] Societal sanctions imposed upon lesbians affect the freedom of all women, insofar as negative attitudes toward lesbians reflect a restriction of lifestyle choice for all women. The theme of choice and challenge to the patriarchal system is a salient concept in the feminist perspective. Furthermore, the feminist analysis of social conditions is critical in understanding how negative attitudes toward lesbians are maintained and how oppression of lesbians not only causes personal pain but also represents a political issue for both women and men of all sexual orientations.

Women's sexuality, whether expressed within lesbian or heterosexual relationships, has traditionally been defined in male terms. The feminist perspective is one that considers the emancipation of both social and sexual roles for women and men as necessary for human liberation. Laws and Schwartz[55] describe the function of sexual socialization in terms of sexual scripts. They indicate that "sexual scripting governs both sexual behavior and sexual identity . . . alternative scripts are denigrated or denied. This has the function of maintaining the dominance of the dominant or institutionalized script and preventing others from appearing as options." The institutionalized scripts have been heterosexually defined by men with specific roles for women to play.

In contrast, lesbians are women-identified women who invest their emotional, psychic, political, and sexual energies in other women and do not participate in maintaining the patriarchal status quo. Thus the lesbian poses a threat to the phallocentric power structure, which clearly defines women in terms of their relationship to men and dictates "appropriate" role behaviors for women and men. Lesbian feminists present a challenge to sexist and heterosexist assumptions because they do not view heterosexual relationships or privilege as critical for their survival or fulfillment. As a result, lesbians are free to create self-definitions that do not rely exclusively upon socially imposed female roles and are free to structure personal relationships that do not replicate the power imbalances prevalent within traditional heterosexual relationships.

In the feminist perspective, the freedom to choose a lesbian lifestyle is fundamental, regardless of the origins of one's sexual orientation. The basis for choice involves a variety of complex personal and social experiences. Women may arrive at their decisions via many paths, yet there are as many commonalities as there are differences. The bottom line is that women must be free to exercise choice without the restrictions of an externally defined set of rules that outline "appropriate" sexual behavior.

However, for women who choose women as affectional/sexual partners, there is a price to pay. In fact, lesbians experience oppression by the dominant culture for their identity and lifestyle in a variety of ways. They are excluded, for example, from legal protection against discrimination in housing, training and employment opportunities, military service, adoptions, and child custody. They cannot have access to the economic and social supports available to heterosexually married couples. They may often have to deny their existence as lesbians and their lifestyles to family, friends, and employers for fear of reprisals or rejection. Their existence is defiled by pornographers who depict lesbians as sexual creatures for the vicarious satisfaction of men, and their image is distorted to suggest that they are dangerous to other women and children. As a result they are often separated from their heterosexual sisters in the struggle against sexism.

The retributions that confront lesbians and gay men also impact upon the lives of heterosexual women and men. The fear of being labeled lesbian or gay keeps women and men in their "places" with respect to sex role behavior and also maintains the inequities in the power balance within both interpersonal relationships and the structure of society. The patriarchal values enforce a hierarchical structure that fosters classist, racist, ageist, and sexist ideology, limiting and often crushing the ability of all people to reach their full human potential.

In summary, the feminist perspective reflects the belief that sexual preference is a matter of individual choice. Choosing a lesbian lifestyle does not suggest pathology or deviance any more than does choosing a heterosexual lifestyle. Feminists recognize, however, that sexual inequality is maintained by the patriarchal value system, which stigmatizes lesbian lifestyles. Freedom from economic, social, and sexual oppression will not be achieved until all women have the fundamental right to determine how they live their lives and choose their love partners.

Impact of Theories of Lesbianism on Attitudes Toward Lesbians

The traditional biological and psychoanalytic theories of lesbianism reviewed in this article have focused on the etiology of lesbianism. These perspectives hold that lesbianism is a uniform entity that manifests certain characteristics. The process of theorizing about etiology requires conceptualizing lesbianism as a homogeneous construct, and this inherently involves overgeneralization. It is this assumption of homogeneity that has contributed to the formation of stereotypes and misconceptions about lesbians. In addition, by investigating the etiology of lesbianism and by not examining the development of heterosexuality, theorists have implicitly proposed that the development of heterosexuality is a "natural process" requiring no explanation, while homosexuality is not "natural" and must be the result of specific factors.

One of the most significant contributions of the traditional theories of lesbianism has been in describing categories that "define" the lesbian. These categories have served as the basis of stereotypes, and will be summarized here.

Lesbians and "Confused Gender Identity"

Scientific and popular misconceptions abound that lesbians are somehow confused in attitudes, appearances, and behaviors, and are thus distinctly different from nonlesbians. Traditional researchers suggest that lesbians are not "real women" but instead are "pseudomales." The biological theorists in particular have searched in vain for evidence to support the theory that within every lesbian lurks some element of masculinity whether by chromosomes, hormones, or genital disfigurement. Just as the biological theorists look for physiological evidence of masculinization, the psychoanalytic theorists look for psychological evidence of psychic impairment in the lesbian's feminine identity, causing her to adopt a masculine or confused identity. The lesbian is then labeled as either neurotic or immature, having an arrested psychosexual development.

Lesbian Sexuality

Until recently, little distinction has been made in the literature between homosexual behavior and a lesbian/gay identity. As a result, the sexual aspects of lesbianism have dominated the light in which lesbians have been and are perceived. This can be illustrated in two ways. First, individuals who engage in homosexual behavior but do not adopt a lesbian identity have been studied as if they were lesbians. Women who express same-sex sexual behavior without the corresponding lesbian identity (such as prison inmates and women in sex-segregated environments) are very different in their identities and in how they are perceived by others from those who adopt a lesbian identity.[56] Second, other nonsexual aspects of the lesbian's lifestyle have received very little attention from traditional theorists. As a result, the lesbian's concern with sexuality has been exaggerated, serving to further label her as deviant from the traditional role of women as less interested in the sexual aspects of a relationship and more concerned with the emotional qualities of a relationship. Also, when sexuality is isolated from the context of the whole person, there is a tendency to view that person as morally dangerous. Thus, the sexual mythology surrounding lesbianism provides the "justification" for institutional discrimination and persecution of lesbians.

Sexual Orientation as a Permanent State

The belief that sexual orientation is a permanent characteristic of a person's identity has significantly influenced how society perceives the lesbian as well as how the lesbian interprets her own experiences. Viewing human sexuality as a polar construct with homosexuality on one end and heterosexuality on the other accentuates the differences among people and blocks avenues for communication and mutual understanding.

A final issue involves how the theories of lesbianism have impacted on the lives of lesbians. By their influence on attitudes, theories of lesbianism have played an important role in matters regarding social acceptance. The concepts associated with lesbianism have contributed to an image or stereotype that others expect and perceive the lesbian actually to fit. As Hart and Richardson explain, "The imagery associated with lesbianism prevalent in both scientific and popular accounts of homosexuality affects homosexual women both by informing public and private opinion (thus influencing how lesbians are perceived and treated within society) and also by directly influencing how lesbians see themselves. Indeed whether the individual introjects or rejects such images, she must still take them into account in the individual meaning she ascribes to her identification as lesbian."[57]

The attitudes held by the gatekeepers of society, such as the legal, medical, psychological, educational, and informational institutions may directly affect how lesbians and gay men perceive themselves, their lifestyles, their futures, and their emotional and physical health. Effects are also felt by people related to lesbians and gay men such as parents, children, siblings, other relatives, and friends. Although attitudes held by the general society may not create the same formidable legal and institutional oppression that the gatekeepers do, they pose daily interference for the person who does not wish to hide her/his sexual orientation.

Consequently, many lesbians choose to remain hidden. This invisibility reinforces lesbian stereotypes because there are few public role models to combat the stereotypic images. As a result, society maintains its attitudes, and the individual lesbian may feel that she is the only one who experiences a discrepancy between the imagery associated with lesbianism and her own self-concept. This may lead to feelings of isolation and loneliness unless the woman has access to the lesbian community or a supportive family and friendship network.

Conclusion

Although oppression and persecution of lesbians continues today, taking a variety of subtle and not-so-subtle forms, lesbians are no longer isolated from each other in the same ways as before. Lesbians are reclaiming their herstory, establishing their culture through literature, music, art, and communities. Lesbians are sharing ideas, dreams, and energy with each other and with those who are open to hearing and learning. Lesbians are making an impact both personally, on the lives of the people they meet, and institutionally, by challenging old ways of thinking and by refusing to be victims of prejudice. Lesbians will not be pushed back into the closets or be talked about in whispers. Lesbian pride has emerged and lesbians will no longer be invisible.

Notes

1. L. Crompton, "The Myth of Lesbian Impunity: Capital Laws from 1270 to 1791," *Journal of Homosexuality* 6, nos. 1 and 2 (1980−81).

2. J. D. Steakley, *The Homosexual Emancipation Movement in Germany* (New York: Arno Press, 1975).

3. J. J. Congar, "Proceedings of the American Psychological Association, Incorporated for the Year 1974: Minutes of the Annual Meeting of the Council of Representatives," *American Psychologist* 30 (1975): 620−51.

4. R. von Krafft-Ebing, *Psychopathia Sexualis*, trans. C. Chaddock (Philadelphia, Pa.: F. A. Davis, 1884).

5. H. Ellis, *Studies in the Psychology of Sex*, vol. 1, part IV (New York: Random House, 1936).

6. M. Hirschfield, *Sexual Anomalies and Perversions* (London: Francis Aldor, 1936).

7. G. Henry and H. M. Galbraith, "Constitutional Factors in Homosexuality," *American Journal of Psychiatry* 13 (1934): 1249–79.

8. Ellis.

9. G. L. Foss, "The Influence of Androgens on Sexuality in Women," *Lancet* 1 (1951): 667–69; N. K. Gartrell, D. L. Loriaux, and T. N. Chase, "Plasma Testosterone in Homosexual and Heterosexual Women," *American Journal of Psychiatry* 34 (1977): 117–19; P. Griffiths et al., "Homosexual Women: An Endocrine and Psychological Study," *Journal of Endocrinology* 63 (1974): 549–56; F. E. Kenyon, "Homosexuality in the Female," *British Journal of Hospital Medicine* (Feb. 1970): 183–206; J. Loraine et al., "Patterns of Hormone Excretion in Male and Female Homosexuals," *Nature* 234 (1971): 552–54.

10. H. F. L. Meyer-Bahlburgh, "Sex Hormones and Male Homosexuality in Comparative Perspective," *Archives of Sexual Behavior* 6 (1977): 297–325.

11. Gartrell et al.

12. Griffiths et al.

13. H. F. L. Meyer-Bahlburgh, "Sex Hormones and Female Homosexuality: A Critical Examination," *Archives of Sexual Behavior* 8 (1979): 101–19.

14. Ibid.

15. L. Kreuz, R. Rose, and J. Jennings, "Suppression of Plasma Testosterone Levels and Psychological Stress," *Archives of General Psychiatry* 26 (1972): 479–82.

16. A. A. Ehrhardt and J. Money, "Foetal Androgens and Female Gender Identity in the Early Treated Adrenogenital Syndrome," *Johns Hopkins Medical Journal* 122 (1968): 160–67.

17. D. Tanner, *The Lesbian Couple* (Lexington, Mass.: Lexington Books, 1978).

18. R. Bayer, *Homosexuality and American Psychiatry: The Politics of Diagnosis* (New York: Basic Books, 1981).

19. S. Freud, "Female Sexuality," in J. Strachey, ed. and trans., *The Standard Edition of the Complete Psychological Works of Sigmund Freud*, vol. 21 (London: Hogarth Press, 1961).

20. J. Marmor, ed., *Sexual Inversion: The Multiple Roots of Homosexuality* (New York: Basic Books, 1965).

21. K. Horney, *New Ways in Psychoanalysis* (New York: W. W. Norton, 1939); C. Thompson, "Changing Concepts of Homosexuality in Psychoanalysis," *Psychiatry* 10 (1947): 183; C. Wolff, *Love Between Women* (New York: St. Martin's Press, 1971).

22. A. C. Kinsey et al., *Sexual Behavior in the Human Female* (Philadelphia, Pa.: Saunders, 1953).

23. W. H. Masters and V. E. Johnson, *Human Sexual Response* (Boston: Little, Brown, 1966).

24. A. Koedt, "The Myth of the Vaginal Orgasm," in S. Cox, ed., *Female Psychology: The Emerging Self* (Chicago: Science Research Associates, 1976), pp. 284–89.

25. Freud.

26. E. Bergler, *Homosexuality: A Disease or Way of Life?* (New York: Collier Books, 1956).

27. Wolff.

28. A. Adler, "The Homosexual Problem," *Alienist, Neurol* 38 (1917): 268.

29. Cited in F. Caprio, *Female Homosexuality: A Psychodynamic Study of Lesbianism* (New York: Citadel Press, 1954).

30. Caprio.

31. Caprio's magazine citations include the following: "Autobiographical Confessions of Lesbians," *My Confessions*, Sept. 1953; W. Niederfond, "Masculine Women Are Cheating Love," *Coronet Magazine*, May 1953; S. V. Lawton, "Is There a Lesbian in Your Town?" *Male Magazine*, April 1954; T.L.J. (neuropsychiatrist), "Poignant Confessions of a Lesbian," *Life Romance Magazine*, August 1953.

32. Freud; Wolff.

33. Bergler; Caprio; Freud.

34. Freud; Caprio; Bergler.

35. Wolff; Freud.

36. Caprio.

37. H. Deutsch, "On Female Homosexuality," *Psychoanalytical Quarterly* 1 (1932): 484–550; H. Deutsch, *Psychology of Women*, vol. 1 (London: Research Books, 1947); Freud.

38. M. Klein, *The Psychoanalysis of Children* (London: Hogarth Press, 1932); C. W. Socarides, "The Psychoanalytic Theory of Homosexuality with Special Reference to Therapy," in I. Rosen, ed., *Sexual Deviation*, 2d ed. (New York: Oxford University Press, 1979).

39. I. Bieber et al., *Homosexuality: A Psychoanalytic Study* (New York: Basic Books, 1962).

40. D. J. West, "Parental Figures in the Genesis of Male Homosexuality," *International Journal of Social Psychiatry* 5 (1959): 85–97.

41. R. B. Evans, "Childhood Parental Relationships of Homosexual Men," *Journal of Consulting and Clinical Psychology* 33 (1969): 129–35.

42. N. Woodman and H. Lenna, *Counseling with Gay Men and Women: A Guide for Facilitating Positive Lifestyles* (San Francisco: Jossey-Bass, 1980).

43. J. Katz, *Gay American History* (New York: Avon Books, 1976).

44. K. Davis, *Factors in the Sex Life of Twenty Two Hundred Women* (New York: Harper & Brothers, 1929).

45. Kinsey et al.

46. E. Hooker, "The Adjustment of the Male Overt Homosexual," *Journal of Projective Techniques* 21 (1957): 18–31; E. Hooker, "Male Homosexuality in the Research," *Journal of Projective Techniques* 22 (1958): 33–54.

47. C. Ford and F. Beach, *Patterns of Sexual Behavior* (New York: Harper & Row, 1951).

48. V. Armon, "Some Personality Variables in Overt Female Homosexuality," *Journal of Projective Techniques* 24 (1960): 292–309; M. Freedman, *Homosexuality and Psychological Functioning* (Monterey, Calif.: Brooks/Cole, 1971); J. H. Hopkins, "The Lesbian Personality," *British Journal of Psychiatry* 115 (1969): 1433–

36; Hooker; M. T. Saghir and E. Robins, *Male and Female Homosexuality: A Comprehensive Investigation* (Baltimore, Md.: Williams & Wilkins, 1973); M. Seligman, "Adjustment of Homosexual and Heterosexual Women," *British Journal of Psychiatry* 20 (1972): 477–81; C. Thompson, "Changing Concepts of Homosexuality in Psychoanalysis," *Psychiatry* 10 (1947): 183.

49. Bayer.

50. R. Quinney, *The Social Reality of Crime* (Boston: Little, Brown, 1970), p. 244.

51. K. Plummer, *Sexual Stigma: An Interactionist Account* (London: Routledge & Kegan Paul, 1975).

52. B. Berzon and R. Leighton, eds., *Positively Gay* (Millbrae, Calif.: Celestial Arts, 1979).

53. Plummer.

54. For example, see Radicalesbians, "The Woman-Identified Woman," in A. Koedt, E. Levine, and A. Rapone, eds., *Radical Feminism* (New York: Quadrangle Books, 1973), pp. 240–45; S. de Beauvoir, *The Second Sex* (New York: Alfred Knopf, 1952).

55. J. L. Laws and P. Schwartz, *Sexual Scripts: The Social Construction of Female Sexuality* (New York: Holt, Rinehart & Winston, 1977), p. 13.

56. Tanner.

57. J. Hart and D. Richardson, eds., *The Theory and Practice of Homosexuality* (London: Routledge & Kegan Paul, 1981), p. 112.

2

Developing a
Lesbian Identity

JEANNINE GRAMICK

*T*he first stage of the coming-out process for lesbians and gay men is the formation of a homosexual identity. Before a person can *come out* or reveal a same-sex orientation to family members, friends, work associates, members of the gay community, or the general public, the individual must have some understanding or awareness of her or his homosexual orientation. How does a lesbian arrive at this first understanding of her sexual identity? Does her process of self-identification differ from that of a gay male? I undertook a study of lesbianism with these questions in mind. This article discusses earlier research on this topic, and the subjects, methods, and findings of my own study, within an interactionist theoretical framework.

Definitions of Coming Out

There are many definitions and descriptions of coming out. In the late 1960s, coming out was viewed as a single event or a debut, the first time a homosexually oriented individual identified herself or himself as such to another person. Such a coming out could occur, for instance, in a gay bar setting.[1] The event of coming out was defined in terms of contact with the gay or lesbian subculture; it was a "discovery by the individual that other homosexuals exist, alone and organized in groups, and the subsequent participation in their activities or at least the initiation of some contact with them."[2] Sociologists Gagnon and Simon were the first to recognize that the individual is the initial audience in the coming-out process. They define

Research for this article was supported in part by two grants awarded by the National Institute of Health and Human Services to Dignity/San Diego and to New Ways Ministry, Mt. Rainier, Maryland.

coming out as "that point in time when there is self-recognition by the individual of his [*sic*] identity as a homosexual and the first major exploration of the homosexual community."[3] Dank's study in 1971 was the first systematic and empirical attempt to examine those social conditions by which males learn or decide that they are homosexually oriented.[4] Males begin to view themselves in a new category, that of being homosexual, and use various social contexts to enable such self-identifications. In the opinions of these researchers, coming out seems to occur at a distinct point in time and always in the social environment of the homosexual subculture.

Contrary to the descriptions of coming out offered by these early researchers, my research as well as other studies indicates that coming out to oneself need not occur in the socializing context of the lesbian or gay community. Particularly with lesbians, self-identification and acceptance as homosexually oriented occur prior to involvement and membership in the homosexual subculture.[5] More recent researchers also stress the process notion of coming out, rather than defining it as occurring at a discrete point in time. They describe coming out as "the process through which gay women and men recognize their sexual preference and choose to integrate this knowledge into their personal and social lives."[6] Others describe it as an "emergent identification with homosexuality and growing self-awareness as a homosexual."[7] These approaches emphasize the personal elements in the coming-out process; the social backdrop becomes secondary in importance.

In the late 1970s Lee traced the complete coming-out process through three chronological stages: signification or naming oneself as homosexual, coming out, and going public.[8] He further subdivided each stage into steps, although each individual does not necessarily pass through each step. Lee's stages can be applied to males but make little sense for women. For example, one step in the signification stage, the "anonymous sex" of gay males in parks or restrooms, highway stops or steam baths, is virtually unknown in the lesbian experience. My research indicates that lesbians require emotional bonds before any sexual involvement is initiated.[9] Similarly, the term that Lee uses as the final step of the signification stage, *closet queen*, reveals a masculine bias. This term can be applied to some gay males but never to lesbians. Lee's coming-out stage incorporates not only the concept of debut but also regular involvement in the gay subculture of bars and liberation groups and knowledge of one's sexual orientation by heterosexual friends and work associates. Lee's stage of going public involves an ideological and political stance demonstrated not only by identification in the public media but also by frequent public articulation as a spokesperson for gay concerns.

Another conceptualization of the process of becoming homosexual, developed by Plummer, also involves stages: sensitization, signification, coming out, and stabilization. His description of sensitization strongly resembles some of Lee's steps in his signification stage. While conceptually distinct, Plummer's first two stages prove empirically difficult to distinguish. In his framework, coming out involves being " 'reborn' into the organized aspects of the homosexual community."[10] Although an individual may come to a self-understanding of identity before any contact with the gay world, Plummer believes that interaction with other self-acknowledged homosexuals is crucial in providing coping mechanisms to resolve problems and conflicts that arise in the sensitization and signification stages.

Schäfer defines coming out as a "self-discovery . . . process of perceiving one's self as lesbian."[11] Within this developmental process Schäfer investigates progressive stages: from a "particular interest" in women to the first suspicion of being lesbian to the first physical sexual contact with a woman to the certainty of being lesbian. Other researchers suggest three stages leading to self-identification as homosexually oriented: (1) realization of same-sex desires, (2) initial sexual experience, and (3) acknowledgment of lesbian orientation.[12]

As one can see from the above account, researchers take various approaches to coming out. Although Lee's signification stage is similar to Dank's and to Schäfer's concepts of coming out, different researchers define coming out in different ways. I describe coming out as a continual developmental process of sexual self-discovery and self-revelation of same-sex preferences. Although I prefer Lee's broad categories of signification, coming out, and going public, I identify different components within each of those stages. This article focuses on the first stage, signification or sexual self-identification. For a young female or male coming to an awareness of a homosexual identity, which conflicts with established sexual norms, the process is invariably characterized by anguish, frustration, confusion, or denial, and may often be postponed until postadolescence. A strong sense of sexual identity, no matter how long it may take to achieve, is a prerequisite for the unfolding of psychosocial intimacy.

An Interactionist Theory of Lesbian Signification

The first step in developing a theory to understand the process of arriving at a lesbian signification or lesbian identity is to investigate "those first conscious and semi-conscious moments in which an individual comes to perceive of himself [*sic*] potentially as a homosexual."[13] In hindsight one may construct sexual meanings to explain events, feelings, or actions apparently devoid of sexual content at the time of occurrence. Rather than intuitively and automatically knowing he or she is homosexually oriented, an individual relies on a post hoc interpretation of previous factors to come to an understanding of a same-sex identification. An interactionist must analyze the social situations that influence an individual to give a sexual meaning to her/his responses to feelings, fantasies, and experiences.

Because sexuality is intimately connected to genital or other kinds of physical expression and emotional or affectional content, these sources provide clues to naming oneself as homosexual. For example, strong affectional or emotional attachments to individuals of the same sex, frequent fantasies of a same-sex erotic nature or intense same-sex physical or romantic attractions may provide a basis for later reflection on the possibility of a homosexual orientation. However, a homosexual meaning is not immediately imputed to such experiences. Meanings are continually being modified and reconstructed.

Initially females do not impute a lesbian interpretation to strong emotional bonds or attachments to other females, to an early preference for female company, to a sense of more comfortableness with women, or to a certain "warm feeling" associated with female friendships. Romantic feelings or crushes on teachers or girlfriends and sexual dreams or fantasies only later assume a homosexual translation. For example, some young girls may fantasize about "rescuing the princess from the dragon." While some heterosexual girls may collect photos and scrapbooks of their favorite male movie celebrities, others may express "mad passions" for some female stars. Gradually, through interaction with peers, adults, and the social milieu, the young female begins to sense a feeling of "being different." From television, books, magazines, school discussions, or even hushed conversations with peers, she learns that lesbians exist in society. Though she may cognitively understand the nature of homosexuality, she still does not render any homosexual meaning to her own initial clues.

In adolescence, her physical or erotic attractions become more manifest. She may "fall in love with" a woman, without attempting to satisfy any of her sexual attractions. Since she is socialized into heterosexual social roles and behavior by a strong emphasis on heterosexual dating during this period, homosexual identification is obscured or delayed. Repression or even denial of same-sex feelings and attractions may result from societal expectations, particularly from family and peers, of heterosexual patterns. Because she operates primarily in the heterosexual and heterosocial world, which insists that female sexual satisfaction is dependent upon a male, she does not recognize her own homosexual sources. She may even marry heterosexually or become physically involved with a male. Eventually, however, the young woman encounters others known by her to be homosexually oriented. It is at this point and thereafter that potential sources of homosexual signification become more evident.

Although other social factors undoubtedly come into play, those inter-actions that are most explicitly sexual in nature directly influence a homo-sexual self-conception. Sexual attachments and sexual commitments con-firm increasing suspicions of a lesbian identity. That is, genital behavior and establishment of a physical relationship with another woman directly influence the woman to identify herself as lesbian.

In many instances well-grounded friendships may exist for several years before the advent of a physical relationship. Although some women have described their first lesbian relationships as "stormy," "unhealthy," or "a disaster," the experience is generally helpful and meaningful, often val-idating a homosexual lifestyle, increasing the woman's self-esteem and self-acceptance as a lesbian. Lesbian relationships often break down because of social coercion to conform to "normal" heterosexual patterning, family pressure or family commitments, lack of social support for the isolated lesbian couple, guilt, or rejection of a homosexual orientation. As in het-erosexual couple situations, other factors may include jealousy or possess-iveness, lack of communication, political or value differences, alcoholism, death of one partner, or a third-person disruption of the relationship.

"From an interactionist perspective, however, an important part is likely to be played by identification with significant others who enable an individual either to neutralize his [sic] homosexual potential or to build it up. The strength of the drive is less important than access to supportive others!" asserts Plummer.[14] "Access to supportive others" may, but does not generally, include an active participation in the homosexual subculture prior to the stabilization of a lesbian identity. Unlike males, homosexual as well as heterosexual females tend to interact socially in small, private set-tings. Lesbian sexual behavior generally precedes involvement in the homo-sexual community "by a considerable period of time."[15] For the most part, then, a young woman makes the acquaintance of her lesbian partners in nongay circumstances; for example, through introduction to relatives, friends, or neighbors, in work situations, at social gatherings, or at school or rec-reational activities. During the entire first stage of the coming-out period, social problems of isolation and loneliness confront most lesbians. Without benefit of a reference group to lend support and to provide occasions for communication and discussion of similar problems and concerns with others, it is remarkable that most lesbians cope with their growing social-sexual awareness as well as they do.

After many years of increasing suspicions coupled with denial and repression, the woman is ready to make a lesbian declaration. There is no blinding revelation, only the gradual, increasing awareness by which the woman finally admits, "I am a lesbian." She comes to recognize that her relationships with males have been less fulfilling than her same-sex ones; no "fireworks" occur with men in comparison to her female encounters. She concedes a desire to be "special" to another woman, just as her adolescent girlfriends yearned to be first in the affections of some male.

A lesbian self-declaration does not imply achievement of complete self-acceptance. As a conflictual period of the coming-out process, acknowledgment of one's lesbian orientation is usually characterized by an emotional reaction of happiness on the one hand and troubled feelings with fear regarding the future on the other. Although feelings of guilt are uncommon and disgust rare, there is still relatively little calm or feeling of pride at the final realization and self-admission of a lesbian orientation.[16]

The process of arriving at a lesbian identity is constantly modified and negotiated through social interactions, but the roles played by supportive others contribute most significantly to a homosexual construction. In particular, episodic sexual encounters as well as longer-lasting sexual relationships provide the social context by which a lesbian signification develops. While such a theory seems plausible, what empirical data can be advanced to support it?

Collecting Data

In addition to providing a means to test the interactionist theory just described, my research was also designed to correct two critical deficiencies of previous sociological surveys involving lesbians. First, most of these previous studies included respondents who were self-stated lesbians; they did not employ any techniques to determine the actual sexual orientation of their volunteer subjects.[17] One study incorporated a self-rating index of sexual orientation and reported that 12 percent of the sample rated themselves bisexual or more heterosexual than lesbian; however, the 12 percent was then included in the "lesbian data" analysis![18] The same substantive criticism can be leveled against Masters and Johnson, who further obfuscate results by limiting their definition of sexual orientation to sexual performance and behavior.[19] Only one previous study eliminated respondents with a heterosexual or bisexual orientation from the sample data.[20]

In reality, all individuals' sexual feelings, fantasies, and behaviors vary from opposite-sex to same-sex along a continuum, but it is necessary to establish some distinction between homosexual and heterosexual orientations for statistical purposes. For my research, the method of determining sexual orientation was based on three indices adapted from Kinsey's homosexual-heterosexual continuum and the CHEER Sexual Orientation Rating

Scale.[21] The three indices were (1) sexual feelings and attractions, (2) romantic or erotic dreams or fantasies, and (3) physical/genital behavior. Each of the three scales could be rated 1 (only opposite sex), 2 (predominantly opposite sex), 3 (equally opposite and same sex), 4 (predominantly same sex), 5 (only same sex). For example, the woman was asked to consider her sexual feelings and attractions over her entire life span and to rate them (1, 2, 3, 4, or 5) according to the above criteria. The woman was then asked to evaluate her erotic fantasies, using the same range (1 through 5). Similarly, a score was determined for her physical/genital behavior. If the respondent's average score on these three rating scales was at least 3.3, she was designated homosexually oriented.[22]

Second, in scientific studies of homosexuality, sampling is virtually always a problem since it is impossible to identify clearly the total homosexual population. How representative a sample of the lesbian population can be obtained when so many lesbians are reluctant to disclose the fact of their sexual orientation? The most covert and quiescent lesbians are most assuredly underrepresented in all homosexual samples to date. Many closet lesbians refuse to be interviewed. Even though the foregoing sampling problems are formidable, sociological reports of lesbians could be based on more diverse samples. Previous studies have incorporated samples with disproportionate numbers of younger women, probably because younger lesbians seem more open about their orientation and therefore more accessible to researchers. Few subjects in their forties or fifties have been included while the median age of most lesbian samples is mid-twenties.[23] Black women are neglected by researchers on lesbianism.[24]

From a pilot study I obtained abundant data on middle-class Protestant lesbians but little or no data on lesbian mothers. In an effort to improve upon previous skewed samples, I particularly attempted to include in my investigation a fair representation of lesbians relative to age, race, ethnic background, religion, economic class, and maternal status.

Between February and May 1979, personal interviews with 118 women in the Baltimore-Washington, D.C. area were conducted by a team of 6 qualified interviewers. One male interviewer met only with those women who indicated agreement or comfortableness with a male interviewer. Interviewees were not paid for their time, which usually involved approximately one and a half hours. Eighteen women were evaluated as bisexual or predominantly heterosexual in orientation. The data I discuss in this article were obtained from 97 of the 100 lesbians—the 97 who responded to all questions concerning initial homosexual awareness and same-sex socializing patterns.

Demographic Characteristics of Participants

Black women constituted 24 percent of the sample, in sharp contrast with previous studies of lesbians, which utilized almost exclusively Caucasian samples. A little over two-thirds of this sample (68 percent) were Caucasian while 2 percent were Hispanic. Although the representation of Catholic (17 percent), Protestant (22 percent), and Jewish (4 percent) subjects occurred in expected proportions, half the participants indicated no current religious affiliation.[25] Forty percent of the sample earned an annual personal income of less than $7,000 while only 7 percent made $26,000 or more. The women in the sample ranged in age from 18 to 76 with approximately half (47 percent) the sample between 18 and 29, and almost a third (31 percent) over 45 years of age. Both economic and age distributions were fairly diverse and reflected greater proportions of lower income and older women than did previous studies.

Although the sample was generally well educated, subjects of prior surveys were more so, even though they were generally younger.[26] In the present study, 39 percent held college or graduate degrees. One participant had never enrolled in high school and 8 percent had not completed high school. The sample had a high incidence of occupational prestige positions, a probable reflection of the relatively high educational levels: almost half (47 percent) of the participants were employed in professional, technical, managerial, or administrative duties.[27] These high levels of educational and occupational achievement should not be construed to represent the entire lesbian population since these results may merely indicate that only those individuals educated enough to understand the value of research volunteered for the study.

Approximately two-fifths (42 percent) of the participants had been heterosexually married.[28] The frequency of previous heterosexual marriage among lesbians may be partially explained by societal conditions. Because women are socialized to recognize and to articulate their sexual desires somewhat beyond adolescence, they continue the expected heterosexual socializing patterns and experience the subsequent problems and pain associated with sexual identity awareness in a marriage context. By this time children are often involved as a result of the heterosexual marriage.[29]

Developing a Stage-Sequential Model

According to the theory of lesbian signification described earlier, I named a number of factors in the process of arriving at an acknowledgment of lesbian activity. Some of these factors, such as erotic feelings, are more internal to the individual; others, such as physical/genital behavior, are more external or involve social interaction with other individuals. From the social interactionist perspective, however, even the more logically internal or individual factors require social interaction before the person absorbs or translates this information into sexual terms.

More specifically, in the research design eight factors that provide clues or indications of a possible lesbian identity were named. Data were collected from 97 subjects concerning the ages at which each subject experienced each of these factors. Each interviewee was asked at what age she first:

1. Felt she was "different" or suspected that she might be lesbian (feeling "different")

2. Became aware of or realized that there were lesbians (cognitive awareness)

3. Met another lesbian (lesbian acquaintance)

4. Had a strong emotional attraction toward another female (emotional attraction)

5. Had a strong physical attraction toward another female (physical attraction)

6. Had physical contact with another woman that she recognized as a lesbian experience (physical contact)

7. Had a lesbian relationship lasting at least six months (lesbian relationship)

8. Said to herself, "I *am* a lesbian" (self-acknowledgment)

Mean ages for these eight factors were determined and the factors were rearranged so that they appeared in chronological order. The ordered factors are: emotional attraction (14.5), feeling "different" (15.8), cognitive awareness (16), physical attraction (17.4), lesbian acquaintance (20.6), physical contact (20.7), lesbian relationship (23.2), and self-acknowledgment (23.8). It is clear, for example, that the average age at which the women had a physical or lesbian contact with another woman was about 20.7 years. The statistics indicate that as many women under 21.5 years of age admitted to themselves that they were lesbian, as women over 21.5.

Previous studies also yielded age data on a number of salient factors associated with lesbian identity. In one study subjects manifested a "particular interest" in other females at a median age of 14.6.[30] This emotional attraction or "particular interest" included no proper perception of sexual desires but is more appropriately described as affection or desire for closeness to a person in which a need for friendship and tenderness predominates. The same study likewise established the age of first physical/homosexual contact at late adolescence or young adulthood by reporting a median age of 19.8.[31] It also supports my findings that awareness of sexual attraction occurs prior to physical contact. Finally, another study established a median age of 20 for developing an initial lesbian relationship.[32]

To recognize any sort of developmental pattern in a person's lifelong erotic biography, longitudinal recording is necessary. But no serious research to date had undertaken the task of constructing a stage-sequential model to organize and to explain the complex process of developing a lesbian identity. Having identified eight factors logically associated with homosexual signification, I then constructed a multi-stage model wherein each stage is defined as the period between the occurrence of one factor and the occurrence of the next factor. For example, if a subject reported that her first emotional attraction to another female occurred at age 10 and that she first felt "different" from her peers at age 13, then the period between ages 10 and 13 is her stage of feeling "different." The stages so constructed allow for individual deviations from the assumed general ordering of factors: Each woman may not have progressed through these stages in the order listed.

The analysis used correlation and regression methods. A path analysis, used to interpret relationships among the various stages, revealed that only physical/genital contact and the establishment of a long-term lesbian relationship have substantial direct influence on acknowledgment of a lesbian identity; that is, lesbian behavior and commitment in a lesbian relationship stabilize a potential homosexual identity. These results support the theory that social interactions are of prime importance in the formation of a lesbian identity. Furthermore, a second path analysis showed that the development of a lesbian relationship is the primary predictor of self-acknowledgment; physical/sexual contact is second.

There was no attempt to analyze the resolution of identity, that problematic period between self-acknowledgment and final self-acceptance. Such a coalescense lag lasted on an average of one year among the reported sample.

Discussion of the Findings

My concept of adopting a lesbian identity is based on the ordering and importance of stages within a woman's erotic and affectional biography. While the particular sequence of occurrence may vary considerably from one woman to another, there is a general pattern or order among factors. Initial cues such as feelings, interests, same-sex attractions, and associations with homosexually oriented individuals, are continually reinterpreted and reevaluated. Homosexual meanings are constructed as the person socially interacts with others; such a provisional sexual identity is reconsidered in the wake of subsequent experiences with significant others.

It is important to distinguish between recurrence and relative frequency in arriving at a lesbian identification. The often repeated statement, "Homosexual acts do not a homosexual make," indicates that the mere *recurrence* of genital same-sex behavior is not sufficient to define a woman as lesbian. However, if such behavior is engaged in often enough or relatively frequently, then such activity may be important and direct evidence of a lesbian identity. Simply stated, "The best indicator of my being is what I do most often."[33]

The interactionist theory of developing a lesbian identity is quite distinct from the "gay trajectory" approach. The gay trajectory framework postulates an atemporal series of five elements: a subjective feeling of being different, a realization of lesbian signification, acceptance of such a label, identification with a homosexual community, and involvement in a sexual-emotional lesbian relationship. The first three are viewed as primary. Sexual behavior is acknowledged as "only one criterion" while emotional and sexual attractions to the same sex are considered as "ultimately more important" in the social construction of lesbian identity.[34] This constitutes a major conceptual difference from an interactionist theory of homosexual identification. My analysis indicates that sexual behavior, in terms of relative frequency, and lesbian relationships play a larger and more important role than gay trajectory theory allows.

The path analysis reveals that relationships in the data are consistent with my theory. A period of physical/sexual contact and the development of a long-term lesbian relationship constitute particularly salient experiences toward lesbian identification. Early apprehensions about sexual feelings and even same-sex erotic attractions contribute only indirectly to sexual self-knowledge. While knowledge of homosexuality, as well as the practical enlightenment gained through meeting homosexual people, enables a person to understand better the complexities involved in human sexuality, such factors represent only transitional phases and do not directly influence lesbian self-labeling. Only when such experiences culminate in frequent same-sex behavior, do they contribute to a lesbian identification. There seems to be a certain congruity between maintaining a stable lesbian relationship and sexual identity. Sociosexual interaction with significant others confirms a potential lesbian orientation.

The role of the homosexual community in developing a lesbian identity needs exploration. More than three-fifths of the present sample arrived at a lesbian signification *before* their entry into gay or lesbian circles, which occurred on an average of three years later. It thus appears that the homosexual community may not function as a significant factor in developing lesbian awareness. This seems to differ from the socializing context of the coming-out process for gay males.[35]

This stage theory with the empirical verification pertains only to lesbians and not to gay men. While some elements involved in sexual self-discovery may be common to both genders, their sequence and relative importance are not. Women entertain increasing suspicions of a lesbian orientation and experience same-sex feelings before engaging in physical behavior; the order is generally the opposite for males. Same-sex genital activity tends to precede intellectual awareness of homosexuality for males, but is consequent to an understanding of the term for females.[36]

Social factors from educational or familial structures, which young girls internalize, seem to operate more stringently on females than on males to inhibit sexual awareness and subsequent sexual behavior. A much greater degree of emotional involvement with and commitment to another person must be present for women than for men before physical/genital contact is initiated and sustained. This prerequisite emotional bond may explain the relative durability of lesbian couple relationships. When sexual excitement and novelty wane, the emotional attachment may remain or even increase. In the present study, for example, the first significant relationship of 14 percent of those interviewed endured between 4 and 9 years while another 8 percent revealed a duration of 14 to 32 years, with several stating that the relationship was still continuing. "For females the 'discovery' of love relations precedes the 'discovery' of sexuality while the reverse is generally true for males," state Simon and Gagnon.[37] These gender differences seem to be "consistent with the sex-role socialization of our society in general."[38]

Notes

1. Evelyn Hooker, "The Homosexual Community," in John H. Gagnon and William Simon, eds., *Sexual Deviance* (New York: Harper & Row, 1967), pp. 167–84.

2. Marcel T. Saghir and Eli Robins, "Homosexuality I. Sexual Behavior of the Female Homosexual," *Archives of General Psychiatry* 20 (Feb. 1969): 192–201. See particularly page 194.

3. John H. Gagnon and William Simon, "Homosexuality: The Formulation of a Sociological Perspective," in Mark Lefton, James K. Skipper, Jr., and Charles H. McCaghy, eds., *Approaches to Deviance* (New York: Appleton-Century-Crofts, 1968), p. 356.

4. Barry M. Dank, "Coming Out in the Gay World," *Psychiatry* 34 (May 1971): 180–97.

5. See Jack H. Hedblom, "Dimensions of Lesbian Sexual Experience," *Archives of Sexual Behavior* 2 (Dec. 1973): 329–41; and Siegrid Schäfer, "Sexual and Social Problems of Lesbians," *Journal of Sex Research* 12 (Feb. 1976): 50–69.

6. Carmen de Monteflores and Stephen J. Schultz, "Coming Out: Similarities and Differences for Lesbians and Gay Men," *Journal of Social Issues* 34 (1978): 59–72. See page 60.

7. Hedblom, p. 333.

8. John Alan Lee, "Going Public: A Study in the Sociology of Homosexual Liberation," *Journal of Homosexuality* 3 (Fall 1977): 49–78.

9. See also Hedblom's article. More than 90 percent of his lesbian sample required emotional attachments before there could be any sexual involvement.

10. Kenneth Plummer, *Sexual Stigma: An Interactionist Account* (London: Routledge & Kegan Paul, 1975), p. 147.

11. Schäfer, p. 51.

12. Deborah Belote and Joan Joesting, "Demographic and Self-Report Characteristics of Lesbians," *Psychological Reports* 39 (1976): 621–22.

13. Plummer, p. 135.

14. Plummer, p. 137.

15. Hedblom, p. 336.

16. Schäfer.

17. For example, see Hedblom, and Belote and Joesting. Also see Janet S. Chafetz et al., "A Study of Homosexual Women," *Social Work* 19 (Nov. 1974): 714–23; Wayne L. Cotton, "Social and Sexual Relationships of Lesbians," *Journal of Sex Research* 11 (May 1975): 139–48; and Letitia Anne Peplau et al., "Loving Women: Attachment and Autonomy in Lesbian Relationships," *Journal of Social Issues* 34 (1978): 7–27.

18. Schäfer.

19. William H. Masters and Virginia E. Johnson, *Homosexuality in Perspective* (Boston: Little, Brown, 1979).

20. Joyce C. Albro and Carol Tully, "A Study of Lesbian Lifestyles in the Homosexual Micro-Culture and the Heterosexual Macro-Culture," *Journal of Homosexuality* 4 (Summer 1979): 331–44.

21. Petra Liljestrand, Robert P. Peterson, and Russell Zellers, "The Relationship of Assumption and Knowledge of the Homosexual Orientation to the Abridgment of Civil Liberties," *Journal of Homosexuality* 3 (Spring 1978): 243–48.

22. Item-scale analysis indicated a high degree of scale reliability (Cronbach's alpha = .80).

23. Hedblom; Chafetz; Belote and Joesting; Schäfer; Albro and Tully; Peplau et al.

24. Hedblom included only one black woman. Only Alan P. Bell and Martin S. Weinberg, *Homosexualities: A Study of Diversity Among Men and Women* (New York: Simon and Schuster, 1978), have included an adequate representation of black lesbians in their work.

25. Reporting similar findings, Albro and Tully state that this religious disaffiliation may possibly be related to "basic religious proscriptions of homosexuality" (p. 334).

26. Albro and Tully state that 76 percent of their subjects held college or graduate degrees.

27. This professional bias among lesbian women is confirmed by Hedblom, and Albro and Tully. Hedblom attributes the need for educational attainment and occupational advancement to economic necessity: "The lesbian cannot look to a well-educated male to support her during her life, nor can she become a housewife and rely on her femininity to provide for her" (p. 333).

28. This statistic is considerably higher than those reported by Hedblom, Schäfer, and Albro and Tully. However, it replicates the findings of Cotton, and Bell and Weinberg.

29. The proportion of lesbian mothers in our sample (24 percent) is much higher than the 6 percent reported by Hedblom but much lower than the 38 percent of Bell and Weinberg.

30. Schäfer.

31. Somewhat earlier ages for first physical/homosexual contact are reported by Hedblom while somewhat later ages are given by Saghir and Robins. Belote and Joesting note that physical contact occurred between the ages of 15 and 19 for 51 percent of their sample and between the ages of 20 and 24 for another 25 percent.

32. Peplau et al.

33. David Matza, *Becoming Deviant* (Englewood Cliffs, N.J.: Prentice-Hall, 1969), p. 169.

34. Barbara Ponse, *Identities in the Lesbian World: The Social Construction of Self* (Westport, Conn.: Greenwood, 1978), p. 124.

35. See Dank.

36. See Dorothy I. Riddle and Stephen F. Morin, "Removing the Stigma," *APA Monitor* 16 (1977): 28. Women seem to act on their same-sex feelings on an average of three to five years later than men. See also Schäfer.

37. William Simon and John H. Gagnon, "The Lesbians: A Preliminary Overview," in John H. Gagnon and William Simon, eds., *Sexual Deviance*, pp. 247–81.

38. de Monteflores and Schultz, p. 68.

3

The Coming-Out Process: Violence Against Lesbians

RUTH BAETZ

*T*he term *coming out* can have many meanings: a woman's first sexual experience with another woman, a woman's self-realization of sexual feelings for another woman, a woman's acceptance of the label *lesbian*, a woman's declaration to anyone or everyone that she is a lesbian, or any combination of these possibilities. However coming out is defined, it requires a woman to take a stand against a cultural taboo.

When I wrote *Lesbian Crossroads*,[1] I saw coming-out situations that lesbians have to confront as involving merely personal decision-making processes. In reality, however, each decision-making crossroad is not simply a time for choice based on personal preference, but a culturally constructed mine field intended to eliminate or impede the lesbian lifestyle. How do you choose between possible disownment by your parents or a dwindling relationship riddled with half-truths, if those are your choices? How much of your time and energy do those decisions take, and what pain do they cause you and your loved ones? You can see why I have referred to the coming-out process as violence against lesbians. The fact that lesbians are forced to risk cultural retribution over and over again in order to relate intimately is violence against lesbians and causes tremendous pain and damage in lesbian lives. The fact that the violence is masked, we believe that we have power over and can maneuver through personal decisions correctly if we try hard enough, makes the process especially sinister.

Given that we are talking simultaneously about two things—personal life decisions and culturally constructed mine fields—let us look at what this coming-out process is all about. How does a woman arrive at the realization that she is a lesbian? The journey to this realization runs into some of society's most deadly weapons:

Silence: Often there are no role models and no sense of lesbian existence or lesbian herstory. How can a woman realize that she is something if that something does not exist?

Lies: If the silence has been broken, a woman may have seen lesbian reality distorted by the way the mass media covers lesbian and gay pride marches or butch/fem couples, or by films like *Windows* (released by United Artists in 1980), where the lesbian is a rapist. How can a woman name her pleasurable emotional and physical feelings with the same lesbian label as these specters of perversion?

Isolation: Without the freedom to gather and be open as lesbians, women cannot share or strategize to end heterosexist and homophobic oppression. Who do lesbians talk to about their confusing feelings if they see no others who have felt similarly?

Intimidation: As women come closer to identifying themselves as lesbians, society's opposition becomes more overt, running the continuum from ridicule and jokes to legal threats of prison and custody battles.

Physical violence: Society's final weapon is actual violence. From street attacks to electroshock therapy to denial of life's necessities (such as employment and housing)—violence has been one of the most devastating influences on lesbian existence.

Imagine for a moment a woman beginning to realize that she is a lesbian. If you can consider the effect of these societal weapons on her emotional well-being, you have some idea of the toll that coming out may take on her. During the realization process, she may have to deal with a loss in self-confidence, self-hatred, physical illness, nervous breakdown, alcoholism, marriage attempts, realization of wasted years of trying to be someone she isn't, numerous therapy sessions, and suicide attempts. This is euphemistically called coming out to yourself. It could more accurately be described as waging a major battle against an invisible internal enemy that has been culturally constructed.

To balance this perspective, let me make it clear that all lesbians do not experience all the effects of violence. For many lesbians different crossroads are easy, enriching, and welcomed as personal growth or political progress. The truth is, however, that society intends coming out to be difficult, and the potential for violence is always present.

We have just explored the first lesbian crossroad, self-realization, along with its hazards and potential consequences. Since looking at the coming-out process from the perspective of violence can be a heavy dose of depressing reality, we will look at the other crossroads and points of violence more briefly. I have listed nine crossroads, and under each noted some common considerations, on a continuum from subtle to blatant or from irritating to deadly. I am sure that your own imagination and experiences can fill in many more examples.

1. **Coming out to parents and siblings**
   Loss of choice: forced to lie or face consequences
   Living in fear that they may find out
   Destruction of honest relationship
   Forbidden to see lover (younger lesbians)
   Thrown out of house
   Disowned
   Beaten

2. **Coming out to children**
   Staying closeted to keep kids (and related stresses)
   Living under the threat of endless custody battles
   Expensive custody battles, losing custody
   Losing visitation
   Children kidnapped
   Disowned by children
   Ex-husband's physical intimidation, beating

3. **Coming out at school and work**
   No gay youth groups or literature
   Robbed of lesbian herstory—never mentioned in school
   Staying in closet and hearing lezzie jokes
   Losing friends
   Blackmail
   Expelled from school
   Threats of rape and switchblade fights
   Losing professional license (nursing, social workers, teachers)
   Dishonorable military discharge
   Getting fired

4. **Religion**
   Years of guilt (can also affect relationships)
   Intimidation (hell)
   Excommunication
   Religious "deprogramming"

5. **Therapy**
   Trivialization of what lesbians face
   Unqualified therapists
   Not challenging internalized self-hatred

Patronizing/pity/not taking lesbianism seriously ("just a phase")
Treating lesbianism as the problem
Incarceration in mental hospital
Mental hospital harassment
Shock therapy

6. *Discrimination/harassment*

Stares, whispers, jokes
Not served in restaurants
Car window smashed
Porno and news images that incite fear in us and violence against us
Phone threats
Job loss
Housing destroyed or denied or eviction
Economic oppression that forces us to live in dangerous areas
Street threats and fights
Rape

7. *Politics and the law*

Fear of violence keeps us in line
Immigration hassles
Police harassment
Probation officer hassles
Physical and psychological violence in prisons, especially toward "butches"
Police brutality
Illegality in many states—prison, blackmail, eviction, job loss

8. *Culture*

Immigration hassles
Possible deportation
Triple minority status
Isolation: few role models, no writings in ethnic literature, racism in lesbian community, heterosexism in ethnic community, effectiveness in ethnic movement jeopardized
Whole family may lose face in community
Thrown out into racist society alone if disowned
All the violence previously cited in other crossroads, often to a greater degree

9. *Lesbian community/social life*

Internalized homophobia (calling lesbian dances "women's" dances)
Quarrels in relationships due to external stresses
No recognition of divorce or lover's death

Isolation of young lesbians if no alcohol-free meeting place exists
Illegality of relationships with underaged lesbians
Violence, both psychic and physical, turned inward—high suicide
    and alcoholism rates
Isolation—nonexistent or hidden community

Looking at the numerous hazards present at lesbian crossroads raises the question, Why are they there? There are several theories. One says society is ignorant about lesbians and fears and tries to tame or destroy anything it is ignorant of. Another states that this society is based on sameness and it discriminates against anyone who is different. Still another suggests propaganda against minorities of all kinds is used as a way to keep workers divided so we don't challenge the ruling class.

From a feminist perspective, I see violence against lesbians as one of the patriarchy's ways of maintaining its power. Lesbianism is the ultimate rebellion against male authority since lesbians can choose not to need men for approval, self-image, money, or physical necessities. It makes sense that a patriarchy would want to prevent women from becoming lesbians, and to keep lesbian energy directed toward basic survival. In this sense, keeping lesbians in line keeps all women in line, just as rape keeps all women in line. All independent single women can be threatened with the lesbian label as long as that label carries such dire consequences, and such women will therefore be more inclined to marry or at least to be connected to men in some way. Lesbians, as women who don't have the drain of fighting sexism in their intimate relationships, as women who have no stake in upholding male privilege, are a powerful threat to the male-dominated status quo.

Whichever analysis is used, it is clear that society puts up definite roadblocks to prevent lesbians from existing, if possible, or being free. So how do lesbians survive and why do some women actually decide to become lesbians? The search for our true selves may actually be an innate drive. Possibly loving other women counteracts society's woman-hating socialization so that we begin to love ourselves in the process, freeing up energy not only to survive but also to grow and create. Sometimes women are lucky enough to have other women's nurturing and support to encourage us in our quest for sexual identity; at other times, the struggle itself can clear our vision and strengthen us. Lesbians who have gone through the various crossroads have gained immense self-knowledge and survival skills. While obvious damage is done, lesbians have learned what radical change is and how to use compromise and strategy. We, as lesbians, have often built strong networks to make life easier for ourselves and other women in the process of coming out.

Coming out is, in fact, a heroic journey against formidable odds that changes both the journeyer and the world around her. For me, coming out meant stepping into a world without sex roles where personal choices and personal growth abound. I could see a world view that made sense of my previous experiences—one that helped put into perspective the oppression of all minority groups. This world view gave me guidelines and a strong commitment to work against oppression because I could see that my life and the lives of the women I love depend on it.

Note

1. Ruth Baetz, *Lesbian Crossroads: Personal Stories of Lesbian Struggles and Triumphs* (New York: William Morrow, 1980). Also available in paperback from Naiad Press, Inc., P.O. Box 10543, Tallahassee, FL 32302.

4

Lesbian Relationships: A Struggle Toward Partner Equality

BARBARA SANG

Most couple relationships are in transition. As a result of the women's movement, homosexual as well as heterosexual couples are in the process of reevaluating how they relate to one another. Many couples are trying to create relationships of equality—that is, relationships in which both persons have the opportunity to realize their potentials.

Lesbians as a group have managed to obtain autonomy and wholeness as individuals despite the oppression of women in this society.[1] Thus, lesbians may come to couple relationships from a unique vantage point in that both members of the couple expect to be treated as equals. Many of the same issues that have long been familiar to lesbian couples are now becoming familiar to nonlesbians as they themselves work toward self-realization in committed relationships. If this observation is valid, lesbian couples have been ahead of their times in attempting to develop relationships that combine intimacy and equality.

Some of the themes that emerge frequently in lesbian relationships will be explored in this article. Many observations relate to the female socialization process and to homosexual oppression. Other relationship issues reflect lesbians' development of new ways of relating in couples so as to accommodate the needs and potentialities of both partners. It is my hope that as lesbians come to understand more fully how they are interacting with one another, they will be in a better position to create relationships that are more rewarding and fulfilling. Although many of my observations may seem critical, my intention is to deal openly with those aspects of lesbian relationships that interfere with growth and fulfillment.

In describing lesbian relationships, I have intentionally tried to report my observations in the language and style of my experience rather than with reference to existing relationship frameworks. Nearly all relationship models are based on a heterosexual perspective and generally, theoreticians in this area have been male. In order to highlight certain points or to show the uniqueness of lesbian relationships, I do make comparisons between heterosexuals and homosexuals. However, I've attempted to keep such comparisons to a minimum to avoid setting up heterosexual relationships as the norm.

Roles and the Decision-Making Process in Lesbian Relationships

Most lesbian couples today do not identify themselves as either male/female or butch/fem. A conversation between the mothers-in-law of a lesbian couple illustrates such a change. One mother-in-law asks the other to help her figure out who plays what role. The other mother-in-law replies, "Don't you know that roles are no longer in fashion these days!" When role-playing or a double standard is found to exist, it is usually related to such variables as age, socioeconomic background, and geographical location.[2] Also, in some experimental studies lesbians have been found to label themselves *male*. However, this term has often been forced on a subject if she views herself as independent and self-directed. Experimenters sometimes pose questions in such a way that subjects have no other choice but to categorize themselves into stereotypical sex roles.

Studies on lesbian relationships indicate that a small minority of lesbians view themselves in stereotypic roles. Sociologist Donna Tanner studied twelve lesbian couples in the Chicago area who had been living together from six months to twelve years. Half the couples had been in relationship for two years or longer. The subjects ranged in age from twenty to thirty-five and occupations ranged from nurse's aide to college instructor. The dyadic relationships were categorized into three types:

1. *Traditional complementary:* Fits a traditional marriage model. One partner assumes the head-of-the-household role and its attendant responsibilities. A number of the women in this type of relationship had been previously married heterosexually.

2. *Flexible nurturing and care-taking:* There is no stereotypic sexual division of labor and duties. However, the definition of the relationship appears to be somewhat dependent on emotional and financial conditions. Some of the women in this group were students and were consequently temporarily dependent on their lovers' economic support. The majority of couples were reported to fall into this middle, more flexible, and less defined category.

3. *Negotiated-egalitarian prototype:* Is free from gender role stereotypes and traditional sexual division of labor. Reciprocity is stated as the key to the relationship. There is much mutual dependence and role-switching. Tanner reported that this type of relationship is most vulnerable to breaking up because many of the mutual needs on which most dyadic relationships are based are no longer relevant to these couples.[3]

In another study, Karla Jay and Allen Young's *The Gay Report: Lesbians and Gay Men Speak Out About Sexual Experiences and Lifestyles,* some lesbians from varying parts of the country responded to a questionnaire that specifically asked, "How often do you role play butch/fem, male/female, husband/wife, dominant/submissive in your relationship?" Subjects categorized their responses on a seven-point scale from "always" to "never." The majority of lesbians reported that sexual role-playing (76 percent) and other-than-sexual role-playing (79 percent) "never occurs" or "occurs very infrequently."

Although obvious role-playing is less likely to be a means for one woman to obtain power over another, power dynamics between lesbians do exist. In one study conducted by psychologist Letitia Peplau, virtually all subjects believed that, ideally, both partners should have exactly equal say in the relationship. Only 64 percent, however, felt that their current relationships lived up to this ideal.[4]

The double standard in today's lesbian couple may take on more subtle form. The concept of oppression of one person by another[5] may provide another way of looking at the "oneuponeship" that occur in relationships when one person believes herself to be more important, knowledgeable, skillful, or correct. If individual members of a couple tend to view differences between themselves in an either/or fashion, this manner of thinking is likely to result in negative value judgments such as, "My way of doing things is better, stronger, or more adult." It is this kind of power dynamic that can cause discord in couples. In a society that has placed greater values on male qualities and the male role, it is not surprising that a person, male or female, whose qualities come closer to the male stereotype may attempt to dominate or feel superior to a person who has fewer of these qualities. For example, one member of a couple by virtue of her background, interests, or talents, may be highly skillful in mechanics whereas her lover may be less adept in this area. The partner who is accomplished in a field that women have been traditionally excluded from may feel herself to be the more successful or knowledgeable person. If her partner cannot accept her differences and perceive herself as equally worthwhile, she is likely to relegate her more mechanically inclined mate to a superior position. In doing so, she will simultaneously feel resentful and controlled.

Many of the qualities that have been associated with the female role such as expression of emotions and nurturing may be devalued in importance by persons who cannot respect individual differences in ability, interest, and style. It is significant to note that lesbians were aware of the complexities underlying so-called male-female qualities in a given relationship long before it became a fashionable topic of study among academics. This understanding is strikingly illustrated in the following quote from a relatively unknown study by the Daughters of Bilitis of San Francisco:

> A number of persons indicated specifically that they recognized both "masculine" and "feminine" elements in themselves. It is probable that a large majority of persons, Lesbian and otherwise, have such a mixture of elements, but that awareness of this mixture, as well as the mixture itself, varies from person to person. It also seems likely that awareness of either the "masculine" or the "feminine" qualities may be heightened by contrast with a partner who has a different combination of them.[6]

Another way of analyzing inequality in lesbian couple relationships is expressed by Kay Whitlock in her article entitled "Striving Toward Equality in Loving Relationships." She proposes that relationship inequality is a derivative of heterosexist ideology. Whitlock believes that gay persons need to understand the pressures on them to conform and adopt the heterosexual model, which includes emphasis on finding fulfillment through another person and the fact that women are not taught to develop a strong sense of personal autonomy.[7] The traditional romantic myth leads women to assume that by working to take care of all the emotional and physical needs of their husbands and children, they will feel fulfilled, loved, and cherished in ways that will satisfy their own emotional needs.[8] Thus, women are taught to "submerge their own identities in relationships" and to "perform for the benefit of others." Heterosexual relationship norms also encourage possessiveness and ownership with regard to one's mate ("my woman"). These aspects of relating relegate women to positions of powerlessness and helplessness.

How are decisions made as to who does what in a lesbian relationship since tasks are not assigned on the basis of gender? In most lesbian relationships, chores are performed according to skills, interests, and time availability of each person. In describing chore and financial management, subjects in Lena Furgeri's study on couple relationships reported:

> "If she cooks I do the dishes. She has more time off because she teaches so she shops and does the wash."
>
> "Sometimes both of us do something. Sometimes both of us do nothing. Certain chores get done according to who feels like it and the need to get it done; we both cook because we both like to. If one cooks the other does the cat litter. At times we both eat out because we're busy."[9]

Division of labor based on each other's individual needs, preferences, and abilities is not always easy to carry out. Often, a couple must spend time and energy learning how to function best in combination with each other. Good communication is essential in relationships where chores are not automatically determined on the basis of gender role. Each woman needs to clarify her own interests and make them explicit to her partner. This process of negotiation can strengthen a lesbian couple relationship in the following three ways: first, each person gets to do what she enjoys and therefore brings a sense of contentment to the relationship; second, each woman gets a chance to realize her own potential as a person rather than fitting herself into a stereotyped role; and third, effective communication on certain basic tasks can be applied to other situations where good communication is necessary.

Female couples are likely to have more in common than heterosexual couples, as a result of their socialization as women. Two people with similar values and interests can pool their skills for the betterment of both. However, when two individuals are equally invested in one area there can be cause for disagreement. One way in which couples can get stuck is not being able to agree on an alternative solution to a problem.

Another role-related source of tension in lesbian relationships can be the quest for self-actualization. Many lesbians have translated feminist ideology into a need to become the all-knowing, skilled, and diversified person, regardless of their own needs and limitations. Lesbians who do not measure up to this new and unrealistic notion of what it means to be an independent adult put unnecessary pressure on themselves and their partners. Respect for each other's individual capabilities and limitations is particularly important if women are to create an emotional climate in which each person is free to develop her individuality.

Some Partner Expectations in Lesbian Relationships

Psychological and sociological studies tend to suggest that female couple relationships are more emotionally satisfying than couple relationships between women and men.[10] Psychologist Alan Bell and sociologist Martin Weinberg report that the monogamous, "close-coupled" lesbians that they studied tended to be less lonely in their relationships than heterosexual women.[11] Psychologist Letitia Peplau's study found that the majority of women, a diverse sample of 137 lesbians, reported considerable closeness in the relationship and about 75 percent indicated that they and their current partner were "in love."[12]

Females have been socialized to value emotional communication and to place importance on creating satisfying relationships. As a result, two women are often more willing to work on the emotional aspects of their coupling than a heterosexual couple. Because women have the capacity to give of themselves emotionally, two women frequently expect a lot from each other. In more traditional relationships, women are not as apt to expect as much from men emotionally.

One of the most salient couple issues that emerges in working with lesbians in therapy is one's feeling that the other is not caring enough. Examples of some of the kinds of interactions that illustrate this are as follows: The partner is expected to know that her lover needs a particular service or form of support without being directly told. One partner goes out of her way to give to the other and *expects* the other to reciprocate in the appropriate manner. This expectation may or may not be explicit, and the partner feels obligated to give of herself and be there for the other person despite the fact that she may not want to or be unable to do so.

The process by which women are socialized to meet the needs of others is well described in Jean Baker Miller's *Toward a New Psychology of Women* and Carol Gilligan's *In a Different Voice: Psychological Theory and Women's Development.*[13] Both authors point out that women are constantly concerned with the question of whether they are giving enough. Women have traditionally built a sense of self-worth on activities that involve taking care and giving to others. Women have also been trained to believe that they should want to respond to others at all times; they don't feel they have the right to call a halt to these demands. Frequently, when a woman does not meet all her partner's expectations she wonders whether she is selfish.

Two lesbians may expect more from one another because women are supposed to care for others. It takes more strength in female relationships to take care of one's own needs and not always be there for the other. If women are to go beyond this variation of the romantic myth they will have to become more aware of this powerful relationship dynamic.

Aloneness and Togetherness

The most frequent problem theme in lesbian couple relationships has to do with time together and time alone. Many lesbians feel that if they are in a committed relationship they will not have time to be by themselves. A variation on this dilemma is expressed by Ruth Falk in her book *Women Loving:* "I have often been afraid if I got close to someone I would lose my independence—partly because they would make demands on my space and partly because I would want to be with them and would not take the space I needed."[14]

Female socialization fosters the need for togetherness. Many women do not know how to take time for themselves or are afraid of the prospect of being alone. Having more in common can make it difficult for lesbians to separate from the relationship to pursue their own individual interests. A primary reason why two women do not take time away from each other appears to be related to the pressure to be there or take care of one another. Each woman assumes that if she were to go out on her own, her partner would be bored, lonely, or angry. Not infrequently, each member of the couple will separately express the need for time away from the relationship but fears that if she were to take that time, her lover would feel resentful. Many women seem to equate time together with caring, regardless of how that time is spent. For couples to be able to separate from each other, each individual must believe that she has the right to spend time on her own and trust that her partner can take care of herself. Bell and Weinberg found that lesbians were more likely than male homosexuals to spend more of their leisure time at home.[15] If this is the case, one option for women may be to learn how to pursue separate interests in the home without being distracted by one another's presence.

In traditional heterosexual relationships, it is the male who is usually offered the option of time alone. Women are not expected to take time away from the relationship to pursue their own interests; thus, separation is not as much of an issue. In fact, separateness is often built into these relationships as a function of role specialization: The female's domain is in the home and the male's domain is in the business world.

A solution to the problem of obtaining time alone is to discuss it honestly. Couples frequently fail to let each other know when they will will be available, which can lead to discord. Since all individuals vary in their need for privacy and time with others, couples need to take into account style differences. The person who prefers more social contact may have to socialize on her own. One recurring question that couples often raise is, How much time away from the relationship is justified? Although this is a decision that each couple must make for themselves, the real issues have to do with trust and good communication.

Another reason that lesbian couples may become overly dependent on each other has to do with social ostracism and/or lack of opportunity to meet other lesbians. Some lesbians might isolate themselves from other women for fear of losing their partner to another lesbian. This issue will be discussed in another section.

Lesbians and Work

Many lesbians report having known from an early age that they would have to be economically self-sufficient as adults. Statistics show that the majority of lesbians are self-supporting and are often deeply involved in the work they do. A substantial proportion of lesbians sampled through homophile organizations, friendship networks, and bars have been found to be professional women.[16]

In traditional heterosexual relations, the female is expected to give her support and aid to the male. Since lesbians value each other's work, they are more likely to facilitate the realization of each other's potential. Interest in one another's work may be manifested by sharing job experiences and problems, and by providing support and suggestions to one another.

As a result of the feminist movement, more women are seeking to realize their potential through rewarding careers and greater professional responsibility. If one woman in a lesbian relationship feels unfulfilled in her work, however, she might be overly resentful and critical of a career-satisfied partner. Conversely, some women may put pressure on their partners to achieve more in the work area, despite the partner's lack of interest in such advancement. In still other relationships, women may be vocationally competitive with one another; both women feel threatened if one does not have the same job status or success as the other. Since job and economic status have traditionally defined one's role and status in a relationship, this can be a particularly sensitive area for the lesbian couple.

Relationship problems can arise when one woman believes her work to be more important or valuable than the other person's work. This imbalance is more likely to occur when one person has attained more education or a higher occupational position. In traditional heterosexual relationships it is taken for granted that the man will be more successful and make more money. One difficulty that may arise when two women work is related to possible relocation decisions based on job offerings.

Couple Economics

Although lesbians as a group appear to earn more than traditional women, women as a class are economically oppressed. Job insecurity and financial crises can make for additional stress in lesbian relationships.

Several summers ago I spent a few weeks at a small family resort. Being in a situation where I could compare the financial circumstances of heterosexual couples with those of lesbian couples, I clearly realized how much less economic mobility lesbian couples of a similar age and professional status have. The following factors appear to be responsible for lowering a lesbian couple's standard of living: Women continue to earn less than men for the same jobs, and fewer of the higher-paying jobs are open to them. Homosexual couples cannot benefit from one another's insurance policies or take advantage of discounts in transportation or memberships that come with family status. Women tend to know less about the ways of investing the money they earn, and there is usually less money to invest. Many lesbians have not had financial support for schooling or other life ventures as a result of their sexual orientation. Many female couples may be afraid to pool their assets for fear of the relationship breaking up. Each time a lesbian moves to a new living arrangement with another woman, she may have to give up some of her belongings, thus incurring a loss. The more a lesbian's social and professional contacts are with other women and gays, the less likely she is to learn about the existence of higher-paying positions. Some lesbians choose to maintain separate residences to avoid being known as living with another woman; such an arrangement does not permit the couple to benefit from sharing expenses.

One common financial problem that a female couple faces is how to handle finances when there is a disparity in income. Without a clear understanding as to what arrangements are acceptable to each partner, there is likely to be discord. The woman who earns less money may feel guilty, less responsible, and unworthy of making decisions. The woman who takes home the larger salary could feel herself to be exploited or to have a greater financial burden. A possible solution is for each to pay expenses in proportion to her earnings. When one person is working and the other person is not, financial problems can be intensified unless both women can openly deal with their feelings.

Dealing With Differences

It has been my observation that many lesbians are in relationships with partners who differ from them on the basis of class, religion, race, and nationality. One of the largest studies on couple relationships, Lena Furgeri's "The Lesbian/Feminist Movement and Social Change," confirms my impression.

Most lesbians have had to transcend considerable social barriers in the search for their own sexual identification. Consequently, they may be more receptive to forming relationships with partners who differ significantly from themselves. Another possible explanation for such diversity in a couple's background may have to do with the heterogeneity of the lesbian community where women meet. It is also possible that the basis for attraction between lesbians may differ from traditional heterosexual standards of attraction. This seems to be an unexplored area that needs to be researched.

Differences in background can permit considerable richness and skill sharing, thereby enhancing what each individual has to offer. Both women get a chance to see the world from a different perspective. Differences in backgrounds, however, can also be the source of misunderstandings. By acknowledging differences in socialization, couples are often able to put what appear to be personal disagreements into a nonthreatening context.

In any couple relationship, two individuals are bound to differ in personal style or preference. By spelling out differences between individuals in simple language, couples can avoid negative judgments inherent in such labels as *dependent, childish, helpless,* and *selfish.*

Other possible differences between lesbian partners relate to their oppression as women and as gays. The following are a few potential areas of difference that most lesbians must cope with: One woman is able to be more public about her lesbianism. One member of the couple is accepted by her family and the other is not. One woman believes it important to be politically gay, whereas the other does not. One woman has more relationship experience by virtue of having come out at an earlier age. One is not sure if she actually wants to be in a lesbian relationship due to its social stigma or her own personal doubts. One has more skills that have traditionally been defined as male in a society that devalues skills traditionally associated with the female role. One member of the pair is more accepting of her lesbianism than her partner. One woman does not want any social contact with men whereas the other woman does.[17] These differences between partners can lead to one person having more power than the other. This in turn leads to interpersonal oppression. For example, the woman who is able to be more open about her lesbianism could put the other down for being uptight or uncourageous. Uniting to face common oppression, however, can bring a lesbian couple closer if they are careful not to direct their own frustration and rage against one another. Psychotherapist Robyn Posin has observed that women who come to lesbian relationships in their later years are more self-accepting but even these women bring a core of self-negation as a result of their devaluation as women in American society.[18]

Friendships

It has been noted that lesbian friendship networks contain a large number of women who have been lovers. Thus, at any one party, everyone in a room may be related to everyone else through former lovers. At one time and in more isolated geographical regions, the so-called incestuousness of lesbian networks was attributed to the fact that there were not many other available options. Today, in large cities, despite the women's movement opening up more avenues for social contact, friendship patterns do not appear to have changed significantly. Jean Weber, writing in the *Christopher Street* magazine, has questioned whether the "inbreeding" among lesbians may be related to "the fear of going outside the safe, familiar and often circumscribed surroundings."[19] One function that the tightly knit friendship network has been reported to serve is that of extended family.[20] By group affiliation, each lesbian is assured of continued contact with the lesbian world. Over time the group provides individuals with a sense of continuity and history. Also, as sociologists William Simon and John Gagnon point out, the community provides each individual with an ideology that helps her resist the societal negative image.[21]

Many lesbians in couple relationships may feel threatened when their partner enters into a close friendship with another woman. A problem that continues to exist for lesbian couples is that for women, the boundary between friends and lovers is not always clear; every woman could be a potential lover. In traditional heterosexual relationships, friendships with one's own sex are not suspect in this way; two traditional heterosexual women are expected to have an emotionally close relationship. Women in our society have been permitted to embrace warmly, hold hands, and regard one another affectionately without such behavior having romantic implications. For most lesbians, on the other hand, love relationships start off as friendships. Unless lesbian couples can work out an understanding about female friends and feel secure with one another, friends are likely to become a source of conflict. Seeing her partner behaving warmly with a friend can be particularly upsetting to a member of a couple who has just been fighting. Resentment can also occur when a woman who has been physically and emotionally cold to her partner is overly attentive and affectionate to a female friend. It also appears that couples need a clearer understanding of the meaning of one another's behavior so that two friends who are acting affectionately are not perceived as courting. One recurring problem for many lesbians is knowing how to tell if someone is interested in them as a lover or as a friend. Courting rituals for women appear to be vague or subtle, and therefore it is not always possible for one woman to decipher another's communication. For many women, a period when the relationship is not defined seems to occur before romantic feelings develop.

It is fairly common for lesbians to maintain friendships with one another after the couple has broken up. Often such former lovers are referred to as family. Ex-lovers may be seen during holidays, at lesbian social functions, and for recreational companionship. Furgeri noted that the termination of a lesbian relationship or coupling does not seem to involve the same animosity and bitterness that heterosexual partings often entail. She suggested that relationship continuity is possible because of the quality of communication that existed when the women were a couple. Women can have much in common, even if they are no longer relating sexually to one another.

Tanner hypothesized that maintaining friendships with past lovers serves a survival function—ensuring contact with other lesbians—as well as serving an adaptive function since it is not easy to avoid contact with former lovers within the confines of the lesbian community.

Many relationships between former lovers may become more rewarding as the pressures and expectations of couple intimacy are no longer operating. It is perhaps for this reason that ex-lovers may pose a threat to current partners. When the new couple is not getting along, the relationship with the ex-lover may look more loving, more harmonious, and less complicated.

Not all ex-lovers choose to be friends. Sometimes, for the very same reasons that an intimate relationship is not possible, a friendship is not possible. Some women need a period of separation before a friendship can develop. The timing may be different for both parties; the person who is no longer invested in the relationship in a romantic way may be unable to understand why her former lover cannot just be friendly.

Couple Issues Related to Monogamy and Nonmonogamy

The question of open relationships has been discussed ad infinitum in most books on lesbian and gay lifestyles. In this section I do not want to concern myself with whether nonmonogamy is better, more rewarding, freer, or more mature. My belief is that open or closed relationships are a matter of individual choice. What I would like to address are some of the problems that arise in couple relationships when there is a discrepancy between one's ideology and personal needs. More specifically, many couples believe that they *should* be able to maintain sexual relationships with other women in addition to their primary relationship. More often than not, once a member of a couple actually does become involved sexually with another person, her partner finds herself feeling hurt, insecure, angry, and jealous. What makes these feelings more painful is that one is not supposed to have them. The rationale underlying nonmonogamy for many lesbians is that one person cannot satisfy all of another's needs. Many lesbians want to be free to relate to other women sexually so as not to get caught up in the same kind of possessiveness that characterizes some heterosexual relationships.

The presence of a third party often prevents a couple from working out what is disturbing them in their own relationship. Instead of dealing with what is happening between them, the focus in the relationship is on fighting about the third person. Often, the person who has taken the outside lover assumes a position of power in the primary relationship. Some lesbians seem to equate sexual freedom with the ability to be one's own person. Such women experience monogamous sexual relationships as taking away something from them. However, relating to just one person need not signify dependency, loss of autonomy, or nonflexibility. Inner freedom need not be given up in relating solely to one person. As individual lesbians learn other ways of obtaining a realistic sense of identity and their own separateness, committed relationships with one person do not seem so threatening. It is significant that some studies of lesbian relationships have reported that couples in committed relationships experience less insecurity in the relationship and are more likely to remain together longer.[22]

Today's lesbian has considerably more opportunity to relate emotionally and sexually to a wide variety of women. Although the term *dating* may be obsolete, it appears to be important for lesbians to experience different women before they view themselves as ready to be part of a committed couple. By allowing themselves a more undefined period to get to know one another, women may be in a better position to choose partners with greater long-term potential. Such an interim period would also serve to lessen the feeling of failure when a relationship does not work.

Many lesbians do want to form long-term satisfying relationships. The question is how to make these relationships work better, particularly since there are so few adequate homosexual or heterosexual role models. We need to learn more about the ways in which women can be both self-sufficient and part of a fulfilling couple relationship. At present, many lesbians and feminists are trying to create a new female model of experience that includes strength and emotional closeness as well as the ability to be vulnerable and sensitive. In the future we may well see the impact of this new way of being as women on the nature and quality of women's relationships. In other words, as women change themselves, this change will be reflected in the way they relate to one another in lesbian couple relationships.

Notes

1. See June Hopkins, "The Lesbian Personality," *British Journal of Psychiatry* 115 (1969): 433–36; Mark Freedman, *Homosexuality and Psychological Functioning* (Monterey, Calif.: Brooks/Cole, 1971); and Andrea Oberstone and Harriet Sukoneck, "Psychological Adjustment and Life Style of Single Lesbians and Single Heterosexual Women," *Psychology of Women Quarterly* 2 (1976): 171–88.

2. See Del Martin and Phyllis Lyon, *Lesbian/Woman* (San Francisco: Glide Publications, 1972); Karla Jay, "Surviving Gay Coupledom," in Karla Jay and Allen Young, eds., *After You're Out* (New York: Pyramid Publications, 1977), pp. 35–

43; and Lena Furgeri, "The Lesbian/Feminist Movement and Social Change: Female Homosexuality, A New Consciousness," unpublished doctoral dissertation, City University of New York, 1976. [Editors' Note: Joan Nestle, of the Lesbian Herstory Archives, provides a different perspective of butch-fem relationships in her article "Butch-Fem Relationships: Sexual Courage in the 1950's." *Heresies* 3, no. 4, pp. 21–24. To quote Nestle, "Butch-fem was an erotic partnership, serving both as a conspicuous flag of rebellion and as an intimate exploration of women's sexuality." She strongly disagrees with lesbian feminists who believe butch-fem to be a reproduction of heterosexual models.]

3. Donna Tanner, *The Lesbian Couple* (Lexington, Mass.: Lexington Books, 1978).

4. Letitia Anne Peplau et al., "Loving Women: Attachment and Autonomy in Lesbian Relationships," *Journal of Social Issues* 34 (1978): 7–27.

5. Barbara Sang and Lila Lowenherz, "Personism: Toward the Elimination of Interpersonal Oppression," paper presented at the meeting of the American Psychological Association, Chicago, 1975.

6. Daughters of Bilitis, "DOB Questionnaire Reveals Some Facts About Lesbians," *The Ladder* 3, no. 12 (1959): 22.

7. Kay Whitlock, "Striving Toward Equality in Loving Relationships," in Ginny Vida, ed., *Our Right to Love: A Lesbian Resource Book* (Englewood Cliffs, N.J.: Prentice-Hall, 1978), pp. 63–66.

8. Lila Lowenherz, "Women and the Myth of the 'Other'," unpublished paper, 1976.

9. Furgeri, p. 79.

10. See Ruth Falk, *Women Loving* (New York: Random House, 1975); Diane Greene, "Women Loving Women: An Exploration Into Feelings and Life Experiences," unpublished doctoral dissertation, City University of New York, 1976; Oberstone and Sukoneck; and Furgeri.

11. Alan P. Bell and Martin S. Weinberg, *Homosexualities: A Study of Diversity Among Men and Women* (New York: Simon & Schuster, 1978).

12. Peplau et al., p. 19.

13. Jean Baker Miller, *Toward a New Psychology of Women* (Boston: Beacon Press, 1976); Carol Gilligan, *In a Different Voice: Psychological Theory and Women's Development* (Cambridge, Mass.: Harvard University Press, 1982).

14. Falk, p. 465.

15. Bell and Weinberg, pp. 180–86.

16. See Daughters of Bilitis; Freedman; Furgeri; Oberstone and Sukoneck; and Tanner.

17. For a more detailed analysis of the effects of gay oppression on the development of lesbian relationships, see Sidney Abbott and Barbara Love, *Sappho Was a Right-On Woman: A Liberated View of Lesbianism* (New York: Stein & Day, 1972); and Barbara Sang, "Psychotherapy with Lesbians—Some Observations and Tentative Generalizations," in Edna Rawlings and Dianne Carter, eds., *Psychotherapy for Women: Treatment Towards Equality* (Springfield, Ill.: Charles C. Thomas, 1977), pp. 266–75.

18. Personal communication.

19. Jean Weber, "Lesbian Networks," *Christopher Street* (April 1979): 51–54.

20. See Furgeri; Tanner; and Weber.

21. William Simon and John Gagnon, "Femininity in the Lesbian Community," *Social Problems* 15 (1967): 212–21.

22. Peplau et al.; and Tanner.

5

The Older Lesbian: Love Relationships and Friendship Patterns

SHARON RAPHAEL
MINA ROBINSON

*T*his article explores the subject of intimacy and aging by studying a heretofore neglected population of women, lesbians over the age of 50. The authors focus particularly on the patterns of support and nature of relationships that appear to exist for the women studied, whose ages range from 50 to 73. Much of the data presented question popular prevailing myths about older lesbians, especially those that picture the older lesbian as lonely, totally isolated, and without anyone to love or care about her in old age. Special attention is given to two areas that contribute to an understanding of support and intimacy in later life: (1) love relationships and (2) friendship patterns.

Other issues which this article will touch upon include the following:

a. Are uncoupled lesbians single by choice or through just not having found the right person? What decisions have these lesbians who are now over the age of 50 made about their love relationships?

b. What are long-term relationships between lesbians like? Does sexuality continue into old age? Does sexuality change as lesbians age, and in what ways?

c. When the sampled older lesbians ended a long-term relationship (equivalent to divorce), did they get the support (emotional or financial) they needed? Were friends, or relatives, or co-workers told of the breakup? What role did each group play in providing comfort or understanding? Indeed, was there any support at all, from anyone? How

This article is reprinted from *Alternate Lifestyles*, vol. 3, no. 2 (May 1980), pp. 207–29, by permission of Human Sciences Press, Inc. (72 Fifth Ave., New York, NY 10011), and the authors. Copyright © 1980.

does a closeted lesbian cope when she has lost a mate and the people around her are aware only of the more minimal loss of a "roommate"?

d. Where do older lesbians meet other lesbians? In what kind of settings did the respondents meet their mates?

e. In what ways do the lives of feminist lesbians differ from the lives of nonfeminist lesbians?

Wolf (1978), in reporting preliminary trends in her research on close friendship patterns of older lesbians, contends that because older lesbians have less chance than heterosexuals for close family ties due to social stigma and because they are also less likely to have children, they have developed close friendships which offer support. Lowenthal and Haven (1968) refer to the lifelong need for intimacy:

> Lowenthal and Haven show that a single intimate friendship is an effective "buffer" against demoralization produced by the three major kinds of social losses that beset older people: widowhood, retirement, and diminished social participation. Indeed, the morale of people who are more isolated in old age, *but who have one intimate friendship,* is as high as that of people with increased social participation. Only for those *without* a confidant does more social participation help to forestall demoralization in old age. One intimate friendship, in short, was as effective as several less intimate ones for safeguarding morale after role exit [Blau, 1973: 71–72].

Blau also states:

> Friendships with peers are more effective alternatives to marriage and work roles than are relationships with children, though only the latter are defined as institutionally significant. Indeed, because friendship rests on mutual choice and mutual need and involves a voluntary exchange of sociability between equals, it sustains a person's sense of usefulness and self-esteem more effectively than filial relationships. . . . Bonds of friendship, as a rule, develop only between people who view each other as equals and who have interests and experiences in common that they can freely share with one another. For these reasons friendships are usually confined to people of the same generation and at a similar stage of life [Blau, 1973: 67–68].

And Raphael notes:

> Being misunderstood and rejected by "straight" people who have previously been close increases the social barrier between Gay and non-Gay. The lesbian who has "come out" finds it more comfortable and more meaningful to look for friendships and support from within the Lesbian and Gay community [Raphael, 1974: 97].

With these considerations in mind, we will explore in some detail the love relationships and friendship patterns of 20 older lesbians.

Sample and Research Design

The sample employed here consists of 20 women over the age of 50 who identify themselves as lesbians. Of the women, 13 range in age from 50 to 59 and seven from 60 to 73. Exactly half of the respondents live in the San Francisco Bay area of California, and the other half live in the Los Angeles area.

The sample was selected by means of the "snowball technique." An attempt was made to minimize the bias in using this approach by making contact with the initial respondents from as broad a base as possible. This was done by advertising in lesbian, feminist, and older women's publications as well as by receiving referrals from friends and associates. There were two criteria for acceptance as a participant: The women were required to be 50 years of age or older and had to define themselves as lesbians.

All of the respondents are Caucasian, though of various ethnic backgrounds. Eleven of the women were single at the time of the interview and nine were coupled. Five of those who were coupled did not have mates in this sample. (Two couples were interviewed.) Seven of the women have children. Only one had a child still living at home. Five of the women had had heterosexual marriages of significant duration (19–33 years) and another six had short marriages (from three weeks to three years). The short marriages took place primarily when the women were in their twenties and, in several cases, were to gay men for the purpose of "passing" for heterosexual. Fifteen of the women state they have "always known they were lesbian." Two of the women "came out" in their sixties, three in their fifties, one at 48 and one at 38. The other 13 came out in their teens or early twenties.

Thirteen of the respondents had either attended or graduated from college. Six of these had master's degrees. Two had some grade school and two had some high school. Three women were high school graduates.

Nine women were professionals, three were small business owners, two were office administrators, four were in retail sales or office work, one was a real estate saleswoman, and one was an artist. Seven of the 20 are fully retired.

The religions the respondents were raised in were Catholic, three; Protestant, eight; Jewish, six; none, three. The religious convictions they currently hold are Protestant, two; Jewish, one; Science of Mind, two; belief in God, two; 11 had no affiliation or were atheistic.

The interviews took from one to four hours with each respondent. An interview schedule was used which explored four general topic areas: attitudes toward and preparations for aging, kinship/friendship networks, friends and lovers, and identity and community (Robinson, 1979). Discussion within this article will be limited to the material specifically pertaining to intimacy, friendship, and aging.

The data presented here are not intended necessarily to be generalizable to a larger population. Rather, the import of qualitative analysis is to show the richness, diversity, and complexity of the situations of individuals under study. We believe we accomplish this task. Further research can utilize the data offered here for the generation of specific hypotheses to be tested on larger samples of older women.

Love Relationships

What are the ways in which our interviewees structure their love relationships? To what extent is sexuality central to such relationships? Has the importance of sexuality changed over time for these women? These are the questions which will be explored in this section.

Patterns of Intimate Relationships

Although the dominant pattern that intimate relationships followed in our data was one of serial monogamy, there were some respondents with nontraditional preferences. All the lesbians have been in at least one major relationship. Three of the women sampled have been in only one relationship, and two of them are still in that relationship. All three are late-blooming lesbians.

Sixteen of the women in the sample, including the nine women currently in love relationships with women they live with, said they prefer being in a coupled relationship. The primary reasons they gave included companionship, sharing, and support. However, some women had more nontraditional ideas. One woman stated: "I want a lover, a monogamous relationship, but I don't want to live with her." Another single woman said: "What I would like best is a steady girlfriend but not living together." One single, feminist, late-blooming lesbian stated:

> I prefer being single. I have idiosyncracies and I don't want to change how I love. Being coupled would be supportive and psychologically good but I'm too old [she is 63]. I would like a relationship but not someone to live with. It would be exciting to live in a retirement community with other lesbians.

Several women talked about wanting to live collectively and have non-monogamous relationships. Two of them said:

> I don't want to live with a lover. I want a primary relationship. I want to share experiences and goals but not a monogamous relationship. I want to live in a rural women's community.

> I would like to live in a collective. I would like nonmonogamous, plural relationships.

A feminist woman in a coupled relationship stated:

> I have mixed feelings. I love being single, but I also love sharing. . . . After we were together for three years we decided to try nonmonogamy. It didn't work out very well, although we tried for almost four years. Being nonmonogamous is demanding and time-consuming on your primary relationship. We give each other primary support, but I also get support from other friends. We are monogamous again, but I think we'll come to nonmonogamy again when we're both ready.

Sexuality

Sexuality continues to play a part in the lives of all of the women in the sample. Some of these women have experienced changes in the emphasis they place on the importance of sexuality in their lives. This sometimes appears to be caused by the entrance of a new partner.

> Sexuality wasn't important to me before meeting _____ . I was in a forty-year relationship, but the last thirty years we had no sex at all. I'm seventy-three years old and feel thirty-five. I have at last achieved what I looked for all my life in finding someone to love me. Our sex life is very active.

> Sexuality is important to me now. It has changed. It's now happy, fulfilling, marvelous. The frequency has increased since coming out [at sixty-two].

A single woman who was in a 23-year relationship stated:

> Sexuality is very important to me. I'm not able to be sexual with women I don't care about, and sometimes I have a hard time finding women who want sexuality to be a part of their lives. My sexual needs increase as I grow older. I think as women grow older we grow more sexual. We are getting in touch with our basic natures. I love to touch and be touched. I'm not so bothered now by what people think. Whoever I get involved with has to be very spontaneous about lovemaking. I've just started to realize this.

A single, late-blooming lesbian stated:

> It's more important now [the last few years] than before. I want more sex in my life. I'm willing to put more energy into sexuality, instead of in my head. I don't find it easy to be sexual in a casual way. It is the most personal and private thing you can give to anyone. When I am in a relationship I am very sexual.

Another late-blooming lesbian who is in her first lesbian relationship after a 25-year marriage to a man reported: "Sexuality is very important in my life. But then I've got a damn good partner. Sex sure has gotten better!"

For one 72-year-old single woman, finding a partner is a problem.

> Sexuality has been extremely important in my life. I still occasionally have a wet dream. My libido hasn't really changed, but my sex life has gone downhill the past three years, since my last relationship ended. If you don't have a partner, well . . .

A 60-year-old single woman stated:

> Sexuality is fairly important to me but not something I have much of. There was a definite decline when I was going through menopause, from my early forties to my early fifties, but then it came back. There has been a slight decline in my libido in recent years.

Another single long-time lesbian reported:

> I have to love someone before I can have sex. Within long-term relationships it has played a major part in the relationship. My sexuality has stayed the same. Aging hasn't changed anything.

Two women in the study, both feminists, talked about celibacy. The first, a long-time lesbian, responded:

> I was celibate for over a year. Sexuality isn't nearly as important as I was prepared to think. I am relating to another woman now. I decided to be celibate at a time when I wanted to put a lot of energy into things I was doing and not into love relationships. It worked well for me.

The other woman, a late-blooming lesbian, stated:

> My sexuality was transformed into spiritual energy. I have been celibate now for the longest time since I was seventeen [for the past one and one-half years]. I will remain celibate unless I meet someone very special. I do masturbate. My orgasmic drive has diminished. Three years ago I broke my ankle and the shock was so great to my system that I went through instant menopause. That's when my sexual need diminished. Now I'm content with four to six orgasms a week. That didn't used to be enough. Sexuality shaped my life in my thirties and forties, but in my fifties it hasn't [she came out at 51].

The problems that occur in long-term relationships seem to transcend sexual preference:

> It's not the strongest thing in my life. It's less important than it used to be. We make love less often. I think it has to do with the long hours at work, my age [60], and the length of our relationship. I was fifty-three when I started feeling less sexual. We had been together twelve years at that time [twenty years now].

Another woman reported:

> It was more important at one time. Not anymore. Sometimes I feel like going out and just picking somebody up. I feel I need that. Once in a while I

feel restless. But I don't want to hurt _____ . I don't want to risk our relationship [of 20 years]. My sexuality changed with menopause. I don't feel so sexy anymore. It might have something to do with my relationship. I love _____ . But I don't stay with her for sex. I think sometimes couples put too much stress on sex. But sex isn't everything.

A long-time lesbian who has been in seven major relationships talked about her feelings after five years in her current relationship:

Sexuality is not the predominant factor in my life. My libido seems to change with my partners. Sexuality doesn't stand alone. It depends on circumstances. My libido has decreased, but the longer the relationship, the less important sexuality.

A 50-year-old lesbian who has been living with her 30-year-old lover for the past six years stated:

It has decreased. Partially because we've been together for a long time; it gets boring. Partly because we don't work at it. I'm not sure I was ever all that attracted to _____ . We still make love periodically. We are intimate but we have something else. We are companions. Sex has been important in other relationships. The last affair I had [when she and her lover were being non-monogamous] was very sexual. She was older and very erotic, very experienced. We got together for sex. That was the purpose. My libido is decreasing. The quality is more intense, more emotional, but not the driving force it was. I feel the decrease is due to my relationship. I need a woman as aggressive and self-confident and competent as I am. An older woman.

Thus, the myth of a sexual and emotional desert for lesbians in old age has been shown by our data to be false. The findings show that sexuality does continue into old age. Some of the respondents have found life partners at advanced ages. Women who find themselves single in middle or old age continue to seek new partners and in many instances find them. Unlike many older heterosexual men who prefer younger women to older women, the findings show that older lesbians prefer and seek out other older women as partners. Just as Laner's (1979) research comparing lesbians with nongay women tended to dispute notions of ageism within the lesbian community, our study has demonstrated that older lesbians prefer to relate both sexually and socially with members of their own age cohort.

The findings on sexuality in our study compare favorably with the results described in the Duke Longitudinal Study (Verwoerdt et al., 1969) which uncovered patterns of variability in sexual activity in later life. One significant difference that stands out is that the unmarried heterosexual women in the Duke study were almost totally sexually inactive, whereas the older uncoupled lesbians showed a high degree of sexual interest and had realistic expectations of finding sexual partners in the future.

Many of the single women in the sample follow the pattern that Gagnon and Simon (1967) found in their study of lesbians of all ages. These women feel the need for the development of a strong emotional bond before they feel comfortable in allowing sexuality to enter the relationship.

However, several of the respondents who are in long-term committed relationships with women they love state they are bored sexually and feel the need to look elsewhere to have their sexual needs met. Several other single women have stated that the type of relationship they would prefer to be in is a nonmonogamous one, preferably in collective women's communities. Older lesbians in our study who are working on the establishment of nonmonogamous relationships with women's collectives clearly represent examples of the concept of neogamy,

> a seldom-used term meaning new forms of intimate bonding . . . meant here specifically to signify new and therefore alternative forms of intimacy and bonding among individuals which may or may not be sexual [Dressel and Avant, 1978: 13].

Friendship Patterns

To examine the data to see whether friendships develop between equals (Roscow's [1967] term meaning similar status) and whether lesbians, after coming out, look for support within the lesbian community, we will determine the age range of friends and who friends are (gay, straight, men or women) for our respondents.

Two of the 20 women sampled either were in or had recently been in a love relationship with a woman considerably younger than themselves (about 20 years' difference). But all of the women who seek out friends do so among women in the same age cohort. Only one woman listed gay men among her very closest friends, and she considered them to be more like kin than friends. They fulfilled kin roles in her life, such as taking care of her when she was ill and calling daily to check up on her.

Among the nine women in the sample who are currently in love relationships, only one said she had no need for additional friends outside of her love relationship, and she describes herself as a loner. The other eight all have, and wish to continue to have, friends, particularly older lesbian friends, in addition to the relationship they have with their lovers. All nine women view their lovers as their best friends as well as companions and mates.

The seven single feminist women who are actively involved in organizations and who make new friends with women they meet at those organizations are all involved in age-segregated organizations that were formed intentionally to meet the needs of older women.

In general, how do older women meet other lesbians? How important are straight friends? During stressful times, what natural support systems are available to older lesbians? And to what extent is one's self-esteem related to friendship ties? The following sections address these questions.

Meeting Other Lesbians

The respondents were asked how they meet other lesbians. Their answers ranged from "I don't" to "In all the activities I participate in." Several of the women compared the way things used to be with the way they are now in their responses.

> It's hard. I don't like to drink. Bars depress me. I found when I broke with _____ [23-year relationship] I didn't know what to do. I went to bars. It was demoralizing. . . . [Now] I'm in women's and lesbians' groups. I meet them through that, but that's new. It is a problem.

> I meet them at Alcoholics Together (gay AA) meetings. In the past, going to gay bars was the only place I could meet my own kind.

> It's difficult to meet other lesbians. I'm glad for the women's movement. I don't like bars.

> I came to the city to meet other older women. The first year I was here I worked with a neighborhood food co-op, but all I met were younger straight men and women, so then I got involved with older women's groups.

Only three of the women responded in the negative, saying they didn't meet other lesbians. All three, since the time of the interview, have met other older lesbians by going to lesbian and women's movement activities and meetings.

The women in the sample were asked if they had any lesbian friends. The women who are coupled appear to have fewer close friendships with lesbians (other than their lovers) than do single lesbians. Many more coupled lesbians answered the question of friendship with lesbians with the responses, "Quite a few, but I don't see them very much," "A lot, but not close," and "Several, but they are really social acquaintances." The single women, on the other hand, tended to answer with, "Yes, five or six very close friends" or "Lots, all since I came out six years ago."

That the single women in the sample appeared to have more close lesbian friends than the coupled women is quite understandable. One's lover in the lesbian world is almost always a lesbian's best friend, confidant, and constant companion. Therefore, all other lesbian friends take on a less important status almost automatically. Exceptions are found among feminist women, particularly those who believe in nonmonogamy or plural relationships.

About one-third of the women in the sample have met and continue to meet lesbian friends (and potential lovers) in the organizations in which they participate. Another third of the respondents meet other lesbians through friends. The few women who stated they were not able to meet any other lesbians have, since the interviews, met other lesbians at organizations they were directed to by the researchers. This is additional evidence to help destroy the myth that says lesbians are isolated in later life. A few of the respondents were relatively isolated from the lesbian community and did not have many lesbian friends. However, given the information on where they could contact other older lesbians and what organizations existed they were quick to follow up with participation in the lesbian community.

Mates were met in similar settings, generally through friends or within organizations in which they participated. Some of the respondents were friends with their mates for a long period of time before becoming interested in forming a love relationship, while others were immediately attracted to their mates as potential lovers.

Straight Friends

When asked if they had any straight friends, one woman answered, "Only casual acquaintances, but they don't come over." Three women said, "Neighbors" or "People I work with." One woman responded with "Many," but when asked who they were, she said, "The grocer and church people." She does not attend a church at this time.

Half of the women in the sample reported they have had close, long-time friendships with at least one heterosexual woman, but when questioned, they state they have never come out with these close friends. Most of the women in the sample reported they have only one or two straight friends, while they have many lesbian friends. Only one of the six late-blooming lesbians had made any new straight women friends since she had come out. None had made straight male friends. However, all but one had made new lesbian friends since coming out.

Blau's (1973) statement that friendships develop between equals would tend to be supported by the evidence that all of the respondents, when seeking out friends, do so within their own age cohort. That most of the women sought lesbians as friends also supports Raphael's (1974) statement that a lesbian who has come out will find it more comfortable and more meaningful to look for friendships and support within the lesbian community. During the course of the interviews, many of the women spoke specifically to the point of having to look very hard at times to find lesbians their own age, because most of the lesbians in organizations were younger women, but they definitely expressed the need for friends of their own age.

When the respondents were asked about straight friends, many gave a different type of answer than they gave when asked about lesbian friends.

With a few exceptions, they tended to qualify their respondents with comments that served to nullify their answers, such as "I'm friendly with all my neighbors, but they don't come over." One possible explanation for the difference in the type of answer given is that at least some of the women were not comfortable with stating directly that they had no straight women friends. Another possibility is that people define the word "friend" differently. To some, a friend is anyone toward whom one is friendly. To others, a deep bond of commitment that can only be established with time is a necessary ingredient for friendship. Other women appeared to include anyone with whom they spent social time as their friends. Some described friends as the people with whom they worked on common goals in organizations. Thus, a number of reasons may account for the variations in responses.

Support System Availability When Love Relationships End

One way of determining one's support system is to examine a stressful event and the relevant people one relies upon in such a situation. A major trauma in most individuals' lives is the ending of a love relationship. This research attempts to find if the sampled lesbians had the support of friends or family at these times in their lives. Another area of interest is the support systems for lesbian "widows"; however, only one of the respondents had ever suffered the loss of a mate through death, and that death was a suicide. Instead of being given support, the surviving woman was blamed for the death of her mate by their friends. The only support she received was from one old woman who lived next door. There was no will, and the house they lived in, which was in her lover's name, went to the deceased's mother. They had been in the relationship for five years.

Two women in the sample had never experienced the end of a major love relationship with another woman. Both are still in their first relationship. The other 18 respondents had gone through the experience of having a lesbian relationship end at least once in their lives.

There have been major changes in the support women used to receive and what they now receive. It appears that these changes are a consequence of the lesbian's being more out of the closet, at least with people she considers friends, than she used to be. An example of this is the response from one woman when asked what support, if any, she received when her relationship ended:

> None. None of our friends knew we were Gay. It was a shock to them, but they thought we were just friends who decided after twenty-three years of living together that we didn't want to be roommates any more. We did remain friends and gave each other support, but mostly I gave her support. When

that relationship ended, I was broken up. I do feel I had friends around, but I don't ask for help. My friends are straight. I couldn't go to them and say I just broke up with a lover. My best friends are straight. And that's where I should look for support. My intimate friends are not gay, so I could not tell them. Lesbians did invite me to parties, and one I went places with. I got more from them because they knew what happened. The next relationship I had was still in the closet and so was she, so we had no supports. By the time my last relationship ended, I was involved in groups [older women's liberation groups] and I had told a few good friends [straight] about being gay. I got support.

Other women had similar stories to tell.

When my first relationship ended, I had no one to talk to. I was afraid her parents would make trouble on my job. There was one gay woman where I worked that helped. She gave me support. My last relationship before the one I'm in now I wanted to end. She had a serious drinking problem, and I am an alcoholic, but don't drink anymore. I couldn't handle it. By this time I was out and I did get a lot of support from friends. I had no support at all. When a relationship ended, I drank. Things are different now. I don't drink. I have friends. If I were to break up now, well, it would be different.

Three of the respondents had different experiences. Two talk about the phenomenon of looking for friends and finding unwanted potential lovers.

Right after the war [World War II] a woman broke up with me. I went to pieces. My friends all sympathized but they all wanted to go with me them- selves. But I played the field for a while.

Most of the time I've gone directly into another relationship, but I do have friends I can talk to but one time I didn't, so I went to some meetings hoping to make some new friends, but all the women wanted me for a lover, not a friend. I resented it and felt they should have known better. If I were interested in someone sexually, they would have known it because it would have been obvious.

Six other women reported that they have never had support when a relationship ended. Two of them reported:

I had no support at all when we broke up. I was afraid my sister would say "I told you so" and she was the only one who knew. I wrote my feelings in a journal. It was kind of childish stuff but I had nothing else. We had no friends.

There was never enough support. I was not out. Most of my friends were straight, and they didn't know anything. There was a lot of hurt. Nothing you could do about it in those days.

Several of the women received other forms of support. Two of them reported.

When I broke up, my gay male friends kept me busy. They took me out. I also threw a party to meet new people and it worked.

We had each other. We continued to live together.

In examining the data, then, we find that 11 of the women state they had very little or no support whatsoever. Eight of these women, however, state that things are different for them now. Some of the women have more friends to turn to, and others are no longer in the closet (at least to the degree they once were), so they can now confide in friends, where once they could not. The ideology of the gay liberation movement, which has stressed coming out, has clearly made an impact in this area.

An ever-increasing number of women have been able to come out, at least with people they consider their friends. Future generations of older lesbians should be reporting fewer and fewer instances of lack of support when relationships end, if the coming-out trend continues. Attempts to put lesbians and gay men back in the closet, such as the defeated California Proposition 6, have potential ramifications far beyond loss of job, even extending to the seemingly unrelated area of support system availability.

Self-Esteem and Friendship Ties

In the interviews conducted with the respondents, the women were asked for their self-image—how they saw themselves. Their verbal responses were rated positive, mixed, or negative, depending upon their answers. In analyzing their answers, three categories were used: strong self-esteem, moderate self-esteem, and weak self-esteem. The responses were assigned to a category in the following manner.

To be assigned to the strong self-esteem category, the respondent must have primarily used words and phrases commonly understood to express positive values. An example is "strong, bright."

To be assigned to the moderate self-esteem category, the respondent must have used words and phrases commonly understood to express both positive and negative values. An example of this is "I guess I'm no worse than anybody else except for my weight. But at least I know myself pretty well."

To be assigned to the weak self-esteem category, the respondent must have primarily used words and phrases commonly understood to express negative values. An example of this is "If I was to see me walking down the street, I wouldn't bother turning my head."

These self-assessments were then compared with the respondents' frequency of interaction with kin (siblings and children) and friends. On the basis of these responses, relationships were categorized as strong, moderate, or weak.

The modal findings are as follows:

a. Most respondents reported weak sibling ties and strong friendship ties.

b. Most respondents with children reported strong ties with children and with friends.

c. The strongest assessments of self-esteem came from those individuals with weak sibling ties and strong friendship ties. And the stronger the friendship ties, the more likely the older lesbian is to have high self-esteem.

Another way of viewing this is that if one has high self-esteem, one is likely to have strong friendship ties. This is another finding that helps to dispel the myth that lesbians, because of weak or absent family ties, spend their later years friendless, lonely, and with low opinions of themselves. It does appear that lesbians in the age cohort sampled for this study show a much lower incidence of strong ties to vertical kin than do Stehouwer's (1968) respondents, who represent the general population. However, Wolf (1978) is correct when she states that missing kin ties are most often replaced with close friendship ties.

Five of the 10 women in the category of weak sibling and strong friendship ties have very purposefully sought to build friendship networks. They have done so by being involved with feminist organizations and in attempting to form living collectives. All five of these women are single.

The other five respondents who fit into the category of weak sibling ties and strong friendship ties have not joined feminist organizations or planned collectives. They have not purposely set out to form friendship networks, and four of the five are not single but are in love relationships. Four of the five women would not describe themselves as feminists.

There are several possible explanations as to why the feminists and nonfeminists were found to be in the same category—weak sibling ties and strong friendship ties. The one explanation that makes the most sense to the writers is that lesbianism, not feminism, is the common denominator which unites the women in this sample in relation to their friendship patterns. For the older lesbian, the development of close friendship ties can be looked at as a type of adaptation to aging. Friendship ties often serve as an important support system which can enable the women to survive in an otherwise hostile environment. It seems that older lesbians have adapted well to aging as minority group members regardless of their relationship status or political ideology.

Summary and Conclusion

By way of summarizing, it was found that serial monogamy was the dominant life pattern. All the women in the sample had had at least one major relationship during a lifetime and most preferred coupled relationships. Some held nontraditional feminist views about relationships, and expressed interest in nonmonogamous, supportive, and collective-type friendship networks.

Our findings on sexuality showed that it continues to play an important part in the lives of all the women in the sample. Level of sexual activity was greatly influenced by availability of partners. The older lesbians in the study expressed a strong preference toward other older lesbians as partners. The uncoupled lesbians, unlike their heterosexual counterparts, had realistic expectations of finding new partners and expressed little difficulty in finding sexual partners in their own age group.

Regarding friendships, it was found that lesbians who "came out" in later life had fewer straight friends than before "coming out" and chose to seek friends from among their lesbian peers. Single lesbians have more close lesbian friends than do coupled lesbians. The lesbian in a coupled relationship views her partner as her best friend.

Our study found significant differences prior to gay liberation regarding support system availability. Often when a long-time lesbian relationship ended pre-gay liberation, there was often no recognition by friends or relatives that a relationship had existed. Those lesbians who had experienced gay liberation and feminism tended to be more "open" about such relationships and more prepared to share feelings with both gay and nongay intimates who they knew to be supportive.

Finally, this study found that lesbians with high self-esteem tended to have weak sibling ties and strong friendship ties. This finding tends to dispel the myth that because of the loss of family ties the older lesbian would find herself in later years friendless, alone, and with low self-esteem.

A final note should be made regarding feminist ideology and the women in our sample. The data have shown that the nonfeminist women are living out their lives in ways which are satisfying to them and which are not so different from those of the feminist women. There would appear to be three major differences between feminists and nonfeminists. Feminists tend to be active in organizations, while nonfeminists are not active. Nonfeminists tend to be in long-time monogamous relationships, while feminists tend to be single. Finally, feminists are interested in the concept of collective living, while nonfeminists are not.

One way to describe the differences between feminists and nonfeminists is to view the nonfeminists as traditional-thinking women and the feminists as non-traditional-thinking women who believe that new ways can be found to deal with old problems. Another way to view feminists and nonfeminists in this sample is to recognize that the primary difference between the two groups, except for organizational involvement and differing views on monogamy and collective living, is one of conscious ideology.

It would seem to the researchers that nonfeminists in many cases live out the same ideology as do feminists—that is, their supportive relationships with friends. However, the nonfeminists do not see a connection between their lifestyle and the philosophy of feminism.

Regardless of political orientations, however, all of our respondents in their own ways represent positive role models for future age cohorts of older women who are seeking nontraditional supports and living arrangements in later life.

References

Blau, Z. (1973) *Old Age in a Changing Society.* New York: New Viewpoints.

Dressel, P., and W. R. Avant (1978) "Neogamy and older persons: an examination of alternatives for intimacy in the later years." *Alternative Lifestyles* (February): 13–36.

Gagnon, J., and W. Simon (1967) "The lesbians: a preliminary overview," pp. 247–282 in *Sexual Deviance.* New York: Harper & Row.

Laner, M. (1979) "Growing older female: heterosexuality and homosexuality." *J. of Homosexuality,* 4 (Spring).

Lowenthal, M., and C. Haven (1968) "Interaction and adaptation: intimacy as a critical variable," *Amer. Soc. Rev.* 33: 20–30.

Raphael, S. (1974) "Coming out: the emergence of the movement lesbian." Ph.D. dissertation. Cleveland: Case Western Reserve University.

Robinson, M. (1979) "The older lesbian." M.A. thesis. Los Angeles: California State University, Dominguez Hills.

Rosow, I. (1967) *Social Integration of the Aged.* New York: Free Press.

Stehouwer, J. (1968) "The household and family relations of old people," pp. 177–226 in E. Shanas, P. Townsend et al. (eds.) *Old People in Three Industrial Societies.* New York: Atherton.

Verwoerdt, A., E. Pfeiffer, and H. S. Wang (1969) "Sexual behavior in senescence." *Geriatrics* 24 (February): 137–153.

Wolf, D. (1978) "Close friendship patterns of older lesbians." Presented at Gerontological Society meetings, Dallas, November.

6

Beloved Women:
The Lesbian in American
Indian Culture

PAULA GUNN ALLEN

Beloved Women

It is not known if those
who warred and hunted on the plains
chanted and hexed in the hills
divined and healed in the mountains
gazed and walked beneath the seas
were Lesbians
It is never known
if any woman was a Lesbian
so who can say that
she who shivering drank
warm blood beneath wind-blown moons
slept tight to a beloved of shininghair
curled as a smile within crescent arms
followed her track deep into secret woods
dreamed other dreams
and who would record these things
perhaps all women are
Lesbian though many try
to turn knotted sinew and stubby cheek
into that ancient almostremembered scene
perhaps all know the first
beloved so well
they can shape the power
to reclaim her

The portents in the skies—
the moons forever growing and falling

away, the sun's concentric orbits
daily crossing themselves like a nun—
who's to say that these are signs
of what has always been?
And perhaps the portents are better
left written only in the stars,
etched on cave walls, rosewindows,
the perfect naves of brooding
cathedrals. Perhaps
all they signify is best left
unsaid.

Nobody knows whether those women
were Lesbians. Nobody
can say what such an event
might mean.

June 1980

The lesbian is to the American Indian what the Indian is to the Caucasian—invisible.[1] Among the Sioux there were women known as Manly-hearted Women who, it seems, functioned as warriors. Whether they were lesbians is not mentioned in references to them. Indeed, their existence was a pretty well-kept secret, and little is made of it. Among the Cherokee there were women known as Beloved Women who were warriors, leaders, and influential council members. But among the Cherokee, all women had real influence in tribal matters until reorganization was necessitated by American removal attempts. It is not known, however, whether the Beloved Women were lesbians.

In my reading about American Indians, I have never read an overt account of lesbians, and that reading has included hundreds of books and articles.[2] The closest anyone has come, to my knowledge, is a novel by Fred Manfred entitled *The Manly-Hearted Woman,* and though its protagonist dresses as a man and rejects her feminine role, and though she marries a woman, the writer is very explicit: ɔhe and her "wife" do not share intimacies—a possibility that seems beyond the writer's ability to envision. Indeed, she eventually falls in love with a rather strange young warrior who is possessed of enormous sexual attractiveness (given him by spirit-power and a curious genetic circumstance). After the warrior's death, the Manly-Hearted Woman divorces her wife and returns to woman's garb and occupation, discarding the spirit stone that has determined her life to that point.[3]

Because there are few direct references to lesbians or lesbianism among American Indians that I am aware of, much of my discussion of them here is necessarily conjectural. The conjectures are based on secure knowledge of American Indian social systems and customs, which I have gathered from study and from personal information on the American Indian people—of whom I am one—and on my knowledge of lesbian culture and practice.

Certainly, the chances that aboriginal American women formed affectional alliances are enormous. It is equally likely that such relationships were practiced with social sanction, though no one is presently talking about this. The history of Native America is selective; and those matters pertaining to women that might contradict a Western patriarchist world view are carefully selected out.

But it is certain that many tribes have recorded stories concerning daughters born to spirit women who dwelt alone on earth. These daughters often became the mothers of entire tribes. In one such tale, first mother was "born of the dew of the leaf of the beautiful plant."[4] Such tales point to a time prior to the advent of the patriarchy. While historical and archeological evidence suggest that this time predated European contact in some regions of the Western Hemisphere, the change in cultural orientation was already proceeding. The tribes were becoming more male-oriented and more male-dominated. At Zūni, and Hopi, for example, the Deity, who was once perceived as female, started to be seen as male, having passed through a phase of androgyny.[5] As this process continued, less and less was likely to be said by American Indians about lesbians among them. Indeed, less and less about women in any position other than that sanctioned by missionaries was likely to be recorded.

A number of understandings about the entire issue will be important in my discussion of American Indian women—heterosexual or lesbian. It is my contention and belief that those two groups were not nearly as separate as modern lesbian and straight women are. My belief is based on my understanding of the cultures and social systems in which women lived. These societies were tribal, and tribal consciousness, with its attendant social structures, differs enormously from that of the contemporary Western world.

This difference requires new understanding of a number of concepts. The concept of family, the concept of community, the concept of women, the concept of bonding and belonging, and the concept of power were all distinctly understood in a tribal matrix; and those concepts were/are very different from those current in modern America.

The primarily spirit-directed nature of the American Indians must be understood before the place of women, and the place of lesbians, will be comprehensible. Without that understanding, almost anything about American Indians will seem trivial, obscure, or infuriating. To put it simply, the tribes believed that all human and nonhuman activities were directly related to the spirit world. They believed that human beings belonged in a universe that was alive, intelligent, and aware, and that all matters were as much in the province of the spirits as of human beings.

This perception was not based on fantasy or on speculation. It did not spring from some inarticulate longing planted deep within the savage breast by some instinctive human need to understand and manipulate reality. That scholars and folklorists can believe that it did testifies to their distance from a tribal world. In fact, the American Indian people, of whatever tribe, grounded their belief in the spirit world firmly upon their own personal, direct, and communal experience. Those who are traditionals today still place the same construction on actual events. They speak directly to a spirit being, as directly as you might speak to a lunch companion.

Because this is so, their understanding of bonding, sexual relationships, power, familial order, and community was quite different from a modern Christian's view. Included in one's family were a number of spirit people. Among those who shared intimately in one's personal and private reality were one or more personal spirit guides; on the advice of these guides rested many of the decisions and activities in which any person engaged.

Family and Community in American Indian Life

Much of modern society and culture among American Indians results from acculturation. Christianity has imposed certain imperatives on the tribes, as has the growing tendency to "mainstream" Indians through schooling, economic requirements, and local, state, and federal regulation of their lifestyles. The Iroquois, for example, changed the basic structure of their households after the American Revolution. The Americans determined that they had defeated the Iroquois nation—though they had not even fought. Social disorder of enormous magnitude ensued. Handsome Lake, a Seneca prophet, received a series of visions that were to help his people accommodate to the white man. Handsome Lake decreed that a woman should cleave to her husband and they should share a dwelling separate from her mother's (clan) longhouse, and thus the central relationship of mother-daughter was destroyed.[6]

Among American Indians, spirit-related persons are perceived as more closely linked than blood-related persons. Understanding this primary difference between American Indian values and modern Euro-American Judeo-Christian values is critical to understanding Indian familial structures and the context in which lesbians functioned. For American Indian people, the primary value was relationship to the spirit world. All else was determined by the essential nature of this understanding. Spirits, gods and goddesses, metaphysical/occult forces, and the right means of relating to them, determined the tribes' every institution, every custom, every endeavor and pastime. This was not peculiar to inhabitants of the Western Hemisphere, incidentally; it was at one time the primary value of all tribal people on earth.

Relationship to the spirit world has been of primary value to tribespeople, but not to those who have studied them. Folklorists and ethnographers have other values which permeate their work and their understandings, so that most of what they have recorded or concluded about American Indians is simply wrong. And while there can be little question about the fact that most women married, perhaps several times, it is important to remember that tribal marriages bore little resemblance to Western concepts of that institution. Much that has been written about marriage as practiced among American Indians is wrong.

Among the many tribes divorce was an easy matter for both women and men, and movement of individuals from one household to another was fluid and essentially unconstrained. There are many exceptions to this, for the tribes were distinct social groups; but many had patterns that did not use sexual constraint as a means of social control. Within such systems, individual action was believed to be directed by spirits (through dreams, visions, direct encounter, or possession of power objects such as stones, shells, masks, or fetishes).

In this context it is quite possible that lesbianism was practiced rather commonly, as long as the individuals cooperated with the larger social customs. Women were generally constrained to have children, but in many tribes, childbearing meant empowerment. It was the passport to maturity and inclusion in womanculture. An important point is that women who did not have children because of constitutional, personal, or spirit-directed disinclination had other ways to experience spirit instruction and stabilization, and to exercise power.

Family did not mean what is usually meant by that term in the modern world. One's family might have been defined in biological terms as those to whom one was blood-kin. More often it was defined by other considerations; spiritual kinship was at least as important a factor as blood. Membership in a certain clan related one to many people in very close ways, though the biological connection might be so distant as to be practically nonexistent. This facet of familial ordering has been much obscured by the presence of white Christian influence and its New Testament insistence that the term *family* refers to mother, father, and children, and those others who are directly related to mother and father. In this construct, all persons who can point to common direct-line ancestors are in some sense related, though the individual's distance from that ancestor will determine the degree of relationship to other descendants of that ancestor.

Among many American Indians, family is a matter of clan membership. If clan membership is determined by your mother, and if your father has a number of wives, you are not related to the children of his other wives unless they themselves happen to be related to your mother. So half-siblings in the white way might be unrelated in an Indian way. Or in some tribes, the children of your mother's sister might be considered siblings, while those of your father's brother would be the equivalent of cousins. These distinctions should demonstrate that the concept of *family* can mean something very different to an Indian than it does to a non-Indian.

A unified household is one in which the relationships among women and their descendants and sisters are ordered. A split household is one in which this is not the case. A community, then, is an ordering of sister-relationships, which determine who can depend on whom for what. Male relationships are ordered in accordance with the maternal principle; a male's spiritual and economic placement and the attendant responsibilities are determined by his membership in the community of sisterhood. A newcomer in town might be asked, "Who is your mother?" The answer identifies the person and determines the ensuing relationship between the questioner and the newcomer.

Again, *community* in the non-Indian modern world tends to mean people who occupy a definable geographical area and/or who share a culture (lifestyle) or occupation. It can extend to mean people who share an important common interest—political, avocational, or spiritual. But *community* in the American Indian world can mean those who are of a similar clan and spirit; those who are encompassed by a particular spirit-being are members of a community. In fact, this was the meaning most often given to the concept in traditional tribal cultures. So it was not impossible that members of a community could have been a number of women who "belonged" to a given medicine society, or who were alike in that they shared consciousness of a certain spirit.

Women and Power

Any discussion of the status of women in general, and of lesbians in particular, cannot hope for accuracy if one misunderstands women's power in tribal societies. It is clear, I think, that the ground we are here exploring is obscure: women in general have not been taken seriously by ethnographers or folklorists, and what explorations have been done have been distorted by the preconceptions foisted on us by a patriarchal world view, in which lesbians are said not to exist, and women are perceived as oppressed, burdened, and powerless.

In her discussion of the "universal" devaluation of women, Sherry Ortner, for example, cites the Crow, a matrilineal American Indian tribe that placed women highly in their culture. Ortner points to the fact that Crow women were nevertheless required to ride "inferior" horses during menstruation, and were prohibited from participating in ceremonies during their periods.[7] Ortner marshalls this and other impressive evidence to support her claim that Crow women were believed to be inferior to men. But I suspect that the vital question is not whether women have been universally devalued, but when and how and why this came about. I further suspect that this devaluation has resulted from the power which women are perceived to have, and that evidence supporting this contention is at least as massive as the evidence of our ignominy.

Ortner concludes that the Crow prohibited women at prescribed times from certain activities because of a belief that menstruation is unclean. The truth of the matter is quite different. Tribal people view menstruation as a "medicine" of such power that it can cause the death of certain people, such as men on the eve of combat. Menstruating (or any other) Crow women do not go near a particularly sacred medicine bundle, and menstruating women are not allowed among warriors getting ready for battle, or those who have been wounded, because women are perceived to be possessed of a singular power, most vital during menstruation, puberty, and pregnancy, that weakens men's powers—physical, spiritual, or magical. The Crow and other American Indians do not perceive signs of womanness as contamination; rather they view them as so powerful that other "medicines" may be cancelled by the very presence of that power.

The Oglala Holy Man John Lame Deer has commented that the Oglalas do not view menstruation, which they call *isnati* ("dwelling alone"), as "something unclean or to be ashamed of." Rather it was something sacred; a girl's first period was greeted by celebration. "But," he continues, "we thought that menstruation had a strange power that could bring harm under some circumstances. This power could work in some cases against the girl, in other cases against somebody else. . . ."[8]

Power, among tribal people, is not perceived as political or economic, though status and material possessions can and often do derive from it. Power is conceived of as being supernatural and paranormal. It is a matter of spirit, involvement, and destiny. Woman's power comes automatically, by virtue of her femaleness, her natural and necessary fecundity, and her personal acquaintance with blood. The Arapaho felt that dying in war and dying in childbirth were of the same level of spiritual accomplishment. In fact, there are suggestions in the literature on ritualism and tribal ceremony that warriors and male initiates into medicine societies gain their super-natural powers by imitating ritually the processes that women undergo naturally.

Maternity was a concept that went far beyond the simple biological sense of the word. It was the prepotent power, the basic right to control and distribute goods because it was the primary means of producing them. And it was the perfect sign of right spirit-human relationship. Among some modern American Indians this principle is still accepted. The Keres, for example, still recognize the Deity as female, and She is known as Thought Woman, for it is understood that the primary creative force is Thought.

The power of women can only be controlled and directed by other women, who necessarily possess equal power. A woman who is older is more cognizant of what that power entails, the kinds of destruction it can cause, and the ways in which it can be directed and used for good. Thus, adolescent women are placed under the care of older women, and are trained in manners and customs of modesty so that their powers will not result in harm to themselves or the larger community. Usually, a woman who has borne a child becomes an initiate into the mysteries of woman-hood, and if she develops virtues and abilities beyond those automatically conferred on her by her nature, she becomes a medicine woman. Often, the medicine woman knows of her destiny in early childhood; such chil-dren are watched very carefully so that they will be able to develop in the way ordained for them by the spirits. Often these children are identified by excessive sickliness, which leads them to be more reflective than other children and which often necessitates the added vigilance of adults around them.

Eventually, these people enter into their true profession. How and when they do so varies tribe by tribe, but they are usually well into their maturity before they are able to practice. The spirit or spirits who teach and guide them in their medicine work do not appear for them until they have stabilized. Their health usually improves, and their hormone-enzyme fluc-tuations are regularized. Very often this stabilization occurs in the process of childbearing and nursing, and this is one reason why women usually are not fully accepted as part of the women's community until after the birth of a first child.

Lesbians in Tribal Life

Lesbianism and homosexuality were probably commonplace among the old Indians. But the word *lesbian,* when applied to traditional Indian cul-ture, does not have the same meaning that it conveys today. The concepts are so dissimilar as to make ludicrous attempts to relate the long-ago women who dealt exclusively with women on sexual-emotional and spiritual bases to modern women who have in common an erotic attraction for other women.

This is not to make light of the modern lesbian, but rather to convey some sense of the enormity of the cultural gulf that we must confront and come to terms with when examining any phenomenon related to the American Indian. The modern lesbian sees herself as distinct from society. She may be prone to believe herself somehow out of sync with "normal" women, and often suffers great anguish at perceived differences. And while many modern lesbians have come to see themselves as singular but not sick, many of us are not that secure in our self-assessment. Certainly, however, we come to terms with our sexuality; we are not in the position of our American Indian foresister who could find safety and security in her bond with another woman because it was perceived to be destined and nurtured by nonhuman entities, and was therefore acceptable and respectable (albeit, perhaps terrifying) to others in her tribe.

Simple reason dictates that lesbians did exist in tribal cultures, for they exist now. Because they were tribal people, the terms on which they existed must have been suited to the terms of tribal existence. Certainly, American Indian women had abundant opportunities to form erotic bonds with other women.

Spheres of influence and activity in American Indian cultures were largely divided between the sexes: there were women—goddesses, mothers, sisters, grandmothers, aunties, shamans, healers, prophets and daughters; and there were men—gods, fathers, uncles, shamans, healers, diviners, brothers, sons. What went on in one group was often unknown to the other. There were points of confluence, of course, such as in matters pertaining to mundane survival; family-band-clan groups interacted in living arrangements, in the procural or production of food, weaponry, clothing, and living space, and in political function. Men and women got together at certain times to perform social and ceremonial rituals, or to undertake massive tasks such as hunts, harvests, or wars. There were certain reciprocal tasks they performed for one another. But in terms of any real sense of community, there were women and there were men.

In such circumstances, lesbianism and homosexuality were probably commonplace. Indeed, same-sex relationships may have been the norm for primary pair-bonding. Families did not consist of traditional nuclear units in any sense. There were clans and bands or villages, but the primary personal unit tended to include members of one's own sex rather than members of the opposite sex.

Women spent a great deal of time together, outside the company of men. Together they spent weeks in menstrual huts; together women tilled their fields, harvested wild foods and herbs, ground grains, prepared skins, smoked or dried foodstuffs, and just visited. Women spent long periods together in their homes and lodges while the men stayed in men's houses or in the woods, or were out on hunting or fishing expeditions. Young women were often separated from the larger groups for periods of months or years, as were young men. It seems likely that a certain amount of sexual activity ensued. It is questionable whether these practices would be identified as lesbian by the politically radical lesbian community of today; for while sex between women probably occurred regularly, women also regularly married and raised children—often adopting children if they did not have any. There were exceptions to this rule. The Objibway, for example, recorded several examples of women who lived alone by choice. These women are not said to have lived with other women; they lived alone, maintaining themselves and shunning human society.

The women who shared their lives with women did, as a matter of course, follow the usual custom of marrying. The duration of marriage and the bonding style of marriage differed among tribes. Many peoples practiced serial monogamy; others acknowledged the marriage bond but engaged in sexual activities outside of it. Adultery was not a generally recognized concept in American Indian cultures, although some tribes did punish severely a woman who "transgressed" the marriage bond. Among many tribes paternity was not very important; one was identified by the identity of the mother and her clan. This practice was once widespread in North America and today persists in many regions, including the southwestern United States.

Because traditional American Indian women spent the preponderance of their time with women, and because attitudes toward sex were very different from modern Western views, it is likely, in my opinion, that lesbianism was an integral part of American Indian life. This seems reasonable given the fact that lesbianism is a widespread practice even in cultures that have more rigid notions about "appropriate" sexual and bonding behavior. However, relationships among women did not depend only on opportunity. Lesbianism must be viewed in the context of the spiritual orientation of tribal life.

It may be possible to distinguish between those women who took advantage of the abundant opportunities to form erotic bonds with other women, and those women whose relationships with women were as much a matter of spirit direction as of personal preference (though the two were one in some senses). It might be that some American Indian women could be seen as dykes, while some could be seen as lesbians, if you think of a dyke as one who bonds with women in order to further some spirit and supernatural directive, and a lesbian as a woman who is emotionally and physically intimate with other women. (The two groups would not have been mutually exclusive.)

American Indian tradition holds that one who is chosen/directed by the spirits for a particular task must carry out that task. Whoever does not do so is subject to physical and/or psychological destruction. This is not, by the way, because spirits are naturally vindictive, but rather because it is the nature of supernatural/paranormal power to act; if it is denied proper expression, it will express inappropriately, and this might (and often does) result in dire events to the chosen one, her loved ones, and/or her people.

Essentially, the way is dependent on the kind of power the woman possesses, the kind of spirit to whom she is attached, and the tribe to which she belongs. Her initiation will take the course that that of males takes: she will be required to pass grueling physical tests; she will be required to lose her mundane persona and transform her soul and mind into other forms. She will be required to follow the lead of spirits and to carry out the tasks they assign her. The Lakota have a word for some of these women, *kŏska-laka*, which is translated as "young man," and "woman who doesn't want to marry." I would guess that its proper translation is "lesbian" or, colloquially, "dyke." These women are said to be the daughters (the followers/practitioners) of *wiya numpa* or Doublewoman. Doublewoman is a spirit/divinity who links two women together making them one in Her power. They do a dance in which a rope is twined between them and coiled to form a "rope baby."[9] The exact purpose or result of this dance is not mentioned, but its significance is clear. In a culture that values children and women because they bear them, two women who don't want to marry (a man) become united by the power of *wiya numpa* and their union is validated by the creation of a rope baby. That is, the rope baby signifies the potency of their union in terms that are comprehensible to their society, which therefore legitimizes it.

It is clear that the *kŏskalaka* are perceived as powerful, as are their presumed male counterparts, the *winkte*. But their power does not give them the right "to determine [their] own and others' actions" as Jane Fishburne Collier incorrectly says it does.[10] Rather, it gives them the ability to manipulate physical and nonphysical reality toward certain ends. When this power is used to determine others' actions, it at least borders on black magic or sorcery.

To clarify the nature of the power I am talking about, let us look briefly at what Lame Deer has to say about the *winkte*. Lame Deer is inclined to speak rather directly, and tends not to romanticize either the concept of power as it is understood and practiced by his people, or the *winkte* as a person who has certain abilities that make him special. He says that a *winkte* is a half-man/half-woman, perhaps even a hermaphrodite with both male and female organs. In the old days, *winktes* dressed like women and lived as women. Lame Deer admits that though the Lakotas thought people are what nature, or dreams, make them, still men weren't happy to see their sons running around with *winktes*. Still, he says that there are good men among the winktes, and that they have special powers. He took Richard Erdoes (co-author of *Lame Deer: Seeker of Visions*) with him to a bar to interview a *winkte*. The *winkte* told Lame Deer and Erdoes that a *winkte* has a gift of prophecy and that he himself could predict the weather. The Lakota go to a *winkte* for a secret name, and such names carry great power, though they are often off-color. "You don't let a stranger know [the secret name]," Lame Deer says. "He would kid you about it."[11] A *winkte's* power to name often wins him great fame, and usually a fine gift as well.

The power referred to here is magical, mysterious, and sacred. That does not mean that its possessors are to be regarded as priestly-pious people, for this is hardly the case. But it does mean that those who possess "medicine power" are to be treated with a certain cautious respect.

It is interesting to note that the story—one of the few reliable accounts of persons whose sexual orientation differs from the heterosexual—concerns a male, a *winkte*. The stories about *kŏskalaka* are yet to be told. It seems to me that this suppression is a result of a series of coincidental factors: the historical events connected with the conquest of Native America; the influence of Christianity and the attendant brutal suppression of medicine people and medicine practices; the patriarchal suppression of all references to power held by women; Christian notions of "proper" sexual behavior; and, recently, a deliberate attempt on the part of American Indian men to suppress all knowledge among their own people of the traditional place of women as powerful medicine people and leaders in their own right. The medicine-lesbian (to coin a term) has become anathema; her presence must remain hidden until all power she held has been totally blanketed by silence.

Conclusion

Womanculture is unregulated by males, and is misperceived by ethnographers. Perhaps this is so because it is felt—at least among ethnographers' tribal informants—that it is wise to let sleeping dogs lie. There may also be fear of what power might be unleashed if the facts about American Indian lesbianism were discussed directly. A story that has recently come to my attention might best clarify this statement.

Two white lesbians, feminists and social activists, were determined to expand their activities beyond the lesbian and feminist communities, and to this end became involved in an ecological movement that centered on American Indian concerns. In pursuit of this course, they invited a Sioux medicine man to join them, and arranged to pick him up from the small rural town he was visiting. When he saw them, he accused them of being lesbians, and became very angry. He abused them verbally, in serious and obscene terms. They left him where he was and returned home, angry and confused.

A certain amount of their confusion was a result of their misperception of Indians and of this particular medicine man. I have friends in the primarily white lesbian community who seem to think that Indian men, particularly medicine men, are a breed apart who are naturally just. Like other Americans, Indians are inclined to act in ways that are consistent with their picture of the world, and, in this particular Indian's picture, the world was not big enough for lesbians. The women didn't announce their sexual preference to him, by the way; but he knew a *kŏskalaka* when he saw one, and reacted accordingly.

A friend who knew the women involved asked me about this encounter. She couldn't understand why the medicine man acted the way he had. I suspect that he was afraid of the lesbians' power, and I told her that. An American Indian woman to whom I recounted the story had the same reaction. *Kŏskalaka* have singular power, and this medicine man was undoubtedly aware of it. The power of the *kŏskalaka* can (potentially, at least) override that of men, even very powerful medicine men such as the one in my story. I know this particular man, and he is quite powerful as a medicine man.

Not so long ago, the American Indians were clearly aware of the power that women possessed. Even now there are those among traditionals (those who follow the old ways) who know the medicine power of women. This is why a clear understanding of the supernatural forces and their potential in our lives is necessary. More than an interesting tour through primitive exotica is to be gained.

Before we worry about collecting more material from aborigines, before we join forces with those who are in a position to destroy us, and before we decide that belief in ancient matriarchal civilization is an irrational concept born of conjecture and wish, let us adjust our perspective to match that of our foresisters. Then, when we search the memories and lore of tribal peoples, we might be able to see what eons and all kinds of institutions have conspired to hide from our eyes.

The evidence is all around us. It remains for us to *dis*cover what it means.

Notes

1. I use the term American Indian, rather than Native American. While Native American was the usage introduced on college campuses in the sixties and seventies, American Indian is the preferred term of Indian communities and organizations.

2. Jonathan Katz, in *Gay American History* (New York: Crowell, 1976), included a chapter on "Native Americans/Gay Americans, 1528–1976" (pp. 281–334). Fourteen entries in that chapter relate to women. Several of these refer to Indian women who dressed in male clothing. Others cite studies or accounts of the Kutenai Indians, the Crow, the Klamath, the Yuma, and the Kaska that document or suggest the existence of lesbian relationships. Other entries cite Indian legends involving lesbian relationships.

3. Frederick Manfred, *The Manly-Hearted Woman* (New York: Bantam, 1978).

4. Hamilton A. Tyler, *Pueblo Gods and Myths* (Norman: University of Oklahoma Press, 1964), pp. 116–24.

5. Anthony Purley, "Keres Pueblo Concepts of Deity," *American Indian Culture and Research Journal* 1, no. 1 (1974): 28–30.

6. For a detailed discussion of this, see Anthony Wallace, *Death and Rebirth of Seneca* (New York: Alfred A. Knopf, 1969).

7. Sherry B. Ortner, "Is Female to Male as Nature Is to Culture" in Michelle Zimbalist Rosaldo and Louise Lamphere, eds., *Woman, Culture and Society* (Stanford: Stanford University Press, 1974), pp. 65–71.

8. John (Fire) Lame Deer and Richard Erdoes, *Lame Deer, Seeker of Visions: The Life of a Sioux Medicine Man* (New York: Simon & Schuster, Touchstone Books, 1972), pp. 148–49.

9. Elaine A. Jahner and J. DeMollie, *Lakota Belief and Ritual,* Part III, *Narratives* (Lincoln: University of Nebraska Press, 1980).

10. Jane Fishburne Collier, "Women in Politics," in Rosaldo and Lamphere, p. 90.

11. Lame Deer, p. 150.

7

Reclamation: A Lesbian Indian Story

BETH BRANT

October 1975

Tonight I heard Audre Lorde speak. It seems as if all day I have been moving towards this moment. This conference has me spinning around, and is forcing me to look at things that have been hiding inside me. Audre read a love poem. I felt a yearning. Tonight I became a lesbian. A snake sheds her skin, and I'm shedding my old life. This realization that "equality" and civil-rights feminism has been a restriction on me. Becoming a lesbian is not a "personal solution." It's a freedom to explore my feelings, my thoughts, my politics. I feel a sense of relief, a sense of joy. I'm an outlaw that just escaped the posse! I became a lesbian tonight.

January 6, 1976

I look in the mirror and see more wrinkles around my eyes. I'll soon be thirty-five. It seems like my eyes are getting darker. But no, the same old blue-gray. I had a dream about Grandma last night. Her eyes were dark and wet. Her braids had come loose, and were hanging down her back. She was wearing moccasins. This was not like Grandma! I only saw her in cotton dresses. Maybe on Sunday she'd wear one of those shiny rayon dresses. Her braids were always firmly anchored, and on Sundays, a hat would cover her head. Grandma believed in God. A white God whose agents took her name away, jailed her family on Mohawk reservations in Canada, and stole her rituals. But, maybe she carried her rituals around somewhere inside her. When she sang "In the Garden" or "Rock of Ages," who knows what she was seeing in her mind?

April 18, 1976

I was at another meeting tonight. So many interminable meetings; organizing, trying to make feminist changes in too many places in too short a time. Sometimes I hate it. I want to stay home, eat shit food, watch TV, make love all night. A black was speaking. She said, "You white women. . ." I sat there agreeing with her. It wasn't till I came home that I thought, "But I'm not white!" I went to the mirror. All I could see was my mother's face looking out at me. My white mother's face. I searched for traces of my father, my grandparents. I guess they are somewhere. I just can't find them yet. I suddenly realize that I have passed for white. I feel strange, sort of like a collaborator. My stomach hurts. I went upstairs to check on my daughters. They are growing up. Sixteen, twelve, and eleven. I have been neglecting them. In my newfound life, I think I have left them behind. I love them so much, but I hunger for freedom too. So I go to meeting after meeting. Go to the bars once in a while. Dance like crazy. I have a lover for an evening or two. Nothing serious, but at the same time, not transient or impersonal. Always caring. I want my daughters to come with me, in my new skin, but I think they won't. Why is it so hard? Why do I feel like crying? I want my mother. I really want Grandma. Please Grandmother, hold me.

July 25, 1976

I am in love with Denise! She is wonderful. She is earthy, brilliant, beautiful, and Polish. I love her. We're going to live together and make a rich life. When we're old, old women, we will live in a little home with no children, and rock in our rocking chairs, and make love, and sleep intertwined like morning glories. We will make a feminist world from love. I am so happy! There is a magic between us, a language we both speak. I feel cherished.

September 1976

Denise and I are becoming adjusted to each other's rhythms. The kids like her. She is a good and wise woman. She wants to share motherhood. I can't believe such happiness. How did this happen? I want to hold onto this feeling, keep it with me.

January 20, 1977

Today we were talking about our childhoods. My family was big and extended. I was very happy in it. I was indulged, as were all the kids. There was always someone around to listen, to teach. I was a sick child. Rheumatic fever. Most of my world was contained in the little room where my bed was made up. My mom had other women to help with the care I required. I never realized the importance of those women. They were so beautiful. Coal-black hair. Grandma with her silver braids. Mother, pale and English looking. She wasn't frail though. Denise wants to know everything. Most of this stuff is buried inside my head and heart. It makes me strangely uncomfortable. I am afraid to face my own racism. I have a need for things to be nicey-nice. I can't look too deeply. It means a change in everything. I'm so happy with my life as it is now. Will this be jeopardized? What is going on?

May 16, 1977

We had a bad fight. About children, about us, about our defensiveness towards each other. Where does this come from? We're like two cats that curl up to each other, then wake to spit and hiss and hurt. I hate this. Denise looks so unhappy. I made her cry such heart-wrenching sobs. I hate myself. I am so mean. I feel like a cornered animal.

My mother called and we talked. She finds gentle fault with the way I raise my daughters. I told my mother that we are different. I came away from the phone irritated and upset. Denise says I *am* raising the children like my mother would. Spoiling them rotten! Dear heart. Every act of rebellion on Denise's part was met with the belt, or the ritual washing out her mouth with soap. Her spirit remains unbroken. Her undaunted faith in us, in women, in feminism, is a testimony to courage, to the rebel in us all. I am promising myself I will be more fair to Denise. She tries hard to see my side of things. I lash out; hurting, injuring.

December 21, 1977

My blood pressure is high again. The Indian's disease. My dad has diabetes. Grandma had everything wrong with her. She died of a heart attack. Too much corn soup and fry bread. It scares me, but I don't take good care of my body. Smoking, eating too much, the stress of living in a city like Detroit. Fear all around us. When one of the kids is late coming home, I experience a terror that leaves me shaking. I worry about money. We work so hard.

Denise and I find comfort in one another, but I still feel alone, unfinished. I'm not sure who I am. Is this possible? I dream of Grandmother, and now, Denise has dreams of her.

May 3, 1978

After a period of not reading, I find I am devouring everything in sight. So many important words are being spoken. I read about racism and anti-racism, and try to find the words that will heal me and let me off the hook. I don't want to waste time and emotion on white guilt. (But I'm not white!) My anger at myself, for what I see as betrayal of my family, is eating at me. The pain of being at war with myself is spilling out onto the relationships I value. I love Denise, my daughters, my friends, but I don't want to see anyone. I just want to read and make peace with me. Are there other women like myself? Two races melding into one woman. By some twist of genetic fate, I came out light-skinned, blue-eyed. The color that counts is white. Once, in therapy, years and years ago, I expressed a desire to adopt an Indian child (o liberal humanist). My therapist, a white man, interpreted this to mean that I wanted to give birth to my father's child. Fool, fool! I wanted to give birth to myself! The thing I hated in my mother was her whiteness. In a world that demands we hate our mothers, this was the reason I had singled out. Mother defied her family to marry Dad. Maybe she was disappointed in our lack of color. Or maybe she was relieved to know our lives would be easier because of light skin and blue eyes. She will never say, believing it to be disloyal to speak of such things. Disloyal to whom?

January 12, 1979

I tentatively begin talking again about the past. Denise listens, encouraging me. I talk more and more about Grandma. I cry when I remember small bits and scraps that seem to come out of the air. I remember Grandpa's death. I loved him. I remember a dress with daisies on it. Mama and Grandma had worked on it together. Grandpa picked me up in his arms, hugged me tight, and called me "a masterpiece, our masterpiece." He taught me Mohawk, and told me countless stories. Now I can at last mourn him, and let him go. I feel like a stone has been lifted from my heart.

Ultimately, lesbian/feminism means a new way of putting things right. A turning away from the inventions of patriarchy that have made us crazy and uncertain.

April 1980

I am in a discussion group. Tonight we talked about racism. A woman asked, "What was your first encounter with racism?" I began to speak on my girlhood. When I was eight or nine, my friends started to bug me about my family. They taunted me. I didn't understand. One asked me if my father did rain dances. Another asked if my Grandma slept in a tipi. In fear and self-defense, I made up stories about my father. I made fun of Grandma (forgive me, forgive me). My friends laughed. I had appeased them. I had learned the secret of how to placate the monster of racism. As I told my story, the tears began to flow. Denise took my hand. My dearest friend, my love. As I wept, and related my feelings of having betrayed the woman I loved, I felt a sense of power growing in that room. Each woman was struggling with her own brand of guilt, her own assumptions; coming to a feminist understanding of our place in this thing, our responsibility to each other. It's not a phony humanist or ACLU attitude; one that hides or glosses over the woman-hatred everywhere. Our movement goes deeper. It challenges, it doesn't settle for skirmishes won in courtrooms, or amendments to patriarchal constitutions. The core of our movement is our love for each other, the justice that pervades our theory, our poetry, our struggles to be fair in our relationships with lovers, friends, our children, our mothers. I feel exhilarated tonight. I think I can hold onto this. I know I have to begin talking and writing and reaching out to others like myself. I have laid some ghosts to rest. I read somewhere that the ancient meaning of reclamation means to protest, or a cry of opposition. This is the kind of reclaiming I'm engaged in. Actively and forcefully seizing my life out of the hands of those who would destroy me and all women like me. By saying no to them, I have said yes to us.

Postscript: February 1983

In three years I have taught myself to name myself in many ways. As Indian, as lesbian, as mother, as writer. And I look over my shoulder as I write this. The four do not go together. It is "wrong" to be a lesbian Indian, a lesbian mother. It is even more of a breach to write about it.

I can't take sanctuary in the definition "artist." It is too tame a word for what I do. It doesn't carry enough weight. It doesn't breathe, sweat, eat, make love.

"Cultural worker" comes close, yet misses. It is too loose, too temporary a description. It fails to take in the guts and blood of making words *mean* something. Of translating language into magic. Of transforming magic into action.

So, I am an Indian, a lesbian, a mother, a writer.

Three years have made me angrier, have made me sadder. I am struck by how much naive hope I had. How much I wanted there to be solutions to problems that had yet to be named. My unrelenting optimism in the idea of love and feminism being the answer to human and planet suffering. But I *do* believe in love and feminism. I also believe in responsibility. And love without responsibility is a travesty. Feminism without love is self-aggrandizement.

It is impossible to separate love and feminism from where I live, Detroit. The environment surrounding me and my family is one of hunger, unemployment, polluted sky, rotten lakes, food that is unfit to eat. I cannot pretend that the couple who live next door has nothing to do with me. He has been out of work for months. She works for minimum wage filling candy machines in a school. He says, "I only want to work. Why don't they want me to work?" She is expecting another child. They have no insurance for the birth. If she believed in abortion, there wouldn't be money anyway. *This has everything to do with me, with us.* Why is the issue of class a dirty topic, not to be touched, except by leftists, and then, only in peripheral language—"workers" or "ruling class." Why is it taking so long to see our complicity in the very oppressions we rail against?

And why has racism become a proving ground for white feminists to contest with each other over who is more antiracist, who is more self-righteous? Why, my sisters and I repeatedly ask, are Indians not reckoned with? A well-known white feminist, giving a speech, talked about blacks, Latinas, Asians. Where was I? Where were my sisters? Do we not count when the talk turns to racism? Is it okay to be racist towards us, but not the others? What else can I infer from our constant negation, our being written off in regards to the women's movement? Our being discounted and made invisible at every turning? I think I look over my shoulder to see if my shadow follows. Or else, I may not exist, except in my own imaginings.

In three years my daughters have grown. One no longer lives at home. All have jobs that are considered shit work. One is a secretary. One is a cashier. One is a kitchen girl in a restaurant. One went to college for a year. All are heterosexual. Denise recently lost her job; fired because of her lesbianism. Her job was not a fancy one, but it supported us and kept us going. I do not have a job. At least, not one that requires me to be in one place every day, doing the same thing daily. My work is here, on the page, in the pen, in front of Indian audiences, feminist audiences. However, my work does not pay me. I doubt whether it will be possible to earn a living this way. Denise believes in me, and backs up that belief by being the wage-earner.

My eldest daughter is getting married this summer. The fact of this lesbian mother, watching her eldest and beloved girl make preparations for the ritual of marriage, is a reality I have not yet begun to deal with. My emotions are conflicted. I have joy for her, but I want to scream—"Don't do it, don't do it!" Yes, Denise and I made far too many mistakes in wanting to be fair, to be liberal. Our daughters love us, and tolerate who we are. There has been an uneasy truce in our home. A very wise woman said, "The best way to insure having heterosexual children, is for them to have a lesbian mother." I am a lesbian mother. I will always be a lesbian mother.

Three years later, I still hold hope for the possibilities of love and feminism. There is much work to do. And I am already tired. Spirit keeps me going. Indian spirit, lesbian spirit, mother spirit, writer spirit. They make up a whole. And I am that whole.

8

The Puerto Rican Lesbian in the United States

HILDA HIDALGO

*T*he Puerto Rican lesbian is probably the person most invisible in the literature addressing the sexual lifestyles of Puerto Ricans. Based on 1980 official census figures and using the Kinsey Scale,[1] we can estimate that there are 210,000 Puerto Rican homosexuals living in the continental United States and that over half of these are lesbians. If we accept the premise that each of these Puerto Rican lesbians and gay men has at least four other nonlesbian, nongay significant others—members of the Puerto Rican community who are in some meaningful way affected by their lifestyle—the issues related to this minority affect 50 percent of the Puerto Rican population in the United States. Sexuality and its expression is a major force in personality development, in the dynamic functioning of the individual, in mental health and self-actualization. Thus, issues of gay and lesbian Puerto Ricans deserve much more attention from human services professionals than they have been given in the past.

The focus of my study is the Puerto Rican lesbian in the continental United States. Specifically, the data and insights gathered are directed toward exploring the following issues:

1. The organizational roots, contexts, and implications of the lesbian Puerto Rican community in the United States

2. The meaning to Puerto Rican families of having an identified lesbian member

3. The effects of class and ethnicity on lesbian lifestyles in the Puerto Rican community, and interaction with the dominant lesbian culture

4. The implications of my findings for psychotherapy

Brief Overview of the Puerto Rican Community in the United States

A brief overview of the Puerto Rican community is necessary to locate Puerto Rican lesbians within their cultural context. The Puerto Rican community in the United States has characteristics that stem from the political, social, and economic colonial relationship that has existed between the United States and Puerto Rico since 1898. Puerto Rican culture is the result of the dynamic intermingling of four cultures: Taino, African, Hispanic, and Anglo-American. Puerto Rican migration to the U.S. reflects the effects on individuals of a technological age of production, creates a "commuter-migration" frame of reference that keeps many Puerto Ricans "island centered,"[2] and is met with racism in the United States.

Puerto Ricans are United States citizens by birth; they have access to the continental United States. The exodus of Puerto Ricans to the United States mainland between 1945 and 1970 was so great that it has been referred to as one of the largest population movements in modern history. Considering the size of the Puerto Rican population, the exodus of the islanders to the continental United States represents the equivalent of fifty million United States citizens leaving the United States to settle elsewhere.[3] Puerto Ricans (on the island as well as in the continental United States) have been the target of massive institutional programs to Anglicize or Americanize them. The resistance of Puerto Ricans to this forced acculturation has been noted by various social scientists like Nathan Glazer, who described Puerto Ricans as "island centered." In spite of collective and individual resistance to being Anglicized, Puerto Ricans residing in the United States for extended periods of time have been influenced by the dominant culture to the degree that island Puerto Ricans have minted a new word to describe them: *New Yoricans.*

According to the 1980 census, 2.1 million Puerto Ricans live in the continental United States—almost as many Puerto Ricans as resided on the island of Puerto Rico in 1960 (2.3 million). As a group, Puerto Ricans are at the bottom of the economic totem pole. The Bureau of the Census reports that in 1979 the annual median income for Puerto Rican families was $7,163, substantially lower than the median income for Irish-American families ($12,518) and Italian-American families ($12,520). Another study by the Bureau of the Census reveals that 38.9 percent of the Puerto Rican population in the continental United States are living with incomes below the official poverty level.

Migration to the continental United States has not made most Puerto Ricans surrender their dream of returning to a few acres of land on an island romanticized and idealized by the diaspora, and to the peace of belonging. The reality is that it is more and more difficult for the Puerto Rican to return and make an easy adjustment to the island society. The Puerto Rican lesbian, more than her heterosexual sister, seems to have accomplished the psychological task of clearly saying to herself, "I am going to stay within continental United States society; I will incorporate in the larger society and in the lesbian culture without suicidal or shameful renunciation of my Puerto Rican identity."

Methodology

I have been studying Puerto Rican lesbians for the last ten years, and have conducted in-depth interviews with three hundred Puerto Rican lesbians. Two hundred fifty of these lesbians have resided in the continental United States for more than ten years. The resources available to one precluded the possibility of a random representative sample. No study of Puerto Rican lesbians has included a larger sample or a representative sample.

To complement the data and insights gained from the in-depth interviews, I have observed and participated in a variety of events involving the Puerto Rican lesbian/gay community. The events have been of a political and/or social nature, organized by individuals and organizations. Examples of these events are a meeting of COHLA—Comité Organizador de Homosexuales Latino-Americanos—the first and second National Conference of Third World Lesbians/Gays, the National Gay/Lesbian March, Washington, D.C. (October 1979), and Gay Pride Marches (1975–81) in New York City and Boston.

Profile of the Puerto Rican Lesbian in the United States

The following profile of the Puerto Rican lesbian in the United States is based on my interviews and observations. I compare the data with data available from other sources on the Puerto Rican population in the United States.[4]

Place of Birth

Eighty percent (N = 240) of the sample were born and raised in the United States. Of these, 230 were first-generation United States born, of Puerto Rican parents; 10 were second-generation; and 60 were born in Puerto Rico. Length of residence in the United States varied from 2 years to 40 years. This distribution follows the trend reported in a 1970 study that found that 31 percent of the population studied had been born on the island.

Age
Lesbians in the sample ranged from 16 to 65 years of age. Seventy-five percent were in the 21 to 30 age bracket; fifteen percent in the 31 to 45 age bracket. In this respect the lesbian sample represented an older population since the median age of members of the Puerto Rican community in the United States is 18.

Education
Ninety-eight percent (N = 294) had completed high school, 37 had completed college, with 10 having graduate and/or professional degrees at the post-baccalaureate level. One hundred and twenty-five had vocational training (secretarial, medical technician, computer, etc.) either as part of their high school education or after high school. The 2 percent in the 16 to 20 age bracket were still in school. The lesbians in the sample were better educated than the majority of the Puerto Rican community since only about 33.3 percent of Puerto Ricans in the United States (ages 15 to 24) have completed high school. In New Jersey, statistics compiled by Aspira Inc. indicate that about 2 percent of Puerto Rican youth attend college. Christensen[5] found in a 1975 study he made in Puerto Rico that women's educational level was higher than men's.

Economics
The median income in the lesbian sample was $12,780, exceeding the median income of Puerto Ricans by $5,617. The higher income was reflective of their higher level of employment and educational achievement. The lesbians were very aware of their need to be economically independent of welfare agency/male/lover/husband/family of origin support.

Family Characteristics
In this respect, the lesbians followed more closely the pattern in the general Puerto Rican population, 32 percent having four to seven siblings and 50 percent coming from families headed by females. Seventy-five of the women were presently married or had been married and were now divorced. Ten were living with their husbands at the time they were interviewed and had no plans to separate or end the marriage. Two hundred and fifty-five (85 percent) contributed financially to the support of parents or siblings. Forty-five of the lesbians in the sample lived in the same household with members of their family of origin (parents, married siblings, and so on).

Degree of Incorporation

The degree of incorporation (adopting characteristics of the dominant Anglo society without abdicating their identity as Puerto Ricans) was determined by the following indicators:

1. The use of English as the language of preference, and fluency
2. The frequency of their visits to Puerto Rico
3. Their involvement and association with organized groups in the Puerto Rican community
4. Their participation in social and recreational activities where the participants were predominantly, if not exclusively, Puerto Rican

I developed a rudimentary scale of 1 to 10 to measure incorporation using the four indicators listed, with a score of 10 representing maximum incorporation. It is significant that 72 percent scored at the midpoint of the scale or higher.

Organizational Affiliations of Puerto Rican Lesbians in the United States

In the interviews I asked about organizational affiliations and activity. I divided organizations into six categories: (1) political, (2) professional, (3) feminist, (4) religious, (5) social-recreational, and (6) lesbian.

The highest organizational activity was related to the lesbians' professions or jobs. In this category 99 percent of the sample were "in the closet" and felt that identification as lesbians in these organizations would hurt them professionally. It is interesting that the professionals in the group were predominantly members of the human services professions: social workers, nurses, teachers, lawyers, psychologists, and medical doctors.

Religious organizations ranked second in terms of organizational affiliations. Sixty-nine (69 percent) of those with religious affiliations seemed to have made accommodations that allowed them to practice a lesbian lifestyle and still belong to religious groups that consider homosexuality a sin, without exhibiting high levels of conflict and/or guilt. Two persons in the sample belonged to Dignity (a Roman Catholic lesbian-gay organization).

While the affiliation of Puerto Rican lesbians with lesbian-gay political activist groups is low, the participation in gay-lesbian civil rights marches has increased. I made a rough head count of Latino participation in the Gay Pride Marches of 1978, '80, and '81, and the numbers of Latinos and Puerto Ricans participating in these events more than doubled from 1978 to 1981. Some of the organizations joined by Puerto Rican lesbians are Salsa Soul Sisters, New York; El Comité Latino de Lesbianas y Homosexuales, Boston; and Comité Homosexual Latino-Americano, New York. Juanita Ramos, a Puerto Rican lesbian, was one of the speakers at the National Gay-Lesbian March in Washington, D.C. (1979).

The data indicate that Puerto Rican lesbians involved in political activities tended to be members of progressive political organizations that included as a major aspect of their political agenda the political status of Puerto Rico. These organizations were predominantly pro-independence for Puerto Rico and for a socialist democratic or communist form of government. Although these organizations stated that they accepted the lesbian/gay lifestyle, many lesbian and gay activists were frequently asked to remain in the closet because the organization believed that open identification of lesbian/gay members would hurt its political goals. After being very active in these political groups, a number of lesbians left the organizations out of frustration at placing their liberation as lesbians as a hidden agenda in the main political agenda. Consistently, lesbians and gays reported overt and covert sexist and homophobic behavior on the part of these political organizations and their leaders.

One of the most revealing findings in the research was the high number of Puerto Rican closeted lesbians in positions of leadership in many of the most respected and established Puerto Rican institutions and organizations. My personal experience, as one of the leaders of the Puerto Rican community in the state of New Jersey and in the nation, is that my influence and status in the Puerto Rican community was not diminished when I publicly came out as a lesbian. The trend in the young Puerto Rican lesbian community is in the direction of becoming more visible, political, and organized. Their influence and force will undoubtedly increase in the Puerto Rican community.

Puerto Rican Families and Identified Lesbian Members

Puerto Rican lesbians believe that young Puerto Rican women, married or single, are more accepting of their (the lesbians') sexual orientation than men are. Young men are also viewed by them as more accepting than older men. My findings indicate that sex and age are viewed by lesbians as important variables of acceptance, while marital status is not perceived as having much influence.

Half of the sample said that their families knew of or suspected their homosexuality. They perceived their families as having a "silent tolerance" in which there was seldom an open acknowledgment of their particular lifestyle. Siblings and cousins appeared to be more understanding and accepting. A few subjects indicated that they had talked about their sexual orientation with sisters and cousins without experiencing rejection. There were strong indications that family acceptance or tolerance, rather than rejection, of homosexual members was related to the overall tone of the family relationship. For example, where the family was warm, with close ties of understanding for all its members, the homosexual member was not singled out for rejection; but when family members related to each other with hostility, sexual orientation offered a rationale for rejection.

As an illustration of how the Puerto Rican culture transmits double messages, some gay women stated that they often received praise from the family and the community for not being "boy crazy" and for being dedicated to their studies, jobs, or professions. At the same time, they were teased for not getting married. The phrase "te vas a quedar jamona" (you are going to become an old maid) often followed the words of praise.

The highest degree of nonacceptance was experienced by lesbian mothers. They tended to be more closeted than single lesbians and more fearful of rejection by their family if their identity as a lesbian became known. They also feared losing custody of their children.

In 1976, I reported my initial findings from a sample of sixty-one Puerto Rican lesbians.[6] Subsequent research and interviews have shown trends different from those reported in 1976: (1) The acceptance of lesbians in the Puerto Rican family structure has improved as Puerto Rican women and their families are influenced by and are becoming more accepting of the sexual revolution of this decade. (2) Puerto Rican women are more free in expressing sexuality—this is true of lesbian and nonlesbian Puerto Rican women in Puerto Rico and the United States. (3) Female members of the family in general are more accepting of lesbian family members than are male family members.

Puerto Rican lesbians have also created extended family relationships with other Puerto Rican lesbians and progressive nonlesbian women. These "extended families" are very important support systems to lesbians; indeed, most lesbian social life takes place in the homes of members of the extended family.

Class, Ethnicity, and Lesbian Lifestyles in the Puerto Rican Community

Puerto Rican culture has strong roots in the Judeo-Christian tradition and in patriarchy. Therefore, the traditional position articulated in the culture is rejection of lesbianism and homosexuality. Homophobia plays a major role in the official culture. (Homosexuality and lesbianism are criminal offenses in Puerto Rico.) However, indicators point to a greater acceptance in the Puerto Rican community of lesbianism and homosexuality (for instance, many gay/lesbian bars operate openly in the Latino community in the United States and in Puerto Rico). Perhaps one of the Puerto Rican tools of survival is the ability to compromise and make compatible positions that seem by logic to be incompatible (for example, to be an "emotional" *independentista* and nationalist and a "rational" *estado-librista* or *estradistra*).

My observations support the conclusion that exposure of the Puerto Rican community to lesbians plays a more important role in acceptance of a lesbian lifestyle than does social class. Individuals who have positive interactions with lesbians are most accepting and supportive of a lesbian lifestyle, regardless of the class and educational level of either the lesbian or the heterosexual person.

The lesbian/gay community reflects the racist and sexist attitudes of the larger community. Within the Puerto Rican gay community, racism, Puerto Rico style, is evident. However, the Puerto Rican lesbian experiences more overt racism from the Anglo gay community. Whatever issue, situation, activity the Puerto Rican lesbian confronts, she usually processes it from the perspective of her Puerto Rican identity.

Politically aware Puerto Rican lesbians and gays have many demands made on them to become involved in organizations and activities in the Puerto Rican community and in the non-Puerto Rican community. They are likely to be overextended. Unlike their non-Third World counterparts, Puerto Rican lesbians/gays can find it difficult, if not impossible, to devote all or a major portion of their energies to lesbian and gay issues and concerns. They might subordinate the lesbian/gay issue of oppression to fighting oppression based on race and ethnicity. Being overextended, they may have difficulties meeting deadlines, or because of priorities they might default in following through on a previously agreed-to task (giving first attention to a crisis or issue that subsequently develops and is related to the Puerto Rican community). These actions can be misinterpreted by non-Third World persons as lack of interest or lack of responsibility. Lack of awareness and understanding of Puerto Rican lesbian realities and priorities by the greater lesbian/gay community often negatively affects conditions and networking with other groups.

Implications for Psychotherapy

Given the importance of the sexual drive and physical expression of this drive for the mental health of individuals, the findings discussed have implications for the human services professions and for psychotherapy.

In spite of the change approved in 1973 by the American Psychiatric Association that removed homosexuality from the list of mental disorders, the great majority of psychotherapists base their clinical practice in homophobic theories of personality development such as neo-Freudian, Adlerian, and Gestalt therapy. Even those therapists who consider themselves liberal and accepting—including feminist therapists—assume that a lesbian or homosexual lifestyle is a second-best adaptive alternative for those who can't deal with or refuse a heterosexual lifestyle. This homophobic attitude makes responsive and constructive psychotherapy difficult, if not impossible. In addition, most therapists have a limited understanding of Third World culture and Puerto Rican culture specifically. Women in my sample who were members of professions related to mental health stated that they perceived remaining in the closet as a professional survival strategy. In choosing a psychotherapist the Puerto Rican lesbian must test the therapist's knowledge, sensitivity, and respect for the Puerto Rican culture and for the lesbian lifestyle. Psychotherapist Bernice Goodman has developed a set of questions as guides for selecting a nonhomophobic therapist.[7] I consider Goodman's instrument for selecting a nonhomophobic therapist to be such a valuable resource for lesbians that I have obtained permission to include it in this article.

How to Choose a Nonhomophobic Therapist

Private Practice

1. What firsthand knowledge does the therapist have about the lesbian and gay culture? How many lesbian/gay clients? How long has the therapist been working with lesbian/gay clients?

2. How much understanding and knowledge does the therapist have about racism, sexism, and homophobia in our society?

3. Is the therapist committed to a concept of "difference" rather than "sameness"?

4. Is this therapist free to challenge self-oppressive attitudes that you hold about yourself and to support new self-creative and expansive feelings about yourself?

5. How, and in what way, does this therapist participate in the lesbian and gay community?

6. Is this therapist willing to engage with clients in community activities outside of the therapy interaction? Can the therapist understand the qualities that are different in these two types of interactions?

7. Do you like this person? Does this person generate a feeling of trust and safety? Does this person seem secure and free and happy to participate as a therapist in the interactional process of therapy?

8. How willing is this therapist to negotiate terms and means of payment (for example, sliding scale, barter, work exchange, etc.)? Does he or she

give you the impression that the payment is more important than you are?

9. Does this therapist understand that institutional homophobia is an illness and that lesbian/gay people are victims of the social illness?

10. Can this therapist articulate the differences between real societal oppressions and appropriate behavior responses related to this, and real intrapsychic difficulties that a lesbian/gay person may be experiencing?

11. Can this therapist distinguish between programmed negative definitions of self as a woman and internal, positive organic psychic feelings of self as woman?

12. Can this therapist help men deal with feelings about differing from societally defined and imposed images of being a "real man"? Is this therapist able to raise questions within the gay male community in terms of the "economically reinforced macho image" vs. an attitude of not acknowledging oppression as men.

Agency Practice

1. The same criteria for choosing a therapist in private practice apply for choosing a therapist within an agency.

2. Does the waiting room have lesbian/gay magazines and literature?

3. Does written material descibing agency services include lesbian/gay people and their needs?

4. Ask the therapist how many staff meetings are devoted to lesbian/gay issues, as well as to other alternate lifestyles.

5. Ask how many open lesbian/gay professionals/workers are on the staff of their agency.

6. Ask for a therapist who is knowledgeable about lesbian/gay culture and who has been retrained to recognize homophobic attitudes, values, and practices.

In the last analysis, the goal of any therapeutic intervention is for the patient or client to become her own authority in charge of her individual and community life. Self-actualization of the Puerto Rican lesbian client occurs when her feelings, her internal harmony as a lesbian and a Puerto Rican become freed.

Conclusions

Research on the Puerto Rican lesbian and gay population is difficult. Too often Puerto Ricans have experienced the punitive use of research findings. Being a Puerto Rican lesbian feminist with a recognized track record of community involvement helped me get access to subjects and gain their trust. While the resources available to me precluded the possibility of a random sample, the findings clearly indicate trends and directions in the attitudes and lifestyles of Puerto Rican lesbians and in how they are perceived by the larger Puerto Rican community. Three hundred Puerto Rican lesbians stood up and were counted, a clear indication that the Puerto Rican lesbian will become more visible and more actively involved politically, and that the seed of her rebellion against her triple oppression (as a Puerto Rican, as a woman, as a lesbian) has taken root and will flourish.

Notes

1. Alfred C. Kinsey et al., *Sexual Behavior in the Human Female* (New York: Simon & Schuster, 1965), pp. 468–72.
2. Nathan Glazer, *New York Puerto Ricans* (Cambridge, Mass.: Harvard University, Joint Center for Human Studies, 1963).
3. Luis Nieves Falcón, *El Migrante* (San Juan, Puerto Rico: Editorial Edil, 1975).
4. *Puerto Ricans in the Continental United States: An Uncertain Future* (Washington, D.C.: U.S. Commission on Civil Rights, 1976).
5. Edward W. Christensen, "The Puerto Rican Woman: The Challenge of a Changing Society," *Character Potential* 7 (March 1975).
6. Hilda Hidalgo and Elia H. Christensen, "The Puerto Rican Lesbian and the Puerto Rican Community," *Journal of Homosexuality* 2 (Winter 1976): 109–21.
7. Bernice Goodman, "Out of the Therapeutic Closet," in Hilda Hidalgo and Travis Peterson, eds., *NASW Resource Manual on Gay and Lesbian Issues* (in preparation).

Section Two

Oppression

9

Compulsory Heterosexuality and Lesbian Existence

ADRIENNE RICH

I

Biologically men have only one innate orientation—a sexual one that draws them to women—while women have two innate orientations, sexual toward men and reproductive toward their young.[1]

. . . I was a woman terribly vulnerable, critical, using femaleness as a sort of standard or yardstick to measure and discard men. Yes—something like that. I was an Anna who invited defeat from men without ever being conscious of it. (But I am conscious of it. And being conscious of it means I shall leave it all behind me and become—but what?) I was stuck fast in an emotion common to women of our time, that can turn them bitter, or Lesbian, or solitary. Yes, that Anna during that time was . . .

[Another blank line across the page:][2]

The bias of compulsory heterosexuality, through which lesbian experience is perceived on a scale ranging from deviant to abhorrent, or simply rendered invisible, could be illustrated from many other texts than the two just preceding. The assumption made by Rossi, that women are "innately sexually oriented" toward men, or by Lessing, that the lesbian choice is simply an acting-out of bitterness toward men, are by no means theirs alone; they are widely current in literature and in the social sciences.

I am concerned here with two other matters as well: first, how and why women's choice of women as passionate comrades, life partners, coworkers, lovers, tribe, has been crushed, invalidated, forced into hiding and disguise; and second, the virtual or total neglect of lesbian existence in a

This article was first published in *Signs: Journal of Women in Culture and Society,* vol. 5, no. 4 (Summer 1980), pp. 631–60. Copyright is held by Adrienne Rich, and the selection is reprinted by permission.

wide range of writings, including feminist scholarship. Obviously there is a connection here. I believe that much feminist theory and criticism is stranded on this shoal.

My organizing impulse is the belief that it is not enough for feminist thought that specifically lesbian texts exist. Any theory or cultural/political creation that treats lesbian existence as a marginal or less "natural" phenomenon, as mere "sexual preference," or as the mirror image of either heterosexual or male homosexual relations, is profoundly weakened thereby, whatever its other contributions. Feminist theory can no longer afford merely to voice a toleration of "lesbianism" as an "alternative life-style," or make token allusion to lesbians. A feminist critique of compulsory heterosexual orientation for women is long overdue. In this exploratory paper, I shall try to show why.

I will begin by way of examples, briefly discussing four books that have appeared in the last few years, written from different viewpoints and political orientations, but all presenting themselves, and favorably reviewed, as feminist.[3] All take as a basic assumption that the social relations of the sexes are disordered and extremely problematic, if not disabling, for women; all seek paths toward change. I have learned more from some of these books than from others; but on this I am clear: each one might have been more accurate, more powerful, more truly a force for change, had the author felt impelled to deal with lesbian existence as a reality, and as a source of knowledge and power available to women; or with the institution of heterosexuality itself as a beachhead of male dominance.[4] In none of them is the question ever raised, whether in a different context, or other things being equal, women would *choose* heterosexual coupling and marriage; heterosexuality is presumed as a "sexual preference" of "most women," either implicitly or explicitly. In none of these books, which concern themselves with mothering, sex roles, relationships, and societal prescriptions for women, is compulsory heterosexuality ever examined as an institution powerfully affecting all these; or the idea of "preference" or "innate orientation" even indirectly questioned.

In *For Her Own Good: 150 Years of the Experts' Advice to Women* by Barbara Ehrenreich and Deirdre English, the authors' superb pamphlets, *Witches, Midwives and Nurses: A History of Women Healers,* and *Complaints and Disorders: The Sexual Politics of Sickness,* are developed into a provocative and complex study. Their thesis in this book is that the advice given American women by male health professionals, particularly in the areas of marital sex, maternity, and child care, has echoed the dictates of the economic marketplace and the role capitalism has needed women to play in production and/or reproduction. Women have become the consumer victims of various cures, therapies, and normative judgments in different periods (including the prescription to middle-class women to embody and preserve the sacredness of the home—the "scientific" romanticization of the home itself). None of the "experts' " advice has been either particularly scientific or women-oriented; it has reflected male needs, male fantasies about women, and male interest in controlling women—particularly in the realms of sexuality and motherhood—fused with the requirements of industrial capitalism. So much of this book is so devastatingly informative and is written with such lucid feminist wit, that I kept waiting as I read for the basic proscription against lesbianism to be examined. It never was.

This can hardly be for lack of information. Jonathan Katz's *Gay American History*[5] tells us that as early as 1656 the New Haven Colony prescribed the death penalty for lesbians. Katz provides many suggestive and informative documents on the "treatment" (or torture) of lesbians by the medical profession in the nineteenth and twentieth centuries. Recent work by the historian Nancy Sahli documents the crackdown on intense female friendships among college women at the turn of the present century.[6] The ironic title, *For Her Own Good*, might have referred first and foremost to the economic imperative to heterosexuality and marriage and to the sanctions imposed against single women and widows—both of whom have been and still are viewed as deviant. Yet, in this often enlightening Marxist-feminist overview of male prescriptions for female sanity and health, the economics of prescriptive heterosexuality go unexamined.[7]

Of the three psychoanalytically based books, one, Jean Baker Miller's *Toward a New Psychology of Women*, is written as if lesbians simply do not exist, even as marginal beings. Given Miller's title I find this astonishing. However, the favorable reviews the book has received in feminist journals, including *Signs* and *Spokeswoman*, suggest that Miller's heterocentric assumptions are widely shared. In *The Mermaid and the Minotaur: Sexual Arrangements and the Human Malaise*, Dorothy Dinnerstein makes an impassioned argument for the sharing of parenting between women and men and for an end to what she perceives as the male/female symbiosis of "gender arrangements," which she feels are leading the species further and further into violence and self-extinction. Apart from other problems that I have with this book (including her silence on the institutional and random terrorism men have practiced on women—and children—throughout history, amply documented by Barry, Daly, Griffin, Russell and van de Ven, and Brownmiller,[8] and her obsession with psychology to the neglect of economic and other material realities that help to create psychological reality), I find utterly ahistorical Dinnerstein's view of the relations between women and men as "a collaboration to keep history mad." She means by this, to perpetuate social relations which are hostile, exploitive, and destructive to life itself. She sees women and men as equal partners in the making of "sexual arrangements," seemingly unaware of the repeated struggles of women to resist oppression (our own and that of others) and to change our condition. She ignores, specifically, the history of women who—as witches, *femmes seules,* marriage resisters, spinsters, autonomous widows, and/or lesbians—have managed on varying levels *not* to collaborate. It is this history, precisely, from which feminists have so much to learn and on which there is overall such blanketing silence. Dinnerstein acknowledges at the end of her book that "female separatism," though "on a large scale and in the long run wildly impractical," has something to teach us: "Separate, women could in principle set out to learn from scratch—undeflected by the opportunities to evade this task that men's presence has so far offered—what intact self-creative humanness is."[9] Phrases like "intact self-creative humanness" obscure the question of what the many forms of female separatism have actually been addressing. The fact is that women in every culture and throughout history *have* undertaken the task of independent, nonheterosexual, woman-connected existence, to the extent made possible by their context, often in the belief that they were the "only ones" ever to have done so. They have undertaken it even though few women have been in an economic position to resist marriage altogether; and even though attacks against unmarried women have ranged from aspersion and mockery to deliberate gynocide, including the burning and torturing of millions of widows and spinsters during the witch persecutions of the fifteenth, sixteenth, and seventeenth centuries in Europe, and the practice of suttee on widows in India.[10]

Nancy Chodorow does come close to the edge of an acknowledgment of lesbian existence. Like Dinnerstein, Chodorow believes that the fact that women, and women only, are responsible for child care in the sexual division of labor has led to an entire social organization of gender inequality, and that men as well as women must become primary carers for children if that inequality is to change. In the process of examining, from a psychoanalytic perspective, how mothering-by-women affects the psychological development of girl and boy children, she offers documentation that men are "emotionally secondary" in women's lives; that "women have a richer, ongoing inner world to fall back on. . . . men do not become as emotionally important to women as women do to men."[11] This would carry into the late twentieth century Smith-Rosenberg's findings about eighteenth- and nineteenth-century women's emotional focus on women. "Emotionally important" can of course refer to anger as well as to love, or to that intense mixture of the two often found in women's relationships with women: one aspect of what I have come to call the "double-life of women: (see below). Chodorow concludes that because women have women as mothers, "The mother remains a primary internal object [*sic*] to the girl, so that heterosexual relationships are on the model of a nonexclusive, second relationship for her, whereas for the boy they recreate an exclusive, primary relationship." According to Chodorow, women "have learned to deny the limitations of masculine lovers for both psychological and practical reasons."[12]

But the practical reasons (like witch burnings, male control of law, theology, and science, or economic nonviability within the sexual division of labor) are glossed over. Chodorow's account barely glances at the constraints and sanctions which, historically, have enforced or ensured the coupling of women with men and obstructed or penalized our coupling or allying in independent groups with other women. She dismisses lesbian existence with the comment that "lesbian relationships do tend to re-create mother-daughter emotions and connections, but most women are heterosexual" (implied: more mature, having developed beyond the mother-daughter connection). She then adds: "This heterosexual preference and taboos on homosexuality, in addition to objective economic dependence on men, make the option of primary sexual bonds with other women unlikely—though more prevalent in recent years."[13] The significance of that qualification seems irresistible—but Chodorow does not explore it further. Is she saying that lesbian existence has become more visible in recent years (in certain groups?), that economic and other pressures have changed (under capitalism, socialism, or both?), and that consequently more women are rejecting the heterosexual "choice"? She argues that women want children because their heterosexual relationships lack richness and intensity, that in having a child a woman seeks to re-create her own intense relationship with her mother. It seems to me that on the basis of her own findings, Chodorow leads us implicitly to conclude that heterosexuality is *not* a "preference" for women; that, for one thing, it fragments the erotic from the emotional in a way that women find impoverishing and painful. Yet her book participates in mandating it. Neglecting the covert socializations and the overt forces which have channelled women into marriage and heterosexual romance, pressures ranging from the selling of daughters to postindustrial economics to the silences of literature to the images of the television screen, she, like Dinnerstein, is stuck with trying to reform a man-made institution—compulsory heterosexuality—as if, despite profound emotional impulses and complementarities drawing women toward women, there is a mystical/biological heterosexual inclination, a "preference" or "choice" which draws women toward men.

Moreover, it is understood that this "preference" does not need to be explained, unless through the tortuous theory of the female Oedipus complex or the necessity for species reproduction. It is lesbian sexuality which (usually, and, incorrectly, "included" under male homosexuality) is seen as requiring explanation. This assumption of female heterosexuality seems to me in itself remarkable: it is an enormous assumption to have glided so silently into the foundations of our thought.

The extension of this assumption is the frequently heard assertion that in a world of genuine equality, where men were nonoppressive and nurturing, everyone would be bisexual. Such a notion blurs and sentimentalizes the actualities within which women have experienced sexuality; it is the old liberal leap across the tasks and struggles of here and now, the continuing process of sexual definition which will generate its own possibilities and choices. (It also assumes that women who have chosen women have done so simply because men are oppressive and emotionally unavailable: which still fails to account for women who continue to pursue relationships with oppressive and/or emotionally unsatisfying men.) I am suggesting that heterosexuality, like motherhood, needs to be recognized and studied as a *political institution*—even, or especially, by those individuals who feel they are, in their personal experience, the precursors of a new social relation between the sexes.

II

If women are the earliest sources of emotional caring and physical nurture for both female and male children, it would seem logical, from a feminist perspective at least, to pose the following questions: whether the search for love and tenderness in both sexes does not originally lead toward women; *why in fact women would ever redirect that search;* why species-survival, the means of impregnation, and emotional/erotic relationships should ever have become so rigidly identified with each other; and why such violent strictures should be found necessary to enforce women's total emotional, erotic loyalty and subservience to men. I doubt that enough feminist scholars and theorists have taken the pains to acknowledge the societal forces which wrench women's emotional and erotic energies away from themselves and other women and from women-identified values. These forces, as I shall try to show, range from literal physical enslavement to the disguising and distorting of possible options.

I do not, myself, assume that mothering-by-women is a "sufficient cause" of lesbian existence. But the issue of mothering-by-women has been much in the air of late, usually accompanied by the view that increased parenting by men would minimize antagonism between the sexes and equalize the sexual imbalance of power of males over females. These discussions are carried on without reference to compulsory heterosexuality as a phenomenon let alone as an ideology. I do not wish to psychologize here, but rather to identify sources of male power. I believe large numbers of men could, in fact, undertake child care on a large scale without radically altering the balance of male power in a male-identified society.

In her essay "The Origin of the Family," Kathleen Gough lists eight characteristics of male power in archaic and contemporary societies which I would like to use as a framework: "men's ability to deny women sexuality or to force it upon them; to command or exploit their labor to control their produce; to control or rob them of their children; to confine them physically and prevent their movement; to use them as objects in male transactions; to cramp their creativeness; or to withhold from them large areas of the society's knowledge and cultural attainments."[14] (Gough does not perceive these power-characteristics as specifically enforcing heterosexuality; only as producing sexual inequality.) Below, Gough's words appear in italics; the elaboration of each of her categories, in brackets, is my own.

Characteristics of male power include:

the power of men

1. *to deny women* [our own] *sexuality*
   [by means of clitoridectomy and infibulation; chastity belts; punishment, including death, for female adultery; punishment, including death, for lesbian sexuality; psychoanalytic denial of the clitoris; strictures against masturbation; denial of maternal and postmenopausal sensuality; unnecessary hysterectomy; pseudolesbian images in media and literature; closing of archives and destruction of documents relating to lesbian existence];

2. *or to force it* [male sexuality] *upon them*
   [by means of rape (including marital rape) and wife beating; father-daughter, brother-sister incest; the socialization of women to feel that male sexual "drive" amounts to a right;[15] idealization of heterosexual romance in art, literature, media, advertising, etc.; child marriage; arranged marriage; prostitution; the harem; psychoanalytic doctrines of frigidity and vaginal orgasm; pornographic depictions of women responding pleasurably to sexual violence and humiliation (a subliminal message being that sadistic heterosexuality is more "normal" than sensuality between women)];

3. *to command or exploit their labor to control their produce*
   [by means of the institutions of marriage and motherhood as unpaid

production; the horizontal segregation of women in paid employment; the decoy of the upwardly mobile token woman; male control of abortion, contraception, and childbirth; enforced sterilization; pimping; female infanticide, which robs mothers of daughters and contributes to generalized devaluation of women];

4. *to control or rob them of their children*
[by means of father-right and "legal kidnapping";[16] enforced sterilization; systematized infanticide; seizure of children from lesbian mothers by the courts; the malpractice of male obstetrics; use of the mother as "token torturer"[17] in genital mutilation or binding the daughter's feet (or mind) to fit her for marriage];

5. *to confine them physically and prevent their movement*
[by means of rape as terrorism, keeping women off the streets; purdah; foot-binding; atrophying of women's athletic capabilities; haute couture, "feminine" dress codes; the veil; sexual harassment on the streets; horizontal segregation of women in employment; prescriptions for "full-time" mothering; enforced economic dependence of wives];

6. *to use them as objects in male transactions*
[use of women as "gifts"; bride-price; pimping; arranged marriage; use of women as entertainers to facilitate male deals, e.g., wife-hostess, cocktail waitress required to dress for male sexual titillation, call girls, "bunnies," geisha, *kisaeng* prostitutes, secretaries];

7. *to cramp their creativeness*
[witch persecutions as campaigns against midwives and female healers and as pogrom against independent, "unassimilated" women;[18] definition of male pursuits as more valuable than female within any culture, so that cultural values become embodiment of male subjectivity; restriction of female self-fulfillment to marriage and motherhood; sexual exploitation of women by male artists and teachers; the social and economic disruption of women's creative aspirations;[19] erasure of female tradition];[20] and

8. *to withhold from them large areas of the society's knowledge and cultural attainments*
[by means of noneducation of females (60 percent of the world's illiterates are women); the "Great Silence" regarding women and particularly lesbian existence in history and culture;[21] sex-role stereotyping which deflects women from science, technology, and other "masculine" pursuits; male social/professional bonding which excludes women; discrimination against women in the professions].

These are some of the methods by which male power is manifested and maintained. Looking at the schema, what surely impresses itself is the fact that we are confronting not a simple maintenance of inequality and property possession, but a pervasive cluster of forces, ranging from physical brutality to control of consciousness, which suggests that an enormous potential counterforce is having to be restrained.

Some of the forms by which male power manifests itself are more easily recognizable as enforcing heterosexuality on women than are others. Yet each one I have listed adds to the cluster of forces within which women have been convinced that marriage, and sexual orientation toward men, are inevitable, even if unsatisfying or oppressive components of their lives. The chastity belt; child marriage; erasure of lesbian existence (except as exotic and perverse) in art, literature, film; idealization of heterosexual romance and marriage—these are some fairly obvious forms of compulsion, the first two exemplifying physical force, the second two control of consciousness. While clitoridectomy has been assailed by feminists as a form of woman-torture,[22] Kathleen Barry first pointed out that it is not simply a way of turning the young girl into a "marriageable" woman through brutal surgery: it intends that women in the intimate proximity of polygynous marriage will not form sexual relationships with each other; that—from a male, genital-fetishist perspective—female erotic connections, even in a sex-segregated situation, will be literally excised.[23]

The function of pornography as an influence on consciousness is a major public issue of our time, when a multibillion-dollar industry has the power to disseminate increasingly sadistic, women-degrading visual images. But even so-called soft-core pornography and advertising depict women as objects of sexual appetite devoid of emotional context, without individual meaning or personality: essentially as a sexual commodity to be consumed by males. (So-called lesbian pornography, created for the male voyeuristic eye, is equally devoid of emotional context or individual personality.) The most pernicious message relayed by pornography is that women are natural sexual prey to men and love it; that sexuality and violence are congruent; and that for women sex is essentially masochistic, humiliation pleasurable, physical abuse erotic. But along with this message comes another, not always recognized: that enforced submission and the use of cruelty, if played out in heterosexual pairing, is sexually "normal," while sensuality between women, including erotic mutuality and respect, is "queer," "sick," and either pornographic in itself or not very exciting compared with the sexuality of whips and bondage.[24] Pornography does not simply create a climate in which sex and violence are interchangeable; *it widens the range of behavior considered acceptable from men in heterosexual intercourse*—behavior which reiteratively strips women of their autonomy, dignity, and sexual potential, including the potential of loving and being loved by women in mutuality and integrity.

In her brilliant study, *Sexual Harassment of Working Women: A Case of Sex Discrimination*, Catharine A. MacKinnon delineates the intersection of compulsory heterosexuality and economics. Under capitalism, women are horizontally segregated by gender and occupy a structurally inferior position in the workplace; this is hardly news, but MacKinnon raises the question why, even if capitalism "requires some collection of individuals to occupy low-status, low-paying positions . . . such persons must be biologically female," and goes on to point out "the fact that male employers often do not hire qualified women, *even when they could pay them less than men* suggests that more than the profit motive is implicated" [emphasis added].[25] She cites a wealth of material documenting the fact that women are not only segregated in low-paying, service jobs (as secretaries, domestics, nurses, typists, telephone operators, child-care workers, waitresses) but that "sexualization of the woman" is part of the job. Central and intrinsic to the economic realities of women's lives is the requirement that women will "market sexual attractiveness to men, who tend to hold the economic power and position to enforce their predilections." And MacKinnon exhaustively documents that "sexual harassment perpetuates the interlocked structure by which women have been kept sexually in thrall to men at the bottom of the labor market. Two forces of American society converge: men's control over women's sexuality and capital's control over employees' work lives."[26] Thus, women in the workplace are at the mercy of sex-as-power in a vicious circle. Economically disadvantaged, women—whether waitresses or professors—endure sexual harassment to keep their jobs and learn to behave in a complaisantly and ingratiatingly heterosexual manner because they discover this is their true qualification for employment, whatever the job description. And, MacKinnon notes, the woman who too decisively resists sexual overtures in the workplace is accused of being "dried-up" and sexless, or lesbian. This raises a specific difference between the experiences of lesbians and homosexual men. A lesbian, closeted on her job because of heterosexist prejudice, is not simply forced into denying the truth of her outside relationships or private life; her job depends on her pretending to be not merely heterosexual but a heterosexual *woman*, in terms of dressing and playing the feminine, deferential role required of "real" women.

MacKinnon raises radical questions as to the qualitative differences between sexual harassment, rape, and ordinary heterosexual intercourse. ("As one accused rapist put it, he hadn't used 'any more force than is usual for males during the preliminaries.'") She criticizes Susan Brownmiller[27]

for separating rape from the mainstream of daily life and for her unexamined premise that "rape is violence, intercourse is sexuality," removing
rape from the sexual sphere altogether. Most crucially she argues that "taking rape from the realm of 'the sexual,' placing it in the realm of 'the violent,'
allows one to be against it without raising any questions about the extent
to which the institution of heterosexuality has defined force as a normal
part of 'the preliminaries.' "[28] Never is it asked whether, under conditions
of male supremacy, the notion of 'consent' has any meaning."[29]

The fact is that the workplace, among other social institutions, is a place
where women have learned to accept male violation of our psychic and
physical boundaries as the price of survival; where women have been educated—no less than by romantic literature or by pornography—to perceive
ourselves as sexual prey. A woman seeking to escape such casual violations
along with economic disadvantage may well turn to marriage as a form of
hoped-for protection, while bringing into marriage neither social or economic power, thus entering that institution also from a disadvantaged position. MacKinnon finally asks:

> What if inequality is built into the social conceptions of male and female
> sexuality, of masculinity and femininity, of sexiness and heterosexual attrac-
> tiveness? Incidents of sexual harassment suggest that male sexual desire itself
> may be aroused by female vulnerability. . . . Men feel they can take advantage,
> so they want to, so they do. Examination of sexual harassment, precisely
> because the episodes appear commonplace, forces one to confront the fact that
> sexual intercourse normally occurs between economic (as well as physical)
> unequals . . . the apparent legal requirement that violations of women's sex-
> uality appear out of the ordinary before they will be punished helps prevent
> women from defining the ordinary conditions of their own consent.[30]

Given the nature and extent of heterosexual pressures, the daily "erotici-
zation of women's subordination" as MacKinnon phrases it,[31] I question
the more or less psychoanalytic perspective (suggested by such writers as
Karen Horney, H. R. Hayes, Wolfgang Lederer, and most recently, Dorothy
Dinnerstein) that the male need to control women sexually results from
some primal male "fear of women" and of women's sexual insatiability. It
seems more probable that men really fear, not that they will have women's
sexual appetites forced on them, or that women want to smother and devour
them, but that women could be indifferent to them altogether, that men
could be allowed sexual and emotional—therefore economic—access to
women *only* on women's terms, otherwise being left on the periphery of
the matrix.

The means of assuring male sexual access to women have recently
received a searching investigation by Kathleen Barry.[32] She documents

extensive and appalling evidence for the existence, on a very large scale, of international female slavery, the institution once known as "white slavery" but which in fact has involved, and at this very moment involves, women of every race and class. In the theoretical analysis derived from her research, Barry makes the connection between all enforced conditions under which women live subject to men: prostitution, marital rape, father-daughter and brother-sister incest, wife-beating, pornography, bride-price, the selling of daughters, purdah, and genital mutilation. She sees the rape paradigm—where the victim of sexual assault is held responsible for her own victimization—as leading to the rationalization and acceptance of other forms of enslavement, where the woman is presumed to have "chosen" her fate, to embrace it passively, or to have courted it perversely through rash or unchaste behavior. On the contrary, Barry maintains, "female sexual slavery is present in ALL situations where women or girls cannot change the conditions of their existence; where regardless of how they got into those conditions, e.g., social pressure, economic hardship, misplaced trust or the longing for affection, they cannot get out; and where they are subject to sexual violence and exploitation."[33] She provides a spectrum of concrete examples, not only as to the existence of a widespread international traffic in women, but also as to how this operates—whether in the form of a "Minnesota pipeline" funneling blonde, blue-eyed midwestern runaways to Times Square, or the purchasing of young women out of rural poverty in Latin America or Southeast Asia, or the providing of *maisons d'abattage* for migrant workers in the eighteenth arrondissement of Paris. Instead of "blaming the victim" or trying to diagnose her presumed pathology, Barry turns her floodlight on the pathology of sex colonization itself, the ideology of "cultural sadism" represented by the vast industry of pornography and by the overall identification of women primarily as "sexual beings whose responsibility is the sexual service of men."[34]

Barry delineates what she names a "sexual domination perspective" through whose lens, purporting objectivity, sexual abuse and terrorism of women by men has been rendered almost invisible by treating it as natural and inevitable. From its point of view, women are expendable as long as the sexual and emotional needs of the male can be satisfied. To replace this perspective of domination with a universal standard of basic freedom for women from gender-specific violence, from constraints on movement, and from male right of sexual and emotional access is the political purpose of her book. Like Mary Daly in *Gyn/Ecology,* Barry rejects structuralist and other cultural-relativist rationalizations for sexual torture and antiwoman violence. In her opening chapter, she asks of her readers that they refuse all handy escapes into ignorance and denial. "The only way we can come out of hiding, break through our paralyzing defenses, is to know it all—the full extent of sexual violence and domination of women. . . . In *knowing,* in facing directly, we can learn to chart our course out of this oppression, by envisioning and creating a world which will preclude female sexual slavery."[35]

"Until we name the practice, give conceptual definition and form to it, illustrate its life over time and in space, those who are its most obvious victims will also not be able to name it or define their experience."[36]

But women are all, in different ways and to different degrees, its victims; and part of the problem with naming and conceptualizing female sexual slavery is, as Barry clearly sees, compulsory heterosexuality. Compulsory heterosexuality simplifies the task of the procurer and pimp in worldwide prostitution rings and "eros centers," while, in the privacy of the home, it leads the daughter to "accept" incest/rape by her father, the mother to deny that it is happening, the battered wife to stay on with an abusive husband. "Befriending or love" is a major tactic of the procurer whose job it is to turn the runaway or the confused young girl over to the pimp for seasoning. The ideology of heterosexual romance, beamed at her from childhood out of fairy tales, television, films, advertising, popular songs, wedding pageantry, is a tool ready to the procurer's hand and one which he does not hestitate to use, as Barry amply documents. Early female indoctrination in "love" as an emotion may be largely a Western concept; but a more universal ideology concerns the primacy and uncontrollability of the male sexual drive. This is one of many insights offered by Barry's work:

> As sexual power is learned by adolescent boys through the social experience of their sex drive, so do girls learn that the locus of sexual power is male. Given the importance placed on the male sex drive in the socialization of girls as well as boys, early adolescence is probably the first significant phase of male identification in a girl's life and development. . . . As a young girl becomes aware of her own increasing sexual feelings . . . she turns away from her heretofore primary relationships with girlfriends. As they become secondary to her, recede in importance in her life, her own identity also assumes a secondary role and she grows into male identification.[37]

We still need to ask why some women never, even temporarily, "turn away from heretofore primary relationships" with other females. And why does male-identification—the casting of one's social, political, and intellectual allegiances with men—exist among lifelong sexual lesbians? Barry's hypothesis throws us among new questions, but it clarifies the diversity of forms in which compulsory heterosexuality presents itself. In the mystique of the overpowering, all-conquering male sex drive, the penis-with-a-life-of-its-own, is rooted the law of male sex-right to women, which justifies prostitution as a universal cultural assumption on the one hand, while defending sexual slavery within the family on the basis of "family privacy and cultural uniqueness" on the other.[38] The adolescent male sex drive, which, as both young women and men are taught, once triggered cannot take responsibility for itself or take no for an answer, becomes, according to Barry, the norm and rationale for adult male sexual behavior: a condition of *arrested sexual development.* Women learn to accept as natural the inevitability of this "drive" because we receive it as dogma. Hence marital rape, hence the Japanese wife resignedly packing her husband's suitcase for a weekend in the *kisaeng* brothels of Taiwan, hence the psychological as well as economic imbalance of power between husband and wife, male employer and female worker, father and daughter, male professor and female student.

The effect of male-identification means

> internalizing the values of the colonizer and actively participating in carrying out the colonization of one's self and one's sex. . . . Male identification is the act whereby women place men above women, including themselves, in credibility, status, and importance in most situations, regardless of the comparative quality the women may bring to the situation. . . . Interaction with women is seen as a lesser form of relating on every level.[39]

What deserves further exploration is the double-think many women engage in and from which no woman is permanently and utterly free: However woman-to-woman relationships, female support networks, a female and feminist value system, are relied on and cherished, indoctrination in male credibility and status can still create synapses in thought, denials of feeling, wishful thinking, a profound sexual and intellectual confusion.[40] I quote here from a letter I received the day I was writing this passage: "I have had very bad relationships with men—I am now in the midst of a very painful separation. I am trying to find my strength through women— without my friends, I could not survive." How many times a day do women speak words like these, or think them, or write them, and how often does the synapse reassert itself?

Barry summarizes her findings:

> . . . Considering the arrested sexual development that is understood to be normal in the male population, and considering the numbers of men who are pimps, procurers, members of slavery gangs, corrupt officials participating in this traffic, owners, operators, employees of brothels and lodging and entertainment facilities, pornography purveyors, associated with prostitution, wife beaters, child molesters, incest perpetrators, johns (tricks) and rapists, one cannot but be momentarily stunned by the enormous male population engaging in female sexual slavery. The huge number of men engaged in these prac-

tices should be cause for declaration of an international emergency, a crisis in sexual violence. But what should be cause for alarm is instead accepted as normal sexual intercourse.[41]

Susan Cavin, in a rich and provocative, if highly speculative, dissertation ("Lesbian Origins," Ph.D. diss., Rutgers University, 1978, unpublished), suggests that patriarchy becomes possible when the original female band, which includes children but ejects adolescent males, becomes invaded and outnumbered by males; that not patriarchal marriage, but the rape of the mother by the son, becomes the first act of male domination. The entering wedge, or leverage, which allows this to happen is not just a simple change in sex ratios; it is also the mother-child bond, manipulated by adolescent males in order to remain within the matrix past the age of exclusion. Maternal affection is used to establish male right of sexual access, which, however, must ever after be held by force (or through control of consciousness) since the original deep adult bonding is that of woman for woman.[42] I find this hypothesis extremely suggestive, since one form of false consciousness which serves compulsory heterosexuality is the maintenance of a mother-son relationship between women and men, including the demand that women provide maternal solace, nonjudgmental nurturing, and compassion for their harassers, rapists, and batterers (as well as for men who passively vampirize them). How many strong and assertive women accept male posturing from no one but their sons?

But whatever its origins, when we look hard and clearly at the extent and elaboration of measures designed to keep women within a male sexual purlieu, it becomes an inescapable question whether the issue we have to address as feminists is, not simple "gender inequality," nor the domination of culture by males, nor mere "taboos against homosexuality," but the enforcement of heterosexuality for women as a means of assuring male right of physical, economical, and emotional access.[43] One of many means of enforcement is, of course, the rendering invisible of the lesbian possibility, an engulfed continent which rises fragmentedly to view from time to time only to become submerged again. Feminist research and theory that contributes to lesbian invisibility or marginality is actually working against the liberation and empowerment of women as a group.[44]

The assumption that "most women are innately heterosexual" stands as a theoretical and political stumbling block for many women. It remains a tenable assumption, partly because lesbian existence has been written out of history or catalogued under disease; partly because it has been treated as exceptional rather than intrinsic; partly because to acknowledge that for women heterosexuality may not be a "preference" at all but something that has had to be imposed, managed, organized, propagandized, and maintained by force, is an immense step to take if you consider yourself freely and "innately" heterosexual. Yet the failure to examine heterosexuality as an institution is like failing to admit that the economic system called capitalism or the caste system of racism is maintained by a variety of forces, including both physical violence and false consciousness. To take the step of questioning heterosexuality as a "preference" or "choice" for women— and to do the intellectual and emotional work that follows—will call for a special quality of courage in heterosexually identified feminists but I think the rewards will be great: a freeing-up of thinking, the exploring of new paths, the shattering of another great silence, new clarity in personal relationships.

III

I have chosen to use the terms *lesbian existence* and *lesbian continuum* because the word *lesbianism* has a clinical and limiting ring. *Lesbian existence* suggests both the fact of the historical presence of lesbians and our continuing creation of the meaning of that existence. I mean the term *lesbian continuum* to include a range—through each woman's life and throughout history— of woman-identified experience; not simply the fact that a woman has had or consciously desired genital sexual experience with another woman. If we expand it to embrace many more forms of primary intensity between and among women, including the sharing of a rich inner life, the bonding against male tyranny, the giving and receiving of practical and political support; if we can also hear in it such associations as *marriage resistance* and the "haggard" behavior identified by Mary Daly (obsolete meanings: "intractable," "willful," "wanton," and "unchaste" . . . "a woman reluctant to yield to wooing")[45]—we begin to grasp breadths of female history and psychology which have lain out of reach as a consequence of limited, mostly clinical, definitions of "lesbianism."

Lesbian existence comprises both the breaking of a taboo and the rejection of a compulsory way of life. It is also a direct or indirect attack on male right of access to women. But it is more than these, although we may first begin to perceive it as a form of nay-saying to patriarchy, an act of resistance. It has of course included role playing, self-hatred, breakdown, alcoholism, suicide, and intrawoman violence; we romanticize at our peril what it means to love and act against the grain, and under heavy penalties; and lesbian existence has been lived (unlike, say, Jewish or Catholic existence) without access to any knowledge of a tradition, a continuity, a social underpinning. The destruction of records and memorabilia and letters documenting the realities of lesbian existence must be taken very seriously as a means of keeping heterosexuality compulsory for women, since what has been kept from our knowledge is joy, sensuality, courage, and community, as well as guilt, self-betrayal, and pain.[46]

Lesbians have historically been deprived of a political existence through "inclusion" as female versions of male homosexuality. To equate lesbian existence with male homosexuality because each is stigmatized is to deny and erase female reality once again. To separate those women stigmatized as "homosexual" or "gay" from the complex continuum of female resistance to enslavement, and attach them to a male pattern, is to falsify our history. Part of the history of lesbian existence is, obviously, to be found where lesbians, lacking a coherent female community, have shared a kind of social life and common cause with homosexual men. But this has to be seen against the differences: women's lack of economic and cultural privilege relative to men; qualitative differences in female and male relationships, for example, the prevalence of anonymous sex and the justification of pederasty among male homosexuals, the pronounced ageism in male homosexual standards of sexual attractiveness, etc. In defining and describing lesbian existence I would hope to move toward a dissociation of lesbian from male homosexual values and allegiances. I perceive the lesbian experience as being, like motherhood, a profoundly *female* experience, with particular oppressions, meanings, and potentialities we cannot comprehend as long as we simply bracket it with other sexually stigmatized existences. Just as the term "parenting" serves to conceal the particular and significant reality of being a parent who is actually a mother, the term "gay" serves the purpose of blurring the very outlines we need to discern, which are of crucial value for feminism and for the freedom of women as a group.

As the term "lesbian" has been held to limiting, clinical associations in its patriarchal definition, female friendship and comradeship have been set apart from the erotic, thus limiting the erotic itself. But as we deepen and broaden the range of what we define as lesbian existence, as we delineate a lesbian continuum, we begin to discover the erotic in female terms: as that which is unconfined to any single part of the body or solely to the body itself, as an energy not only diffuse but, as Audre Lorde has described it, omnipresent in "the sharing of joy, whether physical, emotional, psychic," and in the sharing of work; as the empowering joy which "makes us less willing to accept powerlessness, or those other supplied states of being which are not native to me, such as resignation, despair, self-effacement, depression, self-denial."[47] In another context, writing of women and work, I quoted the autobiographical passage in which the poet H.D. described how her friend Bryher supported her in persisting with the visionary experience which was to shape her mature work:

. . . I knew that this experience, this writing-on-the-wall before me, could not be shared with anyone except the girl who stood so bravely there beside me. This girl had said without hesitation, "Go on." It was she really who had the detachment and integrity of the Pythoness of Delphi. But it was I, battered and dissociated . . . who was seeing the pictures, and who was reading the writing or granted the inner vision. Or perhaps, in some sense, we were "seeing" it together, for without her, admittedly, I could not have gone on.[48]

If we consider the possibility that all women—from the infant suckling her mother's breast, to the grown woman experiencing orgasmic sensations while suckling her own child, perhaps recalling her mother's milk-smell in her own; to two women, like Virginia Woolf's Chloe and Olivia, who share a laboratory;[49] to the woman dying at ninety, touched and handled by women—exist on a lesbian continuum, we can see ourselves as moving in and out of this continuum, whether we identify ourselves as lesbian or not. It allows us to connect aspects of woman-identification as diverse as the impudent, intimate girl-friendships of eight- or nine-year-olds and the banding together of those women of the twelfth and fifteenth centuries known as Beguines who "shared houses, rented to one another, bequeathed houses to their room-mates . . . in cheap subdivided houses in the artisans' area of town," who "practiced Christian virtue on their own, dressing and living simply and not associating with men," who earned their livings as spinners, bakers, nurses, or ran schools for young girls, and who managed— until the Church forced them to disperse—to live independent both of marriage and of conventual restrictions.[50] It allows us to connect these women with the more celebrated "Lesbians" of the women's school around Sappho of the seventh century B.C.; with the secret sororities and economic networks reported among African women; and with the Chinese marriage resistance sisterhoods—communities of women who refused marriage, or who if married often refused to consummate their marriages and soon left their husbands—the only women in China who were not footbound and who, Agnes Smedley tells us, welcomed the births of daughters and orga- nized successful women's strikes in the silk mills.[51] It allows us to connect and compare disparate individual instances of marriage resistance: for example, the type of autonomy claimed by Emily Dickinson, a nineteenth- century white woman genius, with the strategies available to Zora Neale Hurston, a twentieth-century black woman genius. Dickinson never mar- ried, had tenuous intellectual friendships with men, lived self-convented in her genteel father's house, and wrote a lifetime of passionate letters to her sister-in-law Sue Gilbert and a smaller group of such letters to her friend Kate Scott Anthon. Hurston married twice but soon left each husband, scrambled her way from Florida to Harlem to Columbia University to Haiti and finally back to Florida, moved in and out of white patronage and poverty, professional success, and failure; her survival relationships were all with women, beginning with her mother. Both of these women in their vastly different circumstances were marriage resisters, committed to their own work and selfhood, and were later characterized as "apolitical." Both were drawn to men of intellectual quality; for both of them women provided the on-going fascination and sustenance of life.

If we think of heterosexuality as the "natural" emotional and sensual inclination for women, lives such as these are seen as deviant, as pathological, or as emotionally and sensually deprived. Or, in more recent and permissive jargon, they are banalized as "life-styles." And the work of such women—whether merely the daily work of individual or collective survival and resistance, or the work of the writer, the activist, the reformer, the anthropologist, or the artist—the work of self-creation—is undervalued, or seen as the bitter fruit of "penis envy," or the sublimation of repressed eroticism, or the meaningless rant of a "manhater." But when we turn the lens of vision and consider the degree to which, and the methods whereby, heterosexual "preference" has actually been imposed on women, not only can we understand differently the meaning of individual lives and work, but we can begin to recognize a central fact of women's history: that women have always resisted male tyranny. A feminism of action, often, though not always, without a theory, has constantly reemerged in every culture and in every period. We can then begin to study women's struggle against powerlessness, women's radical rebellion, not just in male-defined "concrete revolutionary situations"[52] but in all the situations male ideologies have not perceived as revolutionary: for example, the refusal of some women to produce children, aided at great risk by other women; the refusal to produce a higher standard of living and leisure for men (Leghorn and Parker show how both are part of women's unacknowledged, unpaid, and ununionized economic contribution); that female antiphallic sexuality which, as Andrea Dworkin notes, has been "legendary," which, defined as "frigidity" and "puritanism," has actually been a form of subversion of male power—"an ineffectual rebellion, but . . . rebellion nonetheless."[53] We can no longer have patience with Dinnerstein's view that women have simply collaborated with men in the "sexual arrangements" of history; we begin to observe behavior, both in history and in individual biography, that has hitherto been invisible or misnamed; behavior which often constitutes, given the limits of the counterforce exerted in a given time and place, radical rebellion. And we can connect these rebellions and the necessity for them with the physical passion of woman for woman which is central to lesbian existence: the erotic sensuality which has been, precisely, the most violently erased fact of female experience.

Heterosexuality has been both forcibly and subliminally imposed on women, yet everywhere women have resisted it, often at the cost of physical torture, imprisonment, psychosurgery, social ostracism, and extreme poverty. "Compulsory heterosexuality" was named as one of the "crimes against women" by the Brussels Tribunal on Crimes against Women in 1976. Two pieces of testimony, from women from two very different cultures, suggest the degree to which persecution of lesbians is a global practice here and now. A report from Norway relates:

> A lesbian in Oslo was in a heterosexual marriage that didn't work, so she started taking tranquillizers and ended up at the health sanatorium for treatment and rehabilitation. . . . The moment she said in family group therapy that she believed she was a lesbian, the doctor told her she was not. He knew from "looking into her eyes," he said. She had the eyes of a woman who wanted sexual intercourse with her husband. So she was subjected to so-called "couch therapy." She was put into a comfortably heated room, naked, on a bed, and for an hour her husband was to . . . try to excite her sexually. . . . The idea was that the touching was always to end with sexual intercourse. She felt stronger and stronger aversion. She threw up and sometimes ran out of the room to avoid this "treatment." The more strongly she asserted that she was a lesbian, the more violent the forced heterosexual intercourse became. This treatment went on for about six months. She escaped from the hospital, but she was brought back. Again she escaped. She has not been there since. In the end she realized that she had been subjected to forcible rape for six months.

(This, surely, is an example of female sexual slavery according to Barry's definition.) And from Mozambique:

> I am condemned to a life of exile because I will not deny that I am a lesbian, that my primary commitments are, and will always be to other women. In the new Mozambique, lesbianism is considered a left-over from colonialism and decadent Western civilization. Lesbians are sent to rehabilitation camps to learn through self-criticism the correct line about themselves. . . . If I am forced to denounce my own love for women, if I therefore denounce myself, I could go back to Mozambique and join forces in the exciting and hard struggles of rebuilding a nation, including the struggle for the emancipation of Mozambiquan women. As it is, I either risk the rehabilitation camps, or remain in exile.[54]

Nor can it be assumed that women like those in Carroll Smith-Rosenberg's study, who married, stayed married, yet dwelt in a profoundly female emotional and passional world, "preferred" or "chose" heterosexuality. Women have married because it was necessary, in order to survive economically, in order to have children who would not suffer economic deprivation or social ostracism, in order to remain respectable, in order to do what was expected of women because coming out of "abnormal" childhoods they wanted to feel "normal," and because heterosexual romance has been represented as the great female adventure, duty, and fulfillment. We may faithfully or ambivalently have obeyed the institution, but our feelings—and our sensuality—have not been tamed or contained within it. There is no statistical documentation of the numbers of lesbians who have remained in heterosexual marriages for most of their lives. But in a letter to the early lesbian publication, *The Ladder,* the playwright Lorraine Hansberry had this to say:

> I suspect that the problem of the married woman who would prefer emotional-physical relationships with other women is proportionally much higher than a similar statistic for men. (A statistic surely no one will ever really have.) This because the estate of woman being what it is, how could we ever begin to guess the numbers of women who are not prepared to risk a life alien to what they have been taught all their lives to believe was their "natural" destiny—AND—their only expectation for ECONOMIC security. It seems to be that this is why the question has an immensity that it does not have for male homosexuals. . . . A woman of strength and honesty may, if she chooses, sever her marriage and marry a new male mate and society will be upset that the divorce rate is rising so—but there are few places in the United States, in any event, where she will be anything remotely akin to an "outcast." Obviously this is not true for a woman who would end her marriage to take up life with another woman.[55]

This *double-life*—this apparent acquiescence to an institution founded on male interest and prerogative—has been characteristic of female experience: in motherhood, and in many kinds of heterosexual behavior, including the rituals of courtship; the pretense of asexuality by the nineteenth-century wife; the simulation of orgasm by the prostitute, the courtesan, the twentieth-century "sexually liberated" woman.

Meridel LeSueur's documentary novel of the Depression, *The Girl,* is arresting as a study of female double-life. The protagonist, a waitress in a St. Paul working-class speakeasy, feels herself passionately attracted to the young man Butch, but her survival relationships are with Clara, an older waitress and prostitute, with Belle, whose husband owns the bar, and with Amelia, a union activist. For Clara and Belle and the unnamed protagonist, sex with men is in one sense an escape from the bedrock misery of daily life; a flare of intensity in the grey, relentless, often brutal web of day-to-day existence:

> . . . It was like he was a magnet pulling me. It was exciting and powerful and frightening. He was after me too and when he found me I would run, or be petrified, just standing in front of him like a zany. And he told me not to be wandering with Clara to the Marigold where we danced with strangers. He said he would knock the shit out of me. Which made me shake and tremble, but it was better than being a husk full of suffering and not knowing why.[56]

Throughout the novel the theme of double-life emerges; Belle reminisces of her marriage to the bootlegger Hoinck:

> You know, when I had that black eye and said I hit it on the cupboard, well he did it the bastard, and then he says don't tell anybody. . . . He's nuts, that's what he is, nuts, and I don't see why I live with him, why I put up with him a minute on this earth. But listen kid, she said, I'm telling you something. She looked at me and her face was wonderful. She said, Jesus Christ, Goddam him I love him that's why I'm hooked like this all my life, Goddam him I love him.[57]

After the protagonist has her first sex with Butch, her women friends care for her bleeding, give her whiskey, and compare notes.

> My luck, the first time and I got into trouble. He gave me a little money and I come to St. Paul where for ten bucks they'd stick a huge vet's needle into you and you start it and then you were on your own. . . . I never had no child. I've just had Hoinck to mother, and a hell of a child he is.[58]

> Later they made me go back to Clara's room to lie down. . . . Clara lay down beside me and put her arms around me and wanted me to tell her about it but she wanted to tell about herself. She said she started it when she was twelve with a bunch of boys in an old shed. She said nobody had paid any attention to her before and she became very popular. . . . They like it so much, she said, why shouldn't you give it to them and get presents and attention? I never cared anything for it and neither did my mama. But it's the only thing you got that's valuable. . . .[59]

Sex is thus equated with attention from the male, who is charismatic though brutal, infantile, or unreliable. Yet it is the women who make life endurable for each other, give physical affection without causing pain, share, advise, and stick by each other. *(I am trying to find my strength through women— without my friends, I could not survive.)* LeSueur's *The Girl* parallels Toni Morrison's remarkable *Sula,* another revelation of female double-life:

> Nel was the one person who had wanted nothing from her, who had accepted all aspects of her. . . . Nel was one of the reasons [Sula] had drifted back to Medallion. . . . The men . . . had merged into one large personality: the same language of love, the same entertainments of love, the same cooling of love. Whenever she introduced her private thoughts into their rubbings and goings, they hooded their eyes. They taught her nothing but love tricks, shared nothing but worry, gave nothing but money. She had been looking all along for a friend, and it took her a while to discover that a lover was not a comrade and could never be—for a woman.

But Sula's last thought at the second of her death is, "Wait'll I tell Nel." And after Sula's death, Nel looks back on her own life:

> "All that time, all that time, I thought I was missing Jude." And the loss pressed down on her chest and came up into her throat. "We was girls together," she

said as though explaining something. "O Lord, Sula," she cried, "Girl, girl, girlgirlgirl!" It was a fine cry—loud and long—but it had no bottom and it had no top, just circles and circles of sorrow.[60]

The Girl and *Sula* are both novels which reveal the lesbian continuum in contrast to the shallow or sensational "lesbian scenes" in recent commercial fiction.[61] Each shows us woman-identification untarnished (till the end of LeSueur's novel) by romanticism; each depicts the competition of heterosexual compulsion for women's attention, the diffusion and frustration of female bonding that might, in a more conscious form, reintegrate love with power.

IV

Woman-identification is a source of energy, a potential springhead of female power, violently curtailed and wasted under the institution of heterosexuality. The denial of reality and visibility to women's passion for women, women's choice of women as allies, life companions, and community; the forcing of such relationships into dissimulation and their disintegration under intense pressure have meant an incalculable loss to the power of all women *to change the social relations of the sexes, to liberate ourselves and each other.* The lie of compulsory female heterosexuality today afflicts not just feminist scholarship, but every profession, every reference work, every curriculum, every organizing attempt, every relationship or conversation over which it hovers. It creates, specifically, a profound falseness, hypocrisy, and hysteria in the heterosexual dialogue, for every heterosexual relationship is lived in the queasy strobelight of that lie. However we choose to identify ourselves, however we find ourselves labeled, it flickers across and distorts our lives.[62]

The lie keeps numberless women psychologically trapped, trying to fit mind, spirit, and sexuality into a prescribed script because they cannot look beyond the parameters of the acceptable. It pulls on the energy of such women even as it drains the energy of "closeted" lesbians—the energy exhausted in the double-life. The lesbian trapped in the "closet," the woman imprisoned in prescriptive ideas of the "normal," share the pain of blocked options, broken connections, lost access to self-definition freely and powerfully assumed.

The lie is many-layered. In Western tradition, one layer—the romantic—asserts that women are inevitably, even if rashly and tragically, drawn to men; that even when that attraction is suicidal (e.g., *Tristan und Isolde*, Kate Chopin's *The Awakening*) it is still an organic imperative. In the tradition of the social sciences it asserts that primary love between the sexes is "normal," that women *need* men as social and economic protectors, for adult sexuality, and for psychological completion; that the heterosexually constituted family is the basic social unit; that women who do not attach their primary intensity to men must be, in functional terms, condemned to an even more devastating outsiderhood than their outsiderhood as women. Small wonder that lesbians are reported to be a more hidden population than male homosexuals. The black lesbian/feminist critic, Lorraine Bethel, writing on Zora Neale Hurston, remarks that for a black woman—already twice an outsider—to choose to assume still another "hated identity" is problematic indeed. Yet the lesbian continuum has been a lifeline for black women both in Africa and the United States.

> Black women have a long tradition of bonding together . . . in a Black/women's community that has been a source of vital survival information, psychic and emotional support for us. We have a distinct Black woman-identified folk culture based on our experiences as Black women in this society; symbols, language and modes of expression that are specific to the realities of our lives. . . . Because Black women were rarely among those Blacks and females who gained access to literary and other acknowledged forms of artistic expression, this Black female bonding and Black woman-identification has often been hidden and unrecorded except in the individual lives of Black women through our own memories of our particular Black female tradition.[63]

Another layer of the lie is the frequently encountered implication that women turn to women out of hatred for men. Profound skepticism, caution, and righteous paranoia about men may indeed be part of any healthy woman's response to the woman-hatred embedded in male-dominated culture, to the forms assumed by "normal" male sexuality, and to *the failure even of "sensitive" or "political" men to perceive or find these troubling.* Yet woman-hatred is so embedded in culture, so "normal" does it seem, so profoundly is it neglected as a social phenomenon, that many women, even feminists and lesbians, fail to identify it until it takes, in their own lives, some permanently unmistakable and shattering form. Lesbian existence is also represented as mere refuge from male abuses, rather than as an electric and empowering charge between women. I find it interesting that one of the most frequently quoted literary passages on lesbian relationship is that in which Colette's Renée, in *The Vagabond,* describes "the melancholy and touching image of two weak creatures who have perhaps found shelter in each other's arms, there to sleep and weep, safe from man who is often cruel, and there to taste *better than any pleasure, the bitter happiness of feeling themselves akin, frail and forgotten* [emphasis added]."[64] Colette is often considered a lesbian writer; her popular reputation has, I think, much to do with the fact that she writes about lesbian existence as if for a male audience; her earliest "lesbian" novels, the Claudine series, were written under compulsion for her husband and published under both their names. At all events, except for her writings on her mother, Colette is a far less reliable source on lesbian existence than, I would think, Charlotte Brontë, who understood that while women may, indeed must, be one another's allies, mentors, and comforters in the female struggle for survival, there is quite extraneous delight in each other's company and attraction to each others' minds and character, which proceeds from a recognition of each others' strengths.

By the same token, we can say that there is a *nascent* feminist political content in the act of choosing a woman lover or life partner in the face of institutionalized heterosexuality.[65] But for lesbian existence to realize this political content in an ultimately liberating form, the erotic choice must deepen and expand into conscious woman-identification—into lesbian/ feminism.

The work that lies ahead, of unearthing and describing what I call here "lesbian existence" is potentially liberating for all women. It is work that must assuredly move beyond the limits of white and middle-class Western women's studies to examine women's lives, work, and groupings within every racial, ethnic, and political structure. There are differences, moreover, between "lesbian existence" and the "lesbian continuum"—differences we can discern even in the movement of our own lives. The lesbian continuum, I suggest, needs delineation in light of the "double-life" of women, not only women self-described as heterosexual but also of self-described lesbians. We need a far more exhaustive account of the forms the double-life has assumed. Historians need to ask at every point how heterosexuality as institution has been organized and maintained through the female wage scale, the enforcement of middle-class women's "leisure," the glamorization of so-called sexual liberation, the withholding of education from women, the imagery of "high art" and popular culture, the mystification of the "personal" sphere, and much else. We need an economics which comprehends the institution of heterosexuality, with its doubled workload for women and its sexual divisions of labor, as the most idealized of economic relations.

The question inevitably will arise: Are we then to condemn all heterosexual relationships, including those which are least oppressive? I believe this question, though often heartfelt, is the wrong question here. We have been stalled in a maze of false dichotomies which prevents our apprehending the institution as a whole: "good" versus "bad" marriages; "marriage for love" versus arranged marriage; "liberated" sex versus prostitution; heterosexual intercourse versus rape; Liebeschmerz versus humiliation and dependency. Within the institution exist, of course, qualitative differences of experience; but the absence of choice remains the great unacknowledged reality, and in the absence of choice, women will remain dependent upon the chance or luck of particular relationships and will have no collective power to determine the meaning and place of sexuality in their lives. As we address the institution itself, moreover, we begin to perceive a history of female resistance which has never fully understood itself because it has been so fragmented, miscalled, erased. It will require a courageous grasp of the politics and economics, as well as the cultural propaganda, of heterosexuality to carry us beyond individual cases or diversified group situations into the complex kind of overview needed to undo the power men everywhere wield over women, power which has become a model for every other form of exploitation and illegitimate control.

Notes

1. Alice Rossi, "Children and Work in the Lives of Women" (paper delivered at the University of Arizona, Tucson, February 1976).
2. Doris Lessing, *The Golden Notebook* (New York: Bantam Books [1962], 1977), p. 480.
3. Nancy Chodorow, *The Reproduction of Mothering* (Berkeley: University of California Press, 1978); Dorothy Dinnerstein, *The Mermaid and the Minotaur: Sexual Arrangements and the Human Malaise* (New York: Harper & Row, 1976); Barbara Ehrenreich and Deirdre English, *For Her Own Good: 150 Years of the Experts' Advice to Women* (Garden City, N.Y.: Anchor Press/Doubleday, 1979); Jean Baker Miller, *Toward a New Psychology of Women* (Boston: Beacon Press, 1976).
4. I could have chosen many other serious and influential recent books, including anthologies, which would illustrate the same point: e.g., *Our Bodies, Ourselves*, the Boston Women's Health Collective's best-seller (New York: Simon & Schuster, 1976), which devotes a separate (and inadequate) chapter to lesbians, but whose message is that heterosexuality is most women's life preference; Berenice Carroll, ed., *Liberating Women's History: Theoretical and Critical Essays* (Urbana: University of Illinois Press, 1976), which does not include even a token essay on the lesbian presence in history, though an essay by Linda Gordon, Persis Hunt, et al. notes the use by male historians of "sexual deviance" as a category to discredit and dismiss Anna Howard Shaw, Jane Addams, and other feminists ("Historical Phallacies: Sexism in American Historical Writing"); and Renate Bridenthal and Claudia Koonz, eds., *Becoming Visible: Women in European History* (Boston: Houghton Mifflin Co., 1977), which contains three mentions of male homosexuality but no materials that I have been able to locate on lesbians. Gerda Lerner, ed., *The Female Experience: An American Documentary* (Indianapolis: Bobbs-Merrill Co., 1977), contains an abridgment of two lesbian/feminist position papers from the contemporary movement but no other documentation of lesbian existence. Lerner does note in her preface, however, how the charge of deviance has been used to fragment women and

discourage women's resistance. Linda Gordon, in *Woman's Body, Woman's Right: A Social History of Birth Control in America* (New York: Viking Press, Grossman, 1976), notes accurately that: "It is not that feminism has produced more lesbians. There have always been many lesbians, despite high levels of repression; and most lesbians experience their sexual preference as innate . . ." (p. 410).

5. Jonathan Katz, *Gay American History* (New York: Thomas Y. Crowell Co., 1976).

6. Nancy Sahli, "Smashing: Women's Relationships before the Fall," *Chrysalis: A Magazine of Women's Culture* 8 (1979): 17–27. A version of the article was presented at the Third Berkshire Conference on the History of Women, June 11, 1976.

7. This is a book which I have publicly endorsed. I would still do so, though with the above caveat. It is only since beginning to write this article that I fully appreciated how enormous is the unasked question in Ehrenreich and English's book.

8. See for example, Kathleen Barry, *Female Sexual Slavery* (Englewood Cliffs, N.J.: Prentice-Hall, Inc., 1979); Mary Daly, *Gyn/Ecology: The Meta-Ethics of Radical Feminism* (Boston: Beacon Press, 1978); Susan Griffin, *Woman and Nature: The Roaring Inside Her* (New York: Harper & Row, 1978); Diana Russell and Nicole van de Ven, eds., *Proceedings of the International Tribunal of Crimes Against Women* (Millbrae, California: Les Femmes, 1976); and Susan Brownmiller, *Against Our Will: Men, Women and Rape* (New York: Simon & Schuster, 1975). *Aegis: Magazine on Ending Violence Against Women* (Feminist Alliance Against Rape, P.O. Box 21033, Washington, D.C. 20009), continues to be a valuable resource.

9. Dinnerstein, p. 272.

10. Daly, pp. 184–85; 114–33.

11. Chodorow, pp. 197–98.

12. Ibid., pp. 198–99.

13. Ibid., p. 200.

14. Kathleen Gough, "The Origin of the Family," in *Toward an Anthropology of Women*, ed. Rayna [Rapp] Reiter (New York: Monthly Review Press, 1975), pp. 69–70.

15. Barry, pp. 216–19.

16. Anna Demeter, *Legal Kidnapping* (Boston: Beacon Press, 1977), pp. xx, 126–28.

17. Daly, pp. 132, 139–41, 163–65.

18. Barbara Ehrenreich and Deirdre English, *Witches, Midwives and Nurses: A History of Women Healers* (Old Westbury, N.Y.: Feminist Press, 1973); Andrea Dworkin, *Woman Hating* (New York: E. P. Dutton, 1974), pp. 118–54; Daly, pp. 178–222.

19. See Virginia Woolf, *A Room of One's Own* (London: Hogarth Press, 1929), and *Three Guineas* (New York: Harcourt Brace & Co., [1938] 1966); Tillie Olsen, *Silences* (Boston: Delacorte Press, 1978); Michelle Cliff, "The Resonance of Interruption," *Chrysalis: A Magazine of Women's Culture* 8 (1979): 29–37.

20. Mary Daly, *Beyond God the Father* (Boston: Beacon Press, 1973), pp. 347–51; Olsen, pp. 22–46.

21. Daly, *Beyond God the Father,* p. 93.

22. Fran P. Hosken, "The Violence of Power: Genital Mutilation of Females," *Heresies: A Feminist Journal of Art and Politics* 6 (1979): 28–35; Russell and van de Ven, pp. 194–95.

23. Barry, pp. 163–64.

24. The issue of "lesbian sadomasochism" needs to be examined in terms of the dominant culture's teachings about the relation of sex and violence, and also of the acceptance by some lesbians of male homosexual mores. I believe this to be another example of the "double-life" of women.

25. Catharine A. MacKinnon, *Sexual Harassment of Working Women: A Case of Sex Discrimination* (New Haven, Conn.: Yale University Press, 1979), pp. 15–16.

26. Ibid., p. 174.

27. Brownmiller (n. 8 above).

28. MacKinnon, p. 219. Susan Schecter writes: "The push for heterosexual union at whatever cost is so intense that . . . it has become a cultural force of its own that creates battering. The ideology of romantic love and its jealous possession of the partner as property provide the masquerade for what can become severe abuse" (*Aegis: Magazine on Ending Violence against Women* [July–August 1979], pp. 50–51).

29. MacKinnon, p. 298.

30. Ibid., p. 220.

31. Ibid., p. 221.

32. Kathleen Barry, *Female Sexual Slavery* (see n. 8 above).

33. Ibid., p. 33.

34. Ibid., p. 103.

35. Ibid., p. 5.

36. Ibid., p. 100.

37. Ibid., p. 218.

38. Ibid., p. 140.

39. Ibid., p. 172.

40. Elsewhere I have suggested that male identification has been a powerful source of white women's racism, and that it has often been women who were seen as "disloyal" to male codes and systems who have actively battled against it (Adrienne Rich, "Disloyal to Civilization: Feminism, Racism, Gynephobia," in *On Lies, Secrets, and Silence: Selected Prose, 1966–1978* [New York: W. W. Norton & Co., 1979]).

41. Barry, p. 220.

42. Cavin (see above), chap. 6.

43. For my perception of heterosexuality as an economic institution I am indebted to Lisa Leghorn and Katherine Parker, who allowed me to read the unpub-

lished manuscript of their book, *Woman's Worth: Sexual Economics and the World of Women* (London and Boston: Routledge and Kegan Paul, 1981).

44. I would suggest that lesbian existence has been most recognized and tolerated where it has resembled a "deviant" version of heterosexuality; e.g., where lesbians have, like Stein and Toklas, played heterosexual roles (or seemed to in public) and have been chiefly identified with male culture. See also Claude E. Schaeffer, "The Kuterai Female Berdache: Courier, Guide, Prophetess and Warrior," *Ethnohistory* 12, no. 3 (Summer 1965): 193–236. (Berdache: "an individual of a definite physiological sex [m. or f.] who assumes the role and status of the opposite sex and who is viewed by the community as being of one sex physiologically but as having assumed the role and status of the opposite sex" [Schaeffer, p. 231].) Lesbian existence has also been relegated to an upper-class phenomenon, an elite decadence (as in the fascination with Paris salon lesbians such as Renée Vivien and Natalie Clifford Barney), to the obscuring of such "common women" as Judy Grahn depicts in her *The Work of a Common Woman* (Oakland, Calif.: Diana Press, 1978) and *True to Life Adventure Stories* (Oakland, Calif.: Diana Press, 1978).

45. Daly, *Gyn/Ecology*, p. 15.

46. "In a hostile world in which women are not supposed to survive except in relation with and in service to men, entire communities of women were simply erased. History tends to bury what it seeks to reject" (Blanche W. Cook, " 'Women Alone Stir My Imagination': Lesbianism and the Cultural Tradition," *Signs: Journal of Women in Culture and Society* 4, no. 4 [Summer 1979]: 719–20). The Lesbian Herstory Archives in New York City is one attempt to preserve contemporary documents on lesbian existence—a project of enormous value and meaning, still pitted against the continuing censorship and obliteration of relationships, networks, communities, in other archives and elsewhere in the culture.

47. Audre Lorde, *Uses of the Erotic: The Erotic as Power*, Out & Out Books Pamphlet no. 3 (New York: Out & Out Books [476 2d Street, Brooklyn, New York 11215], 1979).

48. Adrienne Rich, "Conditions for Work: The Common World of Women," in *On Lies, Secrets and Silence* (p. 209); H.D., *Tribute to Freud* (Oxford: Carcanet Press, 1971), pp. 50–54.

49. Woolf, *A Room of One's Own*, p. 126.

50. Gracia Clark, "The Beguines: A Mediaeval Women's Community," *Quest: A Feminist Quarterly* 1, no. 4 (1975): 73–80.

51. See Denise Paulmé, ed., *Women of Tropical Africa* (Berkeley: University of California Press, 1963), pp. 7, 266–67. Some of these sororities are described as "a kind of defensive syndicate against the male element"—their aims being "to offer concerted resistance to an oppressive patriarchate," "independence in relation to one's husband and with regard to motherhood, mutual aid, satisfaction of personal revenge." See also Audre Lorde, "Scratching the Surface: Some Notes on Barriers to Women and Loving," *Black Scholar* 9, no. 7 (1978): 31–35; Marjorie Topley, "Marriage Resistance in Rural Kwangtung," in *Women in Chinese Society*, ed. M. Wolf and R. Witke (Stanford, Calif.: Stanford University Press, 1978), pp. 67–89; Agnes Smedley, *Portraits of Chinese Women* *in Revolution,* eds. J. MacKinnon and S. MacKinnon (Old Westbury, N.Y.: Feminist Press, 1976), pp. 103–10.

52. See Rosalind Petchesky, "Dissolving the Hyphen: A Report on Marxist-Feminist Groups 1–5," in *Capitalist Patriarchy and the Case for Socialist Feminism,* ed. Zillah Eisenstein (New York: Monthly Review Press, 1979), p. 387.

53. Andrea Dworkin, *Pornography: Men Possessing Women* (New York: Putnam, 1981).

54. Russell and van de Ven, pp. 42–43, 56–57.

55. I am indebted to Jonathan Katz's *Gay American History* (n. 5 above) for bringing to my attention Hansberry's letters to *The Ladder* and to Barbara Grier for supplying me with copies of relevant pages from *The Ladder,* quoted here by permission of Barbara Grier. See also the reprinted series of *The Ladder,* ed. Jonathan Katz et al. (New York: Arno Press); and Deirdre Carmody, "Letters by Eleanor Roosevelt Detail Friendship with Lorena Hickok," *New York Times* (October 21, 1979).

56. Meridel LeSueur, *The Girl* (Cambridge, Mass.: West End Press, 1978), pp. 10–11. LeSueur describes, in an afterword, how this book was drawn from the writings and oral narrations of women in the Workers Alliance who met as a writers' group during the Depression.

57. Ibid., p. 20.

58. Ibid., pp. 53–54.

59. Ibid., p. 55.

60. Toni Morrison, *Sula* (New York: Bantam Books, 1973), pp. 103–4, 149. I am indebted to Lorraine Bethel's essay, "This Infinity of Conscious Pain: Zora Neale Hurston and the Black Female Literary Tradition" in *All the Women Are White, All the Blacks are Men, But Some of Us Are Brave: Black Women's Studies,* ed. by Gloria T. Hull, Patricia Bell Scott and Barbara Smith (Old Westbury, N.Y.: The Feminist Press, 1982).

61. See Maureen Brady and Judith McDaniel, "Lesbians in the Mainstream: The Image of Lesbians in Recent Commercial Fiction," *Conditions,* vol. 6 (1979).

62. See Russell and van de Ven, p. 40: ". . . few heterosexual women realize their lack of free choice about their sexuality, and few realize how and why compulsory heterosexuality is also a crime against them."

63. Bethel, "This Infinity of Conscious Pain," op. cit.

64. Dinnerstein, the most recent writer to quote this passage, adds ominously: "But what has to be added to her account is that these 'women enlaced' are sheltering each other not just from what men want to do to them, but also from what they want to do to each other" (Dinnerstein, p. 103). The fact is, however, that woman-to-woman violence is a minute grain in the universe of male-against-female violence perpetrated and rationalized in every social institution.

65. Conversation with Blanche W. Cook, New York City, March 1979.

10

Lesbians and the Law: Where Sexism and Heterosexism Meet

MEREDITH GOULD

> Lesbian is the word, the label, the condition that holds women
> in line. When a woman hears this word tossed her way, she
> knows she is stepping out of line. . . . Lesbian is a label
> invented by the Man to throw at any woman who dares to be
> his equal, who dares to challenge his prerogatives.
>
> RADICALESBIANS, "THE WOMAN-IDENTIFIED WOMAN"[1]

*L*esbians are women. This fact provides the basis for understanding
why certain areas of substantive law seem to have more impact on lesbians
than on homosexual men, and how the laws and legal processes relied on
by heterosexual women often do not operate in the same way for lesbians.
The misogyny of patriarchal society and the homophobia of Western culture
are a deadly combination indeed when reproduced in law and reinforced
by the legal process. The United States is one of the few countries in the
world where the State still actively defines and regulates private sexual
activity between consenting adults. In addition, despite several waves of
women's liberation and a recent decade of feminist struggle, the United
States remains a modern industrial society that defines and regulates many
of the social, political, and economic roles played by its women citizens.

Lesbianism and Law-Sustained Social Reality

In attempting to explain the position of women in contemporary society,
social scientists have pinpointed and elaborated on the relationship between
women's physiological status as female and the economic demands of

industrial society to explain the emergence of gender, which for women is perceived as "femininity." Basically, these explanations focus on women's unique capacity for pregnancy and lactation, then document how the help-lessness of human infants and the emerging complexity of social life united child-rearing with childbearing, relegating women to a sphere of their own—the family. Women, then, are mothers; sexuality is purposeful in that it is procreative; work is centered in the home. Implicit is the primacy of het-erosexuality at the level of procreation and as it is transformed into a world wherein women are traditionally perceived as economically and emotion-ally dependent on men. Decades of social, economic, and psychoanalytic theory bolster this model, and for all intents and purposes this is the social reality sustained by the law today.

Lesbianism is a radical sociosexual lifestyle, striking at the core of this traditional view. As women whose sexual and affectional preferences are located within women's culture, lesbians shatter the link between sexuality and procreation with two major consequences. First, lesbianism challenges dominant perceptions of femininity and the organization of female sexual roles. Female sexuality becomes visible as having a drive of its own inde-pendent from coital activity. In a sexist, sex-negative society such as that which exists in the United States, where women are devalued and sexual expression is debased as vulgar, such a female sexuality is nothing less than revolutionary. Throughout history, the merest glimmer of female sexuality has given rise to gynocide and the genital mutilation of women.[2] During the fifteenth century, for example, thousands of European women were burned as witches. As late as 1948, clitorectomies and ovariotomies were being performed in the United States to "cure" women of libidinous urges. Lesbianism reorganizes female sexuality. Since mutual masturbation, cun-nilingus, and in some instances, tribadism supplant coitus, the sensual is emphasized rather than the business of human reproduction. And it is precisely this separation of the erotic from the procreative that underlies the biblical prohibitions against "unnatural" acts from which sex statutes are derived.

Second, lesbianism challenges the structures and institutions of gender. For example, although many lesbians are, and even choose to become mothers, lesbianism repudiates motherhood in its institutionalized form of bonding to men. Lesbian mothers are also breadwinners, competing with men in the world of work. This, of course, is a social reality shared by heterosexual women. For lesbians, however, marriage with its implied promise of economic support unto death is not realistically an option. In sum, lesbianism shocks precisely because it undermines every dominant sociocultural stereotype of women even if the day-to-day reality of lesbian life appears conventional, as it often does.[3]

Prosecution for Sexual Practice

In the United States, law is an important institution of social control affecting both public and private facets of individuals' lives. Sexual expression and activity between same-sex partners are areas of private life that the law attempts to regulate, but lesbianism is perceived and sanctioned quite differently from male homosexuality. For one thing, the sexism of Judeo-Christian culture has exempted lesbians almost entirely from formal reprobation for sodomy because sexual activity between women has often been viewed as incomprehensible. Sodomy laws prohibiting various forms of oral and anal sex have historically ignored variations of female sexuality.[4]

The medieval language and intent of sodomy laws derive from biblical prohibitions against "unnatural and abominable" sexual activity. Prohibitions outlined in both the Old and New Testaments reflect patriarchal sexism, and were directed against men who dared act out what were perceived as female, and hence degraded, sexual roles. Such roles were considered especially detestable because they were not procreative. In only two instances are women mentioned and prohibited from engaging in bestiality and transvestism. The Penitentials, which catalogued punishments for sexual sins after male homosexuality was declared a capital crime against God and the state during the fourth century, had referred to lesbianism only briefly by the end of the fifth century. Even when secular courts reemerged in England during the sixteenth century, sodomy remained a male criminal offense punishable by death. Lesbianism was not explicitly named, although historical evidence suggests that the designation of witchcraft as a capital crime and the ensuing gynocide for the crime of female sexuality must have included lesbianism. Before it was decriminalized in 1967 at the recommendation of the famous Wolfenden Committee, sodomy was punishable in England by life imprisonment until sentences were reduced to two years late in the nineteenth century. Although the legal status of British women was less than desirable throughout this period, women fortunately escaped prosecution for sodomy. According to one famous anecdote, women were excluded from legal sanction during the nineteenth century because Queen Victoria, on seeing the inclusion of women in the redrafted sodomy laws, resolutely declared that women simply didn't do such awful things and had all references to lesbianism removed.

In the United States, recommendations of the National Association for Mental Health, the Task Force on Homosexuality of the National Institute of Mental Health, and the National Commission on Reform of Federal Criminal Laws led to the decriminalization of consensual sodomy between adults in the Model Penal Code drafted by the American Law Institute in 1955. Yet this section of the code has not been uniformly adopted in the United

States where, in fact, individual states have the constitutional right to establish their own statutes. Women are almost always systematically excluded from sex statutes, which vary from state to state. This mixed blessing protects women from criminal prosecution even as it reflects a deeply entrenched sexism denying women a legal and sexual identity. Reported cases of criminal prosecution for sodomy between women are nearly nonexistent, primarily because the laws do not acknowledge occurrence of such acts. In one of the few reported cases I could find, the Georgia Supreme Court in 1939 maintained that:

> ... sodomy is defined as "the carnal knowledge and connection against the order of nature, by man with man, or in the same unnatural manner with woman". . . . the language of the Code above quoted seems to us to deliberately exclude the idea that this particular crime may be accomplished by two women. . . . That the act here alleged to have been committed is just as loathsome when participated in by two women does not justify us in reading into the definition of the crime something which the lawmakers omitted.[5]

It is, ironically, the trivialization of female sexuality that has spared lesbians much of the virulent police entrapment and harassment to which male homosexuals have been subjected. This is not to say that lesbians escape the intrusion of law into private life or its regulation of public careers; nothing could be further from the case. Law, so ill-equipped to deal with the changes in women's roles fostered by the contemporary women's liberation movement, is even less prepared to deal with lesbianism. Lesbians share the legal problems of heterosexual women—and then some. While feminist women struggle to challenge and change restrictive gender role socialization and stereotyping, lesbian women must combat those sexist restraints as well as their homophobic extensions. Little wonder lesbians have always been passionately involved with the fight for women's legal and political rights.

Challenging the Norm: Divorce and Custody

Of all the gender role stereotypes lesbians must confront, those entrenched in the practice of family law cause perhaps the most pain in the battle for civil rights and liberties. In this sexist society it often seems as if the entire thrust of female socialization is toward the ultimate goal of marriage and child-rearing. Studies describe how girls are encouraged to play house by their parents, teachers, and peers, and observers note how the pressure to act out a heterosexual script intensifies during adolescence. Marriage has traditionally been viewed as an important, even essential, part of the female life cycle. And although alternative family lifestyles have emerged from time to time, they are variations on heterosexual modes of behavior. Realistically speaking, women are never *encouraged* to include lesbianism among their options. Since many lesbians do become involved in traditional heterosexual marriages at some point, the decision to live exclusively within the gay world means inevitable contact with the legal processes of divorce, alimony, and if minor children are involved, custody. What is often difficult for heterosexual women can become positively nightmarish for lesbians.

Divorce, for example, is usually organized as an adversarial proceeding. One partner accuses the other of some "fault" that provides a rationale for ending the marriage. In 1971, the Uniform Marriage and Divorce Act outlined a "no-fault" system of divorce eliminating the demonstration of guilt. Under this system, "irretrievably broken" marriages can be dissolved by either spouse without contest, and spouses need not demonstrate the other's criminality, adultery, cruelty, impotence, addiction, or whatever. Yet although the no-fault system seems more humane in that it recognizes the improbability of eternal couplehood and exonerates both parties for marital failure, no state has adopted it totally and only a dozen states have adapted their divorce laws to include a no-fault procedure.[6] As a result, lesbians who sue for divorce, or who are sued for divorce by their husbands, often risk having their lesbianism become the central claim in the divorce action. Once that happens, lesbianism, which is considered a form of "sexual cruelty" in divorce law, is a claim that can deeply affect corollary issues of alimony and custody. As far as the courts are concerned, not only is the lesbian wanton and unfaithful, she is a sexual deviant as well. This logic is perhaps best illustrated by one of the few published opinions from a divorce action in which a husband sued for divorce because of his wife's lesbianism. The court declared:

> It is difficult to conceive of a more grievous indignity to which a person of normal psychological and sexual constitution could be exposed than the entry by his spouse upon an active and continuous course of homosexual love with another. Added to the insult of sexual disloyalty . . . is the natural revulsion arising from knowledge of the fact that the spouse's betrayal takes the form of a perversion.[7]

Although more recent cases show some movement away from such negative stereotyping, an admission of lesbianism can influence court orders with regard to alimony.

Contrary to popular belief, alimony is not a right and women do not automatically receive it. In at least two states, alimony has never been granted as part of a divorce, and in most others the amount and duration of the benefit is determined by the length of marriage, earning potential of the wife, her age, and the husband's ability to pay. Moreover, in 1979, whatever belief there was in the routinization of alimony awards to women was sharply undercut by *Orr* v. *Orr,* a case in which the Supreme Court of the United States ruled it unconstitutional to use "sex as a proxy for need," thus opening the way for men to receive alimony benefits as well.[8] As for the length of time any alimony award may remain in effect when enforced by court order, alimony agreements have traditionally stipulated that benefits stop when and if a woman remarries. Since lesbians cannot marry female lovers, and heterosexual marriage is precluded by lesbianism, alimony benefits can logically extend forever. In reality, former husbands have successfully persuaded the courts to reduce or eliminate alimony payments altogether in cases where an ex-wife adopts an exclusively lesbian lifestyle.

For feminists alimony is a complicated issue. Some argue that women should be compensated for the discrimination they experience as wives unable to work continuous careers, or prevented from completing higher education or technical training. Other feminists support the elimination of alimony, claiming it perpetuates gender-based discrimination and inculcates further into the public consciousness an image of female dependency. Although it is not articulated in quite the same way, there is some evidence that courts are shifting from the former to the latter viewpoint. Even so, alimony agreements are successfully negotiated in divorces involving heterosexual partners by using a theory of prior discrimination. As formerly married women, lesbians have been just as limited by the institution of traditional marriage as other women. There seems something fundamentally unfair about denying one category of women the extended compensation to which they might otherwise become entitled. Denying lesbians alimony because of their projected incapability of securing another (male) breadwinner, underscores the heterosexism of judicial reasoning.

The potential unfairness and indignity involved in "simple" lesbian divorce actions fades, however, when compared to that involved in child custody battles.

There have been visible, important changes in both women's roles and family lifestyles during the past decade. Rules have relaxed to the extent that there is a greater public tolerance of alternatives to the nuclear family such as dual-career families, single mothers, single parent adoption, interracial families, and shared parenting among groups of adults. There is, however, significantly less acceptance of lesbians who demand recognition as either single parents or as partners in a lesbian couple.

The standards used to organize custody proceedings acquire additional meaning when the mother is a lesbian. In the language of family law, inherent in the "best interests of the child" standard is a "tender years" presumption maintaining that children need their mothers most during infancy and childhood, and that mothering is best provided by the female parent. In more progressive jurisdictions, lesbian mothers are not automatically prevented from retaining or regaining custody of their children. Nevertheless, lesbian mothers must persuade the courts to set aside deep, pervasive prejudices about lesbianism, and likewise about the nature of motherhood.

The ordinary family court confronted by lesbian mothers holds contradictory images. Sexist law intuitively confers custody on the female parent, while heterosexist law sees conferring custody on a lesbian as morally impossible. Lesbians are considered morally suspect because of stereotypes portraying them as child molesters and cheerleaders for lesbianism, despite empirical data showing pederasty to be exclusively a heterosexual crime and finding that children reared by gay parents usually express a preference for heterosexuality in adulthood.[9] In addition, the psychiatric labeling of lesbians as sick or even severely neurotic conveys the impression that lesbian mothers are emotionally and mentally unstable. In both moral and psychiatric terms, lesbianism has traditionally been synonymous with unfitness, the only characterization that can undermine and invalidate the "tender years" presumption. Consequently, family courts tend to approach lesbian custody in a variety of ways, some of which have been immediately satisfactory but leave much to be desired in the way of eradicating damaging stereotypes.

In *Nadler* v. *Superior Court* (1967), for example, a California Court of Appeals maintained that lesbianism alone could not be the basis for a finding of unfitness.[10] Despite this landmark ruling, the father was awarded custody because the psychiatrist involved testified that the otherwise well-adjusted, loving mother might have difficulty teaching her children conventional morality. This lesbian mother was granted weekly visitation and could meet with her children only in the presence of an adult third party.

Since this decision, courts have been more willing to dismiss the impact of lesbianism as irrelevant even though the visitation and living arrangements they create do make lesbianism an issue. Until the mid-1970s, courts would award a lesbian mother custody of her children with the understanding that she and her lover (and her lover's children) would maintain separate households. In essence the court would simultaneously recognize the lesbian family unit as being in the "best interests of the child," then dismantle that family. In 1974, *Isaacson* v. *Isaacson* and *Schuster* v. *Schuster* became landmark cases establishing important precedent in the negotiation of visitation and custody.[11] After years of litigation and appeal, these women won not only the right to custody but also the right to establish a joint household for their six children.

It seems some of the prejudice against lesbian parenting has eased and it is possible to win child custody. In many instances, however, family courts have simply shifted the focus from the mother's lesbianism to the impact lesbianism may have on the children. In the battle for custody, an ex-husband may argue that although the mother might be well-adjusted, her lesbianism subjects their children to peer-group stigmatization. In response, some courts have decided the potential for embarrassment may be legitimate grounds for denying custody to lesbian mothers. Others have noted that children must routinely cope with the attitudes and prejudices of a community and have ruled in favor of the lesbian family. Occasionally, courts transfer their prejudice from the lesbian mother to the father and are wary of awarding him custody even if he has remarried, reasoning, as has one Circuit Court judge:

> While initially the cardinal feature of a lesbian child custody case appears to be the homosexuality of the mother, an equally serious personality defect of some nature is likely to be found in the father. . . . A husband who selected for his mate a woman with such personality characteristics would also be expected to have some unusual features in his own personality.[12]

Unfortunately, it is difficult to get a true sense of the trends in these cases although at first glance family courts seem more receptive than ever to the reality of lesbian mothering. Many cases are not reported, and proceedings are often sealed to protect the minor children. As a result, precedent, the prior decisions that guide judicial interpretations of law, is scanty. Lacking definitive guidelines in this area of law, each judge is essentially left to his or her own misperceptions about lesbianism as well as about the institution of motherhood.

Work and the Law

Women have worked in the wage labor force throughout history, but changes in traditional conceptions of gender and critical economic conditions since World War II have fostered a dramatic increase in women's labor force participation. As of 1977, the labor force was 47.8 percent female and the United States census estimated that 25.4 percent of all households were headed by women.[13] Women work outside the home because they want to, and because they have to support themselves and their families even if they are conventionally married. Employment statistics for lesbians can only be estimated, but given what is known about incidence, it is probably safe to assume that all employment figures include a fair percentage of lesbians.

Since Title VII of the Civil Rights Act was passed by Congress in 1964, working women have been able to file complaints and ultimately sue employers, labor unions, and employment agencies for sex discrimination. In addition, the Equal Pay Act of 1963 makes it illegal to underpay women for the same work their male counterparts perform. During the past decade women have turned to the Equal Employment Opportunities Commission at the federal level, and to state and local divisions as well, to protest the ways in which they have been prevented from gaining employment in certain occupations and developing careers even in those jobs traditionally thought of as female.

In the United States, occupations are stratified according to sex as well as age, race, and ethnicity. Department of Labor statistics support the popular impression that certain service occupations and virtually all clerical and retail sales occupations are almost exclusively female. Women who do break into the professions are tracked into those such as teaching, nursing, and social work, which require supposedly "feminine" qualities and skills. Within medicine and law, women are encouraged to pursue gender-specific specialties such as pediatrics or family law, and are discouraged from pursuing "masculine" specialties such as surgery or criminal law.

It seems there aren't any female occupations that are readily perceived as lesbian. Even stereotypes of women athletes are fading rapidly with the growth of women's professional and collegiate sports. Lesbians simply do not experience occupational socialization in the same way as male homosexuals who are tracked into sales and the arts, then stigmatized because of it.[14] The occupations women usually hold are so status-devalued to begin with that lesbianism is a subordinate issue. And although both sexism and heterosexism shape the jobs traditionally available for women, for lesbians the fight against employment discrimination is primarily one against sexism.

This is not to say that an admission of lesbianism would escape reprobation. Many of the occupations women hold do require state licensing, and lesbians often cannot risk revealing their identity. Moreover, the stereotypes about child molestation that lesbian mothers must overcome also make it difficult for lesbians to obtain primary and secondary school employment. Here again, there are relatively few reported cases involving the dismissal of lesbian schoolteachers as compared to several well-publicized ones in which gay men have sued homophobic school boards and university administrators. Since litigation is costly, lesbian reluctance to bring such cases to court is probably more related to disposable income than it is to political consciousness.

For the most part, lesbians confront the same employment problems as other women although they take on new dimensions for the lesbian worker. Sexual harassment, for example, a humiliating and damaging work condition just now being addressed by the courts, inflicts an additional layer of trauma for the woman whose lesbianism makes her chances for combatting such harassment that much more formidable. The threat of unemployment can devastate the lesbian mother who, in all likelihood, has a poorly paid job to begin with. The secrecy required for job security prevents lesbians from developing the friendship and support networks that help most women workers sustain the boredom of their jobs. At the managerial and professional levels, lesbians must learn to negotiate the social amenities that usually come with the territory. Some of these conflicts are actionable under Title VII as it now stands, others are not. Legislation is currently being introduced to amend Title VII to include sexual preference. However, until such a clause is specifically included, Title VII does not forbid discrimination against sexual minorities.

Nor is there legislation forbidding discrimination against lesbians in the military. In studying the situation of gay men in the military, Williams and Weinberg found that the sexually active and less discreet serviceman was likely to receive a less-than-honorable discharge.[15] In 1975 Sergeant Leonard Matlovich, a Vietnam veteran and exemplary member of the Air Force, challenged the dishonorable discharge of gay military personnel and lost. Although the information available about lesbians in the military is more myth than fact, it is probably safe to assume that there is a significant lesbian population in the women's armed forces, and the same pseudolegal processes used to coerce confessions from gay men operate against lesbians as well. Despite constitutional court challenges, the Department of Defense issued a revision of its exclusionary policy in January 1981, making mandatory the discharge of homosexuals in the military.[16] Currently, all such discharges are classified as honorable, thus eliminating one source of future job discrimination. Nevertheless, the unilateral discharge of lesbians and gay men from military service has removed what is for some an important means of further education and job training.

Feminist Linkages in Legal Battles

Lesbians have been somewhat less aggressive than male homosexuals in fighting legal battles other than those involving custody. On the other hand, lesbians are an important force in the fight for women's rights. During the past decade, lesbian feminists have compelled the liberal forces for women's liberation to confront their own homophobia. Today the National Organization for Women, one of the most influential women's groups fighting for passage of the recently reintroduced Equal Rights Amendment and other legislation, actively supports lesbian rights and acknowledges contributions made by lesbian feminists. Lesbians and feminists unite around many proposed changes to legislation and challenges to sexist institutions, in recognition of the fact that lesbian oppression cannot be separated from the oppression and exploitation of women in general. Even so, there are some issues around which these two groups of women are notably out of alignment.

Sporadic attempts at winning state sanction for marriage between same-sex partners is one issue that seems curiously out of step with feminist demands for equality and self-determination. Traditional marriage is one of the major sources of women's oppression. In common law, the married woman forfeited her legal and social identity: she lost her name, her right to own property, her right to contract, and the guardianship of her children. Blackstone, in his *Commentaries on the Laws of England,* put it quite succinctly: "By marriage, the husband and wife are one person in law. . . . The very being or legal existence of the woman is suspended during marriage, or at least is incorporated . . . into that of the husband."[17] Despite the fact that contemporary marriage appears more contractual in nature, both custom and law conspire to make the married woman legally subordinate to her husband. If any institution can be singled out as legitimizing and indeed sanctifying heterosexuality, marriage in both its religious and secular form has starred in that role throughout history. Accordingly, feminists have vociferously challenged the legal oppression of married women, trying, albeit unsuccessfully, to have the courts recognize ante-nuptial agreements in which both spouses create their own contractual obligations concerning property, domicile, inheritance, and the like.[18]

Meanwhile, lesbians and male homosexuals are trying to force the law to recognize stable same-sex couples. There are several reasons for this. As a unit, married couples are the recipients of tax benefits, and one spouse is economically protected if the other dies without having prepared a will. Perhaps more important than monetary benefits is the social approval conferred by society on married couples. Gay people attempting to obtain a valid state marriage license often do so for the psychological boost that comes with marriage and to make a political statement about commitment that would contradict negative stereotypes of lesbians and homosexuals as flighty, unstable, and immature.

Courts have stymied all attempts by lesbians to marry, on two grounds. First, courts reinforce the heterosexual norm of marriage by refusing to consider anything but its procreative aspects. Even in states that do not specifically prohibit same-sex marriage, courts have interpreted the statutes to define marriage as "the union of a man and a woman" and reason that same-sex couples "are prevented from marrying . . . by their own incapability of entering into a marriage as that term is defined."[19] Second, courts cannot logically sanction that which has already been labeled criminal. Neither homosexuality nor lesbianism is per se against the law; certain sexual acts are. Gays are harassed by law enforcement officials and prosecuted for sodomy because criminal sex acts are presumed to have occurred. In the United States, coming out gay means coming out criminal. Consequently, the law cannot sanction a marriage whose very consummation is illegal.

Lesbians, following the lead of cohabiting heterosexual couples, have written contracts and sometimes become incorporated to protect joint property. In 1976, the California Supreme Court recognized the rights and obligations of common law spouses in *Marvin* v. *Marvin*.[20] Since then, there has been some movement toward ordering "palimony" and honoring contracts devised by gay couples. In 1978, a California Superior Court judge used the *Marvin* case as a basis for ordering one woman to pay her ex-lover one hundred dollars per month in support.[21] Ruling on yet another strategy pursued by gay couples, a New York City Family Court judge validated the 1981 adoption of one adult homosexual man by another, stating, "There are no public policy or public morality considerations which operate as a bar to such an adoption."[22] Adoption, then, may be a creative alternative to marriage for gay couples seeking to establish those legal and economic ties traditionally acquired through marriage.

These progressive trends should probably be viewed with caution, keeping in mind the regional idiosyncracies of courts, as well as efforts by well-organized conservative groups to repeal gay rights ordinances. Clearly, there is a tension between lesbian and feminist viewpoints in the matter of marriage.

Some lesbians altogether ignore feminist issues that do not seem immediately relevant to their lives. For the most part, however, lesbian feminists are increasingly involved in the women's health movement, establishing shelters for battered women, fighting abortion repeal and sterilization abuse, and providing support services for rape and incest victims. These are realities of women's lives that do not disappear with the discovery and embrace of lesbianism, issues that often end up in the courts.

Conclusion

Contemporary feminists have jolted public consciousness about the status of women, and gay liberation has challenged heterosexist attitudes and beliefs. Lesbians are claimed and supported by both social movements, and yet have suffered losses in the battle for civil rights and liberties.

Oppressed groups have traditionally turned to the legal system, and all too often find the system itself of little or no help. Constitutional victories won by women during the past century have had some impact, but successful litigation, even at the Supreme Court level, has proven to be no guarantor of social change. Lesbians have learned that the virulence of negative stereotyping has often rendered the administration of justice quite useless. Consequently, many lesbians have become involved with politics, working for candidates who take a strong civil rights stand. During the recent Equal Rights Amendment campaign, lesbians affirmed the primacy of womanhood by working for the amendment, even though it was not clear whether the amendment would have had an impact on laws discriminating on the basis of sexual preference. Lesbians also provide a strong constituency for the National Gay Task Force, which has actively lobbied for human rights legislation.[23]

Being a lesbian as well as a woman requires a strategic choice of both battle and arena, and the law is only one tool with which to fight ignorance and fear.

Notes

1. Radicalesbians, "The Woman-Identified Woman," reprinted in Anne Koedt, Ellen Levine, and Anita Rapone, eds., *Radical Feminism* (New York: Quadrangle/New York Times Book Company, 1973), p. 241.

2. For discussions of this history see G. J. Barker-Benfield, *The Horrors of the Half-Known Life* (New York: Harper & Row, 1976); Mary Daly, *Gyn/Ecology* (Boston: Beacon Press, 1978); Andrea Dworkin, *Woman Hating* (New York: E. P. Dutton, 1974); Barbara Ehrenreich and Deirdre English, *For Her Own Good: 150 Years of the Experts' Advice to Women* (Garden City, N.Y.: Anchor Press/Doubleday, 1979).

3. For the classic article underscoring this point, see John H. Gagnon and William Simon, "A Conformity Greater Than Deviance: The Lesbian," in *Sexual Conduct* (Chicago: Aldine, 1973), pp. 176–216.

4. As recently as 1969, Dr. David Reuben in *Everything You Always Wanted to Know About Sex* (New York: Bantam Books, 1969) observed that "one vagina plus another vagina still equals zero" (p. 269).

5. *Thompson v. Aldrege,* 200 S.E. 799 (1939).

6. Lynne Carol Halem, *Divorce Reform* (New York: The Free Press, 1980); Michael Wheeler, *No-Fault Divorce* (Boston: Beacon Press, 1974).

7. *H. v. H.,* 157 A.2d 721 (1959).

8. *Orr v. Orr,* 440 U.S. 268 (1979).

9. Richard Green, "Sexual Identity of 37 Children Raised by Homosexual or

Transsexual Parents," *American Journal of Psychiatry* 135 (June 1978): 692–97; Karen Lewis, "Children of Lesbians: Their Point of View," *Social Work* 25 (May 1980): 198–203.

10. *Nadler* v. *Superior Court,* 255 Cal. App. 2d 323 (1967).

11. *Isaacson* v. *Isaacson,* No. D-36867 (Wash. Superior Court, King County, Sept. 3, 1974); *Schuster* v. *Schuster,* No. D-36868 (Wash. Superior Court, King County, Sept. 3, 1974).

12. Ross W. Campbell, "Child Custody: When One Parent is a Homosexual," *The Judges Journal* 7 (Spring 1978): 40.

13. See generally: U.S. Department of Commerce, Bureau of the Census, *Statistical Abstract of the United States, 1978* (Washington, D.C.: U.S. Government Printing Office, 1978).

14. Eugene E. Levitt and Albert D. Klassen, "Public Attitudes Towar ! Homosexuality," *Journal of Homosexuality* 1 (1974): 29–43.

15. Colin T. Williams and Martin S. Weinberg, *Homosexuals and the Military* (New York: Harper & Row, 1971).

16. "Defense Department Issues Reviser of Anti-Gay Policy," *It's Time* 8 (Jan.–Feb. 1981): 1.

17. Blackstone, *Commentaries on the Laws of England,* 442.

18. Lenore J. Weitzman, *The Marriage Contract* (New York: The Free Press, 1981).

19. *Jones* v. *Hallahan,* 501 S.W. 2d 588 (1973).

20. *Marvin* v. *Marvin,* 134 Cal. Reptr. 815 (1976).

21. Reported in *The Advocate,* July 12, 1978, p. 12.

22. "Homosexual Adopts Another," *New York Times,* 21 Feb. 1981, 42.

23. For information about The National Gay Task Force write: N.G.T.F., 80 Fifth Avenue, New York, New York 10011.

11

Lesbianism and Motherhood: Implications for Child Custody

ELLEN LEWIN

The last two decades have witnessed a number of dramatic changes in the pattern of American family life; the participation of women and particularly mothers in the labor force has grown rapidly (U.S. Department of Labor 1975); the divorce rate has risen steadily while the rate of remarriage has declined (Lipman-Blumen 1976; Norton and Glick 1976; Weiss 1979a); and the proportion of female-headed families has markedly increased (Bane 1976; Keniston 1977; Ross and Sawhill 1975). These developments, among others, have undermined the dominance of the traditional, two-parent nuclear family, and have led to the increased salience of a variety of alternative family forms, including those headed by single parents. Among these single-parent families, perhaps least is known about the lesbian mother and her children.[1] In recent years, however, these families have been brought increasingly into view through publicity surrounding several contested custody cases, most of which resulted in removal of the children from the custody of their mother.[2] While this litigation has generally been centrally concerned with allegations that lesbianism compromises the mother's ability to provide adequate care, little research has addressed the situation of the lesbian mother directly or has examined the questions that the judicial system has raised.

In this paper I examine some of the assumptions that govern the decisions of the courts in custody cases involving lesbian mothers and contrast them with data gathered on lesbian mothers and their families in the San Francisco Bay Area. The findings indicate that the structural positions of lesbian and nonlesbian single mothers place similar constraints on both

This article is reproduced by permission of the author and the Society for Applied Anthropology from *Human Organization*, vol. 40, no. 1 (Spring 1981), pp. 6–14.

populations, giving rise to similar patterns of parental behavior. Actual or threatened custody challenges do, nevertheless, have a differential impact on lesbian mothers, and require them to make distinctive adaptations to what they experience as a source of extreme vulnerability.

Lesbians and Custody Litigation

As the divorce rate has risen, so has the frequency of divorce-related litigation over property, child and spousal support, and custody and visitation rights (Freed and Foster 1974, 1976; Gersick 1979; Weiss 1979b; Westman et al. 1970). The courts are increasingly called on to render decisions affecting family structure and the living arrangements of individual family members. The issues raised in the courts, particularly those brought involving custody disputes, often require judges to determine custody and visitation rights on the basis of assertions made about the lifestyles and values of the individuals involved. Ironically, while states that have adopted "no-fault" divorce legislation (such as California) no longer require that blame be established during ordinary divorce proceedings, child custody hearings may still demand evidence of misconduct in order to determine whether a parent is "unfit" (King 1979). In attempting to serve the "best interests of the child"—the legal standard that applies in custody disputes (Clark 1975)—judges are asked, in essence, to predict both how particular parental characteristics might affect the child's immediate welfare and future development, and whether one or the other party is more deserving of custodial rights. This task is complicated immensely by the adversarial model on which the proceedings are based, and by the nature of evidence in courtroom hearings, where amorphous allegations and reported behavior (the "evidence") must be presented as though they were "facts." These procedures, combined with the discretion permitted judges in custody matters, leave considerable opportunity for the personal biases of judges to play a decisive role in resolving disputes.

When lesbianism is raised in a custody dispute, it tends to be considered sufficient evidence that the mother is an unfit parent, jeopardizing her claim to custody. Most frequently, the issue arises in the context of a divorce proceeding, when custody is being determined along with a property settlement, arrangements for child support, spousal support, and visitation by the noncustodial parent (Boggan et al. 1975).

Traditionally, great latitude and discretion have been permitted judges who preside in custody trials. Because the purposefully vague standard of the "best interests of the child" forms the basis for custody determinations, judges may consider nearly any kind of evidence in deciding with which parent (or other party) to place a child, and with what frequency and under what circumstances to permit or demand visitation (Hunter and Polikoff 1976:693; Goldstein et al. 1973). Custody determinations are never final and whenever a "material change in circumstances" is claimed, the court may be petitioned to reconsider its earlier decision, leading, in some cases, to protracted litigation (Hunter and Polikoff 1976:694).[3]

The courts have explained their reluctance to grant custody to a lesbian mother in a number of ways. In some cases, the issue is explicitly one of morality: the California Court of Appeals ruled in 1959 that a trial judge had acted incorrectly in excluding evidence of a mother's lesbianism and found, instead, that the trial court must inquire into the "moral character, acts, conduct and disposition" of the mother (*Immerman* v. *Immerman*, cited in Hunter and Polikoff 1976).

In other cases, the courts have been preoccupied with the impact of homosexuality on the development of children, and often, implicitly, with the possibility that the children themselves will grow up to be homosexual. In the 1967 case of *Nadler* v. *Superior Court* (California), custody was awarded to the father, with visitation permitted by the mother every Sunday in the presence of an adult third party. The judge commented: "We are dealing with a four-year-old child on the threshold of its development [and] just cannot take the chance that something untoward should happen to it" (Hunter and Polikoff 1976:696).

The fear that children of a homosexual parent will themselves turn out to be homosexual is not the only basis for denying custody to lesbian mothers. In some cases, the issue of stigma has been more prominently discussed, the assumption being that living with a homosexual parent harms a child by exposing him or her to ridicule and teasing, and the hostility of the child's peers. These damaging effects are presumed to occur even if no claims are made that lesbianism disrupts sexual development or constitutes immoral behavior. Removing the child to the custody of the heterosexual parent will, following this reasoning, shelter the child from any stigma resulting from the mother's deviance. While the stigma argument appears to be raised more vigorously when mothers have disclosed their homosexuality in a relatively public manner, or when the custody trial has been the occasion for media coverage, it may be presented even when the alleged exposure is only hypothetical (e.g., *In re Marriage of Ransom*, California 1977). In these decisions, lesbianism alone is not the issue: instead, the extent to which the mother's sexual orientation is publicly acknowledged assumes central importance.

On another level, however, decisions against lesbian mothers often appear to rest on the conviction that homosexuality cannot be combined successfully with the ongoing process of motherhood. In a 1975 Ohio case, for example, the judge stated:

> I don't say that a mother cannot be fit to rear her children even if she is a lesbian, but I wonder if she is fit when she boldly and brazenly sets up in the home where the children are to be reared, the lesbian practices which have been current there, *clearly to the neglect of the supervision of the children*. [Hunter and Polikoff 1976:697. Emphasis added]

The proceedings of the Mary Jo Risher case, probably the only lesbian mother case ever tried by jury, strongly illustrate this same underlying assumption (Gibson 1977). In his examination of the mother, the father's attorney asked repeatedly whether Ms. Risher loved her child or her lover more. This line of questioning culminated in a dramatic moment, with this exchange:

> Attorney: If . . . it came to the choice of the son you've got left and being a homosexual, which would you choose, ma'am?
> Mother: You know, as an *individual* I should not have to answer a question like that. . . .
> Attorney: No ma'am, but as a *mother* you should. [Emphasis added]

Following this reasoning, a lesbian or homosexual liaison is suspected of competing with, and most likely undermining, the provision of maternal care. The language of a number of decisions has made it clear that lesbianism is often assumed to eclipse all other factors in family interaction. In 1975, for example, a California Court of Appeals ruling placed two adolescent children with their maternal grandparents, explaining that "permanent residence in a homosexual household would be detrimental to the [children's] best interests." In justifying this decision, the court reasoned that "children . . . in their most formative and impressionable years . . . [should not have such] an example . . . put before them for emulation" *(Chaffin v. Frye)*. The court's logic, however, did not rest solely on concern with the role models that would be presented to the children; rather, the decision stated that "this factor [homosexuality] is not merely fortuitous or casual, but rather *it dominates and forms the basis* for the household into which the children would be brought if custody were awarded to [the mother]"[4] (emphasis added). While this concern with the sexual relationship as competitive with or polluting of motherhood has not always resulted in removal of the children from the mother's custody, it has frequently led to decisions in which custody was awarded to the lesbian mother only with the stipulation that she limit or end her association with her lover or insulate her children from contact with her lover.[5]

Despite the fact that less is known in general about homosexuality among women than men (Hooker 1972), much of the existing literature has served to exacerbate the court's doubts about lesbian mothers. While recent psychological research has revealed extensive similarities between matched homosexual and heterosexual samples (Adelman 1977; Armon 1960; Hopkins 1970; Freedman 1971; Siegelman 1972) and a number of sociological studies have examined structural and behavioral attributes of lesbian relationships and communities (Gagnon and Simon 1973; Lewin and Lyons 1979; Ponse 1977; Tanner 1978), the outcome of most lesbian mother custody cases suggests that judges continue to be influenced by the traditional (and increasingly outmoded) clinical emphasis on homosexuality as indicative of underlying pathology (Caprio 1967; Cory 1965; Bieber 1962; Fenichel 1945).

This clinical emphasis, and a related preoccupation with sexual behavior, suggests that sexual desire alone is the driving force behind homosexuality. Lesbians are thus popularly viewed as insatiable sexual creatures, all aspects of whose lives are motivated by the relentless pursuit of clandestine pleasures. Fears that such persons might harm or corrupt children have emerged in various local efforts to deny employment to homosexual teachers and health practitioners, as well as in custody litigation and denial of foster and adoptive parenthood to gay men and women.[6]

Recent psychological studies of lesbian mothers and their children raise questions about the accuracy of these popular stereotypes. These studies indicate that parental homosexuality does not give rise to gender-identity confusion, inappropriate gender-role behavior, psychopathology, or homosexual orientation in children. In three separate studies, investigators found that children of lesbian mothers were virtually indistinguishable along any of these dimensions from children of heterosexual single or divorced mothers when such factors as socioeconomic status, age of children, birth order, family constellation, and length of absence of father or adult male were rigorously controlled. Kirkpatrick (1976) and Kirkpatrick, Smith, and Roy (1979, 1980) found that both groups of children perform similarly (and approximately the same as children from two-parent homes) on several measures of mental health and on tests of gender identity. Hoeffer (1979, 1980) found that lesbian mothers were not likely to impose unconventional sex-role behavior on their children and that children of both lesbian and heterosexual mothers were equally likely to choose toys and pastimes that are generally considered to be appropriate for their sex and age. Mandel, Hotvedt, and Green (1979, 1980) report similar findings using some additional measures, as does Green (1978) for children of transsexuals.

While these studies have provided valuable data about the process of sex-role development and have allowed the evaluation of the developmental progress and psychological functioning of children from lesbian mother families, they have not fully described the experience of mothers themselves in heading households, raising families, and resolving the problems associated with these activities. Further, these studies reveal little about the ways in which lesbian mothers cope with the stigma of homosexuality or protect themselves from custody challenges.[7] Are the similarities between children of lesbian and heterosexual single mothers reflective of further similarities in family organization, or do they occur despite the need of lesbian mothers to develop unique strategies to meet the problem of insecure custody?

The existing literature on female-headed families and marital dissolution (Goode 1956; Hetherington et al. 1978; Kriesberg 1970; Ross and Sawhill 1975; Wallerstein and Kelly 1980; Weiss 1975, 1979a) demonstrates that economic difficulties, child care, housing, and role conflicts tend to be pervasive problems for single mothers, and fails to suggest any way in which sexual orientation, or other cultural variations would, in and of itself, alter the impact of these problems. Mothers may attempt to deal with financial uncertainty in a number of ways, tapping both interpersonal and institutional resources as sources of support. The choice of particular living arrangements, entering into romantic involvements, maintaining ties with kin and former affines, and membership in friendship networks are all possible sources of interpersonal support. Reliance on one or more of them requires a judgment as to their reliability or their potential long-range commitment to the mother or to her child. Use of public agencies and participation in community, religious, political, voluntary, and therapeutic groups may provide the mother with institutional support, as well as with possible sources of further interpersonal support.

From this perspective, both heterosexual and homosexual lifestyles may be viewed as potentially affecting maternal adaptation in two ways: (1) by creating particular sorts of interpersonal relationships or networks which may or may not be useful in pursuit of goals and needs; and (2) by limiting or expanding access or perceived access to interpersonal and institutional resources. My concern is thus with sexual orientation as a social phenomenon, rather than as a behavioral manifestation of internal psychological process. Both heterosexuality and homosexuality are approached here as determinants of choices that mothers make, and as the ongoing consequences of choices as they are made. The approach I have used, then, is dynamic and processual, and departs from the more common view of sexual orientation as immutable and not altered by conscious decision making.

The data presented in this paper are drawn from interviews with 80 mothers: 43 lesbian and 37 heterosexual[8] formerly married[9] mothers of children ranging from ages 1 to 18. The interviews were carried out in informants' homes throughout the greater San Francisco Bay Area. Informants included some volunteers who responded to publicity, though most were contacted through personal referrals. Approximately one-half of the lesbian mothers and one-third of the heterosexuals have a coresident sexual partner. In-depth, semistructured interviews lasting between three and six hours were conducted with each mother, focusing primarily on the adaptive strategies pursued by the mothers and the influence of sexual orientation on the resources available to mothers and the choices they make with respect to utilization to these resources. Although the interviews were conversational and quite discursive, each covered a similar range, concentrating on economic issues, interpersonal support systems, institutional support systems, and beliefs and values held by informants about their situations as single mothers.

Lesbian and Heterosexual Mothers Compared

Lesbian mothers, no less than other single mothers (and other people) identify themselves according to a variety of affiliations, including those provided by ethnicity, religion, occupation, social class, political ideology, and their status as mothers. While their lesbianism has been the characteristic that most captures the curiosity of outsiders, lesbian mothers frequently report that other aspects of their identity are more troublesome or more salient than their sexual orientation. For example, a Jewish informant, who had spent her formative years as a refugee, was more attuned to the difficulties that Jews experience in the world than those that might follow from homosexuality. The only abuse or hostility that she perceived herself as having experienced at the hands of her neighbors involved her Jewishness and their anti-Semitism. Another lesbian mother was more intensely involved in the world of a therapeutic self-help group (which she attended several times each week) and with a variety of religious activities (she belonged to two different religious groups) than with anything that might be viewed as the "gay life." Her friends represented those she had met through her spiritual involvements and included other members of the self-help organization (both gay and straight), both of her ex-husbands, a heterosexual roommate (also a single mother), and several relatives (all heterosexual). Although her identification as a lesbian was unambiguous, she experienced it as only one among several sources of personal definition.

The variability among lesbians with respect to the centrality of homosexuality in their definitions of self may also be rooted in the wide variety of personal "coming out" histories related during the interviews. While 21 percent of the lesbian mothers had their first homosexual experience prior to their marriages, the majority said that their first relationship with a woman had taken place while they were married or after the dissolution of the marriage. This suggests that other sources of identity, and particularly that of mother, are likely to have been well established prior to entry into a homosexual lifestyle. Further, not all of the women participate in the activities of the "gay community"; many said that they rarely visit lesbian bars, or attend lesbian cultural events such as concerts, dances, and poetry readings. Only 35 percent of the lesbian mothers belong to lesbian or gay organizations; about the same percentage belong to feminist groups. For some, these patterns of activity are dictated primarily by problems associated with obtaining child care or by lack of money. In as many cases, however, the mothers indicated that these activities were of no great interest to them, or that they were not of sufficient interest to promote regular attendance.

Lesbian and heterosexual mothers display their most striking similarities in the methods by which they establish and maintain systems of social support and in the structural characteristics these systems reveal. Both groups of mothers emphasize affective ties with kin, though only about 10 percent of either receive basic assistance from relatives on a day-to-day basis.

For these few, nevertheless, support from kin may be vital. One heterosexual mother of a 14-year-old daughter, for example, solved the problem of coordinating work and household responsibilities by having her mother move into her home. The grandmother performed many of the routine domestic chores and provided consistent supervision of the informant's daughter. Another mother, who had been laid off from her job, moved into a house owned by her father, and lived there without having to pay rent. Although she would have preferred to have been able to afford to pay for housing, the experience of being dependent on her father was softened by his undemanding attitude.

For others, whose parents or other kin live at a greater distance, the support provided by parents may be primarily economic. One heterosexual informant, whose mother had contributed the money for the down payment on her home, said:

> She helped me a lot financially . . . there were a lot of times when there was just very little money and I was really struggling but the fact that I knew my mother was backing me in some way just made it safer.

Another heterosexual mother looks to her parents for financial support and for help in times of crisis:

> They're very supportive, I could certainly ask them for money and they've given me money . . . in fact, I have to tell them not to give me the money sometimes. . . . When my ex-husband was causing a lot of problems and threatening me and the kids, I left him and went down there. So I have gone to them in crisis situations. . . . I can't think of anything I wouldn't ask of them.

In still other cases, ongoing relationships with family members are a cushion against disaster, a source of emotional support that may be relied on even in the worst of times. A heterosexual mother, whose mother lives next door, described their relationship:

> You know, your family can be a very safe haven for you, especially if you're loaded down with a lot of responsibilities. . . . My mother is the kind of woman that always makes me feel as though I'm just the greatest thing that's ever happened to her in her life. I know that I am just like everybody else . . . but she makes me feel so special. There's a lot of love that she communicates. Sometimes I just bask in it.

Despite the tendency for the exposure of homosexuality to put considerable strain on family relations (Silverstein 1977; Wirth 1978), lesbian mothers are no less likely than heterosexuals to depend heavily on kin, especially parents and siblings, as primary sources of social, emotional, and economic support. As they are for the heterosexual mothers, these ties are particularly central for lesbian mothers whose relatives offer daily child care or regular baby-sitting. For others, the connections with kin offer a sense of stability, an opportunity to continue family tradition and to gain emotional comfort.

One lesbian mother described the reestablishment of her relationship with her mother, which had been disrupted for a time after her mother learned of her homosexuality. The relationship was restored following a family crisis and now is close, and characterized by extensive mutual support.

> When it comes to family things and different crises my mother depends on me a lot . . . she leans on me a lot for support. I'm glad that she can, that I can help her when things are getting her down. When she can't take anymore, she'll lean on me.

This informant sees her mother on the average of once a day. Her child goes to his grandmother's house each day after school and is cared for in the evenings by his grandmother. The informant's relationship with her mother is close, although her mother refuses to visit her home or to recognize the existence of her lover.

Another lesbian mother sees her parents as her most important source of support. Although they live on the East Coast, she sometimes sends her child to them for extended visits and thus is able to have time off by herself:

> I would always feel like, at this point, anyway, that I could turn to them if something was going on for me, and they'd certainly do whatever they could do to try and help me . . . there's just some sense that they care about me, that to me is most helpful. I can really feel miserable and everything, and I always feel like well, I could go to my parents and my mother will take care of me and cook for me and be glad I'm there.

About 84 percent of the lesbian mothers say that most or all of their relatives are aware of their homosexuality. And while considerable turmoil may be generated by the revelation of a mother's sexual orientation, these families seem to come to terms with it after some periods of time. One mother describes a period of several weeks during which her parents either refused to speak to her or harangued her on the phone, begging her to change her ways. After several weeks they relented, and asked her, in essence, to return to the fold:

> Once in a while it will come up, and we'll talk about it. It's real painful for them. They don't want to hear it. So most of the time I don't talk about it. . . . It's a very tight family, and my mother says that we can't disown you. We can be really sad and unhappy about what you're doing, and you are making a big mistake, but we love you and that's that.

The compromises that mothers make with their parents are frequently linked to their relationships with the children. Although relatives are not the most common source of routine child care, they are used at least as often as older children and co-ops or baby-sitting exchanges, and are named at least as often by lesbian mothers as by heterosexuals as their first preference for child care. Relatives also appear consistently for both lesbian and heterosexual mothers as preferred sources of financial assistance, particularly in the event of a serious financial emergency. Seventy-two percent of the heterosexual mothers and 60 percent of the lesbians said that they would rely upon help from their families in the event that they needed funds on an emergency basis. The ongoing importance of relationships with kin is also reflected in the frequency with which holidays (such as Thanksgiving, Christmas, and Passover) are spent with relatives. Seventy percent of the heterosexuals and 56 percent of the lesbians included their relatives in their lists of persons with whom holidays were regularly celebrated.

For both lesbian and heterosexual mothers, child support payments made by the father of the children are likely to constitute an important supplement to the income that they are able to provide on their own.

Nevertheless, about half (46 percent of heterosexuals and 50 percent of lesbians) of the women interviewed in the research report considerable difficulty in obtaining funds, including 23 (9 heterosexuals and 14 lesbians) who receive no financial assistance of any kind from their former husbands.[10] Although child support is not generally their sole or primary source of income, it may make the difference between bare subsistence and the ability to meet some of the special needs children have, such as dental work, music lessons, and eyeglasses. Therefore, the dissatisfaction with child support expressed by mothers tends to center either on problems obtaining agreed payments, or with the inadequacy of the sum the ex-husband pays. Mothers frequently report, for example, that the amount of child support originally awarded remains the same despite inflation and the special needs that children may develop as they grow older. As might be expected, these problems are more pronounced for women who have been separated for longer periods of time.

Despite the popular image of the divorced woman as rapacious and vengeful, scheming to gouge as much money as possible from the ex-husband, both lesbian and heterosexual mothers are likely to accept less than adequate child support payments out of sympathy for the financial difficulties of the father and an acceptance of primary responsibility for the children. The women see the father's new obligations as legitimately diminishing the extent to which he should remain responsible for his children. "Sure," said one heterosexual mother, "I'd like more money, but God—he has a life to live, too."

Others, however, are less sympathetic to the conflicting pressures experienced by their ex-husbands. These mothers speak of sudden reductions in the amount of child support paid and of their inability to combat these instances of paternal capriciousness. One lesbian woman, whose child is severely handicapped, describes her difficulties with child support:

> I was supposed to be getting $100 a week from him . . . after I was out here already he wrote and said that things weren't so good, and that he was going to send me $50 a week. I did some trying to find out if there was anything I could do about that. At that point I was not in very good financial condition. It wound up that I would have to go back to Pennsylvania, and it would cost me a lot of money, and I might lose anyway, and since he owned his own business it was hard to prove what he had.

Not only are many mothers discouraged from seeking legal remedies for their child support problems by the expense of legal action, but also some fear that such action might prompt a child custody challenge or some other form of retaliation by the ex-husband. For lesbian mothers, this fear is particularly acute. One mother, for example, described a series of financial problems and complained about the amount of child support her husband provides:

> I feel like I'm getting ripped off real bad. On the money he gives me, with inflation now, that covers food and some of the bills. It doesn't pay for clothes . . . it doesn't pay for medical expenses. It doesn't put aside any money for her in the event of an emergency. So I have thought about [returning to court].

However, because she is extremely fearful about setting a custody battle in motion and eventually losing her child, this mother has rejected the option of taking legal action to improve her financial status.

Another lesbian mother says that her lawyer gave in to all of her ex-husband's demands at the time of the divorce because of the homosexuality issue. This mother agreed to accept $100-a-month child support with visitation every other weekend. While she never received a single child support payment, she respected the visitation agreement, even driving some 160 km round trip to pick the child up at his father's house at the end of each visit. This visitation arrangement only changed when the child himself started objecting to the visits and the father began to take decreasing interest in his son's life. Despite an apparent lack of parental concern on the part of her ex-husband, who has not sought contact with the child for several years, this mother still worries about custody. "I'm always concerned, it's always in the back of my mind, that he's going to want to go back to court for custody."

Yet another lesbian mother reports accepting a minimal child support payment, never revised, because of the possibility of a custody challenge. Although this mother's ex-husband is a highly paid executive, she receives only $75 per month in child support. She has no plans to seek higher payments, because of the continuing threat of a custody challenge. "Every year or so Bill brings it up. He misses David, he wants him, and all that. He's never done anything legally to try to get him, and he told me he never would. So far he hasn't." These discussions of custody generally arise following the boy's annual visit, for the summer, to his father's home. The mother feels that as the child grows older ("once he was old enough to play ball") his father becomes more and more eager to have custody of him. Although a court battle has not yet developed, she fears that anything she might do to alter the current situation could create the opportunity for such litigation.

The issue of child support frequently becomes confounded with some of the other problems the single mother—whether lesbian or heterosexual—faces in trying to maintain a relationship for her children with their father. The need to keep the payments coming in, even when they are irregular, also means she is forced to maintain a civil relationship with a man for whom she may have very bitter feelings:

> Were it not for the money and the child support thing, I probably would have really told him off a long time ago—just told him to go jump, and it would be fine if I didn't see him again, ever, or hear from him again, ever. But, with the kids, I don't feel like I can do that. I know that I maintain a certain kind of pleasantness, probably with an edge to it, because he's totally capable of never paying another cent. That, in some ways, is the only tie the kids have. They're able to say well, sure he cares about us—look. You know? And I don't want to be responsible for severing that line.

Although lesbian mothers, like other single mothers, are unlikely to count their former husbands among their closest associates, both groups of mothers seek to strengthen the children's relationships with their fathers. Such efforts are frequently made despite displays of disinterest on the part of the fathers. Often, mothers report that their ex-husbands are unwilling to schedule regular visitations, forget children's birthdays, call the children in the middle of the night, and behave in other ways which convince the mothers that their feelings for the children are, at best, ambivalent.

> Interviewer: So he could visit if he wanted to?

> Informant: Yeah, but he chooses not to. It's kind of weird, 'cause he always felt that his father only gave money and never really was there for him. . . . And it wound up that in this case, it's the most blatant of that that you could possibly be. All he does is give money, in his case.

Despite these experiences, the mothers continue to be firm believers in the importance of "male role models" in child development, and most (76 percent of heterosexuals, 74 percent of lesbians) expect their ex-husbands to be central sources of such modeling for the children. While a few heterosexual mothers may also consider boyfriends and other men of their acquaintance to be capable of providing the image of adult maleness that they think their children need, the lesbian mothers had fewer nonkinsmen in their networks. They were as likely, nevertheless, as heterosexual mothers to rely on uncles, grandfathers, and other male family members as sources of masculine influence for their children. Lesbians, then, are as eager as heterosexual mothers that the children's fathers maintain their parental involvement, even when relations between the mother and her ex-husband are particularly strained. Their belief that children need some amount of contact with an adult male and especially with their own father, if they are to develop successfully, militates against their individual need to reduce contact that may be personally stressful and which they fear may lead to a custody challenge.

The need to balance their fear of exposure against their commitment to provide paternal interaction for their children may lead, however, to contradictory situations. One lesbian mother, for example, has accepted her husband's offer to babysit in her home every day while he is unemployed and she is working. On the one hand, this arrangement gives the child an opportunity to form what she considers a meaningful relationship with his father, while relieving the mother of the need to locate and pay for an outside baby-sitter. On the other hand, the constant presence of the husband in her home means that this mother has relinquished whatever privacy she might otherwise have maintained. She feels that she must keep her lesbianism a closely guarded secret even from her child, lest the burden of knowing a secret prove too much for him.

Nevertheless, lesbian mothers' relationships with their ex-husbands are not always distant and stressful; some lesbians, like some heterosexuals, maintain close interaction with their former spouses, gaining not only financial support but continuing friendship:

> I talk to him about decisions about Jane, also about other life decisions, especially if I need money for support. He just lent me half the amount I need for the house and that's like typical of the money arrangements we've made before. I have lent him smaller sums of money before. So I just feel I have a real long-lasting relationship with him. . . . I wish he lived closer by.

In another case, marital separation had not prevented a continuing pattern of extremely friendly relations between the lesbian mother informant, her ex-husband, her parents, and siblings. Rather than eliminating anyone at the time of the separation, the circle widened to include the mother's lover, who joined the entire group on camping excursions and holidays. While the mother's relationship with her former spouse (to whom she was still legally married) had certainly become more restrained and distant than it had been during their marriage, they were able to arrive at an apparently equitable division of child-rearing expenses without the benefit of any formal arrangements.

Although unique individual circumstances influence the particular solutions formerly married mothers make to day-to-day problems, their use of personal networks tends to be relatively consistent. When possible, both lesbian and heterosexual mothers make extensive use of family relationships—with parents, brothers and sisters—to maintain reliable child-care arrangements and assistance with personal and financial emergencies. Further, despite the tensions surrounding their relationships with their former husbands, the two groups of mothers tend to make efforts to strengthen these ties, both to assure the continuity of economic support and to enhance the children's connection with their father.

Implications for Child Custody Determinations

The situations of lesbian and heterosexual mothers are substantially similar, despite the fact that the lesbian mothers' perception of their vulnerability to custody litigation places additional strains on them which may deprive them of the legal rights enjoyed by other divorced or separated mothers. Although no scientific evidence exists that demonstrates that lesbian mothers organize their homes distinctively, that they are unfit parents, or that their children develop differently from those in allegedly heterosexual homes, the notion that something *must* be different—that, in the words of one judge, "homosexuality . . . dominates and forms the basis for the household" *(Chaffin v. Frye)*—continues to pervade the courtroom, and to provide a rationale for removing children from their mothers' custody.

As the frequency of child custody disputes and other divorce-related litigation continues to grow, the courts will doubtless be increasingly called on to resolve the difficult legal questions these cases raise. In addition, however, these same courts are often called on to go beyond resolution of the legal problems and to address the underlying social issues as well. Conflicts of interest become conflicts of values in a forum ill-equipped to deal with the latter (Aubert 1969). Neither the adversarial model that rules custody proceedings, pitting parent against parent, nor the rules of evidence which restrict the exploration of the context in which particular patterns of behavior occur, can provide adequate protection from judicial bias for parents whose lifestyles are unconventional or poorly understood. A shift away from the evaluation of individual parental behavior as "evidence," together with a move toward nonlitigious solutions to custody disputes may help to equalize the status of lesbian mothers in court. Such changes, to which social scientists may make important contributions, may help to eliminate one of the only sources of systematic difference which still exists between families headed by lesbian and heterosexual mothers—the stress which fear of loss of custody produces for lesbian mothers—and the often conflict-laden adaptations they make to this special source of vulnerability.

Notes

1. While the stigma that homosexuals face makes any effort to arrive at population figures highly speculative, Kinsey's figures (1953) can be helpful in establishing some rough estimates. The Kinsey Heterosexual-Homosexual Rating Scale was devised (Kinsey 1948) so that both homosexual and heterosexual aspects of an individual's history could be balanced and so that overly rigid bipolar classificatory systems could be avoided. Both psychological reactions and overt sexual experience are considered—these being weighed with respect to each other and evaluated to produce a rating. Persons rated 0 are classified

as "entirely heterosexual"; those rated 6 are "entirely homosexual." The other ratings represent intermediate types, with 3 defining those whose histories are equally heterosexual and homosexual. Using the scale, Kinsey and his associates demonstrated that a simple determination of how many people are heterosexual or homosexual is not possible. Sexual orientation is more usefully conceptualized as a continuum between two extremes including all intermediate psychological and behavioral types.

Depending on what portion of the scale is selected as representing "homosexual" individuals, the proportion of lesbians in the young adult population may be estimated anywhere between 1 and 20 percent. Hoeffer (1978) applies these data conservatively, calculating the lesbian mother population at 3 percent of the 6.6 million female family heads—about 200,000 in all. She indicates, however, that the true total may lie between this figure and Martin and Lyon's (1972) suggested figure of 3 million, or 30 percent of their estimate of 10 million lesbians in the United States. This larger figure would not only overlap with the populations of female family heads, never married and/or previously married women, but would also include some legally married women and others who do not occupy head-of-household status.

2. Especially in the Isaacson-Schuster case in Washington, the Jullion case in California, and the Risher case (Gibson 1977) in Texas. This latter case was the subject of a network television movie. See Hunter and Polikoff (1976) for further material on the legal situation of lesbian mothers.

3. The Uniform Marriage and Divorce Act includes the following factors among those which can be considered in the course of determining the best interests of the child (Clark 1975:870):

    1. The wishes of the child's parent or parents as to his custody
    2. The wishes of the child as to his custodian
    3. The interaction and interrelationship of the child with his parent or parents, his siblings, and any other person who may significantly affect the child's best interests
    4. The child's adjustment to his home, school, and community
    5. The mental and physical health of all individuals involved

4. The disposition of this case was particularly ironic in that the grandparents, who also had a gay son, might be considered the only people involved in the case who had proved that they were capable of raising a homosexual.

5. For example, in *Mitchell* v. *Mitchell* (1972) a probation officer, a court conciliation counselor, and a psychologist all favored awarding the three children to the mother. The father presented no evidence of the mother's unfitness beyond the fact of her lesbianism and his desire to provide the children with a Christian home. The mother won custody but was ordered not to live with her female lover and only to associate with her when the children were in school or visiting their father. While the judge did not explicitly demand that the relationship be terminated, an order of this type would certainly have the effect of undermining intimacy and mutual support. Similarly, in an earlier decision (since modified) in the joint *Schuster* v. *Schuster* and *Isaacson* v. *Isaacson* case (1974) the judge ordered that the mothers establish separate households with their children. Living together, he reasoned, would promote a "potentially destructive environment" (Hunter and Polikoff 1976:698).

6. The Briggs amendment, which appeared on the California ballot in 1978, exemplifies these efforts. This initiative would have required the dismissal of any teacher or school employee who was either found by school board inquiry to be homosexual or who espoused opinions held to be sympathetic to homosexuals or the granting of civil rights to them. The initiative was defeated; the arguments presented in the campaign, however, rested heavily on the proposition that homosexuals would be "naturally" inclined to sexually molest children or to attempt to "recruit" them into homosexuality. Underlying these arguments is an assumption that sexual impulses among homosexual men and women are extremely powerful and cannot be restrained by ordinary measures.

7. The psychological literature also fails to illuminate the effects on children of different types of custody arrangements. See Ellsworth and Levy (1969) for a detailed critique of the research on divorce and postdivorce families as it can be, and has been, applied to child custody adjudication.

8. Individuals chosen for interviews identified themselves as either lesbian/homosexual or heterosexual and either had had sexual relationships of the corresponding type during the past year, or expressed a preference for the same sex or opposite partners in the event that they begin a relationship. Persons who labeled themselves bisexual or who rejected all labels were excluded from the sample, as were those whose stated sexual behavior directly contradicted the sexual orientation label they had selected.

9. The women in the study had all been legally married to the father of their first child when they conceived or gave birth. Inclusion in the sample required that they be divorced or separated and no longer living with the ex-husband. Some women had subsequent offspring through other unions, both legal and consensual.

10. Studies in various parts of the country have shown that fathers tend to be extremely unreliable in meeting their child support obligations. Ross and Sawhill (1975:47) cite a Wisconsin study which showed that within one year of divorce, 42 percent of the fathers had made no court-ordered child support payments, and that after ten years the percentage had risen to 79 percent. Another study (Citizens' Advisory Council 1972) showed that husbands contributed in only one-third of the cases surveyed, and that 67 percent of fathers did not contribute to their children's maintenance at all.

References Cited

Adelman, Marcy
    1977   Comparison of Professionally-employed Lesbians and Heterosexual Women on the MMPI. *Archives of Sexual Behavior* 6(3):193–201.
Armon, Virginia
    1960   Some Personality Variables in Overt Female Homosexuality. *Journal of Projective Techniques* 24:292–309.
Aubert, Vilhelm
    1969   Law as a Way of Resolving Conflicts: The Case of a Small Industrialized Society. In *Law in Culture and Society*. Laura Nader, ed. Pp. 282–303. Chicago: Aldine.

Bane, Mary Jo
  1976   Marital Disruption and the Lives of Children. *Journal of Social Issues*
    32(1):103–17.
Bieber, I., et al.
  1962   *Homosexuality: A Psychoanalytic Study of Male Homosexuals.* New York: Basic
    Books.
Boggan, E. C., et al.
  1975   *The Rights of Gay People.* New York: Avon.
Caprio, Frank S.
  1967   *Female Homosexuality.* New York: Citadel Press.
Citizens' Advisory Council on the Status of Women
  1972   *Memorandum: The Equal Rights Amendment and Alimony and Child Support
    Laws.* Washington, D.C.
Clark, Homer H., Jr.
  1975   *Domestic Relations: Case and Problems.* St. Paul, Minnesota: West Publishing
    Company.
Cory, Donald Webster
  1965   *The Lesbian in America.* New York: McFadden Bartel.
Ellsworth, Phoebe C., and Robert J. Levy
  1969   Legislative Reform of Child Custody Adjudication: An Effort to Rely on
    Social Sciences Data in Formulating Legal Policies. *Law and Society Review*
    4:167–233.
Fenichel, O.
  1945   *A Psychoanalytical Theory of Neurosis.* New York: W. W. Norton and Company.
Freed, D. J., and H. H. Foster, Jr.
  1974   The Shuffled Child and Divorce Court. *Trial* 10:26.
  1976   Taking Out the Fault But Not the Sting. *Trial* 12:10.
Freedman, Mark
  1971   *Homosexuality and Psychological Functioning.* Belmont, California:
    Brooks/Cole.
Gagnon, John H., and William Simon
  1973   A Conformity Greater than Deviance: The Lesbian. In *Sexual Conduct.* John
    H. Gagnon and William Simon, eds. Pp. 176–216. Chicago: Aldine.
Gersick, Kelin E.
  1979   Fathers by Choice: Divorced Men Who Received Custody of Their Chil-
    dren. In *Divorce and Separation: Context, Causes, and Consequences.* G. Levinger
    and O. C. Moles, eds. Pp. 307–23. New York: Basic Books.
Gibson, Gifford Guy
  1977   *By Her Own Admission.* Garden City: Doubleday.
Goldstein, Joseph, et al.
  1973   *Beyond the Best Interests of the Child.* New York: The Free Press.
Goode, William J.
  1956   *Women in Divorce.* New York: Free Press of Glencoe.
Green, Richard
  1978   Sexual Identity of 37 Children Raised by Homosexual or Transsexual Par-
    ents. *American Journal of Psychiatry* 135(6):692–97.
Hetherington, E. M., et al.
  1978   The Aftermath of Divorce. In *Mother/Child, Father/Child Relationships.* Joseph

Stevens, Jr. and Marilyn Mathews, eds. Pp. 149–76. Washington, D.C.: The National Association for the Education of Young Children.

Hoeffer, Beverly
1978   Single Mothers and Their Children: Challenging Traditional Concepts of the American Family. In *Current Practices in Psychiatric Nursing*. A. Brandt et al., eds. Pp. 175–84. St. Louis: Mosby.
1979   Lesbian and Heterosexual Single Mothers' Influence on Their Children's Sex-Role Traits and Behavior. Paper presented at meetings of the American Psychological Association, New York.
1980   Children's Acquisition of Sex-Role Behavior in Lesbian Mother Families. Paper presented at meetings of the American Orthopsychiatric Association, Toronto.

Hooker, Evelyn
1972   Homosexuality. In U.S. Task Force on Homosexuality, *Homosexuality: Final Report and Background Papers*. John M. Livingood, ed. Pp. 11–21. Rockville, Maryland: NIMH.

Hopkins, June
1970   Lesbian Signs on the Rorschach. *British Journal on Projective Psychology and Personality Study* 15:7–14.

Hunter, Nan D., and Nancy D. Polikoff
1976   Custody Rights of Lesbian Mothers: Legal Theory and Litigation Strategy. *Buffalo Law Review* 25:691–733.

Keniston, Kenneth, and the Carnegie Council on Children
1977   *All Our Children: The American Family Under Pressure*. New York: Harcourt Brace Jovanovich.

King, Donald B.
1979   Child Custody—A Legal Problem? *California State Bar Journal* 54: 156–61.

Kinsey, A. C., et al.
1948   *Sexual Behavior in the Human Male*. Philadelphia: W. B. Saunders.
1953   *Sexual Behavior in the Human Female*. Philadelphia: W. B. Saunders.

Kirkpatrick, M.
1976   A New Look at Lesbian Mothers. *Human Behavior* 36:60–61.

Kirkpatrick, Martha, Katherine Smith, and Ron Roy
1979   Adjustment and Sexual Identity of Children of Lesbian and Divorced Heterosexual Mothers. Paper presented at meetings of the American Psychological Association, New York.
1980   Lesbian Mothers and Their Children: A Comparative Study. Paper presented at meetings of the American Orthopsychiatric Association, Toronto.

Kriesberg, Louis
1970   *Mothers in Poverty*. Chicago: Aldine.

Lewin, Ellen, and Terrie Lyons
1979   Lesbian and Heterosexual Mothers: Continuity and Difference in Family Organization. Paper presented at meetings of the American Psychological Association, New York.

Lipman-Blumen, Jean
1976   The Implications for Family Structure of Changing Sex Roles. *Social Casework* 57:67–79.

Mandel, Jane, Mary Hotvedt, and Richard Green
  1979 The Lesbian Parent: Comparison of Heterosexual and Homosexual Mothers and Children. Paper presented at meetings of the American Psychological Association, New York.
  1980 Entrance into Therapy: Presenting Complaints and Goals of Homosexual and Heterosexual Single Mothers. Papers presented at meetings of the American Orthopsychiatric Association, New York.
Martin, Del, and Phyllis Lyon
  1972 *Lesbian/Woman.* New York: Bantam.
Norton, Arthur J., and Paul C. Glick
  1976 Marital Instability: Past, Present, and Future. *Journal of Social Issues* 32(1): 5–20.
Ponse, Barbara
  1977 Secrecy in the Lesbian World. In *Sexuality: Encounters, Identities, and Relations.* Carol Warren, ed. Pp. 53–78. Beverly Hills: Sage.
Ross, Heather, and Isabel Sawhill
  1975 *Time of Transition: The Growth of Families Headed by Women.* Washington, D.C.: Urban Institute.
Siegelman, Marvin
  1972 Adjustment of Homosexual and Heterosexual Women. *British Journal of Psychiatry* 120:477–81.
Silverstein, Charles
  1977 *A Family Matter.* New York: McGraw-Hill.
Tanner, Donna
  1978 *The Lesbian Couple.* Lexington, Massachusetts: Lexington Books.
U.S. Department of Labor
  1975 *Handbook on Women Workers.* Women's Bureau. Bulletin 297. Washington, D.C.
Wallerstein, Judith S., and Joan B. Kelly
  1980 *Surviving the Breakup.* New York: Basic Books.
Weiss, Robert
  1975 *Marital Separation.* New York: Basic Books.
  1979a *Going It Alone.* New York: Basic Books.
  1979b Issues in the Adjudication of Custody When Parents Separate. In *Divorce and Separation: Context, Causes, and Consequences.* G. Levinger and O. Moles, eds. Pp. 324–36. New York: Basic Books.
Westman, J. C., et al.
  1970 Role of Child Psychiatry in Divorce. *Archives of General Psychiatry.* 23(5): 416–20.
Wirth, Scott
  1978 Coming Out Close to Home: Principles for Psychotherapy with Families of Lesbians and Gay Men. *Catalyst: A Socialist Journal of the Social Services* 1(3): 6–23.

References to Custody Cases

Chaffin v. *Frye*, 45 Cal. App. 3d 39, 119 Cal. Rptr. 22 (1975)

Isaacson v. *Isaacson, Schuster* v. *Schuster,* 585 P. 2d 130, Wash. Sup. Ct. (1974)

Immerman v. *Immerman,* 176 Cal. App. 2d 122, 1 Cal. Rptr. 298 (1959)

Nadler v. *Superior Court,* 255 Cal. App. 2d 323, 63 Cal. Rptr. 352 (1967)

In re Marriage of Jullion and Ceccarielli, No. 490874–4, Cal. Sup. Ct., Alameda Cty. (1978)

In re Marriage of Mitchell, No. 240665, Cal. Sup. Ct., Santa Clara Cty. (1972)

In re Marriage of Ransom, No. 477051–8, Cal. Sup. Ct., Alameda Cty. (1977)

12

Lesbian Childbirth and Woman-Controlled Conception

DEBORAH GOLEMAN WOLF

*T*his article delineates the growing use of insemination, noninstitutionalized medical practices, and home birth among lesbian feminists in the San Francisco Bay Area. Though the number of women using these methods is small, it is significant, for it makes the choice of motherhood available to women who feel that they are strong enough and temperamentally suited to motherhood without necessarily having to be in a dependent relationship with a man.

Why Conceive Artificially?

The role of lesbian mother is not new. Usually, however, women have become mothers in heterosexual relationships and have come to the gay community as self-identified lesbians with their children. Because of this, they have not been appropriate role models for those who want to have children without being in a heterosexual relationship. Since most adoption agencies do not allow single women to adopt and since most lesbians prefer not to have sexual relationships with men, many women have felt that their lesbianism precludes them from having children.

In the last few years, however, a shift has taken place as committed lesbian feminists have become pregnant with the use of artificial insemination, have given birth, and are raising children. Although artificial insemination has been used for at least thirty years, these women are using it

My thanks to Anne, Cathy, Christmas, Jacki, Judy, Karen, Nancy, and to others who could not allow even their first names to be used. Another version of this article appears in *An Anthropology of Human Birth*, edited by Margarita A. Kay (Philadelphia: F. A. Davis, 1981). This article appears here by permission of F. A. Davis Company.

outside the context of the traditional medical establishment. They see themselves as wresting control of fertilization and childbirth away from male dominance and putting it back in the hands of women, to whom it traditionally belonged.

Usually these women are slightly older than many first-time mothers; on the average they are in their late twenties and early thirties. One reason for this is that since they were not in a situation to be *trapped* by pregnancy early in life, they have taken time to develop their own interests, work situation, and lifestyle satisfactorily and have enough income to raise a child. Yet they are aware of the dangers of waiting too long to have children and for many of them their age has been an impetus to get pregnant.

These women are also more educated about the process of pregnancy, birth, and child-raising than are many new mothers, since the process of insemination involves both technical knowledge and planning and since, unlike married women, they are aware that they will have the primary responsibility for the health and well-being of the child.

There is another reason for choosing artificial insemination. Most of the women are aware of child custody cases involving lesbian mothers. Until recently, if the mother's orientation was known, the judges routinely denied her custody of her children because of her orientation, regardless of her qualities as a nurturer, although recently some lesbians have won custody of their children. Still, because of knowledge of these cases, many lesbians opt for alternative fertilization, if only to protect themselves from possible claims of the men who father the children or from intervention on the part of the state.

Other considerations intrude. Sexual intercourse with a man is unpalatable to many lesbians, and therefore alternative insemination is preferable. With the possibility of choice with donors there is also some likelihood of influencing the genetic makeup of the children.

These are practical reasons. There is another, more ideological reason— a woman's choice to conceive and her control over the process is a radical innovation to the usual childbearing situation, and can be a model for other lesbians and for single women who want to have children.

Methods of Conception

Although the use of alternative fertilization is not new, many lesbians who I interviewed were unaware that it was an option for them. They did not personally know of anyone who had used that method for pregnancy and were not sure how to find a doctor who would inseminate them. Therefore, previously, some of these women who decided to become mothers had no alternative to sleeping with a man in order to accomplish this. However, approaching a man was often difficult. One method was to pick up men in bars and sleep with several so that no one man could claim the child as his. Many of the women interviewed preferred sleeping with gay male friends because they felt that they would not regard children as "property" as heterosexual men might and that gay men would not want children to adhere to rigid sex roles.

Women who got pregnant this way sometimes had to deal with subsequent claims on them and their children by the men, who were delighted to have a built-in family whom they could see at their own convenience. Since both the financial and emotional burden of child-raising was on the mother, often the erratic presence of the man in the life of the family was more disruptive than his complete absence.

Because of the problems involved in sleeping with a man in order to conceive, as more has been learned about alternative fertilization, more and more women have considered having children by this method. They can have access to it either from a fertility clinic or from a recently established community-based network of volunteer donors.

Clinic-Based Fertilization

The use of alternative fertilization through the medical establishment in the San Francisco area is well established. This is largely due to the efforts of a family physician who served as a sperm donor when he was in medical school and saw the need to develop a group of such donors for his own patients. He protects both the anonymity of the donor and recipient, and single women can use his service.

Some of the lesbians in the community use this method because by paying for this service, they are not dependent on favors from friends to line up donors, the doctor has screened for various diseases, and the donors can be chosen because of desired characteristics such as coloring.

Disadvantages are that the nature of the insemination in the doctor's office is clinical, that the expense of a monthly insemination until it takes can mount, and that records are kept on the women who use this service, which some women fear might be used against them or their children in the future.

Community-Network-Based Insemination

There are also reasons for relying on the more informal networks of friends who know men who are willing to donate sperm. With this method, women can inseminate themselves in their own homes in comfort, they don't have to pay for a specimen, they don't have to worry about records, and they can use the services of gay men if they want to.

However, many women find it difficult to ask the same favor month after month if they don't get pregnant. And these arrangements can break down down if the potential donor moves or is out of town at the time of ovulation.

In response to the increasing number of women who want to use alternative insemination, a more efficient method of using community donors has been worked out by a feminist facilitator. She has organized a group of gay men who donate sperm for lesbians who want to have children. Consent forms she designed protect both the donor and recipient, but contain a clause that when a child resulting from the insemination reaches legal age, she or he can contact the donor with his permission. This network of donors has become the preferred resource for most lesbians in the community.

Controlling for Gender

Because male and female-producing sperm have different characteristics, techniques have been developed to try to control the gender of the child. Since many lesbians prefer to have female children, they use methods of conception that will favor girls.[1]

The rationale is that X chromosomes, or female-producing sperm, are fatter, slower swimmers, live longer and survive better in an acid environment than the Y chromosomes, or male-producing sperm. To enhance the chances for a daughter, before insemination, a small, natural sponge that has been put in an acidic solution of two tablespoons of white vinegar to one quart of warm water and then squeezed is inserted into the vagina. It is left in place for several hours and removed before the sperm is inserted. The insemination is done within twenty-four hours before ovulation is expected. Because of the acidic environment and the amount of time until ovulation, these methods enhance the survival of the longer-living, acid-compatible female sperm.[2]

It has been estimated that it takes six inseminations or about six months for a pregnancy to take, which is the amount of time it takes women to get pregnant by more traditional methods. This is an average; for some women it may take longer.

As mentioned, there is a stated preference for girls in the lesbian community. One reason is that many women want the chance to raise a daughter in ways more in keeping with feminist principles than the ways they were raised. Another is that since it is a community of women, a daughter fits in better and is more easily socialized, while special thought and arrangements have to be made for a boy to counteract the sexist influence he will be exposed to outside the community. Some women feel that they only want to put their energy into raising daughters and that they will be disappointed if they give birth to a son.

However, the women in the community who have given birth to boys have responded to them eagerly and have loved them without reservation. The presence of boys in the community causes women to more clearly draw the line between thinking all males are sexist and criticizing actual sexist behavior.

The Support Group

In the lesbian-feminist community it is customary for self-help support groups to form in answer to particular needs of community members.[3] Such a group was formed by lesbians who wanted to get pregnant in non-traditional ways and who banded together to help each other. One of the women who started the group talked about how it began:

> A couple of years ago, I started thinking about children in my life and what I wanted to do around children. It never entered my mind that being a lesbian meant you couldn't have children and most lesbians don't think of it as a choice. But I was really into children and had done a lot of child care. . . . I visited some relatives where all the children were being raised to be bigots and I got really depressed about the fact that I had to deny myself a kind of love of children which I knew I could really listen to and raise with love and that the patriarchal system was having this control over me about who I could love. So I got mad and started talking with friends who were lesbians and wanted to have children.

> Having a child is important to me but it isn't my main focus, which is being a full human being, living up to my potential, doing things creatively and working toward social change.

> But I would like to have a child, so we started talking about how there were other women around who wanted to have children and needed a lot of support around it. We decided to start a support group and we put an ad in a women's paper and read a lot of the literature about artificial insemination, but it seemed remote from our lives.

The group continued to meet and collect information but the meetings were becoming repetitive since often women would come once or twice and then go away and other women would replace them. None of the women in the group wanted to have children immediately because of time or financial pressures. They had not yet encountered anyone who had actually gotten pregnant from alternative fertilization. Then:

> Someone got us in touch with a woman who was pregnant with alternative fertilization and we got ecstatic and she came to the group. So we decided to

do a whole new campaign to get women involved and we advertised in the women's papers and with notices at bookstores. . . . And the first meetings were incredible, full of women. We were so excited with this woman because here she was with a full belly and eight months pregnant and a friend of hers came who had had a daughter with alternative fertilization and here was this child sitting there with ten fingers and toes and she looked like everyone else. . . . And we started talking around that and that's how the group has been going since then. . . . There have been six births in the group through alternative fertilization and nine more women are pregnant and several more are trying to get pregnant and then their lovers come so it's really strong.

At the group meetings, women can exchange information about where to find housing, about pregnancy, diet, birth methods, and child-raising. Child care is exchanged; clothes, toys, and equipment are shared or passed on. Many of the women who have children stay in touch with other women in the group because they intend that their children will be friends as they grow up.

The group meetings are fun. There is good food, encouragement for women who are trying to get pregnant, excitement at seeing how the children have changed since the last meeting, joy at another pregnancy announcement, support for the partners of the women, and simply relaxing and being able to be oneself in the context of complete acceptance.

Role of Mother's Lover

Not all women who want to get pregnant are living with lovers; if they are, however, because of the strain of pregnancy and childbirth on a relationship, it is essential that both partners are committed to the decision to have and raise a child and that they have the chance to work through their often conflicting feelings about it.

Women who are living with their lovers usually want to include them in as many aspects of the pregnancy as possible. One woman described how after she was inseminated in her home by a facilitator, she lay still, holding her lover so that her lover too could share the insemination process.

There are many stresses on the lover during the process, yet there are few places she can reveal her feelings. Since the focus is on the pregnant woman, it is often the lover with her own emotional reactions and fears who is ignored and who may feel unworthy if she has ambivalent feelings. Since there is a structural similarity, it is not surprising that some of her fears are similar to those of a husband who is fathering for the first time, such as whether she can take on the extra responsibility of a child who, in this case, is not her biological child; whether the mother will be so wrapped up in the child that there is no emotional room for the lover; whether the child will relate to the lover as affectionately as she/he relates to the mother; and finally, whether the process of pregnancy, birth, and nursing will so tire the mother that she will not want to participate in the outside social activities that the lover might desire. In the support group, the lover is encouraged to meet with other partners and to talk about her feelings.

It cannot be stressed enough how important it is with single mothers who give birth that whoever they designate as important to them be included in the birth process, whenever possible. It is especially important that a lover be included in the process and taken as seriously as a legal husband is. This includes being present during labor and during the birth and having the doctor and nurses address instructions or explanations to her, and being with the mother after birth if there are complications. It is important that the lover, mother, and infant have time together after birth to take comfort in each other, to celebrate the process, and to bond. If the woman does not have a lover but has a very close friend or friends whom she designates as being significant, it is important that they be treated with respect and allowed to participate in the same way.

Relationship with Family

Successful insemination can affect the relationship of lesbians with their own families. One of the reasons that some parents have reservations about a lesbian sexual orientation in their daughters is that they assume they will not have the opportunity to be grandparents—a status enjoyed by most of their contemporaries. Thus, with the increasing use of alternative fertilization, many parents of lesbians become more accepting of their daughters, especially as a relationship with their grandchildren develops.

Women who are using alternative fertilization usually wait until they are pregnant before they let their parents know. Often, the news of a daughter's pregnancy has brought mothers closer to their daughters, since childbirth is an area of interest both can share. One of the women in the group who had always been close to her family was attended during childbirth not only by her lover, midwife, and close friends, but also her mother, brother, sister, and sister-in-law and her children, who had flown across the country to be with her at this important moment.

Ideal Childbirth Situations

The ideal situation for childbirth is in one's home with the help of midwives and in the company of those who are emotionally important, whether these are friends, a lover, other children, or family members. A major concern is the health, comfort, and safety of the baby and mother, and to be in a situation in which one has control and in which one doesn't have to contend with tight schedules or negative attitudes of medical staff. Thus the tendency toward home birth.

When lesbians do give birth in hospitals, they are concerned that people who are important to them be treated respectfully. As one recent mother said:

> First of all, what is important is that your lovers and your friends be treated with respect and that those relationships be treated seriously. It doesn't necessarily have to be your lover, so they see it as a "husband substitute" or something. Because to many of us lesbians—we don't always just mirror a nuclear family—what is essential in our lives is often a friendship group which may or may not include a lover and may change from time to time. We are developing friendship groups that are playing many of the roles that an immediate family does. But that should be respected. At my child's birth, about six people came with me and were sitting in the halls waiting and when my son was born, they took him to the nursery and let everyone see him and the nurse held him up special so my friend could take a picture of him. It was nice.

The Children of Lesbian Mothers

In spite of their growing numbers, lesbians who have children with the use of alternative fertilization are still a small percentage of the parent population. Most of the mothers are aware of this and have thought about how to deal with situations that might arise in the future in response to the children's unusual births. One mother said:

> There are going to be different times in his life when he's going to understand more. What I would like him to understand is that you need sperm to get pregnant but you don't need to live with a man to raise good children, and I'm hoping that the love he gets from us and the support he gets from everybody else is enough so it's not going to be an important question that he know his father is one particular biological father, and I think it'll be more from other kids that he gets the pressure of who his father is and I think he'll end up saying he doesn't know who his father is and that it doesn't matter that he doesn't know. Look how many single women end up raising their kids alone because of the father splitting.
>
> I definitely want him to be around men that I feel good about. Somebody sensitive to our situation and who wants to raise him as a sensitive man and give him some male qualities, who is very physically loving. He could do child care with him, doing things with us and him, or with him alone.

As the child of a lesbian mother gets older, there are other concerns. If it is known that the child is fatherless and being raised by two women, other children may avoid or mistreat the child. Lesbian mothers hope that the child will get enough support and love at home so that the effects of this will not be too damaging, but as the child grows there will be other situations in which the fact of its unusual parentage will have to be dealt with. When the child is small, the mothers can socialize with other lesbians who have children and these children can be the main source of friends for their children. However, when interacting with outsiders, the need for explanation becomes greater. Usually the mother has to go back to work within a few months after birth and it is customary to leave the child with babysitters. The mother's relationship with her lover might affect the attitude of the babysitter toward the child.

As the child grows older and is in nursery school, the reactions of the other children and staff members have to be considered. Sometimes the mothers confront the staff and explain the situation to them and they become more sensitive to it. In other cases, the mothers simply comfort the child if that is necessary or explain that its situation is different from that of most other children but that that should be a source of pride.

Another problem is the public schools. Here women have to decide what they want to put on the official records, how much they want to disclose about the role of the partner in the life of the child, and the degree of participation the partner wants to have in school-centered activities.

However, every time there has to be obfuscation, it is difficult for the partner as well as for the mother and the child. Once again the lack of legitimization of lesbian relationships is damaging. It is therefore important that the family unit be supportive and loving, and that the couple and the child, or children, have outside support systems. These systems can be informal ones such as friends who know their situation and accept it or a group of other lesbian mothers and their partners, and can help to counterbalance the prejudice of the larger culture.

Notes

1. Most of the following information is taken from a pamphlet compiled by two women who have successfully given birth through alternative fertilization. See Anonymous, S. and M., *Woman Controlled Conception*, Womanshare Books, 3929 24th Street, San Francisco, CA 94114. See also M. O'Donnell et al., *Lesbian Health Matters!* Santa Cruz Women's Health Collective, 250 Locust Street, Santa Cruz, CA 95060.

2. L. Galana, "Radical Reproduction: X Without Y," in L. Galana and G. Covina, eds., *The Lesbian Reader* (Oakland, Calif.: Amazon Press, 1975), pp. 122–37.

3. J. Winnow, "Lesbian Mothers: Toward a Non-Institutionalized Mothering," unpublished manuscript, 1978; D. Wolf, *The Lesbian Community* (Berkeley: University of California Press, 1979), p. 138.

13

Lesbians and Contemporary Health Care Systems: Oppression and Opportunity

TRUDY DARTY & SANDEE POTTER

*T*he delivery of health care services to lesbians has been a topic all too frequently neglected by the traditional medical community. As a result of this neglect, lesbians have been forced to be almost totally reliant on a male-dominated heterosexist health care system that has little knowledge or understanding of lesbianism.

While the past fifteen years have seen increased public visibility for the lesbian and gay population in America, the patriarchal medical profession has virtually ignored the health problems of lesbians. The authors' own exhaustive review of the leading medical journals during the last decade revealed less than a dozen articles that focused on the physical health care needs of lesbian clients. Based on the paucity of lesbian health care research found in major medical journals, the reader might make one of two conclusions: that lesbians enjoy incredibly good health and have no need of the services provided by health care practitioners; or that lesbians have the same health care needs as their heterosexual sisters. Both conclusions would be misleading.

The absence of concern over lesbian health care by the medical community can be explained in two ways: first, by the male domination of the American health care system and the medical establishment's attitude toward women of all sexual preference; and second, by the dual oppression of those who are both female and homosexual. The first two sections of this article will explore these dimensions.

A limited alternative to the traditional medical establishment does exist. Within the past decade a grass roots women's health movement has emerged as a result of the resurgence of feminism in the late 1960s. Under the aegis of this new self-help movement, numerous women-controlled health care programs have been developed, the most visible of which are the women-administered health clinics. The ramifications of this challenge to traditional medicine's absolute monopoly on women's gynecological care are tremendous. In the latter sections of this article we will examine the women's health movement, women-controlled health clinics, and lesbian self-help health care.

Male Domination of the American Health Care System and the Medical Establishment's Attitude Toward Women

To understand some of the problems encountered by lesbian clients when dealing with the medical establishment, one must consider the sexual politics of health care in general as well as the specific position and degree of participation of women in the health care system. Males dominate the American health care system. According to 1981 AMA statistics, over 90 percent of the approximately half million practicing physicians in the United States are men; and virtually all administrative and managerial positions are occupied by males. However, three million women currently work in the health sector and over 80 percent of all health service and hospital workers are women. These female workers are paid less than their male counterparts, are in less prestigious medical specialties, have fewer opportunities for professional advancement, and have higher job turnover because of conflicting family and work roles.[1] Clearly, there is an immense power imbalance between the men and women employed in the delivery of health care services.

Male domination of American medicine has not only affected the division of labor in the health care industry but has also resulted in an unequal dichotomy between male doctors and female patients, reflective of traditional sex-role patterns in our society, that has instituted a system of paternal/patriarchal social control. Historically, the Church or organized religion was the prime source of social control, especially the control of the disadvantaged and powerless segments of society. Within the past century, a transfer of power from the religious to the scientific realm has occurred. As Ehrenreich and English have pointed out, medical science has become one of the most powerful sources of sexist and racist ideology in American culture, and medicine's primary contribution to sexist ideology has been to define females as sick, and potentially sickening to males. Natural events in women's lives, such as menstruation, pregnancy, and menopause, are regarded as weakening infirmities. Mixed with the diagnosis of women as sick is the fear of her being contagious to men. Two universal examples of this fear are the menstrual and postpartum taboos.[2]

Sexual feelings, more often than not, have been considered out of place in the lives of "nice" women. In the nineteenth century, a more puritanical era, female sexuality was viewed as unwomanly and, perhaps, pathological. Evidence of female sexual feelings was threatening to nineteenth century males. The guardians of the social order of the time utilized female castration, introduced in the Western world around 1858 by London surgeon Isaac Brown Baker, to impose conventionally expected female patterns of behavior upon women who dared to depart from their circumscribed roles.[3] Sexual surgery or the threat of surgery, such as clitorectomy or ovariotomy, were powerful weapons of social control. Such practices are not as far behind us as might generally be assumed. As recently as 1948, a clitorectomy was performed on a five-year-old child as a cure for masturbation; and total clitoral amputation has continued to be used as part of a surgical procedure to "repair" alleged genital ambiguities.[4] Medicine has consistently employed various means of forcing women to accept their prescribed roles.

The contemporary scene is not vastly improved over the historical one. Healthy women are forced to rely heavily upon the medical profession because of their need for medical care in areas dealing with sexuality and childbearing. Female patients often find the male-dominated health care industry to be very unsympathetic territory. Research by sociologists Scully and Bart found gynecologists defining "what the female role should be in terms of their own values and then labeling as emotionally unstable those women who sought fulfillment in other roles."[5] Additional research by Scully on the education of obstetrician-gynecologists revealed that women are used as "teaching material" by medical residents in teaching hospitals. She reported that it was not uncommon for women to have four or five pelvic examinations during a single clinic visit or during hospitalization, for the sole purpose of providing training for medical students. Scully also noted that women were frequently encouraged to undergo unnecessary surgery so fledgling residents could "master" various surgical skills.

The female patient is expected to play the submissive supplicant role opposite the omnipotent godlike role of the physician. That physicians take their deity status seriously is documented in the following quote by Russell C. Scott, M.D.: "If like all human beings, he the gynecologist is made in the image of the Almighty, and if he is kind, then his kindness and concern for his patients may provide her with a glimpse of God's image."[6] Unfortunately for their patients, physicians tend to be imperfect gods, and blind obedience to physician directives has resulted in medical tragedy for many women: injury, iatrogenic disease, and/or death.

The condescending attitude of male doctors is common throughout the medical establishment, but is especially pronounced in the obstetrician/ gynecologist. The attitude of ob/gyns toward their patients, however, seems not to have hindered their practice of medicine if one measures medical success in terms of dollars. The after-tax income of ob/gyns as a group has passed the median incomes of general surgeons and psychiatrists, establishing obstetrics/gynecology as the highest paid medical specialty; an accomplishment made even more remarkable by America's falling birthrate.[7] The authors suggest that the surgical role of ob/gyns in performing unnecessary hysterectomies and Caesarean sections has certainly had a positive effect on their incomes.

Like the training and textbooks in medical school, medical journals perpetuate condescension toward women and confirm that sexism is alive and well in the medical profession. Both the articles and the advertisements are often offensive to women. In theory the doctor/patient relationship is one of employee/consumer but in reality more closely resembles parent/ child. Prescriptions for mood-altering drugs have replaced the clitorectomy but the objective remains the same—keeping the woman in her male-defined place. Pharmaceutical advertisements and promotions have targeted women as the most likely consumers of mood-altering prescription drugs, like librium, valium, and dexedrine. The success of these promotional campaigns can be measured by the fact that women are the major consumers of such drugs, constituting two-thirds of the market.[8]

It is to this biased medical system that lesbians must entrust themselves for health care. As this brief section has attempted to describe, it is a system permeated with problems for the woman seeking quality and nonsexist health care. If the woman seeking health care happens to be a lesbian the problems are compounded.

Lesbians and Health Care: Double Dilemma

Lesbians requesting health care services from the partriarchal medical system are confronted with a number of difficulties. The basis for these difficulties can be found in both heterosexism, the belief that everyone is or should be heterosexual and that society should be governed by patriarchal norms, and homophobia, the fear of homosexuality in one's self or others.

Heterosexism, and its companion, homophobia, can impact negatively on lesbian health care in many ways. Five are listed and discussed here.

First, lesbians frequently believe that heterosexism prevents them from having the same opportunities for health care services enjoyed by their heterosexual sisters. The obstetrician/gynecologist is considered to be the primary physician to women. The usual entry into the health care system for most women is through routine gynecological visits for periodic examination, prenatal care, and contraceptive counseling. Since the life experiences of many lesbians do not include heterosexual marriage or other sexual relationships that may result in a need for contraceptives or prenatal and obstetrical care, these women have a diminished number of opportunities to initially connect with the health care system.

Also, many lesbians do not go to ob/gyns for fear that their sexual preference will become known. Often physicians feel that it is their duty to inquire about the utilization of specific contraceptive methods, thus putting the lesbian client in a position where she must either reveal her sexual preference or lie about questions pertinent to her medical history. Either course of action is risky. Physician John Whyte and medical student Lisa Capaldini observe:

> Lesbians and gay men have a distressingly accurate sense of double jeopardy regarding their utilization of a health care system that has a history of being indifferent, if not hostile, toward their needs. If they do not disclose their sexual orientation to their physicians, they may subsequently fail to impart important related information necessary for their medical care. If, on the other hand, they do choose to impart this information, they often risk alienating their physicians, and receiving moral pronouncements or insensitive care.[9]

Writing about her preliminary study on factors influencing lesbian gynecologic care, gynecologist Dr. Susan Johnson reported that 40 percent of the study population felt their health care would be adversely affected if their sexual preference were known by their physician. However, among the women involved in the Johnson study who had never discussed their sexual preference with a physician, 64 percent would have liked to have been able to identify themselves as lesbians, no doubt believing that knowledge of sexual preference might permit more intelligent administration of medical services.[10] Coupled with the fear that a physician's homophobia may interfere with the kind of medical care offered to a lesbian is the concern that once a physician realizes that a client is a lesbian, lesbianism will be seen as the *cause* of various health problems, such as ulcers, migraines, alcoholism.

This fear of unpleasant repercussions should her sexual orientation be discovered is also linked to the second negative impact of heterosexism. Because it is assumed that everyone is heterosexual, lesbians cannot ask the following questions specific to their health care and expect to receive adequate answers: What health problems are prevalent among lesbians? What health problems are rare? What forms of lesbian lovemaking are most likely to spread particular types of sexually transmitted diseases? Since there has been so little research conducted on the medical problems of lesbians or the effect of female homosexual activity on gynecologic health, many health providers are too uninformed to competently address such questions. Reviewing the information that is known, it seems that some distinct differences do exist between the health concerns of heterosexual and homosexual women. For example, venereal disease is rare among lesbians.[11] This is in direct contrast to the common belief that all gay people are likely candidates for contracting a venereal disease. If more research were done into all aspects of lesbian health needs, medical science could dispel many of the myths that have evolved out of ignorance and ensure better medical care for lesbians.

Third, because of the assumption that everyone is heterosexual and the extreme deficiency in information concerning lesbian health care, it is easy for physicians to misdiagnose lesbian health problems. One example in the literature is that of a lesbian rushed to an emergency room experiencing acute abdominal pain. Such a patient might be diagnosed as either having appendicitis or a ruptured ectopic pregnancy—that is, pregnancy implanted in the Fallopian tube. If the doctor involved was aware of the patient's lesbianism, he/she could, in most cases, dismiss the pregnancy option and proceed faster with appropriate treatment for appendicitis.[12]

A fourth problem concerns hospital policies that do not recognize a lesbian's lover or friends as her chosen family. In an emergency a lover/partner cannot sign legal consent forms permitting necessary medical procedures as a heterosexual spouse is allowed to do. A critically ill lesbian in an intensive care unit may be denied the loving support of those closest to her because of restrictive visiting rules that mandate only biological family will be admitted. Such rigid inhumane policies often ignore the realities of human relationships and alternative definitions of "family."[13]

Finally, health insurance plans do not have provisions for lesbians to list their lovers as medical dependents—that is, family members. This deprives lesbian couples of the added health protection one could provide for the other and cheats the "legally single" woman out of financial benefits to which she is entitled. Many health insurance plans are employer-funded as part of the benefit package due employees as compensation in addition to wages. Lesbian couples are deprived of the spousal benefits that heterosexually-married couples take for granted.

The Women's Health Movement

From the mid 1800s when the American Medical Association was created and "regular" doctors were established as the only recognized providers of health care,[14] until the 1970s, the traditional male-dominated medical system had a monopoly on the delivery of health care services. The late 1960s, however, saw America's second wave of feminism, which questioned women's relationship to every institution in American society, including the medical establishment. As a result of this critical examination of the structure and quality of women's health care came the women's health movement.

The women's health movement is an umbrella term for the myriad women-controlled health-related groups and projects emerging at a community level across the country. This burgeoning movement is intensely political, loosely structured, lay-controlled, and emphasizes self-help and mutual support. There is no single formal organization to join or any national consensus on policies and goals. Women involved in the movement utilize their collective experiences to expand their individual knowledge and plan strategies for change. The need for the active participation of every woman in her own health care is stressed. Although white middle-class women predominate, women of all ages, social classes, ethnic backgrounds, and sexual preferences have taken active roles in movement activities.[15]

While its earliest beginnings can be traced to the late 1960s, 1971 was a banner year for the women's health movement. The first Women's Health Conference, attended by over eight hundred women, was held in New York in March 1971.[16] Self-help gynecology was introduced by Carol Downer, a member of the Los Angeles Feminist Women's Health Center. Downer invited "empirical observation" by inserting a speculum into her vagina and encouraging the other women in the Los Angeles health group to view her cervix.[17] This radical act of self-examination helped break the barriers of medical mystique that had prevented women from intimately knowing their own bodies. Self-examination and demonstration classes quickly became popular in feminist communities all over the country. Finally, the year 1971 is significant because it marks the opening of the first women-controlled clinics.[18]

Currently, the importance of particular issues and programs is widely varied within the movement. Priorities and long-range objectives are as diverse as the women involved in any particular community. However, there does exist one common goal: a determination to improve health care for all women and to put an end to sexism in the existing health system.[19] Marieskind notes that the "work of the Women's Health Movement falls into three main categories: struggling to change established health institutions, changing consumer and provider consciousness, and providing health-related services."[20] Implementation of the work described by Marieskind can be found in the rapid proliferation of women's health movement activities, which include the following: women-controlled clinics, self-help educational groups, women's health courses, political action groups, research projects, rape counseling and support services, educational films, conferences, newsletters, articles, and books.[21]

The right to abortion and contraception were the first causes around which early movement groups rallied. These two primarily heterosexual issues admittedly commanded most of the energies of the women involved. Gradually services expanded to their present level, encompassing many gynecological procedures and other types of primary care. There is evidence, however, that a continuing heterosexist bias has prevailed.[22]

The question arises: Can a system that evolved from ob/gyn services related to predominately heterosexual reproduction be aware of and responsive to lesbians' specific health care needs? Ruzek substantiates that lesbian complaints are well founded, noting that heterosexual women are often unwittingly insensitive. During her research on women's clinics, Ruzek noted that the issue complained about most frequently by lesbians was the common assumption that every woman used some type of contraceptive.[23] The allocation of scarce resources sometimes does not adequately provide for specifically lesbian needs, concentrating instead on services used primarily by heterosexual women.

Regardless of these shortcomings, the women's health movement and the lesbian community have much to offer each other. Where available, women-controlled health clinics provide a positive alternative for lesbians dissatisfied with traditional health services. Basic movement-wide health issues are relevant to all women, and lesbian energy has made substantial contributions to the women's health movement. As early as 1973, Hornstein wrote of lesbian participation, and since then others have verified continuing lesbian involvement.[24]

Women-Controlled Health Clinics

The most visible aspect of the women's health movement are the women-controlled health clinics, which provide direct primary care services to the public. After more than a decade of struggle, there are less than one hundred clinics in existence, mostly located in university and urban communities. Some of the services offered by these clinics are: routine gynecological care, including pap smears, treatment of vaginitis, and breast exams; pregnancy testing; abortion; family planning and birth control (a limited number of clinics are fitting cervical caps); testing and treatment for venereal disease; health education and consciousness-raising through self-help seminars and literature; referrals to other, often screened, health practitioners; and patient advocacy. A few clinics provide obstetrical care, extended primary care, and mental health counselling, but these services are not widely available.

The authors conducted a national survey of women-controlled health clinics in the spring of 1981. Using a listing provided by the Women's Health Network and supplemental listings from other sources, we mailed questionnaires to sixty-five clinics. Thirty usable questionnaires were returned. Survey data revealed a considerable amount of lesbian participation, both as clinic providers and consumers. In response to the survey question, "Are there any self-identified lesbians on staff at your clinic?" two-thirds of the clinic respondents answered in the affirmative. Two additional clinics said they didn't have any lesbians presently on staff but several had previously been on staff. Four of the clinics reported that lesbians comprised the majority of their staff; one of the four clinics had an exclusively lesbian staff.

Seventeen clinics responded to a survey question asking them to estimate the number of lesbians served by their clinics during the 1980 calendar year, while many of the thirteen nonresponding clinics stated that statistics on sexual orientation were not kept. Of the seventeen clinics responding, sixteen noted that they did have lesbian clients, ranging from a few, about 1 percent, to a high of 70 percent. A review of this data seems to indicate that the percentage of lesbians involved in providing services may be higher than the percentage of lesbians in the clinic populations being served. The reasons for this are not known.

Another area examined in the authors' investigation was special services for lesbians. Fourteen clinic respondents stated that they provided services specifically focused upon meeting the needs of their lesbian consumers, including: lesbian well-woman clinics, availability of lesbian counsellors and staff, conducting patient education on lesbian health care issues, and providing referrals to lesbian and gay therapists.

After reviewing the literature and our research findings, we can state that the women-controlled health clinics have two major strengths and two major weaknesses. The strengths are the clinics' positive self-help feminist perspective and their egalitarian structure. The weaknesses are the scarcity of clinics and their limited services.

As previously stated, one inherent strength of women-controlled clinics is their positive self-help feminist perspective. Each woman is encouraged to take charge of her own body and, indirectly, her life. Patient education, peer-taught in jargon-free language, enables women to evaluate their own physical condition and make informed decisions. The clinics also provide specialized services for distinct groups with special needs, such as the physically challenged, teenagers, and post-menopausal women.

The majority of clinics are administered collectively. Over half of the clinics in our survey had a collective structure, while one-fourth had a hierarchical structure.[25] Even among those clinics that were not collectives, many utilized democratically elected boards and worker-controlled committees to assure community and consumer input. Most clinics also employ some method of client feedback to evaluate their services. All this allows an optimum level of participation for every woman involved, regardless of role. This fluidity of power stands in stark contrast to the hierarchical rigidity of the traditional medical establishment.

One of the most glaring deficiencies in the women's clinic system of health care is the scarcity of the clinics themselves. Most clinics are located only in large cities or university communities. Furthermore, the largest number of clinics are grouped geographically on either the East or West Coast, with California being the leader in the availability of clinics. The deep South and the Southwest are two geographical regions where it would be difficult to find a women-controlled health clinic; in many instances, entire states lack a single facility. This affords very limited access for the majority of women. Lesbians reside in every region of the country, including isolated rural areas. The popular lesbian slogan "We are everywhere" is a valid observation. Most lesbians, like most women, lack the opportunity to make a choice between alternative women-controlled clinics and traditional health care providers.

A second drawback is the limited services currently being offered by the women-controlled clinics. The majority of the proffered services are still gynecologically based. Only rudimentary primary care procedures are performed. Specialized medicine, such as surgery or treatment of life-threatening chronic diseases (like cancer, heart disease, or kidney dysfunction) is not possible within clinic facilities, due to their lack of expensive sophisticated technological equipment and highly trained personnel needed to accomplish such care. The community women-controlled health clinic, often partially staffed by lay healers and volunteers, has a long way to go to compete with any major medical center. Nevertheless, the medical care and education that is provided by the clinics immeasurably aids women in their struggle to reclaim their own bodies from male domination.

Lesbian Self-Help: Sister, Heal Thyself

Realizing the impossibility of women-controlled health clinics being able to meet the needs of all women throughout the life cycle, the lesbian community has responded to the problems of illness and death by developing informal support networks. Lesbians have often survived challenges, both individual and collective, through bonding together as supportive units. There is no reason to face struggles against pain, illness, and physical challenges with anything less than united combativeness. While writing about the Lesbian Illness Support Group of which she is a member, Joan Nestle observed:

> Illness is a betrayer of Lesbian strength, Lesbian self-sufficiency. Its impact clearly marks the limits of rhetoric and forces a clarity about what being a Lesbian means in the deepest sense, the sense of life and death. In the past, whispers of individual afflictions circulated in the community but we were protected by youth and the number of seemingly healthy bodies around us. Illness can be a terrible secret, a gauntlet run daily by the ill woman and her friends and lovers. . . .
>
> As we age as a community, as the chemical poisons of this time and place take their toll, more and more Lesbians will be facing the challenge of illness. We must devise our own way of living with physical change and for us the group is a beginning.[26]

Illness support groups now exist in various cities. These informal groups provide emotional and physical support for ill and physically challenged lesbians, and their lovers and close friends. Regular meetings furnish an outlet for pent-up feelings, fears, and frustrations. Group members learn that they are not alone through revelation of shared experiences. Participants act as advocates for each other, even accompanying each other to medical appointments. Some lesbians may lack the support of their biological family, having been ostracized because of their sexual preference. Lovers and friends often form a new family of choice and play a crucial role in times of crisis.

Tracy Moore, member of an Iowa City lesbian collective, points out that:

> . . . one of the characteristics of our emerging lesbian culture is the voluntary formation of groups to get work done. From project to support to consciousness, whatever the task, lesbians tend to approach it in numbers, sharing responsibility, even when the group and tasks have not been clearly defined.[27]

This truism has even come to include the unavoidable task of facing death. In many instances, communities of women-identified women have rallied around chronically and terminally ill lesbians, providing practical care, emotional help, and even some financial support. An extensive network of volunteers is formed to meet the needs of the ill woman and her household. Food preparation, housekeeping chores, personal care, and transportation is provided by friends working in organized shifts. Requested legal and medical research is done. Even funeral arrangements are made if the woman wishes. At times financial aid has been made available to supplement an inadequate income. One woman, now dead from breast cancer, referred to this financial help as "going on the dyke dole."[28]

Rituals have a defining and cohesive effect on all groups, whether secular or sacred. Philosopher Susanne Langer has explained the role of ritual as:

> ... a symbolic transformation of experiences that no other medium can adequately express. Because it springs from a primary human need, it is spontaneous activity—that is to say, it arises without intention, without adaptation to a conscious purpose; its growth is undesigned, its pattern purely natural, however intricate it may be. ...
>
> Ritual "expresses feelings" in the logical rather than the psychological sense. It may have what Aristotle called "cathartic" value, but that is not its characteristic; it is primarily an *articulation* of feelings. The ultimate product of such an articulation is not simple emotion, but a complex permanent attitude.[29]

Lesbian culture is in the process of developing new rituals—articulating attitudes—in response to the deaths of its members, ones that accurately reflect the values and spiritual needs of the participants.

The self-help efforts of communities of women-identified women have been greatly facilitated by publicity in the lesbian media. The growing popularity of and concern with lesbian health issues is reflected in increased media coverage. Lesbian newspapers, journals, and newsletters promote a nationwide dialogue through articles on health issues, editorials, personal experience stories, letters, and notices of conferences and self-help group meetings.

It has long been a belief in the lesbian community that love and human touch have powerful healing properties. Psychologists have recognized the positive nature of affectionate contact in studies dating back to the 1940s.[30] Lesbians seem to be attempting to blend the benefits of medical technology with the psychological dynamism of love and sisterhood for more effective healing. Incisive lesbian feminist poet Audre Lorde, writing about her personal battle with cancer, has said that after her mastectomy the love of women healed her. She shares with her readers:

> I do know that there was a tremendous amount of love and support flowing into me from the women around me, and it felt like being bathed in a continuous tide of positive energies. ...
>
> ... support will always have a special and vividly erotic set of image/meanings for me now. ... These images flow quickly, the tangible floods of energy rolling off these women toward me that I converted into power to heal myself.[31]

Conclusions

No short-term panaceas exist for the problems of obtaining quality health care for lesbians. As this article documents, there is a wide gulf of misunderstanding, ignorance, and prejudice between health practitioners in the traditional medical establishment and lesbians needing medical services. This chasm is not one that can be easily bridged.

Some positive steps that could be taken are obvious. Both individual physicians and the traditional medical system as a whole need to be educated and sensitized to the realities of lesbian sexuality. Personal biases should be examined and resolved, perhaps within the confines of in-service seminars for practicing health care professionals and through specialized courses for medical and nursing students. Elimination of homophobic prejudices would be an excellent place to begin the healing process.

Much more empirical research is required to discover the subtle differences between health care for lesbians and heterosexual women. Differences do exist; if more were documented, the quality of lesbian health care could be improved. Because health practitioners working within the women's health movement often have greater and more open access to the lesbian community than do traditional medical researchers, collaboration between these two groups could facilitate more innovative and comprehensive medical research. In addition, there is every indication that research conducted by lesbian and gay health professionals could greatly benefit the lesbian community.

Women-controlled clinics should consider keeping accurate records of the medical care provided for lesbians and should encourage their lesbian clients to keep personal medical records; such data could be very useful in clinical studies and lesbian health research projects. The long-range value of such activities to all lesbians warrants cooperation if assurances can be made that research results will be used to good effect.

Emerging alternative health care systems, like the women's health movement, need to be encouraged and supported. Through its activities, programs, and literature, this grass roots movement has provided lesbians with the knowledge and opportunity to challenge the heterosexist monopoly controlling American medical care. However, more is needed than better informed lesbian health care consumers. To maximize the full potential of the women's health movement, the women-controlled clinic system begun in 1971 must be expanded beyond its current limitations of scarce locations, facilities, and services. Lesbians, like other women, need much more than just gynecological procedures. A wider variety of services is imperative.

Finally, lesbians need not be solely dependent on either the traditional medical establishment or the work of those involved in the women's health movement. The actions and words of Joan Nestle, Tracy Moore, and Audre Lorde have shown that individual lesbian communities can extend enormous amounts of care and compassion to their sick and dying sisters. Several lesbian communities have already begun to develop strategies, conferences, and programs to help lesbians who are chronically or terminally ill. Many more lesbian communities need to consider the possibilities. An army of lovers confronting the problems and complexities of modern health care services need not fail.

Notes

1. Helen I. Marieskind, *Women in the Health System: Patients, Providers, and Programs* (St. Louis: C. V. Mosby Company, 1980), p. 127.

2. Barbara Ehrenreich and Deirdre English, *Complaints and Disorders: The Sexual Politics of Sickness* (Old Westbury, N.Y.: Feminist Press, 1973), pp. 5–6.

3. G. J. Barker-Benefield, "The Spermatic Economy: A Nineteenth Century View of Sexuality," *Journal of Feminist Studies* 1 (1972): pp. 45–74.

4. Barbara Ehrenreich and Deirdre English, *For Her Own Good: 150 Years of the Experts' Advice to Women* (Garden City, N.Y.: Anchor Press/Doubleday, 1979), p. 123; Patricia Farnes, M.D., and Ruth Hubbard, Ph.D., "Letters," *Ms.*, April 1981, p. 9.

5. Diana Scully, *Men Who Control Women's Health: The Miseducation of Obstetrician-Gynecologists* (Boston: Houghton Mifflin Company, 1980), p. 107.

6. Russell C. Scott, *The World of a Gynecologist* (London: Oliver & Boyd, 1968), p. 25.

7. Gena Corea, "The Caesarean Epidemic," *Mother Jones*, July 1980, p. 33.

8. Margarete Sandelowski, *Women, Health, and Choice* (Englewood Cliffs, N.J.: Prentice-Hall, 1981), pp. 237–40.

9. John Whyte, M.D., and Lisa Capaldini, "Treating the Lesbian or Gay Patient," *Delaware Medical Journal* 52, no. 5 (May 1980): p. 271.

10. Susan R. Johnson et al., "Factors Influencing Lesbian Gynecologic Care: A Preliminary Study," *American Journal of Obstetrics & Gynecology* 140 (May 1, 1981): pp. 24–25.

11. Alan P. Bell and Martin S. Weinberg, *Homosexualities: A Study of Diversity Among Men and Women* (New York: Simon & Schuster, 1978); Johnson et al., pp. 20–25; Patricia Roberson, M.D. and Julius Schachter, Ph.D., "Failure to Identify Venereal Disease in a Lesbian Population," *Sexually Transmitted Diseases*, February 1981 prepublication draft; Whyte and Capaldini, pp. 271–80.

12. Mary O'Donnell, "Lesbian Health Care: Issues and Literature," *Science for the People*, May–June 1978, pp. 8–19.

13. One way to make the medical profession legally respect a lesbian's choice to have a lover or close friend make medical decisions for her when she is physically incapable is to assign the lover or friend the power of attorney.

14. Peter Conrad and Joseph W. Schneider, "Professionalization, Monopoly, and the Structure of Medical Practice," in Peter Conrad and Rochelle Kern, eds., *The Sociology of Health and Illness: Critical Perspectives* (New York: St. Martin's Press, 1981), pp. 155–65; Barbara Ehrenreich and Deirdre English, *Witches, Midwives and Nurses: A History of Woman Healers* (Old Westbury, N.Y.: Feminist Press, 1973), pp. 21–41.

15. Sheryl Burt Ruzek, *The Women's Health Movement: Feminist Alternatives to Medical Control* (New York: Praeger, 1978), pp. 187–92; Marieskind, p. 291. Ruzek suggests that white middle-class women predominate in the women's health movement while Marieskind notes that there is an increasing diversity of women active in the movement. The research completed by the authors would tend to support Ruzek on this issue.

16. Ruzek, p. 33.

17. Ibid., p. 53.

18. Ibid., p. 61.

19. Helen I. Marieskind, "The Women's Health Movement," in Karen Kowalski, R.N., M.S., ed., *Women's Health Care* (Wakefield, Mass.: Nursing Resources, Inc., 1979), p. 65.

20. Marieskind, *Women in the Health System*, p. 292.

21. Although the specific activities of the women's health movement are too numerous to mention here, the authors would like to cite the following resources: the National Women's Health Network (224 7th Street, S.E., Washington, D.C. 20003), founded in 1975 and considered one of the most important women's health groups in the country; *off our backs* and *Sojourner*, two monthly feminist newspapers that feature women's health articles; and *Our Bodies Ourselves*, a book that is currently being revised for a third edition by the Boston Women's Health Book Collective.

22. Ruzek, p. 190.

23. Ibid.

24. Frances Hornstein, "Lesbian Health Care," unpublished paper; O'Donnell, "Lesbian Health Care: Issues and Literature"; Mary O'Donnell et al., *Lesbian Health Matters!* (Santa Cruz, Calif.: Santa Cruz Women's Health Collective, 1979); Ruzek, p. 190; Darty/Potter, unpublished survey data.

25. Responding to our survey question on the organizational structure of their clinics, sixteen (out of twenty-nine) indicated a collective structure, seven a hierarchical structure, and one a combination of both. Five used some other structure, often democratic and nonauthoritarian in nature.

26. Joan Nestle, "N.Y. Lesbian Illness Support Group: What Being a Lesbian Means in the Deepest Sense," *off our backs* 6, no. 5 (May 1981): p. 8.

27. Tracy Moore, "Because She Died. . . ," *Common Lives/Lesbian Lives: A Lesbian Feminist Quarterly* 1, no. 2 (Winter 1981): p. 46.

28. Tracy Moore, "Linda Knox, Affectionately," *Common Lives/Lesbian Lives: A Lesbian Feminist Quarterly* 1, no. 4 (Summer 1982): p. 5.

29. Susanne K. Langer, *Philosophy in a New Key* (Cambridge, Mass.: Harvard University Press, 1957), pp. 40 and 153.

30. Kingsley Davis, "Final Note on a Case of Extreme Social Isolation," *American Journal of Sociology* 52 (1947): 432–37; Harry F. Harlow, "The Nature of Love," *American Psychologist* 13 (1958): 673–85; R. A. Spitz, "Hospitalism: An Inquiry into the Genesis of Psychiatric Conditions in Early Childhood," in *The Psychoanalytic Study of the Child*, vol. 1 (New York: International University Press, 1945), pp. 53–74.

31. Audre Lorde, *The Cancer Journals* (Argyle, N.Y.: Spinsters Ink, 1980), p. 39.

14

Peril and Promise: Lesbians' Workplace Participation

BETH SCHNEIDER

Lesbians must work.[1] Put most simply, few lesbians will ever have, however briefly, the economic support of another person (man or woman); lesbians are dependent on themselves for subsistence. Thus, a significant portion of the time and energies of most lesbians is devoted to working. Working as a central feature of lesbian existence is, however, rarely acknowledged. As with any significant primary commitment by a woman to job or career, a lesbian's relationship to work is obscured, denied, or trivialized by cultural assumptions concerning heterosexuality.[2]

Moreover, the concept "lesbian" is so identified with sexual behavior and ideas of deviance, particularly in social science literature,[3] that it has been easy to ignore the fact that lesbians spend their time at other than sexual activities; for a lesbian, working is much more likely to be a preoccupation than her sexual or affectional relations. Given the limited research on the sexual behavior of lesbians over the course of their lives, it is no surprise that there is decidedly less known about the working lives and commitments of lesbians.

In asserting the centrality, if not the primacy, of a working life to lesbians, we assume that work provides both a means of economic survival and a source of personal integrity, identity, and strength. While lesbians are certainly not the only women whose identities are at least partially formed by their relationship to work, in a culture defined for women in terms of heterosexual relations and limited control over the conditions of motherhood, most lesbians are likely to have fewer of the commitments and relations considered appropriate and necessary to the prevailing conceptions of women.

On the other hand, work and one's relationship to it is considered a major source of economic and social status, personal validation, and life purpose—certainly for men—in this society.[4] For lesbians then, whose lives will not necessarily provide or include the constraints or the comforts that other women receive ("heterosexual privileges"), working may well take on additional and special meaning. Thus, lesbians' workplace participation is shaped by the possibility of a unique commitment to working, an outsider status by dint of sexual identity, and the set of conditions common to all women workers. The conflicting aspects of these forces define the problematic and often paradoxical context within which lesbians work.

Being a woman worker has many implications for lesbians' material, social, and emotional well-being. Compared to their male counterparts, women employed full-time continue to receive significantly less pay.[5] Most do not have college degrees and enter occupations of traditional female employment where unionization is rare, benefits meager, and prestige lacking.[6] Continued employment in female-dominated occupations maintains women's disadvantage relative to men, since it is associated with lower wages; typically, lower wages keep women dependent on men—their husbands (when they have them) or their bosses.[7] In those situations in which women and men are peers at work, status distinctions remain, reflecting the realities of sexism in the workplace and the society.[8] In general then, women are on the lower end of job and authority hierarchies. In addition, basic to the economic realities of all working women is the need to appear (through dress and demeanor) sexually attractive to men, who tend to hold the economic position and power to enforce heterosexual standards and desires.[9]

Thus, as one portion of the female labor force, lesbians are in a relatively powerless and devalued position, located in workplaces occupied but not controlled by women. Herein lies one paradox of a great many lesbians' working lives. The world of women's labor—with its entrenched occupational and job segregation—creates a homosocial female environment, a milieu potentially quite comfortable for lesbians.

But lesbians must also manage their sexual identity difference[10] at work. As women whose sexual, political, and social activities are primarily with other women, lesbians are daily confronted with heterosexual assumptions at work. The nature and extent of heterosexual pressures (over and above those experienced by all women) condition the nature of their social relationships. Two markedly different dynamics simultaneously affect lesbians in their daily interactions at work.

Negative attitudes toward homosexuality are still widespread in the society. The statements and activities of New Right leaders and organizations and the research results of a number of studies on less politicized populations indicate that lesbians and male homosexuals must continue to be cautious in their dealings with the heterosexual world and to be wary of being open about their sexual identity in certain occupations—especially teaching.[11]

Directly related to these public attitudes, employment-related issues and articles tend to predominate in the lesbian and gay press. Either legislative and political efforts toward an end to discrimination are detailed and progress assessed, or some person or persons who have lost their jobs or personal credibility when their sexual identity has become known or suspected are written up. For example, recently readers of both the alternative press and mass media have seen accounts of the anticipated disastrous financial consequences of a publicly revealed lesbian relationship on the women's tennis tour, community censure of public officials who spoke in favor of antidiscrimination laws, lesbian feminists fired or not rehired at academic jobs, and a purge of suspected lesbians aboard a Navy missile ship, among others.[12]

Nevertheless, there is little systematic evidence that indicates how particular heterosexuals react to lesbians in concrete situations. It is these daily encounters and interactions with heterosexuals that are of crucial concern to lesbians; at work, the disclosure of one's sexual identity might have serious consequences. In a recent study of job discrimination against lesbians, fully 50 percent anticipated discrimination at work and 22 percent reported losing a job when their sexual identity became known.[13] But in addition, lesbians fear harassment and isolation from interpersonal networks; often they live under pressure or demands to prove they are as good or better workers than their coworkers.[14]

Whether anyone is fired or legislation is won or lost, the world of work is perceived and experienced by lesbians as troublesome, ambiguous, problematic. And while it is generally assumed that lesbians are more tolerated than gay men and therefore safer at work and elsewhere, a climate of ambivalence and disapproval pervades the world within which lesbians work; most are not likely to feel immediately comfortable about their relationships to coworkers.

Despite these significant disadvantages and potential troubles, a number of studies consistently show that lesbians have stable work histories, are higher achievers than comparable heterosexual women,[15] and have a serious commitment to work, giving it priority because they must support themselves.[16] These findings suggest, but do not describe or document, that lesbians' workplace survival results from a complicated calculation of the degree to which a particular work setting allows them freedom to be open and allows for the negotiation and development of a support network.

At work and elsewhere, lesbians want and have friendships and relationships with other women; while some research suggests that lesbians are no different than single heterosexuals in the extent of their friendship networks, others describe much greater social contacts for lesbians since they must negotiate two possibly overlapping worlds (work and social life) and most are free of familial constraints that pull other women away from work relationships.[17] Whatever the extent of their networks, it is these friendships and relationships that are a major source of workplace support—and complication—for lesbians, as well as an important facet of their emotional well-being and job satisfaction.

However, there is virtually no research that systematically explores lesbian work sociability, the creation of a support mechanism there, or the conditions under which lesbians are willing to make their sexual identity known. Most of what is known about these problems is based on findings from research on male homosexuals, and therefore does not take into account the greater importance women as a group, and lesbians specifically, attach to emotional support and relationships.[18] Nevertheless, this research indicates that the more a male is known as a homosexual, the less stressful are his relationships with heterosexuals because he does not anticipate and defend against rejection.[19] But economic success frequently requires denying one's sexual identity: research findings over the last decade are consistent in showing that high-status males are less open than low-status males.[20] A combination of avoidance, information control, and role distance are strategies used by homosexuals to preserve secrecy; the result is often the appearance of being boring, unfriendly, sexless, or heterosexual.[21]

In addition to focusing on men, many of these studies were completed prior to, or at the onset of, the gay liberation movement, which has continued to encourage and emphasize "coming out" for reasons of either political principle and obligation or personal health.[22] Certainly, in the last decade many lesbians have taken extraordinary risks in affirming their sexual identities and defending their political and social communities.[23]

In sum, lesbians' relationship to the world of work is both ordinary and unique. Based on findings from a recent study of 228 lesbian workers, a number of previously unexamined aspects of the conditions of lesbian participation at the workplace are explored here. Following a brief description of the research project from which this data is taken and a discussion of the sample generation and characteristics, four aspects of lesbian existence at work are discussed: (1) making friends, (2) finding a partner, (3) coming out, and (4) being harassed.

Research Methods and Sample

The findings are part of a larger research project on working women (both lesbian and heterosexual) and their perspectives and experiences concerning sociability, sexual relationships, and sexual harassment at the workplace.[24] The project was not explicitly designed to directly examine instances of discrimination against lesbians and cannot adequately address that problem. It was designed to explore some of the more subtle interpersonal terrain that all women are likely to encounter at work, as well as those situations of particular concern to lesbians.

The lesbian sample was gathered with the assistance of twenty-eight contacts who provided me with the names, addresses, and approximate ages of women who they thought were lesbians. The contacts provided 476 names. A self-administered questionnaire with 316 items was mailed to 307 of these contacts during the period between January and March 1980. The letter that accompanied the questionnaire did not assume any knowledge of a particular woman's sexual identity. Eight-one percent of these women returned the questionnaire, a very high rate of return that seems to reflect significant interest in all the topics covered.

There were 228 women who identified themselves as either lesbian or homosexual or gay in the question asking for current sexual identity. This sample of lesbians ranged in age from 21 to 58 (median = 29.4); 10 percent were women of color (most Afro-American).[25] The sample was unique in that it was not a San Francisco or New York City based population; 55 percent were from New England, 33 percent from Middle Atlantic states and the rest were from other locations east of the Mississippi River.

The lesbians in this study were employed in all kinds of workplaces. More than half (57 percent) were in professional or technical occupational categories (in such jobs as teaching and social work), with the remaining distributed as follows: administrative and managerial (10 percent), clerical (11 percent), craft (7 percent), service (7 percent), operative (5 percent), and sales (2 percent). Sixty-nine percent worked full-time, 20 percent part-time, and the rest were unemployed at the time of the survey. Fifty-two percent were employed in predominantly (55 to 100 percent) female workplaces, 25 percent in workplaces with 80 percent or more females; 10 percent worked in units with 80 percent or more males. While the educational attainment of this group of lesbians was very high for a population of adult women (82 percent were at least college graduates), their median income was $8800 (in 1979). The low income of the total group reflects a combination of its relative youth and the proportion with less than full-time or full-year employment.

Two questions were asked to determine lesbians' openness about themselves at work, a matter of crucial concern to any understanding of daily workplace experiences. The first asked: "How open would you say you are about your lesbianism at your *present* job?" The choices were: "Totally," "Mostly," "Somewhat," "Not at all." The participants varied widely in the extent to which they felt they were open at work: Only 16 percent felt they were totally open, while 55 percent tended to be and 29 percent were closed about who they were at work.

The second question asked the proportion of each woman's coworkers who knew she was a lesbian. Twenty-five percent estimated that *all* their coworkers knew about their sexual identity,[26] half estimated that at least one or "some" knew, and 14 percent stated that "none knew." The remainder simply "didn't know" if anyone knew they were lesbians, a difficult and often anxiety-provoking situation.

Making Friends

Most lesbians sampled believed it desirable to integrate their work and social lives in some ways.[27] Thus the distinction between public and private life is not terribly useful in describing their lives, despite its persistence as ideology throughout the culture.[28] For example, only one-third maintained that they kept their social life completely separate from their work life, and 39 percent tried not to discuss personal matters with persons from work. Alternately, 43 percent believed that doing things socially with coworkers makes relationships run more smoothly.

There obviously was variability in beliefs. Lesbians who most consistently and strongly held the view that work and social life should be integrated fell into two categories: those who had to—that is, lesbians in professional employment whose jobs required a certain level of sociability and collegiality, and those who had nothing to lose—women in dead-end jobs with no promise of advancement, those with few or no supervisory responsibilities, and those who were already open with persons from work about their sexual identity.

On the other hand, women who could not or did not believe these spheres could be easily or truly integrated were constrained by powerful forces that limited and denied the possibility of such integration: lesbians in male-dominated workplaces and those in worksites with male supervisors and bosses, in which males bond with each other often to the exclusion and detriment of the females.

The beliefs of the lesbians in the sample were quite consistent with the actual extent of their social contacts with persons from work. Most lesbians (in fact, most women) maintained social ties with at least some persons from work—at the job and outside it. Not surprisingly, 84 percent ate lunch with coworkers, but fewer engaged in social activities outside the work setting. For example, 9 percent visited frequently, 55 percent visited occasionally at each other's homes, 8 percent frequently and 47 percent occasionally went out socially with persons from work.

Two aspects of these findings merit further comment. First, the figures for the lesbians differ by less than 1 percent from those of the heterosexual women workers in the larger research project; if lesbians curtail contact or make certain judgments about coworkers as acquaintances or friends, they may do so for different reasons, but they do so to an extent similar to heterosexual women.

Second, certain conditions determine both lesbians' beliefs about, and the extensiveness of, their social contacts. Those in professional employment have more social ties with persons from work than lesbians in working-class jobs (which as a rule require less sociability); lesbians who are older, who have come to be familiar with a particular job setting over a length of time, and those who are open about their sexual identity are much more likely to maintain social contacts with coworkers than their younger or more closeted counterparts. In this particular study, there were no differences of any significance between lesbians of color and whites with regard to sociability; in fact, the lesbians of color had, as a group, more contact with coworkers. This is not surprising in that the networking that produced the original sample reached only as far as a particular group of lesbians of color, who were disproportionately employed in feminist workplaces such as women's centers and women's studies programs, locations that facilitate, however imperfectly, such sociability. Those conditions in which a female culture can develop (granted, often within the limits of a male work world) allow lesbians greater possibilities for being open about their sexual identity with at least some coworkers. Familiar and supportive conditions tend to foster friendships and, as will become clear in the next section, provide the basis upon which more intimate relationships may also develop.

When there is a need to be social, lesbians are; professional jobs require sociability, but very many also require some degree of secrecy as well. This is particularly true for work in traditionally male occupations. In addition, and more important given women's location in the occupational structure, working with children (as teachers, nurses, social workers) can be cause for a relatively closeted existence. In this research, working with children did not seem to influence the extent of lesbian sociability, but it did affect how open they were about themselves at their workplaces. Here lies a classic instance of a highly contradictory situation, one common to many persons in human services and educational institutions. An ideology prevails that encourages (often demands) honesty, trust, and congenial nonalienating working relationships, but a lesbian's ability to actively involve herself in the prescribed ways is often limited or contorted. Frye's description of her experience in a women's studies program captures the essence of the difficulties:

> But in my dealings with my heterosexual women's studies colleagues, I do not take my own advice: I have routinely and habitually muffled or stifled myself on the subject of Lesbianism and heterosexualism . . . out of some sort of concern about alienating them. . . . Much more important to me is a smaller number who are my dependable political coworkers in the university, . . . the ones with some commitment to not being homophobic and to trying to be comprehending and supportive of Lesbians and Lesbianism. If I estrange these women, I will lose the only footing I have, politically and personally, in my long-term work-a-day survival in academia. They are important, valuable and respected allies. I am very careful, over-careful, when I talk about heterosexuality with them.[29]

More traditional workplaces provide even fewer possibilities for support than the one described above.

Finding a Partner

In the last section, brief reference is made to lesbians' sexual relationships at work. The typical story of the office affair seems to have little to do with lesbians. It centers on a boss (the powerful person, the man) and his secretary (the powerless person, the woman); the consequences of this double-edged inequality of occupational status and gender are of prime concern. As the story would have it, the powerful one influences the other's (the woman's) career in such a way that she is highly successful ("She slept her way to the top") or her work and career is permanently ruined. It is rarely acknowledged that relationships at work occur between coworkers or between persons of the same gender, or that the consequences may be close to irrelevant—at least with regard to the job. When acknowledged, it seems that heterosexual affairs are more tolerated than are lesbian or homosexual relations.[30]

But the facts tell another story.[31] Twenty-one percent of the lesbians in this study met their current partners at work; overall, 52 percent of the lesbians had had at least one sexual relationship with a person from work during their working lives. This amazingly high proportion makes sense when it is remembered that the vast majority of women (and lesbians) are employed in female-dominated workplaces. Such a work setting is a good location for a lesbian to find a potential lover. But in addition, there have traditionally been few places—other than bars—for lesbians to meet each other socially; most met, and still meet, through friendship networks (44 percent). While recently the women's and lesbians' communities have provided some alternatives—restaurants, clubs, political activities—employment plays such a significant part in lesbians' lives (and takes such a significant part of their time), that the workplace becomes an important, almost obvious, site for creating and having friendships and more intimate relationships.

Nineteen percent of the currently self-identified lesbians were heterosexual and 9 percent were married at the time of the sexual relationship they reported. This means that 81 percent were lesbians when they entered into at least a somewhat committed (and potentially risky) relationship with a person from work.

The chances that a lesbian will have a relationship with someone at work increase with age. To illustrate, while 79 percent of the sampled lesbians over forty had had a relationship with someone at work sometime in their lifetime, 59 percent in their thirties and 42 percent in their twenties had had such an involvement. In addition, the longer a woman has identified herself as a lesbian (whatever her age), the more likely she is to have an intimate relationship with a person at work. This certainly suggests that some part of the freedom to pursue an involvement in the work setting is an easiness with oneself as a lesbian and a flexibility and wisdom gained from years of managing the complexities of sexual identity difference at work.

Most of the relationships reported were not brief affairs; 60 percent of the lesbians had been or were currently in a relationship of a year or more duration. Having such a relationship can have many effects, many small and predictable, others large and less controllable. Perhaps most obviously, the longer a relationship lasts, the more likely are some people at work (in addition to friends outside work) to know of the involvement. (In contrast to the heterosexuals in the larger study, lesbians tended to be more secretive about the relationship with people from work.)

Since the "office affair" mythology assumes a heterosexual relationship and the dynamic of superior-subordinate, it is useful to examine who in fact the lesbian workers were involved with. Eighteen percent of the lesbians were involved with a man (most, but not all, were heterosexual at the time); the few self-identified lesbians who were nevertheless involved with a man were almost exclusively involved with their boss in relatively brief affairs. Overall, 75 percent were involved with coworkers, 14 percent with boss or supervisor, 6 percent with subordinates, and 5 percent with customers, clients, and the like. With the female boss still very much a rarity, lesbians are less likely to have the option of a relationship with a woman with institutionalized authority over their working lives. This is in contrast to heterosexual women, whose relationships at work tend to be unequal as a result of the mix of gender and status inequality.

There were only a few consistent and predictable patterns in the effects and consequences of these relationships for the lesbians as a group. Seventy-two percent enjoyed their work more than usual. Some involvements improved relationships with other coworkers (25 percent) while others caused problems with coworkers (35 percent) or trouble with a boss or supervisor (20 percent). Much of the difficulty during the course of the relationship seemed to stem from jealousies, irritation at undone work, or inattention on the part of one or both of the parties to others. Also, the involvements often highlighted the lesbians' sexual identity, forcing them to be less closeted. The data suggest that one of the conflicts a lesbian must face in having a relationship at work is a willingness to either engage in massive secrecy and denial of the situation or become more clear about who she is. Many lesbians (39 percent) reported relief at the end of their involvements in part because hostility or gossip was lessened, in part because the pressures of enforced secrecy were removed.

The effects of being and becoming open about one's sexual identity as a consequence of the relationship are mixed and complicated, and often contradictory. For example, 62 percent of the more open lesbians compared to 19 percent of the more closed ones reported significantly greater friction with coworkers and some (22 percent) felt their chances for advancement were diminished. On the other hand, 31 percent of the more open lesbians reported improvement in workplace relations and improved advancement possibilities (10 percent); they enjoyed their work more than the closed lesbians. It is interesting to note that not one lesbian who was closed about her sexual identity at work believed that her chances for promotion were affected one way or the other by her involvement.

Almost everyone reported suffering the usual kinds of emotional problems at the termination of the relationship, obviously the longer the relationship the more so. The work-related consequences of lesbian involvements with women of similar job status are much simpler and less harmful than those with a superior. Thirteen percent of the lesbians resigned or quit because of the breakup; most of the lesbians who resigned were involved with a boss, rather than a coworker, some few of whom were women. A very few lesbians (4 percent) reported losing out on some career-related opportunity, such as a promotion or pay increase; none reported gaining any work benefit. In 15 percent of the instances, the other person left the job at the termination of the relationship; in all these cases, these were female coworkers.

In general, involvements at work are an integral part of a lesbian's emotional commitments to women. This extension of the prescribed limits of relationships beyond friendship is consistent with most other research on lesbians that similarly shows fluid boundaries between friends and lovers and friendship networks of former lovers.[32]

Coming Out

Most lesbians are acutely aware that their openness about their lesbianism is not an all-or-nothing phenomena at work or elsewhere but that it varies depending at the very least on the context and on the particular individuals involved. The lesbians in this study clearly varied in their own sense of how open they *felt* they were at work. As we already saw, being open allowed lesbians greater contact with coworkers, facilitating network-building and support as well as being a basis for (and a possible result of) having a sexual relationship with someone at work.

This study indicates that lesbians tend to be open about their sexual identity when their workplace has a predominance of women and most of their work friends are women, when they have a female boss or supervisor, when they are employed in small workplaces, when they have few supervisory responsibilities, when they have relatively low incomes, and when they are not dealing with children as either students, clients, or patients.

Two aspects of these findings require special comment. First, as noted earlier, the situation of professionally employed lesbians is terribly contradictory. Since the jobs require socializing and contacts with others either at work or in the business or professional communities, lesbians maintain those social contacts; on the other hand, high income professional lesbians are likely to be closeted. The result of this predicament is a well-managed, manicured lie delivered to people with whom one is spending a great deal of time.

Second, the influence of gender proportions is crucial. For example, in workplaces that were heavily female-dominated (80 percent or more women as employees), 55 percent of the lesbians were totally or mostly open about their sexual identity. It is worth noting that this still means that 45 percent tended to be somewhat closeted even in these settings. In contrast, in heavily male-dominated workplaces (80 percent or more men as employees), only 10 percent of the lesbians were open.

A workplace with a predominance of women may include other lesbians to whom a lesbian can be open; they may also become friends or lovers. Of the lesbians who met another lesbian at work, almost all (94 percent) did in fact become friends. But even when there are not other lesbians at work, lesbians take certain risks, trusting at least one hetero-sexual woman to not react negatively to knowledge of her sexual identity. Moreover, most women are not in a structurally powerful position to affect the conditions under which lesbians work. When lesbians do have a female supervisor or boss, they are more often open about their sexual identity than with a male boss. For example, only 21 percent of lesbians with a male boss were open, compared to 47 percent who were open with a female boss. When lesbians were themselves the boss or were self-employed, 88 percent were open about their sexual identity.

How open a lesbian is at her current job is not related to her age or race, or the length of time she has been at that position. However, if she has lost a previous job because she is a lesbian, she is less sociable with people from work at her current job and tends to be more cautious about "coming out" at work. In this study 8 percent of the lesbians reported losing a job when their sexual identity became known and another 2 percent believed (but did not know for certain) they lost a job for this reason. The relatively young age of this sample may account for the lower proportion of job loss than in other studies. Whatever the extent of their openness, 75 percent of all lesbians were concerned that their lesbianism might cause damage to their job or career.

In summary, openness is most likely under conditions that are intimate and safe, free of potentially serious consequences for a lesbian's working life. That is, lesbians are most likely to be open in a small workplace, with a female boss, in a job with relatively little financial or social reward (and possibly few career risks).

The consequences of being open are substantial. Open lesbians have more friends and more social contact at work than closed lesbians; they are more willing to have, and do have, sexual relationships with women from their workplace. In contrast, and almost by definition, lesbians who are closed about their sexual identity at work are more likely to avoid certain situations with coworkers and feel reluctant to talk about their personal life.

While cause and effect is admittedly difficult to disentangle here, open and closed lesbians differ in the extent to which they feel that their sexual identity causes problems in many areas of their life. This research indicates that lesbians who remain closeted at work are obviously more concerned and afraid than open lesbians about losing their jobs. But in addition, closeted lesbians are much more concerned than open ones about losing their friends, harming their relationship with their parents, and where applicable, harming their lovers' careers or child custody situations. Consistent with this is the finding that openness at work is related to a general freedom to be open elsewhere as well: Lesbians who are open at work are more likely to be open with parents and with both female and male heterosexual friends.

Not surprisingly, closed and open lesbians have uniquely different feelings about their positions at work. Closeted lesbians suffer from a sense of powerlessness and significant strain and anxiety at work, while open lesbians have greater emotional freedom. Eighty-four percent of the closed lesbians in the study felt they had no choice about being closeted; two-thirds felt uncomfortable about that decision, and 39 percent felt that the anxiety about being found out was "paralyzing." A significant 36 percent devoted time and emotion to maintaining a heterosexual front at work.

On the other hand, ninety-four percent of the open lesbians felt better since coming out, and while the strength of their feelings varied, most felt they were treated with respect because of their candor. Forty percent reported that their work relationships were a lot better than they were before coming out. Disclosure of one's sexual identity at work allows for the possibility of integrating into the workplace with less anxiety about who one is and how one is perceived. But there are some negative consequences to coming out. Twenty-nine percent of the open lesbians sensed that some coworkers avoided them and 25 percent admitted to working harder to keep the respect they had from their peers. While these consequences seem insignificant in contrast to the benefits of disclosure, it is good to remember that coming out often can be a quite limited communication to a quite limited number of persons; thus, protection is built into the very choice of context and relationship.

Being Harassed

Eighty-two percent of the lesbians studied experienced sexual approaches at work in the year of the study: that is, 33 percent were sexually propositioned, 34 percent were pinched or grabbed, 54 percent were asked for a date, and 67 percent were joked with about their body or appearance by someone at the workplace.[33] These figures are high for one year; they are, however, comparable to those for the heterosexual women in the larger research project who were of similar race and age. Relatively young, unmarried women (this fits the description of most of the lesbians in the study) and those who worked in male-dominated work settings were most often the recipients of these sexual approaches. Ironically enough, the lesbians who tended to be secretive about their sexual identity (therefore presumed to be heterosexual) were more often sexually approached in these particular ways than the more open lesbians. For example, while 32 percent of the more closed lesbians were pinched or grabbed, only 12 percent of the more open were; likewise, 26 percent of the more closed in contrast to 13 percent of the more open were sexually propositioned.

In comments written to the researcher, it became evident that some lesbians were occasionally referring to both women and men in reporting on date requests and jokes, the more prevalent types of interactions. Unfortunately, the data for these experiences did not specify the gender of the initiator, thus making impossible a true profile of all interpersonal dynamics of this sort.

When asked their emotional response to these experiences ("like," "mixed," "dislike"), the great majority (more than 90 percent) reported disliking pinching or grabbing and sexual propositions—whoever initiated them; few lesbians in fact ever reported liking any incident. The one exception was being asked for a date by a coworker, and even here only 9 percent said they liked this interaction, with 46 percent "mixed." Toleration (mixed feelings) was the main response to jokes and date requests. And in all cases, coworkers were the most tolerated group of initiators; some of these coworkers may well be women. Typically, coworkers do not have the institutionalized authority to affect each other's job or career standing though they may nevertheless make life more difficult in these kinds of ways.

We cannot directly infer from these data the meaning of these experiences to lesbian workers. Unwanted sexual approaches can be seen as harassment explicitly targeted at a lesbian because she is a lesbian or as harassment typically experienced by most working women. These sexual approaches highlight the disadvantages of lesbians in a working environment by emphasizing heterosexual norms of intimacy and behavior and accenting further the outsider position many lesbians feel at work. Research that compares lesbian workers with heterosexual women workers indicates that while lesbians and heterosexuals have a quite similar number of such approaches in their daily lives, these interactions are experienced quite differently. Lesbians are more sensitive to the problem of unwanted sexual approaches and are much more willing than heterosexuals to label behaviors of this type as sexual harassment.[34]

Conclusion

This research was an effort using quantitative data to describe the context of daily life at work for lesbians and to understand the sources of lesbian survival at work. It was not a definitive study of the prevalence of lesbian job loss or harassment.

The findings showed fewer difficulties at work than other studies seem to indicate, but like that research, it insufficiently explored the meanings lesbians attach to particular situations. One obvious question that remains is the extent to which a problem or harassment situation at work is attributed specifically to discrimination on the basis of sexual identity rather than understood as a reflection of the general condition of women. In this research (in which all but one of the lesbians indicated that she was a feminist), the interpretation of events is complicated and complex.

Applying a feminist interpretation to certain workplace situations could diminish or exaggerate the extent to which lesbians perceive those instances as resulting from, or in reaction to, their lesbianism. Sexual harassment is a particularly clear case. A lesbian may well wonder why she was hugged by a male coworker: was it a gesture of friendship, harassment specifically directed to her as a lesbian, or harassment similar to that most women encounter at work? If most lesbians considered the variety of harassing experiences at work discrimination against them as lesbians, the proportion reporting workplace problems would surely increase.

While a more complete picture of workplace problems awaits additional research, these findings underscore some important dimensions of lesbians' workplace participation. First, the experience of lesbians is both similar and different from that of heterosexual women workers. It is similar in (1) the creation of a supportive environment of work friends, (2) the experience of unwanted sexual approaches from various parties with whom they interact, and (3) the use of the workplace to meet sexual partners. It is different in (1) the necessity of strategizing in the face of fear of disclosure and possible job loss, and (2) the meanings attached to interactions and events in the workplace.

While the fear of job or career loss or damage is often uppermost in a recitation of workplace problems, most lesbians do not lose their jobs. Two mutually reinforcing aspects of a strategy seem to account for this general lack of this most serious and negative sanction. First, lesbians tend to remain closeted, keeping their sexual identity secret from most persons at work; at the same time, they create an environment that protects them, emotional ties with a few people who contribute to a sense of a less hostile and alienating work world.

Coming out is clearly a process; within any particular institutional context, such as work, an assessment is made as to the degree to which a lesbian can be open about who she is. The extent of disclosure varies, dependent on the particulars of personnel and place; it changes over time. Certainly few are the lesbians and fewer still the workplaces that can manage or tolerate complete disclosure. At the minimum, lesbians come out when they are ready and conditions are good, meaning in some workplaces and with some people. While the exact process is not detailed here, it is clear that coming out occurs when a woman believes that a person is trustworthy, sensitive, or politically aware. This is an assessment over which a lesbian has some control. When a lesbian is known as such at work, a congenial and supportive relationship has typically preceded disclosure.

The ease with which a lesbian is disclosing about her sexual identity reflects historically specific conditions as well. In this sample of highly politicized lesbian women workers in late 1979, 40 percent felt they were totally or mostly open about being lesbians; 75 percent were concerned that their lesbianism might affect their employment situation. In the current climate of conservatism reflected in recent efforts to defend and preserve the "sanctity of the family,"[35] lesbians are forced to constantly weigh the costs of disclosure. Thus, a combination of forces—personal choice, workplace characteristics, and political concerns—continue to define the options and limitations of the workplace environment.

Finally, female support systems at work—allies and networks—can be seen as an integral part of lesbians' emotional commitments to women. While it is certainly ironic and contradictory to exclaim the virtues of "women's work," with its devalued economic and social worth, those workplaces do provide an easier, more congenial atmosphere than is immediately available in more highly paid, male-segregated locations. Many lesbians know these facts and in decisions regarding work may well take them into account.

While the fear and peril of lesbians' workplace situation cannot be denied or diminished, neither can the challenge. Lesbians' participation and relationship to work is similar to the kind of "double vision" shared by other groups who are outsiders:[36] an acute awareness of the strength and force of an oppressive ideology of heterosexuality and its structural manifestations, coupled with an active accommodation and creation of a livable working environment.

Notes

1. The only concern of this article is with lesbians in paid employment. Necessarily excluded are volunteer labor in political activities and unpaid labor of household maintenance and child care responsibilities. While there are seventeen lesbians who are working for wages in consciously organized feminist workplaces, and they are included in the discussion, no effort is made to talk about the particular challenges of working in such locations.

2. The socioemotional climate of work is based on strong cultural assumptions of heterosexuality. An ideology of heterosexuality includes the following beliefs: (1) All persons are heterosexual. (2) All intimate relationships occur between

persons of opposite gender. (3) Heterosexual relationships are better—healthier, more normal—than homosexual relations. With regard to employment, the ideology assumes that every woman is defined by, and in some way is the property of, a man (father, husband, boss); thus, women's work is secondary, since she is, will be, or ought to be supported by a man. See the following for statements concerning the cultural and structural dimensions of heterosexuality: Charlotte Bunch, "Not for Lesbians Only," *Quest: A Feminist Quarterly* 2 (Fall 1975): 50–56; Gayle Rubin, "The Traffic in Women: Notes on the 'Political Economy' of Sex," in Rayna Rapp, ed., *Toward an Anthropology of Women* (New York: Monthly Review Press, 1975), pp. 157–210; Catharine A. MacKinnon, *Sexual Harassment of Working Women: A Case of Sex Discrimination* (New Haven, Ct.: Yale University Press, 1979); Adrienne Rich, "Compulsory Heterosexuality and Lesbian Existence," reprinted in this text; Lisa Leghorn and Katherine Parker, *Woman's Worth: Sexual Economics and the World of Women* (Boston: Routledge & Kegan Paul, 1981).

3. See Anabel Faraday, "Liberating Lesbian Research," and Kenneth Plummer, "Homosexual Categories: Some Research Problems in the Labelling Perspective of Homosexuality," in Kenneth Plummer, ed., *The Making of the Modern Homosexual* (Totowa, N.J.: Barnes & Noble Books, 1981).

4. For a review of the literature on the relationship of work to individual well-being, see Rosabeth Moss Kanter, *Work and Family in the United States: A Critical Review and Agenda for Research and Policy* (New York: Russell Sage, 1977).

5. United States Bureau of Labor Statistics, *Perspectives on Working Women: A Databook*, Bulletin 2080 (Washington, D.C.: U.S. Government Printing Office, 1980).

6. Louise Kapp Howe, *Pink Collar Workers: Inside the World of Women's Work* (New York: G. P. Putnam's, 1977).

7. Heidi Hartman, "Capitalism, Patriarchy, and Job Segregation by Sex," in Zillah Eisenstein, ed., *Capitalist Patriarchy and the Case for Socialist Feminism* (New York: Monthly Review Press, 1979), pp. 206–247.

8. Neal Gross and Anne Trask, *The Sex Factor and Management of Schools* (New York: John Wiley, 1976); and Rosabeth Moss Kanter, *Men and Women of the Corporation* (New York: Basic Books, 1977).

9. MacKinnon.

10. Throughout this article, sexual identity, rather than sexual orientation or sexual preference, is the term used to describe and distinguish heterosexual and lesbian women. As a construct, sexual identity most adequately describes the process of creating and maintaining an identity as a sexual being. In contrast to sexual orientation, it does not assume an identity determined by the end of childhood; in contrast to sexual preference, it does not narrow the focus to the gender of one's partner or to particular sexual practices. See Plummer (n. 3 above) for a recent discussion of the issues and problems of homosexual categorization in the social sciences.

11. Amber Hollibaugh, "Sexuality and the State: The Defeat of the Briggs Initiative," *Socialist Review* 45 (May–June 1979): 55–72; Linda Gordon and Alan Hunter, "Sex, Family and the New Right," *Radical America* 11 (Nov. 1977–Feb. 1978); George Gallup, "Report on the Summer 1977 Survey of Attitudes Toward

Homosexuality," *Boston Globe,* September 10, 1977; Albert Klassen Jr. and Eugene Levitt, "Public Attitudes Toward Homosexuality," *Journal of Homosexuality* 1 (1974): pp. 29–43.

12. See any issue of *Gay Community News* and any newsletter of the National Gay Task Force for a more complete sampling of these types of stories; also see Judith McDaniel, "We Were Fired: Lesbian Experiences in Academe," *Sinister Wisdom* 20 (Spring 1982): 30–43; and J. R. Roberts, *Black Lesbians* (Tallahassee, Florida: Naiad Press, 1981), pp. 74–76.

13. Martin P. Levine and Robin Leonard, "Discrimination Against Lesbians in the Workforce," paper presented at Annual Meetings of the American Sociological Association, September 1982.

14. Sasha Gregory Lewis, *Sunday's Women: A Report on Lesbian Life Today* (Boston: Beacon Press, 1979); Laud Humphreys, *Out of the Closets: The Sociology of Homosexual Liberation* (Englewood Cliffs, N.J.: Prentice-Hall, 1972).

15. Jack Hedblom, "The Female Homosexual: Social and Attitudinal Dimensions," in Joseph McCaffrey, ed., *The Homosexual Dialectic* (Englewood Cliffs, N.J.: Prentice-Hall, 1972); William Simon and John Gagnon, "The Lesbians: A Preliminary Overview," in W. Simon and J. Gagnon, eds., *Sexual Deviance* (New York: Harper & Row, 1967), pp. 247–82.

16. Fred A. Minnegerode and Marcy Adelman, "Adaptations of Aging Homosexual Men and Women," paper presented at Convention of the Gerontological Society, October 1976.

17. For an analysis that suggests a similarity of friendship networks between lesbians and single heterosexual women, see Andrea Oberstone and Harriet Sukoneck, "Psychological Adjustment and Lifestyles of Single Lesbians and Single Heterosexual Women," *Psychology of Women Quarterly* 1 (Winter 1976): 172–88; for one that suggests differences between these two groups, see Alan Bell and Martin Weinberg, *Homosexualities: A Study of Diversity Among Men and Women.*

18. E. M. Ettorre, *Lesbians, Women and Society;* also see Lewis and Bell and Weinberg.

19. Martin Weinberg and Colin Williams, *Male Homosexuals: Their Problems and Adaptations* (New York: Oxford University Press, 1974).

20. Joseph Harry, "Costs and Correlates of the Closet," paper presented at annual meeting of the American Sociological Association, September 1982; also, Humphreys.

21. Kenneth Plummer, *Sexual Stigma: An Interactionist Account* (London: Routledge and Kegan Paul, 1977).

22. Karla Jay and Allen Young, eds., *Out of the Closets: Voices of Gay Liberation* (New York: Pyramid Books, 1972); Karla Jay and Allen Young, eds., *Lavender Culture* (New York: Jove Publications, 1978). See particularly, Barbara Grier, "Neither Profit Nor Salvation," in *Lavender Culture,* pp. 412–20.

23. William Paul et al., eds., *Homosexuality: Social, Psychological and Biological Issues* (Beverly Hills, Calif.: Sage Publications, 1982).

24. For those interested in more detailed statistical and analytical discussion of the findings of this research, see Beth E. Schneider, "Consciousness about Sexual Harassment Among Heterosexual and Lesbian Women Workers," *Journal of*

Social Issues 38 (Dec. 1982): 75–97; and Beth E. Schneider, "The Sexualization of the Workplace," Ph.D. dissertation, University of Massachusetts, 1981.

25. It is difficult to assess the accuracy of the proportion of lesbians of color in this sample since the population is unknown. Moreover, because of racism in the feminist and lesbian communities as well as the varying extent to which sexual identity rather than race or class identity is most salient to lesbians of color, many may not be part of lesbian community networks. Thus, the sampling procedures used here—working through contacts (only two of whom were lesbians of color)—likely proved inadequate to reach them.

26. Ninety-four percent of the lesbians who reported that *all* coworkers knew they were lesbians also reported being "totally" or "mostly open" about their sexual identity. They were employed in all occupations, but a disproportionate number were in human service jobs (40 percent), and 27 percent were in explicitly feminist work organizations. Thirty-one percent were self-employed, in a collective, or were the boss or owner of a workplace; of those who worked for someone else, almost all had a woman supervisor.

27. Women workers' beliefs about the integration of their public and private lives were measured using an index composed of four statements. These were: "The best policy to follow is to keep work separate from friendship," "You try to keep your social life completely separate from your work life," "Doing things socially with coworkers makes work relationships run more smoothly," and "You follow the general rule of not discussing personal matters with people from work." The sociability index combined four behaviors to measure the extent of social contact the women had with people at their current jobs. These four were eating lunch together, talking on the phone after work hours, visiting at each other's homes, and going out socially.

28. For a discussion of these issues, see Kanter (n. 4 above) and Lydia Sargent, ed., *Women and Revolution: A Discussion of the Unhappy Marriage of Marxism and Feminism* (Boston: South End Press, 1981).

29. Marilyn Frye, "Assignment: NWSA-Bloomington-1980: Lesbian Perspectives on Women's Studies," *Sinister Wisdom* 14 (1980): 3–7, esp. 3.

30. For one effort to discuss this distinction, see Richard Zoglin, "The Homosexual Executive," in Martin P. Levine, ed., *Gay Men: The Sociology of Male Homosexuality* (New York: Harper & Row, 1979), pp. 68–77.

31. The results described here are in response to a series of questions about involvement in a sexual relationship at the workplace. The initial item—"Have you *ever* been involved in an intimate sexual relationship with someone from your workplace?"—was followed by a series of descriptive questions about the relationship.

32. Ettorre; Lewis; Sidney Abbott and Barbara Love, *Sappho Was a Right-On Woman: A Liberated View of Lesbianism* (New York: Stein and Day, 1972); Del Martin and Phyllis Lyon, *Lesbian/Woman* (San Francisco: Glide Publications, 1972).

33. Sixteen questions measured the frequency of experiences in the last year of: requests for dates, jokes about body or appearance, pinches or grabs, and sexual propositions by four initiators (boss, coworker, subordinate, and recipient of service). Sixteen additional questions measured levels of dislike of these experiences. In the larger study, there were also questions concerning the general problem of unwanted sexual approaches at work and those behaviors that women most likely define as sexual harassment.

34. Schneider.

35. Zillah Eisenstein, "Antifeminism in the Politics and Election of 1980," *Feminist Studies* 7 (Summer 1981): 187–205; Susan Harding, "Family Reform Movements," *Feminist Studies* 7 (Spring 1981): 57–75; Rosalind Pollack Petchesky, "Antiabortion, Antifeminism and the Rise of the New Right," *Feminist Studies* 7 (Summer 1981): 206–246.

36. See Barry Adam, *The Survival of Domination: Inferiorization and Everyday Life* (New York: Elsevier, 1978); Dorothy E. Smith, "A Sociology for Women," in Julia A. Sherman and Evelyn Torton Beck, eds., *The Prism of Sex: Essays in the Sociology of Knowledge* (Madison: University of Wisconsin Press, 1977); Albert Memmi, *Dominated Man: Notes Toward a Portrait* (Boston: Beacon Press, 1968); Erving Goffman, *Stigma: Notes on the Management of Spoiled Identity* (Englewood Cliffs, N.J.: Prentice-Hall, 1963).

Section Three

Culture and
Community

15

From Accommodation to Rebellion: The Politicization of Lesbianism

ROSE WEITZ

The conception of lesbianism held by lesbians changed dramatically between the 1950s and the early 1970s. In this paper I will explore the nature, sources, and consequences of those changes, using deviance theory as my context.

To sociologists, the term *deviance* refers to behavior that elicits a negative social reaction at a particular time and place. The definition of an act as deviant is separate from any moral judgment of that action; the sociologist is free to view an action as deviant but not immoral, or as immoral but not deviant. This very lack of inherent overlap between deviance and immorality can lead us to important research questions. Thus, while the sociological labeling of an action as deviant derives from an amoral perspective, the study of deviance can illuminate crucial moral and political dilemmas.

A central question for sociologists over the past few decades has been the effect of deviant status on individual identity. From the perspective of interactionist theory, our image of ourselves depends heavily upon the image others have of us. Identity develops through an ongoing interactive process, as social reaction follows individual action and the individual responds to and typically internalizes those social reactions.

Individuals whose actions meet with disapproval may by the same mechanism incorporate the negative reactions of others into their self-concept. Their self-esteem may consequently suffer, as they begin believing that they are indeed weak or bad. This in turn may push individuals farther

A different version of this article will appear in *Studies in the Sociology of Social Problems*, edited by Joseph Schneider and John Kitsuse (Norwood, N.J.: Ablex Publishing Corp., in press).

into deviance, as low self-esteem and the low expectations others hold for them begin to affect their behavior.

Deviance that arises in response to social reactions is referred to as *secondary deviance*. Interactionist theory does not hold that secondary deviance is inevitable. Instead, individuals who engage in deviant behaviors may deflect social sanctions and avoid secondary deviance by accommodating to society—developing excuses and justifications for their actions, passing as "normal," or using various other "stigma management techniques."[1]

Although the interactionist perspective has increased our understanding of deviance, the emphasis on reactive aspects of deviance has obscured the active role of individuals in negotiating their own social position. Far from passively accepting others' valuations, deviants may actively engage in the production of definitions of their own behavior—definitions that may differ greatly from the dominant perspective in the society.

In response to this analytical gap, sociologist John Kitsuse has developed the term *tertiary deviance* to refer to "the deviant's confrontation, assessment, and rejection of the negative identity embedded in secondary deviation, and the transformation of that identity into a positive and viable self-conception."[2] Tertiary deviants reject accommodative strategies and argue that their difference from the norm should in no way limit their civil rights or social worth. In essence, they attempt to redefine the situation so that others will regard them as an oppressed minority group, rather than as deviants. As will be shown in this article, the most rebellious of these individuals may develop a radical critique of society, condemning their condemners and substituting a new ethic that affirms their behavior as sensible, moral, and preferable.

Using these concepts, I will trace the development of lesbian group identity over a period of sixteen years from 1956 to 1972. I will show how during those years, early definitions of lesbianism as an unfortunate fate were replaced by definitions of lesbianism as a valued political choice, and how accommodative strategies were dropped first for civil rights activism and finally for political rebellion.

Methodology

This paper is based on a content analysis of *The Ladder,* the first significant lesbian periodical in America.[3] *The Ladder* appeared almost every month from October 1956 through September 1967 and every two months thereafter, until it ended in 1972. Published by the Daughters of Bilitis (DOB), the first lesbian organization in the United States, *The Ladder* contained a variety of features ranging from political essays and news announcements to poetry, short stories, and book reviews. Among its contributors were DOB founder Del Martin, playwright Lorraine Hansberry, and well-known authors Rita Mae Brown, Jane Rule, and Mary Renault. Joan Nestle, of the Lesbian Herstory Archives, has recently described *The Ladder* (which eventually reached 3800 subscribers) as "the most sustaining Lesbian cultural creation of this period."[4] The only previous research using these data is Lillian Faderman's brief historical overview of the periodical's radicalization.[5]

For most of their history, *The Ladder* and DOB were the only outlet for lesbian writing and the only forum for the development of lesbian philosophy in this country. Although one periodical cannot represent the entire lesbian community, an analysis of *The Ladder* is crucial for understanding the shifting in-group meanings of lesbianism during this time period.

This research focuses on changing definitions of lesbianism, the relationship of these definitions to the homophile and feminist movements, and the consequences of changing definitions of lesbian political activism. As the first step, I took a random sample of sixteen issues (one from each volume of *The Ladder*) and tabulated the nomenclature used by lesbian writers to describe female homosexuals (for example, *homosexual, lesbian, variant, gay*). All issues were searched for statements regarding the cause of lesbianism; the statements were then categorized as describing homosexuality as conscious or unconscious choice, biologically determined, or unchangeably set in early childhood. Fictional accounts of lesbian life and relationships were classified as pessimistic or nonpessimistic; pessimistic stories emphasized isolation, suicide, blackmail, loss of lovers, or rejection by family or friends.

I also looked for data regarding the writers' attitudes toward and level of interest in male homosexuals and the homophile movement. Similarly, the number of feminist articles and editorials per volume was counted; items were defined as feminist if they demonstrated an awareness of women as a social group subject to unequal and unjust treatment or discussed the feminist movement sympathetically. These articles were further divided into those that did and did not discuss lesbian concerns. Items in the news section of *The Ladder* ("Cross Currents") were divided by the same definitions into those that were feminist with no lesbian content, feminist with lesbian content, and lesbian with no feminist content.

Articles and editorials that discussed how best to improve lesbians' position in society were divided according to their suggested policies. Two broad groups of policies resulted: those focused on changing lesbians and those focused on changing society. The former included advocating outward conformity, adjustment to society, reduction in hostility towards heterosexuals, education of lesbians, and the development of greater self-acceptance among lesbians. The latter included advocating decriminalization, research, education of the public, improvement in the status of women, and encouragement of social diversity.

Apolitical Definitions and Accommodative Strategies

While homosexual social clubs have existed for hundreds of years, the organized homophile movement only developed in the United States during the 1950s. According to sociologist Laud Humphreys, this movement became conceivable only after the Kinsey Report on male sexuality demonstrated the prevalence of homosexual behavior. This in turn reduced individuals' sense of isolation, assisted in the redefinition of homosexuality from a personal problem to a social issue, and created the belief that organization for change was possible. The first lasting homophile organization, the Mattachine Foundation, later reorganized as the Mattachine Society, began in 1950. Two years later, ONE, Inc. started as an offshoot of Mattachine.[6] Both organizations were in principle open to women but had almost no women members.

The Daughters of Bilitis began in October 1955, when four lesbian couples met to organize a social club as an alternative to the lesbian bars. At that time, the women of DOB had no knowledge of ONE or Mattachine. The group soon decided to stress education as well as social functions, and in October 1956 began publishing *The Ladder.*[7]

From its start in 1956 through the early 1960s, the writings in *The Ladder* demonstrated strong ties with the male homosexual community and suggested that homosexuality rather than womanhood formed the most salient aspect of lesbian identity. While the publication's audience was overwhelmingly female and its emphasis was on concerns of the female homosexual, the periodical's broader loyalties under editors Del Martin and Phyllis Lyon (and later Barbara Gittings) connected it to the male-dominated homophile movement. Various statements suggested that the founders of DOB and *The Ladder* were motivated neither by feminist sympathies nor by an interest in a separatist lesbian movement but by the belief that a women's organization and journal were the most effective ways to "draw the lesbian into the homophile movement."[8] Periodic notices announced events organized by ONE and Mattachine as well as joint meetings between those groups and DOB. Most of these events featured as speakers male experts in areas such as psychiatry and the law; summaries of the events appeared regularly in the pages of *The Ladder.*

Since *The Ladder* worked towards developing a stronger, more unified homophile movement, rather than towards a separatist lesbian movement, it encouraged male participation in DOB and interest in *The Ladder.*

> We feel that the time has come for still another step in our growth . . . that of working our programs to include the male homosexual. This does not mean membership, but it does mean offering them some of the same situations for group enjoyment and acceptance. We are re-opening our public discussion groups, planning Gab 'n' Javas periodically to include the male homosexual, and are now increasing the social functions which they may attend. . . . Although our magazine has always worked to be of interest to both men and women, we are now running a special "Masculine Viewpoint" section in which we more than ever welcome opinions from our male readers.[9]

The Ladder's writers seemed typically to view lesbians and male homosexuals as belonging to the same membership group and subject to the same socially created fates. Their language accentuated ties to male homosexuals and downplayed any specifically female elements involved. The authors typically used male pronouns as generics to describe the homosexual community without questioning the appropriateness of those pronouns, and used *homosexual* or the more sanitized *homophile* more often than *lesbian* as self-descriptors.

Only vague glimmerings of a feminist consciousness—an awareness of women as a social group subject to unequal and unjust treatment—appeared during these years. Rare exceptions did occur, however, in such divergent places as a review of Betty Friedan's *The Feminine Mystique* and a biographical piece on the troubles of a nineteenth-century lesbian artist.

Since these pages contained no analysis of women's status, *The Ladder* could not develop any theory connecting that status to lesbianism. Instead, reflecting the then-dominant medical model, articles repeatedly described lesbianism as a "process of development," rather than a chosen option. In this model, early childhood experiences in some unspecified way established an unchangeable sexual pattern; lesbianism was not biologically caused, yet was beyond the individual's control and hence not the individual's responsibility. From *The Ladder's* perspective, one could not—and certainly should not—choose to become a lesbian; lesbians were not evil persons, but victims of forces beyond their control. This posture reflected significant ambivalence—if the writers truly regarded lesbianism as morally nonproblematic, they would not need to stress lack of responsibility for it.

This ambivalence was also seen in the fiction writing. More than half of the stories from 1956 through 1964 that described lesbian life and relationships did so pessimistically, focusing on isolation, suicide, blackmail, rejection by family and friends, or the loss of lovers—particularly to a more "natural" love with a man. In a story published in February 1959, for example, rumors start about two young women. In the wake of these rumors, the protagonist leaves her woman friend, is abandoned by her family, moves away to avoid gossip and ridicule, and slowly dies of a broken heart.

In the absence of a political critique of society, *The Ladder* aimed to integrate the lesbian into existing society and held lesbians rather than heterosexual society responsible for reducing homophobic prejudice and discrimination:

> The tendency for the other organizations in the homophile movement is to lay the onus of the problem at the door of a hostile heterosexual society. "They" are the ones who must change, who must learn to understand, because it is "They" who malign, because it is "They" who . . . fail to view homosexuals as persons—human beings. . . . For his own salvation, the homosexual must learn that his life is not directed by the great god, "They," who (sic) he worships and condemns at one and the same time. The homosexual's life is self-directed. . . . He is the product of his own thought, and what others see in him is the image which he projects. If he is hostile, "They" will be hostile. If he hides from himself, "They" will hide from him. If he is fearful, "They" will fear him. If he is hateful, "They" will hate him.[10]

Similarly:

> While ONE and Mattachine have concerned themselves chiefly with public attitudes, this particular approach has been of secondary importance in DOB's concept. Members of DOB have always felt that we can't wait for society to change. Our needs are *now,* and it is possible for homosexuals to accept themselves and the society in which they live and so become productive citizens of the community. . . . We need not wait for society to accept us; we can accept the challenge of society and help to bridge the gap of seeming separation by our own awareness of ourselves as human beings in a society of human beings. *If the public has an image of the homosexual, it is because the homosexual has created this image and continued to project this image* [emphasis mine]. As our own attitudes change, so will society's attitude change.[11]

Presenting a good image thus became all-important. When, for example, in 1960 ONE, Inc. called for a homosexual bill of rights, numerous editorials and articles in *The Ladder* strongly opposed it on the grounds that it would call attention to the homosexual community and incite the wrath of heterosexual society. Instead of a bill of rights, *The Ladder* suggested that the various organizations write "a statement of the purposes and goals of the homophile movement (which would) . . . devote as much space to spelling out the obligations of homosexuals to society as it does to describing society's obligations to the homosexual."[12] Thus, *The Ladder* rejected any confrontation tactics and instead advocated a policy similar to that adopted by other minority groups that believed persecution would eventually cease if they quietly demonstrated their good citizenship.

To achieve its goal of integration into society, *The Ladder* stressed the lack of important differences between lesbians and heterosexuals and encouraged a reduction of surface differences, so as to reduce the saliency of their deviance. Numerous editorials and nonfiction articles from these years declared that lesbians differed from heterosexuals only in their sexual preference:

> The Lesbian is a woman endowed with all the attributes of any other woman. . . . Her only difference lies in her choice of a love partner. . . . To the informed this difference merely means another form of individual adjustment to self and society.[13]

> Remember you are a human being first. Your difference is only in choice of love object, and actually your feelings, emotions, and problems are the same as any heterosexual.[14]

To facilitate acceptance, lesbians were encouraged to minimize the differences and appear as much like traditional heterosexual females as possible. For example, a 1956 letter from a reader declared, "The kids in fly-front pants and with the butch haircuts and mannish manner are the worst publicity that we can get." DOB President D. Griffin replied:

> Very true. Our organization has already touched on that matter and has converted a few to remembering that they are women first and a butch or fem secondly, so their attire should be that which society will accept. Contrary to belief, we have shown them that there is a place for them in society, but only if they wish to make it so.[15]

From this perspective, the homosexual should not deny her "nature," but should realize that visible nonconformity only creates further difficulties while outward conformity and adjustment eventually produce tolerance.

In sum, during these early years *The Ladder* did not encourage pride in a unique and positively chosen lifestyle nor did it present a political critique of society. Instead, it advocated restraint and self-acceptance among lesbians as a means of reducing the saliency of the label *lesbian* and thus developing tolerance among heterosexuals. At the same time, *The Ladder* urged heterosexuals to refrain from condemning lesbians since lesbians differed from heterosexuals only in minor ways and did not choose their unfortunate—but not immoral—fate.

Not just DOB and *The Ladder* but the homophile movement as a whole emphasized outward conformity as the route to social tolerance during these years.[16] This conservative stance must be evaluated in the context of the political climate of those times. Both the popular culture and the government connected the heresies of communism and homosexuality, making employment difficult if not impossible for any known or suspected homosexual. In this context, anything but the most respectably conformist tactics seemed self-destructive.

The Development of Tertiary Deviance

The years 1965 and 1966 saw an increased emphasis in the pages of *The Ladder* on the broader homophile movement. This emphasis reflected the loyalties of then-editor Barbara Gittings, who eventually left DOB to work for the Mattachine Society and who has continued to work with mixed-sex gay groups rather than with lesbian or feminist groups. During these years, few statements appeared from either the editor or DOB. Instead, *The Ladder* seems to have become a forum for announcements and position papers from the East Coast Homophile Organizations (ECHO) and the Mattachine Society. Coverage of the 1965 ECHO conference, for example, filled almost half the pages of three consecutive issues. The "Masculine Viewpoint" column continued and Frank Kameny, president of the Mattachine Society of Washington, D.C., became a regular *Ladder* contributor. *Homosexual* remained the most common self-descriptor, although the term *lesbian* appeared more frequently than in earlier volumes.

The homophile movement of the mid-1960s appears to have been strongly influenced by the growing black civil rights movement, as witnessed by the frequent comparisons between homosexuals and blacks. For example:

> The drive to eliminate discrimination against homosexuals (sex fascism) is a direct parallel to the drive to eliminate discrimination against Negroes (race fascism). These minority movements are not attempts to overthrow the white race, or to destroy the institution of the family, but to allow a fuller growth of human potential, breaking down the barriers against a strange race or sexuality.[17]

Taking their cue from the black civil rights movement, *The Ladder*'s writers focused on actively fighting discrimination against homosexuals in the legal code and in employment (particularly in civil service) so as to obtain their rights as citizens. While in 1960 DOB had strongly opposed the idea of a homosexual bill of rights, DOB now joined fourteen other homophile organizations in issuing the following statement:

> Laws against homosexual conduct between consenting adults in private should be removed from the criminal code. Homosexual American citizens should have precise equality with all other citizens before the law and are entitled to social and economic equality of opportunity. Each homosexual should be judged as an individual on his qualifications for Federal and all other employment.

> The disqualification of homosexuals as a group or class from receipt of security clearances is unjustified and contrary to fundamental American principles. Homosexual American citizens have the same duties and the same right to serve in the armed forces as do all other citizens. . . . For too long, homosexuals have been deprived of these rights on the basis of cultural prejudices, myth, folklore, and superstition. Professional opinion is in complete disagreement as to the cause and nature of homosexuality. Those objective research projects undertaken thus far have indicated that findings of homosexual undesirability are based on opinion, value judgments, or emotional reaction, rather than on scientific evidence or fact. A substantial number of American people are subjected to a second class citizenship, to the Gestapo-like "purges" of government agencies, and to local police harassment. It is time that the American public re-examine its attitudes and its laws concerning the homosexual.[18]

By this point, *The Ladder* no longer emphasized the need to change the behaviors and attitudes of homosexuals as a precondition for social acceptance. However, accommodative strategies were not overtly rejected, as can be seen in the positive comments made regarding the (mandated) conventional dress of protesters at homosexual rights demonstrations.

Articles from the mid-1960s rarely discussed causation of homosexuality beyond stressing that it was not an illness; writers seemed to feel less need than in earlier years to justify their sexual orientation. Ambivalence, however, continued to crop up in the fiction writing towards homosexuality; 61 percent of the stories from 1965 through 1969 gave a pessimistic view of lesbian life and relationships.

In October 1966, "Helen Sanders" (pseudonym) replaced Barbara Gittings as editor of *The Ladder*. At this point, it was announced that:

> Certain changes in editorial policy are anticipated. To date emphasis has been on the Lesbian's role in the homophile movement. Her identity as a woman in our society has not yet been explored in depth. It is often stated in explaining "Who is a Lesbian?" that she is a human being first, a woman second, and a Lesbian only thirdly. The third aspect has been expounded at length. Now it is time to step up *The Ladder* to the second rung.[19]

Subsequent issues typically contained one or two articles regarding discrimination against women in law and employment. These articles stressed that "the Lesbian is discriminated against not only because she is a Lesbian, but because she is a woman."[20] At the same time, *The Ladder* began printing in its news section items regarding the women's movement and women's place in society, without explicitly relating those items to lesbians. Thus, *The Ladder* implicitly suggested that lesbians share a common fate with all women and should work for both women's and homosexual rights. This in turn provided the necessary precondition for the subsequent feminist redefinition of lesbianism.

After this spate of feminist articles, *The Ladder* became generally apolitical, printing few policy statements and devoting an increased number of pages to fiction, humor, and poetry. It only gradually shifted back towards a more political stance in 1969, under new editor Barbara Grier ("Gene Damon"). During 1969, an event took place that radically affected the consciousness of male homosexuals. The coverage of this event in *The Ladder* suggested the changing relationship between the periodical and the homophile movement.

The homosexual community had always accepted police raids on gay bars as a fact of life. In June 1969, however, police raiding the Stonewall, a gay male bar in Greenwich Village, met with fierce physical resistance from the patrons, which resulted in four days of sporadic rioting. This marked the birth of the gay liberation movement.[21]

Prior to this time, the goal of the male homophile movement, like that of DOB, was tolerance from American society and eventually assimilation into that society. The movement had generally used tactics designed not to upset or challenge heterosexuals. The new gay liberation movement, by contrast, used tactics of confrontation adopted from the New Left in order to demand acceptance rather than tolerance, and liberation rather than assimilation.

The Ladder had a lengthy summary of events at the Stonewall in the news section at the back of its October/November 1969 issue. The topic was not, however, picked up in the front pages of that or any subsequent issue nor was it mentioned in other news sections. By contrast, gay male activists identify the Stonewall Rebellion as marking a crucial turning point in their ideological world. It seems, then, that events in the gay male world greatly decreased in significance for the writers of *The Ladder.*

The 1969 discussions regarding DOB's potential membership in the North American Conference of Homophile Organizations (NACHO) provide further evidence of the decreasing importance of the homophile movement to *The Ladder.* Writers uniformly agreed that while DOB and the male homophile groups should work together when it was to their mutual benefit, DOB must first work to improve the status of lesbians and not dissipate its resources by joining an alliance that focused on issues of concern only to male homosexuals. This argument resurfaced in much stronger form in 1970, when the break with the homophile movement was completed.

The Radical Redefinition of Lesbianism

The growing feminist movement of the early 1970s affected not just heterosexual society, but the lesbian world as well. In August 1970, with Barbara Grier as editor, *The Ladder* broke its ties to DOB in order to change officially from a lesbian periodical to a feminist magazine openly supportive of lesbians. According to the new frontispiece: "Initially, *The Ladder's* goal was limited to achieving the rights accorded heterosexual women, that is, full second-class citizenship. . . . *The Ladder's* purpose today is to raise all women to full human status." Thus the focus for change moved officially from the individual lesbian to society as a whole and from homophobia to sexism.

As *The Ladder's* orientation shifted from the homophile to the feminist movement, *lesbian* gradually replaced *homosexual* as the most common self-descriptor, while connections to gay men were de-emphasized and ridiculed. From 1970 on, various editorials exhorted lesbians to stop acting as "the Ladies' Auxiliary to the homophile movement."[22] Concurrently, a series of vituperative statements appeared (with approving editorial comments) from women who denounced and renounced the homophile movement as male-dominated and sexist, and who rejected the possibility of cooperation between lesbians and gay males. The focus of *The Ladder* shifted from homophile to women's liberation, as womanhood became a more salient aspect of lesbian identity than homosexuality. Numerous features appeared during this period that described the oppressed position of women in society and did not discuss lesbians at all—implicitly stressing solidarity among women regardless of sexual preference. Issues published during *The Ladder's* last year contained more feminist, nonlesbian news items than lesbian, nonfeminist items.

New, politicized definitions emerged in these issues, both of women as an oppressed minority and of lesbians as the original, if sometimes nonconscious, feminists. No longer seen as an unfortunate and unchosen fate, lesbianism became defined as a choice women make in response to a sexist society. This new definition of lesbianism was formalized in an article entitled "Woman Identified Woman":

> What is a Lesbian? A Lesbian is the rage of all women condensed to the point of explosion. She is the woman who, often beginning at an extremely early age, acts in accordance with her inner compulsion to be a more complete and more free human being than her society—perhaps then, but certainly later—cares to allow her. . . . She may not be fully conscious of the political implications of what for her began as personal necessity, but on some level she has not been able to accept the limitations and oppression laid on her by the most basic role of her society—the female role.[23]

This statement was simultaneously published in a number of feminist journals, including *The Ladder,* and widely circulated among feminists. *Woman-identified woman* became used as a term for women whose self-concepts are independent of their relationships with men and whose primary energies and loyalties flow toward other women. Although some believe it to be theoretically applicable to heterosexual women, the term is generally used within the feminist community as synonymous with lesbian feminist.

Once lesbianism became defined as a sensible choice, it became reasonable to encourage women to choose lesbianism. "Woman Identified Woman" ended with a call for women to become lesbians as a step toward liberation:

> As the source of self-hate and the lack of real self are rooted in our male-given identity, we must create a new sense of self. . . . For this we must be available and supportive to one another, give our commitment and our love, give the emotional support necessary to sustain this movement. Our energies must flow toward our sisters not backwards toward our oppressors. As long as women's liberation tries to free women without facing the basic heterosexual structure that binds us in one-to-one relationship with our own oppressors, tremendous energies will continue to flow into trying to straighten up each particular relationship with a man, how to get better sex, how to turn his head around—into trying to make the "new man" out of him, in the delusion that this will allow us to be the "new woman.". . .

> It is the primacy of women relating to women, of women creating a new consciousness of and with each other which is at the heart of women's liberation, and the basis for the cultural revolution. Together we must find, reinforce and validate our authentic selves.[24]

Political lesbianism—the conscious, politically-motivated choice to live as a lesbian—was thus encouraged as a way to "dump all roles as much as possible . . . forget the male power system and . . . give women primacy in your life."[25]

In sum, the development of a feminist analysis led to a radical redefinition of lesbianism. Lesbian relationships were extolled because of their potential for equality and personal growth, while heterosexual relationships, mainstream society, and male homosexual society were condemned as sexist and oppressive. The new pride in lesbianism was reflected in the fiction writing; only 39 percent of the fiction stories described lesbian life and relationships pessimistically in the issues published after *The Ladder* became a feminist publication, compared to more than half the stories published before that time.

From these new definitions of the situation, a new political strategy emerged. Editorials and articles described lesbian liberation and women's liberation as interdependent; a new utopian vision called for not only the abolition of the taboo on same-sex relationships, but the abolition of traditional sex roles. Solidarity between lesbians and heterosexual women was therefore essential. Lesbians must understand the costs paid by heterosexual women in living with men on a daily basis, while "straight" feminist groups such as the National Organization for Women must support lesbian rights, particularly since lesbians—the one group "throughout history . . . [which] has had no interest in furthering male power"[26]—formed the backbone of the feminist work force.

Various statements in these last three volumes explicitly disavowed previous tactics of conformity. No longer emphasizing similarities between all persons regardless of sex or sexual preference, *The Ladder* now stressed pride in difference—pride in choosing women in a society that values only men. Whereas earlier issues chastized lesbians for their hostility towards society, once society was defined as misogynist, that hostility became defined as a true class consciousness.

The increasing politicization of *The Ladder* during these years reflected—and perhaps helped create—change in the lesbian world. The changing definition of lesbianism occurred concurrently with the development of lesbian feminist organizations, which began appearing in 1970, such as Radicalesbians, and set the stage for one further change in strategy. Rita Mae Brown called for a separatist lesbian feminist movement in the April/May 1972 issue. Her statement followed logically from the new definition of lesbianism. If lesbianism was a choice, then those who continued to relate to men could be defined as those who refused to choose.[27] The greatest distrust and hostility on the part of lesbians would be reserved for bisexuals, since these women knew they could relate sexually and emotionally to women yet willfully "consorted with the enemy" every time they became involved with men.[28]

Editorial policy of *The Ladder* opposed separatism as self-defeating; the article following Brown's described in glowing terms the possibilities for cooperation between lesbian and heterosexual feminists. Nonetheless, the reality of a separatist movement beginning around this time and based on these definitions was documented not just by occasional writings in *The Ladder,* but by such divergent happenings as concerts open only to lesbians, and the marketing of books and records for sale exclusively to lesbians.

Discussion and Conclusions

When John Kitsuse coined the term *tertiary deviant,* the conceptualization was that of the tertiary deviant coming out of the proverbial closet "not . . . to assume the role of social critic [but] . . . to claim the right to go in and stay *in just like everybody else* [emphasis in original]."[29] The tertiary deviant desires integration into the existing society. Lesbian feminists, however, use their deviance as a springboard for a radical critique of society and as a base for a radical social movement.

Why have lesbian feminists been able to become radical critics of society, while other tertiary deviant groups remain content to work for equal rights within the current social structure?[30] Like other tertiary deviants, lesbian feminists reject prior negative valuations of themselves and substitute new and positive self-conceptions. They differ from other tertiary deviants in defining society as corrupt and in regarding their actions as hidden resistance to that corruption. The following paragraphs delineate some of the factors that have enabled lesbian feminists to become "radical deviants."

First, radical deviance only became possible for lesbians when the nascent feminist movement enabled them to redefine their behavior as consciously or unconsciously chosen. The feminist movement was and is based on the premise that "the personal is political." Working from this principle, heterosexual feminists analyzed all aspects of life as political phenomena, including areas as seemingly private as sexuality. Contact with the emerging feminist movement enabled lesbians to develop politicized counterdefinitions of their own sexuality—definitions that encouraged pride in that sexuality. At the same time, the feminist movement provided a vocabulary that neutralized the dominant society as sexist and corrupt. Thus, lesbians redefined their actions as effective political resistance and their problems with society as injustice rather than as merely personal misfortune. These redefinitions were crucial to the development of a political movement.[31]

Comparisons between gay male and lesbian activists during the early 1970s demonstrate the importance of a new world view—in this case, feminism—in developing radical definitions of deviance. As the gay liberation movement evolved from the homophile movement, gay males adopted, from the hippie counterculture, a belief in the value of personal diversity. Gay males, unlike lesbians, had no larger ideology to provide a context for their homosexuality. Thus the male gay liberation movement never truly developed a political theory of homosexuality and homophobia, but simply created a more activist civil libertarian position. A reading of Laud Humphreys' history of the gay liberation movement, *Out of the Closets: The Sociology of Homosexual Liberation,* and of the various statements generated by that movement amply demonstrates the lack of any political theory comparable to that developed among lesbian feminists.

Finally, the existence of a community of like individuals eased the development of radical deviance among lesbians. Within that community, individuals could share experiences, discover common troubles, and redefine those personal troubles as social problems. The community provided a network of significant others that helped to maintain the newly established politicized definitions of the situation. Thus, the development of radical deviance among lesbians was made possible by a supportive community sharing a definition of a corrupt society in need of radical change, a definition of lesbianism as politically motivated, and a belief that lesbianism is an effective means of resisting society.

In summary, this article has used material from *The Ladder* to illustrate the development of tertiary and radical deviance among lesbians. These data demonstrate the way lesbian writers actively structured their world, developing accounts for their behavior and political strategies based on those accounts. During its early years, *The Ladder* advocated an accommodative stance toward society, urging lesbians to censor outward differences between themselves and heterosexuals and stressing the lack of significant differences between these two groups. With the development of tertiary deviance, lesbians viewed themselves as entitled to civil rights without having to resort to any accommodative strategies. Finally, as a radical deviant stance emerged, deviance was celebrated as honorable resistance and the locus for desired change shifted unequivocally from the individual to the society.

Notes

1. See Marvin B. Scott and Stanford M. Lyman, "Accounts," *American Sociological Review* 33 (Feb. 1968): 46–62; Erving Goffman, *Stigma: Notes on the Management of Spoiled Identity* (Englewood Cliffs, N.J.: Prentice-Hall, 1963).

2. John Kitsuse, "Coming Out All Over," *Social Problems* 28 (Oct. 1981): 1–13.

3. The only previous lesbian periodical, *Vice Versa*, was privately published by Lisa Ben and distributed in the Los Angeles area from June 1947 to February 1948.

4. Joan Nestle, "Butch-Fem Relationships: Sexual Courage in the 1950's," *Hersies* 3, no. 4, issue 12: 24.

5. Lillian Faderman, *Surpassing the Love of Men: Romantic Friendship and Love Between Women from the Renaissance to the Present* (New York: William Morrow, 1981).

6. Laud Humphreys, *Out of the Closets: The Sociology of Homosexual Liberation* (Englewood Cliffs, N.J.: Prentice-Hall, 1972).

7. Del Martin and Phyllis Lyon, *Lesbian/Woman* (San Francisco: Glide Publications, 1972).

8. Del Martin, "And Now We Are Three . . . ," *The Ladder* 3, no. 1 (Oct. 1958): 5.

9. Jaye Bell, "DOB Anniversary Message From the President," *The Ladder* 6, no. 1 (Oct. 1961): 9.

10. Del Martin, "Its Time for a Change," *The Ladder* 7, no. 4 (Jan. 1963): 22.

11. No author listed, "The Dare of the Future: An Appraisal of the Homophile Movement," *The Ladder* 6, no. 8 (May 1962): 9.

12. Del Martin, editorial comment: "How Far Out Can We Go" and "More to the Point," *The Ladder* 5, no. 4 (Jan. 1961): 4–5.

13. Del Martin, "The Positive Approach: Editorial," *The Ladder* 1, no. 2 (Nov. 1956): 8.

14. No author listed, "On 'Growing Up'," *The Ladder* 1, no. 11 (Aug. 1957): 6.

15. D. Griffin, "The President's Message," *The Ladder* 1, no. 2 (Nov. 1956): 3.

16. See Humphreys.

17. Leo Ebreo, "A Homosexual Ghetto?" *The Ladder* 10, no. 3 (Dec. 1965): 8.

18. No author listed, "U.S. Homophile Movement Gains Strength," *The Ladder* 10, no. 7 (April 1966): 4–5.

19. No author listed, "Cross Currents: Another Rung," *The Ladder* 11, no. 1 (Oct. 1966): 24.

20. Shirley Willer, "What Concrete Steps Can Be Taken to Further the Homophile Movement?" *The Ladder* 11, no. 3 (Nov. 1966): 17.

21. See Humphreys.

22. Damon, p. 4.

23. Rita Mae Brown, "The Woman Identified Woman," *The Ladder* 14, no. 11–12 (Aug.–Sept. 1970): 6.

24. Ibid., p. 8.

25. Rita Mae Brown, "Take a Lesbian to Lunch," *The Ladder* 16, no. 7–8 (April–May 1972): 21.

26. Damon, p. 4.

27. For an elaboration of this position see Charlotte Bunch, "Lesbians in Revolt," in Alison Jaggar and Paula Struhl, eds., *Feminist Frameworks* (New York: McGraw-Hill, 1978).

28. See Philip Blumstein and Pepper Schwartz, "Lesbianism and Bisexuality," in E. Goode and R. Troiden, eds., *Sexual Deviance and Sexual Deviants* (New York: William Morrow, 1974).

29. Kitsuse, p. 10.

30. I am not here discussing those countercultural groups whose deviance is initially and overtly defined as political, but rather those groups in which political definitions of deviance only emerge over time to supplant prior negative and apolitical definitions.

31. See Ralph Turner and Lewis M. Killian, *Collective Behavior,* 2d ed. (Englewood Cliffs, N.J.: Prentice-Hall, 1972); Richard A. Cloward and Frances Fox Piven, "Hidden Protest: The Channeling of Female Innovation and Resistance," *Signs: Journal of Women in Culture and Society* 4 (1979): 651–69.

16

Culture-Making: Lesbian Classics in the Year 2000

MELANIE KAYE/KANTROWITZ

What is a classic? Is a classic a book that stays in print? Who decides what stays in print, what gets remaindered, what makes it into paperback, onto the supermarket displays, back into hardbound collected works? Alice Walker's first novel, *The Third Life of Grange Copeland,* was out of print for seven years.[1] *It* didn't change. By what mechanism is it now available in paperback? Pat Parker's *Movement in Black* is out of print, as is Barbara Deming's work.[2] How might their work come back to us? By their deaths? "Discovery" by an influential critic?

In fact, much of the work of Aphra Behn, Emily Dickinson, Christina Rossetti, Angelina Weld Grimké, Willa Cather, Gertrude Stein, H.D., and others, was out of print or hard to come by prior to the second wave of feminism (and who knew that all of these women loved women!) Is this work classic now, but not then? Can we only talk about classics after a suitable passage of time?

One fact is clear. To be a classic, a book must at least get published. A book no one reads has no chance of becoming a classic, no matter how wonderful it is. And while many perhaps worthy books go out of print, many never make it into print in the first place.

But if a book is printed and distributed and well-read and many like it, will it then become a classic? Yes, if—those who read and like it include an editor from Doubleday; a critic from the *New York Review of Books;* a few highly reputed writers; and several professors of literature at prestigious universities who will mention the book in their lectures and in their books, include it on their reading lists and class syllabi, encourage their graduate

Another version of this article appeared in *Sinister Wisdom,* vol. 13 (Spring 1980), pp. 23–34. Copyright is held by Melanie Kaye/Kantrowitz, and this version is used with permission.

students to write dissertations on the author and on the author's circle of friends and colleagues, develop sessions about the author at Modern Language Association meetings to pursue heated discussions about the author's imagery and fictional persona, and, perhaps most insidiously, school the tastes of future writers on the author's perspective and style.[3]

A Historical Digression, By Way of Explanation

Shakespeare in his own time was extremely popular, the best. His popularity developed in the context of a popular theater, a whole audience accustomed to regular play-going; a "hot" audience with a shared and growing frame of reference, like the audience for rock in the late sixties, or, on a smaller scale, women's poetry in the early seventies, exploding with mass energy and creativity.[4] Shakespeare's popularity meant that many of his contemporaries were familiar with his work, language, and ideation. Thus Elizabethan/Jacobean culture, theater, language, literature, conversation—at least around London—incorporated his work, so that he went on being familiar to succeeding generations of writers and audiences.[5] The cultural web around him spun larger and he was part of it. He schooled the ears of those who shaped the language. He gave the storytellers his version of stories that interested him.

Consequently, today his sentences sound "poetic," while those of Ben Jonson—a gifted contemporary—seem peculiar, because Jonson's rhythms and even vocabulary are unfamiliar. The intrigues of *Volpone* (one of Jonson's better plays) are harder to absorb than those of *Romeo and Juliet*, who have, at least on the level of stereotype, passed into mainstream culture.[6] So questions of "greatness" aside (including the question of why Shakespeare *was* more popular than Jonson), no one today approaches the work of Shakespeare and Jonson with an equal headset; Shakespeare is another word for "great writer": Who do you think you are, *Shakespeare*? Nor is anyone likely to experience the pleasurable rush of recognition when confronting Jonson's work: Volpone, Volpone, wherefore art thou Volpone?

It's not that a classic is necessarily great—what's "great"? It's that something large and encompassing grows from it. A classic is a chosen book or writer; and it is also an institution. As an institution, a classic is hard to avoid. It will be crashed into here and there, openly or covertly. We breathe it—a signpost of our culture, or one of its common foods. A classic knits a connection among people of a culture, so that many people can respond with a kind of intimacy and knowledge. The face that launched a thousand ships. Machiavelli. The green-eyed monster. A solid liberal arts education will locate these images at the source. And those who don't respond with intimacy, who remain unfamiliar with the signal or reference, are excluded. Depending on the hierarchy of a situation, this exclusion can be intentional (academic cocktail party) or incidental.

But whatever the intent of this connective tissue and its somewhat mysterious growth, a classic in a given culture always has a supportive relationship to that culture and to those empowered in that culture. A classic may praise or critique, but never ignore, what the people empowered in that culture consider important. Turning once again to Shakespeare: it doesn't matter much what he says about heterosexual love and marriage, or the death of kings. That his plays ask us to obsess on these subjects is enough indication that male Elizabethans took heterosexual coupling and royal death very seriously. Furthermore, though marriage concludes the majority of Elizabethan plays (called comedies), and royal death ends most of the other plays (called tragedies), contemporary Western male criticism has mostly managed to avoid the glaring question: What does it mean when people can envision only two possible ends to any story? Religious parallels of salvation *(The Divine Comedy)* and damnation aside, we can deduce some meaning from the fact that contemporary culture tends to value the "death" plays as higher art than the "marriage" plays. This valuation suggests that the tragedies embody, and are used to tutor us as contemporary evaluators toward, the assumptions of individualism and capitalism (*my* life and what's *mine* matter),[7] and away from the principles of communalism (marriage equals birth equals continuity of life).

In more recent literature, the central plot that emerges as individuals feel far too powerless to matter is the love story, where the individual matters, at least to one other person.[8] But what if the lovers are of the same gender?

Lesbian Culture

Lesbians have been around a long time. And like all people who constitute a group, lesbians have had a culture, albeit a subculture. Even that relatively tiny group of women whose lives are documented—white Western middle-class—offers evidence of women-loving women: witness the elaborate rituals and traditional intensities of women's relationships in the nineteenth century, as detailed by Carroll Smith-Rosenberg; or Nancy Sahli's account of women's passionate crushes on one another, censured only in the last hundred years.[9] In our own century, how many lesbians grew up, alas, haunted by Radclyffe Hall's 1928 novel, *The Well of Loneliness?* Or consider *The Ladder,* for many years many lesbians' only contact with lesbian culture.[10]

But lesbian culture as a context aware of itself, with its own networks and presses and connective tissue, is a recent creation. Contemporary lesbian culture blooms at the convergence of gay liberation and women's liberation, and in the realization by quite a few feminist cultural workers that, as Alix Dobkin bluntly, if musically, put it: "Any woman can be a lesbian."[11] In the consciousness of many heterosexual women, lesbians suddenly ceased to be a third sex, and became—heaven forbid—one's own self. The impact of this convergence of homophiles and feminists on lesbian culture-making has been powerful and pervasive.

For example, one task in creating a culture is to reclaim what one ought to have learned but that somehow went by and was lost. I think of Emily Dickinson's

> Witchcraft was hung, in History,
> But History and I
> Find all the Witchcraft that we need
> Around us, every Day—

Why does a women's studies classroom break into laughter when I read this poem? A flash of feminist resistance? We were not exterminated, we survived. Possible lesbian implications? We are here, hiding, if you knew to see us; implications perhaps suggested by knowledge, recently acquired, that Dickinson loved and desired a woman.

But there is more to the story of Emily Dickinson and her poem. Where did I read the poem? Not in grade school, along with "I'm Nobody, Who Are You?" and "I Never Saw a Moor"; but in an anthology of women's writing gathered by Louise Bernikow because she wanted to uncover the unknown and suppressed work of women writers. Whence this desire? The feminist movement had created or tapped or articulated a need in women readers for women's work. I read Dickinson's poem because of this need, in myself as well as in Bernikow; and because a publisher was astute enough to recognize the anthology as something women needed.[12]

But the story is still not over. I pass over the recent research, sometimes wistful, inconclusive as yet, but provocative and inspiring, on witches and witchcraft; information and possibilities that have sifted into contemporary feminist and lesbian imagination, that suggest lesbianism as one possible deviation among many for which women were tortured and killed. There remains the question: How do I know that Dickinson loved a woman? Because Lillian Faderman rejected the popular mythology in which Dickinson, a pathetically shy spinster, hopelessly in love with Higginson, sent letters to a world that never wrote to her. Instead, Faderman read over Dickinson's letters to discover that Dickinson wrote to her sister-in-law Sue Gilbert in the following terms:

Susie, will you indeed come home next Saturday, and be my own again, and kiss me as you used to? Shall I indeed behold you, not "darkly, but face to face" or am I *fancying* so, and dreaming blessed dreams from which the day will wake me? I hope for you so much, and feel so eager for you. Feel that I *cannot* wait, feel that *now* I must have you—that the expectation once more to see your face again, makes me feel hot and feverish, and my heart beats so fast. . . .[13]

Faderman explains her work on Dickinson: "Six or seven years ago I stopped consenting to the conspiracy to hide lesbian history." Her resolve was facilitated by a newly blooming lesbian culture, and her work contributes to this culture. Thus Emily Dickinson, the oddest duck in American literature, may perhaps be considered in a new light.

In addition, despite the risks involved whenever a writer or teacher (or almost anyone) identifies her/himself as homosexual—and simply mentioning the word is sometimes equated with self-identification—a climate has been established where many culture-makers find it possible to take this risk.[14] When Jan Clausen concludes the title poem in *after touch* with the words "I am a lesbian," we recognize this more accepting climate. When Lorraine Bethel and Barbara Smith write that one lesbian publishing in the journal *Conditions: Five—The Black Women's Issue* felt the need to use a pseudonym, we know we are not accepting enough yet.[15]

Lillian Faderman writes openly of Dickinson's passion for Sue Gilbert; Louise Bernikow supports the possibility that when women say "she" in their love poems, they *mean* "she," and demonstrates that women creators often bond with women in primary intensity; these are facts. Such facts are products of culture; and they are also producers of culture, in a chain extending from Dickinson through Faderman, Bernikow, myself, and all those who may read this combination of materials and talk about what they've read, write books, and think, knowing that Dickinson loved a woman; that love between women was possible and restricted; and that women poets, even those who write in brusque original phrases, are not necessarily loveless and contemptible. The impact that this cluster of information may have on future generations, especially women, especially lesbians, perhaps most especially writers, is incalculable. This is what I mean by culture-making.

And it is happening all around us; by us and to us. While writing this essay, I have been reading *Beginning Book* by Maricla Moyano,[16] which I'd picked up in a women's bookstore (which existed because of a burgeoning feminist culture) and bought because I liked how it looked and because on the back Ti-Grace Atkinson was quoted: "I loved it. It's beautiful. I think it the most beautiful writing to come out of the new women's literature." I recognized Ti-Grace's name—her name *is* a name—because there has been a women's movement; and her praise asks me to read Moyano in a context of feminism and rebellion, a context that until recently was invisible.[17]

The story, about Moyano's "beginning," weaves a childhood narrative against passages that seem to leap out of the narrator's journal, until a second narrative emerges: Moyano abandons a male lover and commits herself to a woman; a spare and slightly surreal coming-out story. Without the gay and women's movement, Moyano's story would probably not have been told, at least not published and republished and flagged by Ti-Grace to me with recognizable signals: *Read this one.*

I read it and find myself delighted by her mind at work/play, by her distinct voice telling a clear honest story. I have learned to value clarity and accuracy. But I was trained in graduate school to mock the concept of "sincerity" in art, to equate art and artifice, as I was steered away from contemporary writers, those untested and unapproved by my betters. No one told me that classics were also *becoming*.

Nor was I told that as a woman with access to print, I would be able to bring literature into a circle of awareness, as I do now with Moyano, by writing about her work; knowing that if her work is widely read by lesbians and loved and used to inspire other writings, or is critiqued and answered with contrasting stories, then *Beginning Book* some twenty or fifty years from now may be considered a lesbian classic. And, conversely, if no one reads it . . .

Classics in Which Lesbian Culture?

But, says the idealist, who believes in the cream theory of greatness (greatness rises to the top, like cream on milk), "Isn't it different with lesbians? None of us runs the *New York Review;* we aren't owned by Shell Oil; some few of us teach college, but not all of us go there. Many of us have other, freer, connections with writing. So won't our great works survive (assuming they get written and published, that is)?"[18]

It's true that lesbian culture, like any culture that matters to people, if not completely suppressed and driven underground, thrives on scanty resources, outside universities and other traditional institutions of cultural production and evaluation. We exchange, are inspired by, and learn from each other's works in a variety of publications, bookstores, classes, grapevines. These alternative institutions exist because of the vitality of lesbian and feminist cultures. Only because of this dynamic, nourishing relationship does the concept of a lesbian classic even arise.

But we should recognize that to the extent that lesbian culture represents the experience, insights, values, and interests of most lesbians, it will have a combative relationship to the dominant culture—as long as in that culture, lesbians are oppressed. *Rubyfruit Jungle* doesn't alter this oppression. Lesbian culture, for it to belong to and represent most lesbians, will be prowoman, pro-working people, and multiracial.[19] This means that a genuine culture of lesbians will always be in danger of repression, co-optation, and absorption, until such time as lesbians have control of their lives.

It's clear that a racist society that makes a best-seller of, for example, Baldwin's *The Fire Next Time*, must have a bizarre and indirect relationship to the content of creative work.[20] The dominant culture can tolerate a few clear thinkers, even revolutionary artists; anthologize their sappiest work ("How Do I Love Thee?" by Elizabeth Barrett Browning, not "Aurora Leigh"[21]); put them on panels; or isolate them, make them stars, interview them on television, deprive them of the deep popular connection that fed their work in the first place and gave them support, information, and, above all, honest criticism. When all else fails, publish their books and don't promote them;[22] destroy their presses or encourage them to destroy one another's; buy film rights to their books and don't film them; or film and distort them.

But not so separate from the dominant culture are the patriarchal outposts in our heads. The fact: whenever we are not consciously fighting against the hierarchies we were born and raised into, we will imitate these hierarchies and reinforce the oppression of other women.

We can say this more simply. How many lesbian or feminist publications, presses, coffee houses, galleries, how many women's studies programs, conferences, how many of our culture-making institutions are controlled by women of color? By women of working class background or without college training? By women who are poor?[23]

White middle-class lesbians can ignore, co-opt, or patronize poor lesbians and lesbians of color. This happens not mysteriously or through moral flaw; but through the facts of oppression. The less oppressed tend to have more access to money, education, and other resources required for cultural nourishment; and to old-girl networks that influence such decisions as what gets printed, heard about, reviewed in which publications, who gets invited to speak at what college on which panel, who gets money to fly to the opposite coast to appear at which conference, who wins which fellow [sic] ships and grants or gets teaching positions where.

The effect of this is much larger than dictating the particular people who do and don't get to make a living off their creative work—though this is large enough. These unofficial networks bear on the questions: Which lesbians will lesbian culture honor and support? Whose experience will come to be represented in the books women will read years from now? Which languages will be preserved and extended and given fruit: The Barbadian-Brooklyn English of Paule Marshall's characters in *Brown Girl, Brownstones?*[24] The witty explosions of Bertha Harris's *Lover?*[25] The working class inflections of Sharon Isabell's *Yesterday's Lessons?*[26]

It's simple. If I teach everyone to talk, future generations will not find a woman's Brooklyn Jewish accent unpoetic or comical. But if British aristocrats—or even William Carlos Williams and Allen Ginsberg—prime our poetic sensibilities, my voice will *never* sound classic.[27]

But the questions extend even further: What kind of consciousness will women have when they pick up which books in which languages representing whose experience? Who will be encouraged to write? Who will be silenced and made invisible? Who will women become, to choose *great/not great?*

Lesbian Classics

In talking about classics, then, I mean who and what will become central to who we, as a people, become, and to what our culture becomes. And we can't know these things yet—though we know that we will become partly *through* our culture. Our classics will be chosen partly because they have shaped the choosers.

But if we can't know, we can suspect which values are significant for us now and what directions our culture may turn. Adrienne Rich's *Women and Honor: Some Notes on Lying,* for example, filled a need and has been taken instantly into the culture.[28] How many lesbians have given a new lover a copy, either to start things off right, or after the first big fight? A value: to be honorable with each other. A form: women and _____ (Susan Griffin's *Woman and Nature;* [29] my "Women and Violence"[30]). All of us asking to be read in a context of women as the lens on the world.

Monique Wittig's *Les Guérillères*[31] seems another core work. The tribal voice ("the women say . . .") made possible, it seems, the collective voice in *Woman and Nature,* as well as the nonlinear form of Griffin's book and much of new women's writing. So that although Wittig's work seemed strange to many women when it first was getting passed around (in the early seventies), it seems less strange now.

Nowhere is this process more evident than in the work of Virginia Woolf. As women readers have articulated not just separate taste, a separate list of best-sellers, favorites, but also a developing network we can call culture, Woolf's role in this culture has become clearer, more obviously key. She wrote about textured lives, the secret currents between women, towards each other, against men, even against each other, but always with a piercing consciousness of sexual conflict. Many of us have imitated/will imitate Woolf to discover what she has to offer in the way of style and vision. And since so many women read and use Woolf, her work becomes familiar, "easier."[32]

Judy Grahn, on the other hand, accessible from the start—language, subject, price—reclaimed the word *common*, a reclamation that continues to echo through our literature: Rich's *The Dream of a Common Language*,[33] my "Are we ready to name/with a common tongue?"[34] Grahn celebrates the speech of ordinary women: "The common woman is as common/as a rattlesnake." Has a sentence ever crackled so across a page?[35] A value, supported in Tillie Olsen's *Silences*, broken; Alice Walker's mother's garden.[36] As long as we cherish the creativity of ordinary women and value what women themselves have valued, we center exactly on the passionately egalitarian vision named in "women's liberation."

But if those who control what gets passed on are antagonistic to this vision, and claim that Grahn's language is flat and a bit rhetorical (instead of powerful and incantatory, which is what I think); or that Rich has lost something (elegance of form? compelling imagery?) by bringing her work progressively towards clarity and accessibility to the vast majority of women; or that Walker has unfortunately fallen prey to white feminist man-hating in her last two splendid articles in *Ms.*;[37] then Rich, Grahn, and Walker may appear in literary history—if at all—as minor writers. And since "lesser" writers whose work connected with theirs in a common tradition will be excluded altogether, none of them will be read in a context of like-minded peers, and their work will seem eccentric rather than central, and will become marginal to the culture that passes on.[38]

Conversely, if tentative explorations are pursued, the original probings will come to seem/be pivotal in the culture. For example, if black and white women confront—in life and in art—the substance of what is between us, historically and currently, separating as well as joining us, so that an authentic bi- or multiracial antiracist tradition is incorporated into lesbian culture, then the relationship between Meridian and Lynn in Alice Walker's *Meridian*, or between Lillian and Sophronia, in Hellman's *An Unfinished Woman*, will be recognized as (painful) beginnings, thus classic.[39]

We can watch a classic becoming. When Audre Lorde tells a room full of women, many lesbians, many black women, "Your silence will not protect you,"[40] and Gloria Hull writes "Poem," dedicated to Audre Lorde, which concludes:

Dear Eshu's Audre,
please keep on
teaching us
how
to speak

> to know
> that now
> "our labor *is*
> more important than
> our silence"

and this poem is chosen to introduce *Conditions: Five—The Black Women's Issue*, we know we're in the presence of something classic. The invocation. The passionate connection. The exhortation to speak.

Similarly, Muriel Rukeyser, recently dead and one of our great poets, celebrates Käthe Kollwitz: "What would happen if one woman told the truth about her life?/The world would split open";[41] and Louise Bernikow lifts these lines to title her anthology of women's poetry over four hundred years, one which makes a point of including women's blues, prison, and work poems—as much truth as she could find.[42]

Or take *Conditions: Five—The Black Women's Issue*, which I have already referred to four times, a sign of its impact. *Conditions: Five* represents another facet of women's truth-telling and is important for its mode of production—the *Conditions* editors gave control of the journal to guest editors, black women—and for the high quality of the gathered work. Smith and Bethel, the guest editors, vigorously solicited material from many women, including some who had not considered themselves writers. The result was twofold: many new writers were included, and *Conditions: Five* not only recorded an emerging black feminist/lesbian culture, but helped to evoke it.

All cultural institutions can open their doors to those who have been excluded. In the past year, *off our backs* and *Heresies* have published issues for and by women of color. If feminist and lesbian institutions—not just journals, but anthologies, women's studies programs, presses, radio programs, and so on—do extend themselves to other communities of women, then *Conditions* and *Heresies* and *off our backs* will be seen as pioneers in Third World feminist and lesbian culture. Otherwise the entire burden of this work of enlarging the circle of women makers will fall to groups like the *Azalea* collective, a group of Third World lesbians, and a multiracial lesbian culture will not flourish. Moreover, if one of our values is inclusion of many different lesbians, and support for personal and cultural uniqueness, then as Asian, Native American, and Latina lesbians, and those in the new immigrant cultures—Vietnamese, Cuban, Haitian—and those yet to come to this country, begin to articulate their cultures, then those of us with access to cultural resources will welcome the opportunity to move on over and expand our circle.[43]

And one of our themes will be how we joined the circle of women.

Coming out, glorious, excruciating, sometimes so natural it went unnamed for years, will occupy a central place in our classics. And since lesbian possibility is often curtailed, then whenever women matter to each other, or choose women, or reject or betray women with a consciousness of pain or necessity, we will discern this possibility.[44] Perhaps our tragedies will be stories where women could not or did not stand by each other, bond together against oppression, or reach out to each other with sufficient strength and tenderness to transform, at least partly, each other's lives. Our comedies would unfold tales of women joining to resist all kinds of damage visited on women in a sexist world, to promote the survival of life on the planet and the creation of a just, generous, multicolored world.

Lesbian Passion

But we stray far from any recognizable boundary of lesbian culture. It may be that on the level of platonic forms, lesbianism means a vast and holy bonding with women. Yet if I were attracted to a particular woman and asked, "Is she a lesbian?" this is not what I'd mean. I would be asking: Might she be open to me? Will she put me down for wanting her?[45]

While love and camaraderie among women have been mocked, discouraged, and often punished, sex between women has been made almost unspeakable, thus unthinkable. In light of this crippling taboo, it's not surprising how little we find in our art that is explicitly sexual, as if we're embarrassed by the sexualness of lesbian sexuality: oceans, flowers, caves, and revolution, okay—but sex?[46] If we remember that some of our people lived—and live—sexless, in terror; and that, as Michaele Uccella has remarked, "To some people, our very existence is pornographic";[47] then as we work to rid our lives of violent offensive pornography, we will be careful at the same time to expand protection for sexual freedom, and to support sexual honesty in our culture.

And one way to expand protection for sexual freedom is to assert this freedom. If our developing culture does support sexual honesty, then perhaps explicitly sexual art and literature will replace exclusively floral interpretations of our cunts. June Arnold's *Sister Gin*[48] will reverberate for us not only as a celebration of female love and middle-aged sexuality and integrity, but also as a depiction of explicit lesbian sexuality. We will laugh with Joan Larkin's " 'Vagina' Sonnet":

> Is "vagina" suitable for use
> in a sonnet? I don't suppose so.
> A famous poet told me, "Vagina's ugly."
> Meaning, of course, the *sound* of it. In poems.[49]

Olga Broumas's poems will make us flush with pleasure; for example:

> ... Marine
> eyes, marine
> odors. Everything live
> (tongue, clitoris, lip and lip)
> swells in its moist shell.[50]

And this incredible poem of Stephanie Byrd's will be honored for the courage it gives us to know our sex:

> I can feel it in my lips
> My ass moves towards warmth
> Press warmth upon my buttocks
>   my breasts
> rub my crotch the lips
> I am warmed, hot water in a bath
> I can feel breath in my throat
> I choke up phlegm
> Lick my chest, the lips
> dart in to make me choke again
> I can feel sight in my eyes
> Push sight into my eyes, the eyelets
> I see writhing eyelets clearer
> Eat me
> Eat me
> Eat me
>   alive[51]

Lesbian Vision

So our culture must allow for both sex and solidarity. From our deepest eroticism to our hardest struggles: if we know ourselves and each other, and that our lives depend on one another, we will cherish "the courage to be there when another woman needs you";[52] we will teach our daughters and our students to believe, and to act on the belief, that "Any woman's death diminishes me."[53] Then lesbians in the year 2000 will read Judy Grahn's "A Woman Is Talking to Death" a bit the way the Greeks, they say, sat around listening to Homer. Grahn's poem will be key in our culture, not just because it is great, but because the values it embodies will be our cultural values—and because Grahn will have helped to make them ours. We will remember that the love we make with each other was called *indecent*. We will have redefined indecent.

> Have you ever committed any indecent acts with women?
> Yes, many. I am guilty of allowing suicidal women to die before
> my eyes or in the ears or under my hands because I thought I could

do nothing, I am guilty of leaving a prostitute who held a knife to my friend's throat to keep us from leaving, because we would not sleep with her, we thought she was old and fat and ugly; I am guilty of not loving her who needed me; I regret all the women I have not slept with or comforted, who pulled themselves away from me for lack of something I had not the courage to fight for, for us, our life, our planet, our city, our meat and potatoes, our love. These are indecent acts, lacking courage, lacking a certain fire behind the eyes, which is the symbol, the raised fist, the sharing of resources, the resistance that tells death he will starve for lack of the fat of us, our extra. Yes I have committed acts of indecency with women and most of them were acts of omission. I regret them bitterly.[54]

Notes

1. First published in 1970 (New York: Harcourt Brace Jovanovich).

2. Pat Parker, *Movement in Black* (Oakland, Calif.: Diana Press, 1978); Barbara Deming, *Prison Notes* (Boston: Beacon Press, 1966); *Running Away from Myself: A Dream Portrait of America Drawn from the Movies of the Forties* (New York: Grossman, 1969); *Revolution and Equilibrium* (New York: Grossman, 1971); *Wash Us and Comb Us* (New York: Grossman, 1972); and *We Cannot Live Without Our Lives* (New York: Grossman, 1974).

3. Louise Bernikow's introduction to her anthology *The World Split Open, Four Centuries of Women Poets in England and America, 1552–1950* (New York: Vintage Books, 1974), gives a lively and accurate description of how literary history gets written.

4. Judy Grahn notes accurately that she, Susan Griffin, and Alta, later joined by Pat Parker, led a renaissance of women's poetry in the early 1970s on the West Coast; in her introduction to selected writings by Alta, *The Shameless Hussy* (New York: The Crossing Press, 1980).

5. Similarly, any writer situated in New York, Boston, San Francisco, or Los Angeles has more chance of influencing the culture than one living in Oshkosh.

6. Jonson's most brilliant play, *Bartholomew Fair,* is practically unintelligible by nonscholars, partly because it is so original, thus unfamiliar; partly because the texture and language of the play reflect so faithfully Jonson's culture. Jonas Barish has remarked on Jonson that never has a poet "been so punished for the crime of not being Shakespeare"; in his introduction to his edition of *Ben Jonson: A Collection of Critical Essays* (Englewood Cliffs, N.J.: Prentice-Hall, 1963).

7. See, for example, R. H. Tawney, *Religion and the Rise of Capitalism* (New York: Harcourt Brace & Co., 1926); and the work of his predecessor, Max Weber, *The Protestant Ethic and the Spirit of Capitalism* (New York: Scribner's, 1958).

8. I received a shot of cultural relativism in 1975, while visiting the People's Republic of China. Some students asked us what American books and movies were about. We described a romantic plot, among some others. They were amazed. "That's all?" they asked. "A whole book just about two people falling in love and getting married?" Their basic plots at the time revolved around a person or small group struggling to transform the world, and succeeding.

9. Carroll Smith-Rosenberg, "The Female World of Love and Ritual: Relations Between Women in Nineteenth-Century America," *Signs* 1 (Fall 1975): 1–29; Nancy Sahli, "Smashing: Women's Relationships Before the Fall," *Chrysalis* 8 (1979): 17–27.

10. Barbara Grier and Coletta Reid have edited three volumes gleaned from *The Ladder,* all published by Diana Press in 1976: *The Lavender Herring: Lesbian Essays from The Ladder; Lesbian Lives;* and *Lesbians' Home Journal.*

11. On the album *Lavender Jane Loves Women,* 1975, from Ladyslipper Music, Box 3124, Durham, N.C. 27705.

12. Bernikow.

13. From the unexpurgated edition of Dickinson's letters, eds. Thomas Johnson and Theodora Ward (1958), cited in Lillian Faderman, "Who Hid Lesbian History?" *Frontiers* 4, no. 3 (1979): 74–76. See also Faderman's article, "Emily Dickinson's Letters to Sue Gilbert," *The Massachusetts Review* 18 (Summer 1977): 197–225.

14. See, for example, Judith Schwarz's recent survey of women researching lesbian history, in *Frontiers* 4, no. 3 (1979): 1–13. Most of the women indicated that they are risking their careers simply by doing this research.

15. Jan Clausen, *after touch* (Brooklyn: Out & Out Books, 1975); Bethel and Smith, "Introduction," *Conditions: Five—The Black Women's Issue* (1979): 12.

16. (New York: Magic Circle Printing, 1979; first published in 1973).

17. Blanche Boyd, a novelist, shared with me her insight that a blurb on a book jacket helps to place the book in the context in which it was meant to be read; conversation, January 1977, in which she was explaining why she especially wanted Tillie Olsen to write an advance notice for her second novel, *Mourning the Death of Magic* (New York: Macmillan, 1977).

18. By *idealist,* I don't mean visionary; a visionary should be clear-sighted. I mean someone who still thinks as she was taught, in terms of essences (Kant, not Hegel); who fails to recognize that what we consider "great" is an historical phenomenon; that *we* are an historical phenomenon.

19. Internationalist as well; Gertrude Stein spoke perhaps more insightfully than she intended: "Patriarchal Poetry is the same as Patriotic poetry" (excerpts from *Patriarchal Poetry* reprinted in Bernikow's anthology).

20. By the sixties, American intellectuals and critics had rejected the idea that content in art mattered, perhaps because (1) a new generation needed new theories to publish new books and to see freshly; (2) McCarthyism had taken its toll—they were suspicious of any political implications, especially "pinkish" tints; and (3) they felt profoundly empty. As Susan Sontag argued, if you're sensually, emotionally, spiritually, morally dead, the priority is to *wake up;* in "On Style," in *Against Interpretation* (New York: Farrar, Straus & Giroux, 1966). The movements of the sixties and seventies brought back to American culture a concern for content.

21. See Bernikow, pp. 29–32, for a discussion of how the Barrett mythology was created.

22. Blanche Boyd's inventive and compelling novel, cited above, received little

promotion from Macmillan, who published it. See also Kathi Maio's account of trying for a year to locate a copy of Andrea Dworkin's *Woman Hating*, published by Dutton in 1974, but unavailable from book distributors for some time; Maio's review of *Woman Hating* in *The Second Wave* 4, no. 1 (1975).

23. I have heard only of *Azalea*, a publication for lesbians of color; see below, discussion of *Conditions: Five*.

24. (First published 1959; republished by the Feminist Press, Old Westbury, N.Y., 1982).

25. (Plainfield, Vt.: Daughters, Inc., 1976).

26. (Oakland, Calif.: Women's Press Collective, 1974.) For a shrewd and sprightly discussion of "nonstandard" English, see Judy Grahn's introduction to volume 1 of *True to Life Adventure Stories* (Oakland, Calif.: Diana Press, 1978), entitled "Murdering the King's English."

27. The first time I heard Muriel Rukeyser read—she was a large woman with a loud New York Jewish accent—my heart sang. I realized I had needed to hear her voice as I had needed to hear women's voices against a drone of male voices. This has implications for all oppressed cultures.

28. Originally published in *Heresies* 1 (Jan. 1977); then as a chapbook by Motheroot Publications (Pittsburgh, 1977); and reprinted in the volume *On Lies, Secrets, and Silence, Selected Prose, 1966–1978*. Sometimes the instant leap into usage encourages the growth of jargon, almost passwords. When women talk about "spinning" as a political activity, without awareness that they're using a metaphor, I know something's out of control (*spinning*, from Mary Daly's *Gyn/Ecology* [Boston: Beacon Press, 1978]); but there's no mistaking our need for our own namings.

29. (New York: Harper & Row, 1978).

30. In *Sinister Wisdom* 9 (Spring 1979): 75–78.

31. Translated into English as *The Lesbian Body* (New York: William Morrow, 1975).

32. Woolf's talent and achievement are so taken for granted now that we risk forgetting that initially she had to publish herself.

33. (1978).

34. From "Naming," in Melanie Kaye, *We Speak in Code* (Pittsburgh: Motheroot Publications, 1980).

35. That these lines barely require citation shows how they've taken hold; but early lesbian publishing efforts should be recorded: *The Common Woman* was distributed in 10¢ mimeographed copies; then printed by the Oakland Women's Press Collective in the early seventies (undated, with *Edward the Dyke and Other Poems*); and now appears in Grahn's collected poems, *The Work of a Common Woman* (Oakland, Calif.: Diana Press, 1978).

36. Olsen, *Silences* (New York: Delacorte Press, 1978); Walker, "In Search of Our Mother's Gardens," *Ms.*, May 1974, 67–70.

37. Walker, "Confronting Pornography at Home—A Fable," *Ms.*, February 1980, 67–70; "Breaking Chains and Encouraging Life," a review of *Conditions: Five* and a tribute to the courage of black lesbians, *Ms.*, April 1980, 35–41.

38. For example, Tillie Olsen tells of returning to writing after decades of abstention to discover that Josephine Herbst (an older contemporary and another rare woman writer on the left) was out of print and virtually unknown. In her own day, Olsen reports, Jo Herbst was as popular and as major a writer as Hemingway or Odets. Perhaps Elinor Langer's biography of Herbst, in progress, will restore her to an appropriate place in our map of American literature.

39. Walker, *Meridian* (New York: Harcourt Brace Jovanovich, 1976); Hellman, *An Unfinished Woman* (Boston: Little, Brown, 1969). Adrienne Rich treats this subject eloquently, in a talk she gave as part of the Lesbians and Literature panel at the 1977 Modern Language Association meeting (on the topic "The Transformation of Silence into Language and Action," published in *Sinister Wisdom* 6 (Summer 1978): 17–24; and, more fully, in her essay "Disloyal to Civilization: Feminism, Racism, Gynephobia," first published in *Chrysalis* 7 (1979), and reprinted in the volume of her collected prose, *On Lies, Secrets, and Silence.*

40. In her talk for the 1977 Lesbians and Literature panel, cited above, also published in *The Cancer Journals*, pp. 18–23.

41. From "Käthe Kollwitz," in Muriel Rukeyser, *The Speed of Darkness* (New York: Random House, 1968).

42. Bernikow.

43. Since I wrote this essay early in 1980, Third World lesbian and feminist activity has born much fruit; for example, the publication of *This Bridge Called My Back: Writings by Radical Women of Color,* edited by Cherríe Moraga and Gloria Anzaldúa (Watertown, Mass.: Persephone Press, 1981); of *Black Lesbians: An Annotated Bibliography,* compiled by J. R. Roberts (Tallahassee, Fla.: Naiad Press, 1981); of a double issue of *Sinister Wisdom* by and for Native American women, edited by Beth Brant (1983); and the creation of Kitchen Table Press and of the Third World Women's Archives (1982). The domino theory is true. In addition, in 1982 I find myself part of a movement of lesbian and feminist Jews; the emergence of a strong proud Jewish identity and the struggle against anti-Semitism begin to gather momentum. The publication of *Nice Jewish Girls: A Lesbian Anthology,* edited by Evelyn Torton Beck (Watertown, Mass.: Persephone Press, 1982), records and accelerates this momentum.

44. Barbara Smith, discussing black women writers, argues that a lesbian perspective emerges when we look for primary female connections; in "Towards a Black Feminist Criticism," *Conditions: Two* (1977): 25–44. Smith's classic essay is also available from Out & Out Books, Brooklyn (1981).

45. Women who were never permitted to express their love for women erotically, or who faced scathing queer-hatred for years, often feel the need for a clear word that means "women who desire women." I'm reminded of Adrienne Rich's pronouncement at the 1976 Modern Language Association meeting: "It is the lesbian in us who is creative. . . ." Dolores Noll, a long-time gay activist, responded that it was all right with her if the word acquired a figurative meaning, but then she wanted a word that expressed who *she* was. See Rich's talk and later remarks on this point in her collected prose.

46. I discuss some reasons for lesbian reticence about explicit sex in "Sexual Power,"

Sinister Wisdom 15 (Fall 1980: 45–50, cocreated with Michaele Uccella): defensiveness; lack of a sense of privacy; and reluctance to feed stereotypes in which lesbians are nothing but sexual beings—these facts explain, in part, our silence.

47. Uccella, conversation, Fall 1979.

48. (Plainfield, Vt.: Daughters, Inc., 1975).

49. From *Housework* (Brooklyn: Out & Out Books, 1975).

50. Broumas, "Amazon Twins," in *Beginning With O* (New Haven, Ct.: Yale University Press, 1977).

51. "I Can Feel It in My Lips," in *25 Years of Malcontent* (Boston, Mass.: Good Gay Poets Press, 1976). Byrd's work deserves mention also as strongly black-identified poetry.

52. Michaele Uccella, defining womanhood, Spring 1979.

53. Adrienne Rich, the last line of "From an Old House in America," in *Poems, Selected and New, 1950–1974*.

54. Grahn, "A Woman Is Talking to Death," in *The Work of a Common Woman*, cited above.

17

The Black Lesbian in American Literature: An Overview

ANN ALLEN SHOCKLEY

*U*ntil recently, there has been almost nothing written by or about the black lesbian in American literature—a void signifying that the black lesbian was a nonentity in imagination as well as reality. This unique black woman, analogous to Ralph Ellison's *Invisible Man,* was seen but not seen because of what the eyes did not wish to behold. In a pioneer article by Barbara Smith entitled "Toward a Black Feminist Criticism," the author candidly lamented:

> Black women are still in the position of having to "imagine," discover and verify Black lesbian literature because so little has been written from an avowedly lesbian perspective.[1]

The ignoring and absence of black lesbians as a literary subject can be attributed to a number of causes. First, white female writers did not know enough about black lesbians to write about them. Secondly, the focus of white women's literature has been on their own volatile positions.

This, of course leaves only the black female writer knowledgeable or sensitive enough to the subject to cultivate and strengthen an undernourished literature. Why have there been so pitifully few black women writers to embrace the topic? The answers are manifold, undergirded by the black female writers who gave top priority to writing about what was seen as their strongest oppression—racism. The literature by late nineteenth- and early twentieth-century black women writers reflects the dominance of this priority.

No doubt, there have been in the contemporary past black female writers who attempted to write about lesbian themes. These, perhaps known only to a few friends and editors, were probably not published because the works came too soon in respect to marketing time. Publishers were not interested in books with lesbian themes, for a productive money-making market was inconceivable. The sociopolitical temper of the times had not given rise to the activism of the women's or gay rights movements of the sixties. In conjunction with this, some of the books were simply not of publishing quality. Then, as now, these women who did not surface, women who might have had something to say, but did not put forth any effort to write, did not have the time, inclination, or ability, even if they had wanted to.

It is my belief that those black female writers who could have written well and perceptively enough to warrant publication chose instead to write about black women in a heterosexual milieu. The preference was motivated by the fear of being labeled a lesbian, even if in some cases they were not.

This threat of being identified as gay, queer, funny, or a bull-dagger in black linguistics is embedded deeply within the overall homophobic attitude of the black community, a phenomenon stemming from social, religious, and biological convictions. The enmity toward homosexuality has long been rampant in black life, and is flagrantly revealed in the words of Minister Addul-Baqui of the male-supremacist Black Muslim religious sect:

> The dressing of man for another man's sexual companionship and the dressing of a woman for another woman's sexual companionship is an evil, lowly, foul thought.[2]

This malevolence has been especially directed toward black lesbians. Blacks have made very few attempts to understand or educate themselves regarding black lesbians. This lack of comprehension has aided in fueling the flames of animosity and misinformation toward them. Just as whites were afraid of and hated blacks because they did not *know* them, so blacks have an inherent bias against lesbians for the same reason.

Stereotypical caricatures of black lesbians abound in the black community, serving to feed antipathies. Formerly, the visible lesbian was the popularly designated "mannish" woman who fitted the stock mold; less stereotypical lesbians were not recognizable, nor did they venture forth to be recognized.

In addition, creating a more obscuring fog was the fact that no conscious efforts were made by knowledgeable individuals who could have documented truths over myths to help others become cognizant of the black lesbian as a person and not a thing. For example, during an oral history interview with a Southern black female gynecologist conducted by this writer, the subject of black women as lesbians was raised. To this, the learned practitioner off-handedly remarked that lesbianism was acquired from white women. (A new disease, perhaps?)

The stereotypical "facts" alias fallacies surrounding black lesbians are ludicrous. They are labeled as being "too ugly to get a man"; "women who have been disappointed in love and turned to women"; "man-haters"; and "man-women" physically.

Muhammad Ali, former world's champion, but still champion of male chauvinism, typified these misconceptions when queried by a female reporter for the *Amsterdam News* about the ERA and the equalizing of economic opportunities. Ali characteristically displayed his lack of enlightenment by replying: ". . . some professions shouldn't be open to women because they can't handle certain jobs, like construction work. Lesbians, maybe, but not women."[3] What is a lesbian if not a woman?

Providing added impetus to the black community's negative concept of homosexuality was the thrust of the sixties. This was the period when the black movement was flourishing, bringing with it the promotion of black male identity to offset the myth of the black matriarchy. Some black women advocated "walking ten steps behind the male," unwittingly encouraging a new master-subserviency at the expense of black woman-hood. The shibboleth of the times was to enhance black manhood.

In view of this, naturally, the independent woman-identified woman, the black lesbian, was a threat. Not only was she a threat to the projection of black male macho, but a *sexual* threat too—the utmost danger to the black male's institutionally designated role as "king of the lovers."

Combining with the stereotypical concepts and black male power thrust of the sixties was the sexism exhibited by black females toward her black lesbian sisters. "Fags" to black women are cute, entertaining, safe, and above all, *tolerated*. Males are expected to venture sexually from the norm. They are *men*, aren't they, and "boys will be boys."

All of these phobias, hostilities, and myths existing around the black lesbian cause a paralyzing *fear* of labels, which has prevented black women writers from writing openly and honestly about lesbianism. Black women writers *live* in the black community and *need* the closeness of family, friends, neighbors, and co-workers to share in the commonality of ethnicity for surviving in a blatantly racist society. This is foremost, superseding the dire need for negating misconceptions and fallacies with voices of truth. For some, it is easier and wiser to live peaceably within the black community by writing about what is socially acceptable.

There is now a trickling of lesbian themes grazing the pages of fiction and nonfiction by and about black lesbians. Even heterosexual black female writers and non-woman-identified women are throwing in, for better or worse, an occasional major or minor lesbian character. Unfortunately, within these works exists an undercurrent of hostility, trepidation, subtlety, shadiness, and in some instances, ignorance culling forth homophobic stereotypes. (In some reviews of my novel I, too, have been accused of character stereotypes.)

Maya Angelou's reminiscences touching upon lesbians in her two autobiographies tend to substantiate black women's conventional views and ideas about lesbians. In her *I Know Why the Caged Bird Sings*, she tells how her introduction to lesbians was made through the enduring classic, *The Well of Loneliness*. Angelou wrote: "It allowed me to see a little of the mysterious world of the pervert."[4] *Pervert?* Her attitude toward the male homosexual is decidedly more flexible, excluding them from this category:

> Of course, I ruled out the jolly sissies who sometimes stayed at our house and cooked whopping eight-course dinners while the perspiration made paths down their made-up faces. Since everyone accepted them . . .[5]

This is a clear example of female sexism pertaining to the double standard. It is all right for men but not women.

After reading *The Well of Loneliness*, Angelou begins to question her own sexuality because of her deepening voice and unfeminine body. She reads more and more on the subject of lesbians in libraries and reasons:

> After a thorough self-examination, in the light of all I had read and heard about dykes and bull-daggers, I reasoned that I had none of the obvious traits— I didn't wear trousers, or have big shoulders or go in for sports, or walk like a man or even want to touch a woman.[6]

In the sequel, *Gather Together in My Name*, Angelou wrote disapprovingly of two lesbians, Johnnie Mae and Beatrice who ". . . were lesbians, which was sinful enough. . . ."[7] Nevertheless, she does not think it sinful to use them for her own monetary advantage by assisting them in an arrangement to entertain their male customers.

Another autobiography by a black woman that describes a lesbian encounter is that of the world renowned singer, Billie Holliday. Recounting the attentions of a rich, white girl:

> She came around night after night. She was crazy about my singing and used to wait for me to finish up. I wasn't blind. I hadn't been on Welfare Island for nothing. It wasn't long before I knew I had become a thing for this girl.[8]

For the girl's enamoredness, Billie offered her explication:

> It's a cinch to see how it all begins. These poor bitches grow up hating their mothers and having the hots for their fathers. And since being in love with

our father is taboo, they grow up unable to get any kicks out of anything unless it's taboo too.[9]

One famous black female singer whose bisexuality is frankly revealed by her biographer is Bessie Smith. The episodes of this gutsy blues singer's sexual affairs with women are frankly told in Chris Albertson's *Bessie* (New York: Stein and Day, 1974).

Over fifty years *after* the publication of the lesbian novel *The Well of Loneliness,* two black novels have appeared with strictly lesbian themes by black female writers: the first, by this author, *Loving Her* (Bobbs-Merrill, Inc., 1974, paperback, Avon, 1978), and *Ruby* (New York: The Viking Press, 1976) authored by the West Indian writer, Rosa Guy.

Ruby is, to use the librarian's professional jargon, a young adult novel leveled for grades eight and up. It was selected as one of the ten best books of 1977 by the American Library Association's Young Adult Services Division. The editors of the *Bulletin of Interracial Books for Children* disagreed with the Young Adult Services evaluation of the book, contending:

> Ruby reinforces sexist stereotypes about heterosexual males, heterosexual females *and* lesbians by implying that *real* lesbians are "masculine" types like Daphne, while "feminine" types like Ruby are destined to "go straight."[10]

The everlasting conundrum of stereotypes leads this writer to pose the question: when do stereotypes begin and end? Stereotypes are found in real life, and isn't fiction supposed to mirror the images of existence?

Rosa Guy's *Ruby* is a continuation of her novel *The Friends* (New York: Holt, Rinehart and Winston, 1973), and is based on the West Indian Cathy family that moved to Harlem. The protagonist, Ruby Cathy, is an eighteen-year-old girl whose mother has died and who is being reared along with her sister by an overprotective and hard-working domineering father. Lonely, she enters into a "more than ordinary friendship" with a pretty, sophisticated mannish high school classmate, Daphne Duprey. The word lesbian is never mentioned throughout the 218-page novel, but "lover" is. The omission causes this writer to wonder if "lesbian" is too obnoxious for young readers, or was there a timidity on the part of the author to categorize the relationship as lesbian?

At the conclusion, Daphne is accepted at Brandeis and announces to Ruby she is "going straight." After an attempted suicide, Ruby, with the help of her father, turns her attention back to an old boyfriend. The reader is left to feel that the whole story was merely an excursion into a Freudian adolescent-stage crush and "all's well that ends well," as both girls go off into the rainbow of heterosexuality. The author has skirted issues without actually disturbing straight waters.

Black lesbian figures seem to be appearing more now as minor characters in novels. Rita Mae Brown, a celebrated white lesbian author, portrays one in her novel *In Her Day* (Plainfield, Vt.: Daughters, Inc., 1976). The inclusion was somewhat of a disaster since the bourgeois professor Adele, a Ph.D. in pre-Columbian art, would hardly have been recognizable as black despite her "little Africa" East 71st Street garden apartment and a white cockatoo named Lester Maddox. Adele talks white without an intentional or unintentional break into black English, which is commonly done by all blacks heedless of education at some time or another. Adele acts white, thinks white, and apparently has no substantial black friends. She could have just been another white character, which, possibly, she should have been.

Gayl Jones, a young black writer, always seems to toss a minor lesbian character or two into her novels. In the first, *Corregidora*, the principal character rebuffs a lesbian advance in bed by a young girl named Jeffy:

> I was drowsy, but I felt her hands on my breast. She was feeling all on me up around my breast. I shot awake and knocked her out on the floor. . . . There was a smell of vomit in the room, like when you suck your thumb.[11]

A lesbian advance is described as so despicable that it is associated with the "smell of vomit." Are unwanted male overtures thusly depicted?

Jones' second novel, *Eva's Man* (New York: Random House, 1976), has the protagonist, Eva, sharing a jail cell with a lesbian. While Eva ruminates over the events leading to her imprisonment for killing her man, the cellmate provides a background, singular Greek chorus litany of ongoing seduction.

Within the short story genre, more stories are developing with black lesbian themes. In her third book, a collection of short stories, *White Rat* (New York: Random House, 1977), Gayl Jones has two stories with explicitly lesbian subjects. One, "The Women," is told from the viewpoint of a young black girl whose divorced mother has a succession of women lovers. When the affairs terminate, the mother tells the daughter they are "a bitches whore." The women lovers are all nebulous characters who do not have any real substance, nor any emotional effect on either mother or daughter. They enter, stay, and leave like ghosts. At the end, the author makes it clear that the daughter, in spite of the mother's lesbian activities, is heterosexual when she prepares to have sex with a boyfriend in her mother's bed.

The second story, "Persona," is a shell-like sketch about a female professor at a predominantly white, all-girls' college who is interested in a black "freshman." The story is murky and extremely subtle, as if the author was afraid to touch it with a heavy pen. Perhaps these stories of Gayl Jones could or *should* have said more.

Pat Suncircle, a pseudonym for a young lesbian writer, has published two short stories in *Christopher Street*. The story "A Day's Growth" (February 1977) is told by a fifteen-year-old girl, Leslie, who is being reared by a religious aunt in the south. On a Saturday, she comes to grips with her sexuality through following in the shadows the lives of Miss Katheryn and Miss Renita, a lesbian couple whom she wants to emulate. The second story, "When the Time Came" (April 1978), is somewhat uneven, centering around a young homosexual boy and his visiting city aunt, who at the end communicate with understanding.

SDiane Bogus, a young California poet, published a short story, "A Measure by June," in the *GPN News* (February 1978). The first person narrative has confessional overtones that follow the storyline of Vy and her relationship with a high school-dropout boyfriend turned con man, June Johnson, to her college years. Concluding with a sexual hotel tryst, Vy informs June she "likes women." The irony of this is that if she did not have the nerve to tell June *before* her sexual act with him, how did she find the courage afterwards?

Short stories are rare occurrences for black lesbian writers, who appear to prefer expressing themselves in poetry rather than prose. Audre Lorde, an established and well-known poet, is the most notable of the muses, paving the way early through her excellent writing and black women courage. Her poetry does not deal with exclusively lesbian themes, encompassing others of love, women, race, family, children and places. The book *From a Land Where Other People Live* (Detroit: Broadside Press, 1973) was nominated for the 1974 National Book Award. Audre's most recent publications are *Coal* (New York: W. W. Norton, 1976), *Between Ourselves* (Point Reyes, Ca.: Eidolon Editions, 1976), and *The Black Unicorn* (New York: W. W. Norton, 1978).

Pat Parker, well known particularly on the West Coast, is also an established poet. In her four books, *Child of Myself* (San Lorenzo, Ca.: Shameless Hussy Press, 1971), *Pit Stop* (Oakland, Ca.: The Women's Press Collective, 1973), *Womanslaughter and Other Poems* (Oakland, Ca.: Diana Press, 1978), and *Movement in Black: The Collected Poetry of Pat Parker, 1961–1978* (Oakland, Ca.: Diana Press, 1978), she writes with a beautifully realistic driving force. Stephanie Byrd, author of *25 Years of Malcontent* (Boston: Good Gay Poets Press, 1976), is a promising newcomer in Roxbury, Massachusetts. Versatile SDiane Bogus stands out best with her poetry, which has been published in magazines and anthologies of which not all have lesbian subjects. Her volumes of poetry, *I'm Off to See the Goddam Wizard Alright* (Inglewood, CA.: SDiane Bogus, 1976) and *Woman in the Moon* (Stamford, Conn.: Soap Box Publishing, 1977), are new entrants in the field. Julia Blackwoman has not yet published a volume of poetry, but is certainly an exciting Philadelphia writer to watch, as indicated by her poem, "Revolutionary Blues," published in *Dyke* magazine's Ethnic Lesbians issue (Fall 1977).

Azalea: A Magazine by Third World Lesbians, published in New York, should become a showpiece and vehicle for new black lesbian writers as well as writers on feminist themes. The preview issue (volume 1, no. 1, winter 1977/78) contains the works of such burgeoning young poets as Donna Allegra, Becky Birtha, Linda Brown, Robin Christian, a.s. Natwa, and editor Joan Gibbs.

There is a wide vacuum existing that must be filled in the area of articles and essays by and about black lesbians. A pioneer and prolific writer utilizing this category is lesbian/feminist Anita R. Cornwell of Philadelphia. The author has appeared throughout the years in the pages of *The Ladder* and other lesbian/feminist publications. Her "Open Letter to a Black Sister" (*The Ladder,* October/November 1971) and "From a Soul Sister's Notebook" (*The Ladder,* June/July 1972), were reprinted in *The Lavender Herring: Lesbian Essays from the Ladder,* edited by Barbara Grier and Coletta Reid (Oakland, Ca.: Diana Press, 1976), and are landmarks for black lesbian writing. Anita's barbed wit is evident throughout when striking out at black male/female relationships or sexism. Her latest, "The Black Lesbian in a Malevolent Society," deploring sexism and black male oppression, appeared in *Dyke* (Fall 1977). Anita R. Cornwell, like Audre Lorde and SDiane Bogus, has not confined herself mainly to lesbian themes, but has written on the subjects of racism and black women as women in a racist/sexist society. Short stories of hers have appeared in established black magazines.

Black lesbian writers are sporadically writing articles for feminist newspapers. Terri Clark, a black lesbian socialist feminist, is an example with her article "Houston: A Turning Point," which was published in *Off Our Backs* (March 1978). The article reported on the Houston Women's Conference from a black feminist perspective. Lea Hopkins, Kansas City poet and writer, has written for the *Kansas City Star.* "Revelation" (*Kansas City Star,* July 24, 1977) pertained to her being gay. The article is a part of her self-published *I'm Not Crazy, Just Different* (Kansas City, n.d.).

It is a pity that so few black women, heterosexual or lesbian, have read or even heard of these writers, with the exception of Audre Lorde. Mainstream publications tend to shy away from their endeavors; therefore the works are usually published by lesbian/feminist publications and publishers, or are self-published.

Regretfully, rarely are any of these writers reviewed, if at all, in black periodicals or newspapers. Herein sexism shows its horns once more. Black books are primarily reviewed in black publications. Black male reviewers tend to scorn books with lesbian themes, citing them as "sick." A striking illustration is the review of my book by a young black male student poet who, obviously incensed by it, wrote: "This bullshit should not be encouraged."[12]

The black female heterosexual reviewers who *could* be sensitive to these works are usually too afraid of their peers to give them any kind of positive review; they are frightened of being tagged a closet lesbian, or a traitor to the black male. As a result, the black female heterosexual reviewer, excluding Alice Walker, either joins the males with all-around negative reviews or elects not to review the work at all.

With established publishers now more openly amenable to lesbian themes, prompted, I fear, more by money than altruism, hopefully a richer and larger body of literature by and about black lesbians will appear through the writings of new as well as established black female writers. There exists an impending need for the planting of additional seeds in what Barbara Smith has termed "a vast wilderness of works. . . ."[13] Surely there are those who can help break through and cause this literature to blossom; it is desperately needed to present another side of the lives of black women.

Notes

1. Barbara Smith, "Toward a Black Feminist Criticism," *Conditions: Two* (October 1977), 39.

2. *Brooklyn Amsterdam News,* 14 January, 1978, p. B1.

3. Cassandra Taylor, "Is Muhammad a Male Chauvinist?" *New York Amsterdam News* (14 January, 1978), p. C2.

4. Maya Angelou, *I Know Why the Caged Bird Sings* (New York: Random House, 1969), p. 265.

5. Ibid.

6. Ibid., p. 272.

7. Maya Angelou, *Gather Together in My Name* (New York: Random House, 1974), p. 54.

8. Billie Holliday and William Duffy, *Lady Sings the Blues* (New York: Lancer Books, 1972), p. 86.

9. Ibid., p. 87.

10. Editors, rev. of *Ruby,* by Rosa Guy, *Interracial Books for Children Bulletin* 8 (1977), 15.

11. Gayl Jones, *Corregidora* (New York: Random House, 1975), p. 39.

12. Frank Lamont Phillips, rev. of *Loving Her,* by Ann Allen Shockley, *Black World,* XXIV (September 1975), p. 90.

13. Smith, "Toward a Black Feminist Criticism," p. 41.

18

Without Approval: The Lesbian Poetry Tradition

BETTY STEINSHOUER

The woman-identified woman has always been involved in poetry. Her heritage is rich with women who expressed themselves in verse, calling upon the power of language to express feelings of love, lust, anger, sorrow, and happiness. Lesbians have been writing poetry since 600 B.C., beginning with Sappho, the first identifiable lesbian poet. This long tradition of lesbian poetry tells a story of struggle for survival and for freedom to write about feelings and experiences that have often been subject to censorship.

Sappho's poetry, like the poetry of many lesbian poets, has been banished, burned, tampered with, and discredited. Of the twelve thousand lines of poetry (nine volumes) estimated to have been written by Sappho, only six hundred lines have survived, most of them in broken fragments of dubious translation. Her most famous poem (and the only complete one we have), "Ode to Aphrodite," is a poem of unrequited love to a young maiden. In 1833, centuries after it was written, a translation became popular in which the maiden had conveniently changed sexes.[1] There will always be "scholars" who refused to acknowledge Sappho's lesbianism, as though to do so would somehow diminish the quality of her work.

The question of quality seems to loom as a large issue when lesbian poets are evaluated by traditional poetry critics. While pointing out the striking absence of lesbian poetry from mainstream literature, it is necessary to address the issue of quality if lesbian poetry is to survive as anything more than a weak facsimile of the real thing.

The fact is that there is a huge body of lesbian poetry. Much of it has been kept out of print for years, and has only begun to surface with the new freedom and awareness brought on by the women's movement and gay liberation of recent decades. While a wide variety of lesbian poetry can be found at feminist and lesbian/gay bookstores, it is rare to find lesbian poetry taught in college literature classes unless it is part of a program in women's studies. If it is there at all, it is likely to be well hidden, either by failure to identify the poet or by selection of poetry that is in itself not recognizable so it can be studied without the subject of lesbianism ever surfacing.

For example, the current edition of the *Norton Introduction to Literature* contains poetry by two lesbians, Audre Lorde and Adrienne Rich.[2] Both Lorde and Rich have long been self-identified as lesbian poets and it is an important element in their work, but in the Norton anthology they are carefully presented in neutral shades.

The two poems by Audre Lorde are "Hanging Fire," which is vaguely feminist, and "Recreation," a love poem possibly written to either sex. In neither poem is there the opportunity to learn about lesbian identity, nor is it mentioned in the biographical description of Lorde.

Norton's treatment of Adrienne Rich is more extensive and so her lesbianism is not as easily concealed. Yet in spite of Rich's strongly lesbian poem "Origins and History of Consciousness," which is reprinted from her book *The Dream of a Common Language*, the only way a student would know for certain from Norton that Adrienne Rich is a lesbian would be to find one tiny sentence at the very end of a long chronology that ends when Rich "leaves Douglass College and New York City; moves to a small town in western Massachusetts with 'the woman who shares my life.' "

In other words, you won't find openly lesbian poets in college English unless you know to search out the tidbit that may or may not be there in the first place. Certainly, there will be no acknowledgment or recognition of lesbian poets as a group or of their work as a permanent, important force in the world of poetry.

Surely there are more than two lesbians writing poetry that is fit to print. But perhaps it is not reasonable or wise to suggest that lesbian poets can or should be accepted for what they are without bringing extra pressures and expectations to bear on their poetry. Why should this poetry have to be singled out and presented differently from any other?

The major difference between lesbian poetry and any other is that it is written from a place outside the realm of male or heterosexual experience. This does not suggest that a special anthology or bookstore section is warranted. The poetry itself must certainly be evaluated according to the popular standards of the time. But the lesbian origin and content must not be clouded if the poetry is to retain its integrity and clarity.

Because it has proven so difficult to secure the lesbian's place in poetry without losing identity in the process, many lesbian poets would not lament their absence from the likes of the Norton anthology. Although there is a certain pride and respectability associated with being "required reading," lesbians have little to gain by seeking approval from traditional (often male) professors who still cannot stomach "women's poetry" and teach with great reluctance such poets as Sylvia Plath and Anne Sexton, classifying their poetry as "emotional" and "confessional" because it tells the truth about women's lives. If heterosexual women cannot write poetry that is taken seriously, how should lesbians go about having their poetry approved in an atmosphere in which their very presence is repugnant or forbidden?

Part of the beauty of the great and ever-flourishing lesbian poetry tradition is that it has happened in spite of and without help or approval from the very sources that can mean life or death to struggling writers. An occasional lesbian wins a male-bestowed award,[3] but the large community of lesbian poets exists for themselves, each other, and the satisfaction (and no small joy) that comes from knowing they have something special to say and the freedom to say it.

Such unrestricted freedom has meant that "bad" poetry is written by lesbians as well as any other poets. The responsibility of recognizing both strengths and weaknesses has brought an even greater freedom: the right to decide and determine new standards for what speaks poetry. Without asking permission from anyone, lesbian poets have taken upon themselves the freedom to build their words from the ground up, and make new forms of the art called poetry.

This poetry of a different sort is not so much a movement as a new genre. Perhaps in future anthologies of literature, it will have a place. For now, the lesbian poetry tradition seems proud and a little relieved to be outside the approval-if-you-do-it-our-way syndrome that has brought women poets up short for ages because they were expected to write like the popular male poets and to keep their womanhood, their pain, and especially their sexuality out of it if they wanted to be approved by the critical eye of the anthology-makers who dole out literature for public consumption.

Whether or not they are fit for a mass audience, lesbian poets have done it. Without approval, they have published one slim volume after another of their own doing. They have written the first explosive poem of their lives and gone on to fill whole volumes with what it means to be woman-loving in a world that does not love women. And they have taken the poems that are not anywhere to be found in "regular" anthologies, and they have anthologized themselves. When *Lesbian Poetry: An Anthology* was published in 1981, it was the first large collection of its kind, although the ground had been broken by a myriad of small volumes containing the work of a few lesbian poets here and there.[4]

Now there is much less scavenging to be done in order to find poets who write well and clearly of their lives as lesbians. In the 1981 anthology alone, there is the work of sixty-four different poets.[5] Here and elsewhere is proof that lesbians are skilled, articulate, and finely tuned poets. Beyond the striking range and depth of the work, there is the sense that this poetry means something more than the page or the words. It has been hard to come by, and in ways too deeply buried to be fully recognized by the casual reader, this poetry contains the spirit of lives that have long been silent.

To sit down with lesbian poetry is to delve into a world of women who have literally run for their lives—away from judgment, away from violence, away from suffocation. To teach their poetry is to force oneself to deal with the life behind the metaphor. Most lesbian poets write out of a personal identity that cannot be separated from their art. Each life is different and the poetry that comes out of that life weaves a story not duplicated in any other place or form.

If the body of lesbian poetry can be divided into manageable categories at all, it can only be seen as representative of all the emotions, frustrations, and wonders of living a life where women are the focus, the substance, and the root. No other group of poets have so given themselves to a task as the lesbians who write down their worst moments, their ecstasy, and the whole gamut of their existence.

The most easily defined lesbian poetry can be placed into niches of thought and feeling without doing it spiritual or rhetorical damage. Most clearly, it is radically political, deeply personal, intensely romantic, and frequently hilarious.

In women's communities that have sprung up in cities and countries everywhere, lesbian poetry can be observed as it is being created. The following poem was written by Pamela Gray of Oakland, California. Previously unpublished, it expresses the wry tolerance that some lesbians develop from living under constant attack.

Questions & Questions

Would you still be one if you weren't with her?
Would you still be one if you weren't in New York?
Would you still say you were one
If someone put hot pokers in your eyes?

Isn't it because you always wanted to be different?
Isn't it because you're easily influenced by friends?
Isn't it because your friends are so much older than you?
Isn't it because you think it goes with being an artist?

Is it because we didn't give you enough attention?
Is it because you went out with the wrong men?

Are you trying to get back at those men?
Are you trying to get back at us?

Why don't you go to a shrink?
Why don't you move out of there and in with a man?
Why won't you even consider our suggestions?
Aren't you too young to know your own mind?
How can you be so damned cocksure?

Did you have orgasms with men?
Do you have orgasms now?
Are you repulsed by a man's touch?
How many men have you been with?
How many women have you been with?

Do you love her?
Does she love you?
Is she faithful?
What else can she give you besides sex?
Do you promise not to tell your brother till after we're dead?
What is a lesbian?
Why must you always take the easy way out?

Copyright © 1983 by Pamela Gray

From questions that are used as weapons to devalue and distort lesbian
lives, to questions that haunt lesbian minds, there develops a profile of the
woman who has chosen to live in danger. It is a private and personal choice,
yet it becomes public and political for the lesbian poet. The next poem,
written by Susanna J. Sturgis of Washington, D.C., and also published here
for the first time, addresses the larger questions of survival and awareness.

This Is a Poem About Eyes Averted

This is a poem about eyes averted
about the day the metro crashed and three people died
and a Florida-bound jet swept commuters off
the 14th Street Bridge and followed them
into the icy river
and I knew
getting home alive
at the end
of the day
was not routine.

Once in Belfast I waited an hour in a rail station
bombed so often I was alone until just before the train left;
ten days later one pub I passed was rubble.
I guess a woman's raped every week
on one of the routes I often walk;
with eyes averted I have the nerve
to leave my house.

"Don't stare."
We polite children learn to turn away
from a scarred face, palsied hands, a woman's cane.
"Color-blindness" is said to be a virtue.
Tell me it's coincidence:
    suburban roads don't run through ghettos
    the interstates bypass stripmined hills
    the textbooks never mentioned us.
Once I heard a woman say
"No woman I know has been raped"
and two of her friends (there were six in the room)
said "I have."

"What you don't know can't hurt you."
An aching tooth, a lump in the breast, an unwritten poem
can't hurt you?

What you don't know about your own oppression
how you oppress
what you won't see
can't hurt you?

"Let sleeping dogs lie."

This friendship strangled in lies,
that one drowned in too much truth.
In fantasy I favor deserts—
endless horizons where nothing hides
save the deep-grown roots of the survivors;
my home New England rock and winter
strip me down to essence
but I live elsewhere,
cliches
are sleeping dogs,
words whose roots have died,
easy to let lie.

Hiking on the South Downs Way I learned
keep your eyes on the horizon and you'll trip on your feet.
At home I step through the thicket
of what all of us see
but pretend we don't:
who did what   to whom   and where,   even why—
from fiery crashes I turn away and think
how averted eyes
allow our survival
and stunt our growth.

Copyright © 1983 by Susanna J. Sturgis

Even the questions without answers are incorporated into the way
lesbians live with each other and cope with the world. The kinship of
lesbians as expressed in the poems seems intense and consuming, with

remarkable combining of young and old into one expanded generation. Mary Ann Daly, another Washington, D.C. poet, expresses this connection with eroticism and tenderness.

My Lover Was a Lesbian Before I Was Born

Purple veins vine the backs of her thighs.
The gap between her teeth sucks me up.
I wake:
who is this old woman in my bed?
The woman no one told me I should love
who works overtime in a gallery
where her own form is never depicted,
her own form
covered by a large man's shirt
who works standing on marble floors
long after her legs have started aching
the marble smooth & richly veined
as she is, but too hard.
Her form is not depicted
unless she comes home feeling good enough
to sit beside a mirror & draw
her big breasts resting on her belly;
I bury my face in her belly;
her smell is all I want until my fingers
find too tender juice coming from her cunt
which is lopsided
one lobe much bigger than the other
o sweet is her sweat.
No one told me I should love this woman
who found me waiting alone in the Club Madame
I depict this for you because you've never seen her
or the two of us
draped fetchingly across a new slick magazine car hood.
And no one suggested that a loved woman's face
might be a little rough with wrinkles & hair,
or that her voice might have a little twang.
No one told me I should love this woman
or any woman
in this way,
that my clitoris might fit so well
in the gap between her teeth.

Copyright © 1983 by Mary Ann Daly

Few lesbian poets are devoid of politics, meaning that they care deeply about what happens to women at the hands of men who batter, rape, and otherwise mutilate an existence that the lesbian would free from the control of heterosexual and patriarchal power. The anger of lesbians is profound in poetry that expresses what women have suffered in the name of femininity.

In *Lesbian Poetry*, the anthology mentioned earlier, Pat Parker pulls name after name of dead women out of "Movement in Black"—legacies of women whose suffering would not be expressed or approved of in traditional poetry. In "Need: A Choral of Black Women's Voices," Audre Lorde describes the living hell of women who hurt too much to live and yet die still fighting for survival. Jewish women who have died in the showers and ovens are immortalized in "Death Camp" by Irene Klepfisz. And "Rape" by Minnie Bruce Pratt tells ugly truths about little girls, young women, and old women alike who have bled and screamed and died because it was supposedly their "lot" as women.

In a few examples that only scratch the surface of the stories told in lesbian poetry, there is evidence of a far-reaching awareness that if anyone will bear witness to women's lives, it will likely be the lesbian poets who are writing their own experiences.

Here can be read the day-to-day torture that many women put themselves through in finding out that being lesbian can be a positive and fulfilling life. The agony of that process underlies much of this poetry, making it sharp with pain and longing for a personal peace. That others may find individual peace and freedom through reading poems that are brief synopses of lesbian lives is in itself justification for the struggle to do this literary work.

The freedom of lesbian love is at the root of these poems. Women find romance with each other as they have never known before. This poetry takes one woman back to her first crush at age thirteen, reminds another woman of a face not looked upon for twenty years.

The poets of the lesbian tradition, whether published or unpublished, whether blessed by formal acceptance of their "calmer" work or denied print because they don't fit in, provide the raw materials with which proud women-identified women can fashion their own culture. In doing so, these poets claim an identity no longer susceptible to the actions of those who find it threatening and unfamiliar. Lesbian poets will not be hampered, dishonored, or destroyed by those who find fault with their mere existence. They will continue to hold fast to their identity and reclaim their power with language in untamed, unapproved verse. And in decades to come, lesbian poetry will have as its most enduring beauty and value not that it duplicates other literature, but that it parallels the separate truths of lesbian lives.

Notes

1. A full discussion of this translation and other aspects of Sappho's work can be found in Dolores Klaich, *Woman Plus Woman: Attitudes Toward Lesbianism* (New York: William Morrow, 1974), p. 137.

2. The Norton anthology is one of the most widely used college texts in required literature courses. References given are from the third edition, 1981.

3. One of the most notable instances happened when Stanley Kunitz was bestowing the Yale Series of Younger Poets Awards. He apparently developed quite a liking for lesbian poetry and encouraged its brief proliferation at Yale University, of all places. Olga Broumas was one of the lesbian beneficiaries, given the award in 1977 for *Beginning With O* (New Haven: Yale University Press, 1977).

4. The largest of earlier collections was published by Out & Out Books (Brooklyn, N.Y.) in 1975. Called *Amazon Poetry,* it contained the work of thirty-eight lesbian poets.

5. Elly Bulkin and Joan Larkin, eds., *Lesbian Poetry: An Anthology* (Watertown, Mass.: Persephone Press, 1981).

19

Lesbians and Women's Music

MAIDA TILCHEN

*T*he most commercially successful and perhaps most spiritually unifying aspect of lesbian feminism has been "women's music," the network of records, record companies, live performances, production companies, and music festivals that has thrived in the last ten years. Women's music has probably been heard by most "out" lesbian feminists all over America and is also a growing influence in the Western European women's communities. Only ten years ago, there wasn't a single lesbian-controlled record album. In 1982, there are dozens of such albums available. Concerts are held regularly in all parts of the United States, even in some small cities in conservative regions. Three large annual music festivals attract thousands of women, with eight thousand traveling to the remote woods of northern Michigan every August for the Michigan Womyn's Music Festival held there. In the fall of 1982, two popular performers, Cris Williamson and Meg Christian, played in New York City's prestigious Carnegie Hall. There are several women-owned record companies with all-women staffs. The largest, Olivia Records in Oakland, California, has produced sixteen albums with worldwide sales of almost one million records. Women's music has provided an opportunity for hundreds of musicians, technicians, producers, and publicists to learn and try out new skills, opportunities that have been denied them in the extremely male-controlled field of commercial music.

Beyond the quantitative success, women's music has been very effective in spreading the messages of lesbianism and feminism. It has been an unparalleled outreach tool, putting the words of lesbian feminism into regular record stores in many cities. It has been played on the radio in many areas, and a documentary film about Olivia Records has been shown by many PBS TV stations. Reviews and articles about women's music have

appeared in many "straight" publications. Women's music concerts, particularly those held on college campuses, have introduced many women and
some men to lesbian liberation and feminism. Performer Holly Near has
been featured in *People* magazine, and appeared on "Sesame Street" and
many local city television shows. Her anti-nuke national concert tour in
1980, and her appearance at the June 12, 1982, massive disarmament
march at the United Nations brought women's music to a whole new audience. Margie Addam has toured many times on behalf of the National
Women's Studies Association and the ERA, reaching an audience familiar
with feminism but not necessarily lesbianism. Some women's music performers reach other music audiences: Robin Flower and Willie Tyson's records sell to country and folk audiences, while Kay Gardner's work is also
intended for New Age enthusiasts.

Issues raised by women's music have affected the women's community
in many ways. Women-only and lesbian-only concerts; accessibility for the
disabled; interpretation for the hearing-impaired; sliding scale fees and work
exchange for poor women; volunteer vs. paid work; political vs. love songs;
collective structures vs. capitalist methods; commercialism vs. intimacy;
outreach to the mainstream vs. cultural independence; politics vs. culture—
many of these issues have been recognized because of women's music events,
and the result has been widespread awareness, controversy, and change on
a national level. Women's music has made it necessary for many women
to translate their abstract political theories and ideals into concrete practices,
and to deal with the many contradictions that arise from such an effort.

In this article, I will attempt to give a brief historical background about
the beginnings of women's music, so that the reader in the '80s can gain
some understanding of the very modest and idealistic circumstances from
which today's women's music scene came. I will then discuss the content
of women's music, in terms of the lyrics and musical styles, also with the
intention of familiarizing newcomers. My intention is to convey the spirit
of what occurred and not to make any attempt at a complete historical
record. The role of lesbians in women's music will also be emphasized. Most
of the remarks quoted in this article come from interviews I did for articles
in Boston's *Gay Community News*.[1] It is my hope that this article will serve
as an informative and enjoyable introduction to women's music for those
who are unfamiliar with it.

The Origins

The Corkroom, a lesbian bar in Los Angeles, spring 1969: The women's
movement was beginning to hit the mass media, and the Stonewall riots
would happen that June. In the bar a regular performer, a woman folk

singer, warmed up the audience with "Freight Train" and some Woody Guthrie tunes. Then she sang a song she had written herself in a sudden impulsive fit of anger:

> I hate not being able
> To hold my lover's hand
> 'cept under some dimly lit table
> Afraid of being who I am
>
> I hate to tell lies
> Live in the shadow of fear
> We've run half of our lives
> From that damn word queer
>
> It's not your wife that I want
> It's not your children I'm after
> It's not even my choice I want to flaunt
> Just want to hear my lover's laughter
>
> Feel like we're animals in cages
> Have you seen the lights in a gay bar
> Not revealing wrinkles or rages
> God forbid we reveal who we are
>
> I hate not being able
> To hold my lover's hand
> 'cept under some dimly lit table
> Afraid of being who I am
> No longer afraid
> In fact damn proud of being
> A lesbian[2]

© 1969, 1977 by Maxine Feldman, Atthis Music Publishers BMF. Used by permission.

The audience was stunned. Their jaws dropped. The bar owner told the performer, Maxine Feldman, "You're making people think, not drink, and that's not what gay entertainment is about."

That's Maxine Feldman's story of how she began to create women's music. The song she sang that night, entitled "Angry Atthis," was the first women's music record to be released, as a 45-rpm single. There had been some records before that marketed to lesbians, and the tunes of lesbian favorites Dusty Springfield and Leslie Gore had been heard at many lesbian parties and in bar jukeboxes, but "Angry Atthis" was clearly the beginning of a new kind of music, music with explicitly lesbian lyrics done by "out" lesbian performers, and produced by lesbian-controlled companies.

Around the same time as the ideas of lesbian liberation were spreading, the second wave of women's liberation was trying to find new ways to reach women with its theories and actions. Susan Abod was probably typical of millions of women who began to think about feminism in 1970, but she went a step further. As she told me:

I was straight, but I was starting to reevaluate my role as a woman in society, and my relationships with men. The ideas of feminism sort of "lit the lightbulb" in my mind. I wanted to work on changing things so they weren't so oppressive. I decided to check out what was happening, and to try to get involved. I heard that a band was starting in Chicago, so I auditioned for them. They liked my singing, and they needed a bass player, so I learned bass and that's how I ended up playing with the Chicago Women's Liberation Rock Band for three years. . . .

Our band spent a lot of time examining the lyrics of rock songs, and the way men performed rock. Lyrics like "Under My Thumb" by the Rolling Stones, and the very macho ways men used their guitars on stage, sometimes fucking them in pantomime, were examined by us. We watched movies and imitated what the men did, but when we did it, everyone would laugh. We'd get down and grind and the audience would respond theatrically and act like groupies. They'd do this whole trip and it was great, there would be this wonderful release of saying, "Look how disgusting this is, and why is it like this, and why can't we change it?"

We played mostly at colleges for white women. The students would get funds to hold meetings or conferences, and we would play at these, in between the meetings and lectures. Naomi Weisstein would give "raps" between our songs, about things like the use of the word "chick" and other consciousness-raising issues. . . . In those early years, at least in Chicago, culture was not deemed important to the feminist movement. The movement saw literature and organizations as the outreach tool to reach the masses, not music.

. . . One typical concert was the second gig we did, a benefit in a tiny restaurant in Chicago. We didn't play very well, but the room was packed and every one of those two hundred or so women and men were jumping up and down and energized. It was primarily women, but also men and kids. Everybody was thrilled that we were doing this, that we were visible, that there was music for what they were all struggling with. It was great.

At this period in women's music, feminism, not lesbianism, was the major focus. As Susan Abod describes her experience:

At the time I first got involved with feminism and the band, I didn't think of lesbianism as an alternative, and I don't think a lot of women did in 1970. There were lesbians in our band, but we didn't talk about it or deal with it. The lesbians were very timid about bringing it up. Nobody ever came up with a lesbian song, and I think, since I was straight then, I would have felt uncomfortable singing one. Our band played mostly mixed benefits, where we didn't deal with lesbianism. I think we also got off the hook because Linda Shear's band, "Family of Women," which was lesbian separatist, was playing in the Chicago area around then. I think, though, that what was happening in our band was a microcosm of what was going on in the feminist movement at the time. Lesbians were timid at first, but their needs were not being met, so finally they walked out and started their own things.

The summer of 1974 brought a landmark event to women's music: the First National Women's Music Festival was held at the University of Illinois campus at Champaign-Urbana. Many women who had been doing music in various parts of the country met there for the first time, and a great deal of networking and energizing occurred. That summer and fall saw the first concert tours by Casse Culver and Margie Addam, who were the first to bring live women's music to many smaller cities. There wasn't any tradition or precedent for the tours, but somehow the performers were able to find volunteers in various towns who would find a place and a sound system, publicize the concert, and try to convince women in their communities to risk their money and see this innovation.

I spoke with Margie Addam after she played to an audience of twenty-three women in Bloomington, Indiana, in the fall of 1974. Her remarks at that time reveal how undeveloped women's music was then:

> I feel that there are a lot of women who are turning to women's culture, because we finally have some artists who are willing to speak from a woman's experience. I've just played a few places in the Midwest, compared that to what I've seen in California, and there's definitely a growing audience. There definitely is a need for it to be made clear what the audience needs in having their experience translated into music.

> In the past year, there have been individual women crisscrossing the country: Cris Williamson, Meg Christian, and Casse Culver. Individually, they are hacking out a loosely-defined network of places to play. I'm gathering information on my tour, which I will communicate to the rest. Right now this network is word-of-mouth. What I envision, and this is one of my dreams, is having a more defined organization, so that women musicians who are interested in traveling and sharing their music all over the country can contact one specific place for information about various cities and local producers. I'd like to be able to set up a tour so that my expenses can be split among several groups in different cities.

These early tours were done in very modest circumstances. Local production was done by volunteers, many of whom had never produced before. The performance spaces were usually college lecture halls, and the sound systems were notoriously poor. Performers usually hoped to earn at least their traveling expenses and a bed for the night, and it was only economically feasible for solo acts to tour. The audiences were small, but growing. Maxine Feldman describes one of her early tours:

> The first time I toured the U.S. it was on the $50 go-anywhere Greyhound pass. I didn't make any money, but I did it so that people would know my name. I played in any small or large town, for any women's center or tiny group that could gather. I met wonderful women all across the country.

Although the expensive business of producing a record seemed remote to women musicians in the early seventies, the goal was getting closer for some. Alix Dobkin, who had played in the straight folk music circuit for ten years, had begun to play music for lesbians in 1972. She found an enthusiastic audience in the New York City area. She formed a band called Lavender Jane with flutist Kay Gardner and bass player Pat Attom. As Alix recounts in her article "Lavender Jane Loves Women":

> Kay and I were constantly asked, "When are you going to make a record?" One night in September 1973, during a cruise on the Hudson River for five hundred lesbians, we were approached by a dozen of them who offered us enough money to make a lesbian record. It was a good place for Lavender Jane to be launched—a boatload of dancing and partying dykes listening to live music from the New Haven Women's Liberation Rock Band.[3]

Alix was able to locate a lesbian sound engineer, Marilyn Ries, instruments were borrowed, songs chosen and arranged, and the record—with a budget of $3,300—was made in November 1973. An organization entitled The Women's Music Network, Inc. was formed, intended to someday realize visionary plans for a "nationwide, nonprofit, corporate empire of women's music" as Alix calls it. "Since we had made a record from practically nothing, we felt that we could accomplish anything." A thousand copies of *Lavender Jane Loves Women* were assembled into their jackets and covers glued on at the first meetings of the Women's Music Network. In 1981, I asked Kay Gardner what she had envisioned happening. She responded:

> When we did *Lavender Jane* we put it all under an umbrella corporation called Women's Music Network because both Alix and I envisioned a large network of women's music. We envisioned that it would grow, and it did, incredibly. When you're a visionary, when you have some of that in you, you know that you are working towards something that's much bigger than anything is at the beginning. And it certainly has grown into something more professional, which can go either way.

The first one thousand copies of *Lavender Jane Loves Women* sold out in three months. There was no distribution system for it, and mainstream record outlets would not carry it, but word-of-mouth, mail order, and feminist and lesbian bookstores all helped disperse the copies.

It soon became apparent that not only was operating capital necessary for women's music to produce records, but that a distribution system would be equally important. At that time, no one had any hopes of getting regular record stores, usually controlled by monopolistic multinational corporations, to carry independent label records of such a radical nature. Furthermore, the politics of many women musicians precluded this. They wanted all aspects of the women's music system to remain in the hands of women.

Not long after the *Lavender Jane* album, Olivia Records was started by Ginny Berson, Meg Christian, Judy Dlugacz, and others. They were inspired by a chance suggestion of Cris Williamson that they start a women's record company. Berson was a member of the Furies, a feminist consciousness-raising group in Washington, D.C. that included writer Rita Mae Brown, photographer JEB (Joan E. Biren), feminist theorist Charlotte Bunch, and Coleta Reid, who founded Diana Press, one of the first lesbian-owned publishing houses. With help from the Furies and others, and despite a lack of experience or money, Olivia released its first record in 1973, a 45-rpm single with sides by Cris and Meg. Sales of the single seeded Olivia's first album.[4]

Olivia recognized the need for a distribution system, and began to develop one. At first, Ginny Berson would ask the audience at each concert for volunteers to sell the record in local areas. Although no money was to be made, help was forthcoming, and gradually a network of distributors was developed. Adding on the women's and lesbian bookstores and mail order sales, Olivia was able to distribute their albums as they came out, starting with Meg Christian's *I Know You Know* in 1974. For some time, Olivia insisted that the distribution system be for Olivia products only. But as more albums began to come out on other independent women's labels, the local distributors rebelled and began to carry all records available. Over the years, the distributors organized their own national organization, the Women's Independent Label Distributors. They agreed to map out exclusive geographical territories so that they would not be competing with each other. Various decisions were made with the record companies that would make the distribution system economically feasible. The increased volume of sales has allowed most distributors to be paid for their time. And the success of women's music has changed the attitude of mainstream stores that once refused to carry records that didn't go through "proper channels." They now get the records on women's terms or not at all. Says distributor Trish Karlinski, who covers the New England region:

> If the straight store in Portsmouth, New Hampshire, didn't carry women's music, all the women in that area would have to drive to Boston to get their albums. They shouldn't have to do that. It's accessibility as well as economics. The mere existence of a women's music network is political, because there are hundreds of women involved in that network who are surviving and making music. We have a network all our own, separate from the mainstream industry, and it went that way because the mainstream industry wouldn't meet our needs and would oppress us to an incredible degree.

The growth of women's music has truly snowballed since the assembly of the distribution system. Many record companies have developed, but Olivia remains the largest. Galaxia Records in Massachusetts also offers records by several different artists. Their record of the New England Women's Symphony Orchestra has sold well to classical record buyers. Most of the other record companies have produced only the records by the artist who runs the company, such as Margie Addam's Pleiades Records, Holly Near's Redwood Records, and Judy Reagan's Wild Patience Records.

Concert production has also moved beyond the volunteer stage. Polly Laurelchild, who produces concerts in Boston, told me,

> I feel that women deserve the best. I'm not going to spend a hundred dollars less and have crummy sound. Another thing is location. The concert should be accessible to many communities. We chose to present Mary Watkins and Linda Tillery at a theater near the black community. There has to be respect for the audience and the artist, and one thing that shows that respect is the quality of performance. You can enhance it by having a good hall and good tech, or make it sound much worse with a poor hall and poor teching. So it is a choice that's political, and artistic, and a matter of pride.

Music festivals have been very important to the growth of women's music. The first national festival held in Champaign-Urbana, Illinois, had an unquestionably catalyzing effect on developing a national network for women's music. This festival was held every year through 1980, and in 1982 it moved to Bloomington, Indiana.

In 1976, some women in Michigan spent four hundred dollars to rent some remote wilderness land for a few days in August on which to hold a music festival. To their surprise, twenty-five hundred women showed up from all over the country. Within a few years, the festival was attracting about eight thousand women to camp on totally undeveloped land with little water and no buildings. The Michigan Womyn's Music Festival has indisputably become *the* annual event for lesbian feminists from all over the world. For four days every year, women can live in a woman-only, idyllic world of sunny days warming bare breasts and starry nights with the full moon shining through the trees and over the stage. Two other large regional festivals are held in northern California and Connecticut. Many small festivals are also held around the country.

Women's music has had astounding growth in the thirteen years since Maxine Feldman shocked the customers of the Corkroom. It is now more often referred to as the women's music industry than as the network of Alix Dobkin and Kay Gardner's visions. The lyrical content and musical styles have also gone in many directions since the days when the Chicago Women's Liberation Rock Band was parodying rock music. In the next section, I will familiarize the reader with the many different styles included in women's music.

What Is Women's Music?

This is a question that has no indisputable answer. For its first few years, even the term *women's music* was not singularly recognized. Maxine Feldman told me of the first time that she realized that there was women's music:

> It was at the 1973 West Coast Lesbian Conference. On stage were myself; Robin Flower; Naomi Littlebear, later of the band Isquierda; Debbie Lempke, later of the Berkeley Women's Music Collective; Family of Women, the Chicago band that included Linda Shear; a local band which became Be Be K'Roche; and Margie Addam. It wasn't called women's music then. We didn't know what to call it. It was just this phenomenon that someone else was making the same music. I think a lot of women didn't want to call it "lesbian music," so they called it "women's music." Lots of terms were going around between '73 and '75: "women-identified women's music," "lesbian feminist music," "feminist music," and finally the word became "women's music." It wasn't the Rolling Stones singing "Under My Thumb"—it was different.

Confusion over what to call it reflects the still ongoing dispute over what is women's music. Some women have always seen it as a "nice name" for lesbian music, a name that permitted performances in space that would otherwise be unavailable and unsafe. It also would draw in listeners who would never attend a "lesbian music" concert. Others say that women's music began in the straight feminist movement, and was taken over by lesbians when they broke away to form their own movement and culture. Certainly, all along there have been straight women performers such as Kristin Lems and Johanna Cazden, who have written and performed to women's and mixed audiences for years. There are also lesbian performers who downplay their lesbianism in order to appeal to wider audiences. In the 1980s, some of the strongest political messages from women musicians have been heard in the punk/New Wave scene, which, like women's music, is an alternative to the multinational record industry. Punk performers and audiences are often mixes of straight, lesbian, and gay men and women. Lesbian punk musicians, many of whom find the musical styles of women's music not to their liking, insist that they are invalidated by a narrow definition of women's music, one that only reflects the lesbian feminist community of the 1970s.

There have been at least four major trends in the content of women's music. These are (1) separatist, (2) innovative, (3) political, and (4) women-produced. (These terms are mine and are intended to be descriptive, not judgmental.) Performers and creators of each of these types of music tend to consider their type as having legitimate claim to being the real women's music, although most recognize the validity of other claims. I shall try to give some idea of each type.

Separatist Music

Separatist music is music performed by lesbians for lesbian-only or women-only audiences. Two names particularly associated with separatist music are Linda Shear and Alix Dobkin. Both have released records marked "This music is for women" or "For sale to lesbians only," and Linda Shear's album says "This album is not for public broadcast (until we control our own airwaves)." At the 1979 Michigan Womyn's Music Festival (and possibly at other festivals) Shear requested that nonlesbians leave the listening audience during her concert. Her explanation was that she wanted to speak to lesbians, and didn't want to worry that she might offend nonlesbians by her exclusivity.

Even within separatist music, there have been disputes over whether performances should be to lesbians only or women only. On her album jacket, Linda Shear explains her evolution from a "wimmin-only" performer to a lesbian-only one. She says that she knew her audiences were mostly lesbians, but that when she began a stated policy of lesbian-only concerts, the quality of the performance changed in a way that she found worthwhile. She felt that the presence of straight women carried lesbian power and energy to the "enemy" (men) and wanted to make it clear that the needs of lesbians are not the needs of all women, and that lesbians need to develop their own culture. She began doing lesbian-only concerts in early 1976.

Alix Dobkin is undoubtedly one of the most influential lesbians of the post-Stonewall years, and one would be hard-pressed to say whether Alix's personal lifestyle set the style for lesbians in the seventies, or if Alix perfectly captured the existing style. Living in the country, shaved head, flannel and denim clothes, lesbian-only space, and uncompromising separatist politics characterize Dobkin's style. Although it was the first lesbian album, *Lavender Jane Loves Women,* for which Alix wrote most of the songs, is still the most blatant statement of lesbian pride on vinyl, with lyrics such as this one from "Talking Lesbian":

> Course it ain't quite that simple, so I better explain
> Just why you've got to ride on the lesbian train
> Cause if you wait for the man to straighten out your head
> You'll all be a-waitin', then you'll all be dead.[5]
>
> © Alix Dobkin

Alix's following albums, released in 1976 and 1981, have continued her separatist stance, although her idealistic visions have been somewhat tempered by the reality of a decade of lesbian feminism. Her 1976 album was titled *Living With Lesbians,* but a song on 1981's *XX ALIX* album is called "Living with Contradictions."

Those who expect women-only concerts to consist of angry man-hating lyrics are quickly disarmed by the warm, intimate, good-humored, and women-affirming style of Alix Dobkin. As of fall 1982, she is one of few musicians who will only perform for women-only audiences. In the 1980s there has been much discussion of the availability and validity of women-only space. Growing consciousness in the lesbian community about racism and sexual minorities has led to a questioning of separatist ideals, and many producers now find women-only and lesbian-only space impossible to justify with their political beliefs. At the same time, a growing dissatisfaction among many lesbians with the dilution of women's music into much less overt lesbian content meant to appeal to broader audiences has led to a slowly growing movement of women hoping to revive women-only concerts.

Innovative Music

Another strain of women's music I have termed *innovative*. Kay Gardner is probably the best-known proponent of this style. Kay began her involvement with women's music by coproducing the *Lavender Jane* album with Alix Dobkin, but the two later went their separate ways. A classically trained musician, Kay has been trying to discover aspects of music that are unique to women. She has done extensive historical research to find out the instruments and styles in which women-only music has been played in many cultures. Her recorded music on such albums as *Mooncircles* includes music played in the obsolete Mixolydian mode, which was said to have been invented by Sappho. She uses instruments such as the flute, finger cymbals, tambourine, and drum, which women can be seen playing in ancient artwork. Most recently, she has been researching the connection between spiritual methods of healing and music, uncovering ancient theories that suggest that specific musical tones have healing effects on specific parts of the body. On the *Mooncircles* liner notes, Kirsten Grimsted writes:

> The concept of music having a biological function diverges sharply from the respected tradition of social protest music from which much of women's music derives. . . . The assumption underlying such criticism is that attunement to nature and to one's biological heritage are by necessity inimical to the cause of social activism. . . . But [*Mooncircles*] is above all not a nostalgic flight away from the pain of reality but rather a journey into awareness of the strength and wholeness in our heritage, which fortifies women for the present and gives impetus to our struggles to regain, come what may, that lost wholeness in our future.[6]

The theme of women's spirituality that pervades Gardner's work does appear in the music of many other musicians—in fact it might be said that it is a women's music convention to have one "goddess" song on every album. Many women musicians do believe that a woman-produced album will generate de facto a style of music unique to women.

Political Music

The most common style in women's music is the topically political style, with *political* being defined broadly. (And the music I have already termed *separatist* and *innovative* is certainly political, too.) Writers such as Holly Near and the Berkeley Women's Music Collective touch on many current concerns of feminists, and serve to communicate messages about events and issues and suggest ways in which women may respond to these. For example, Holly Near's *Imagine My Surprise!* album mentions the following topics in the course of its songs: lesbian liberation; mental illness; the censorship of women's art; violence against women; destruction of the environment; oppression of women in Chile; disabled women; and alcoholic women. It's no wonder that Holly also includes the song "You Bet," in which she justifies writing and singing both love songs, "sweet melodies of women loving," and songs of women "living the lives that inspire the songs of women working/fighting for our senses courageously." Sings Near, "Our everyday lives, the changes inside/Become our political songs."[7] [Lyrics © 1978 by Hereford Music/Thumbelina]

The Berkeley Women's Music Collective, which disbanded in 1979 after six years of performances and two albums, not only sang on political topics but also tried to maintain a collective structure to live out their feminist ideals. A song by Nancy Vogl on their *Tryin' to Survive* album captures the essence of women's music's protest against mainstream music. In the song "California" she begins with lovely verses about the beauties of California, a prevalent topic in pop music, but then goes on to challenge the racist history that has preserved the white-only images of California in popular songs:

> Who lived in California?
> Who worked in California?
> Miwok, Mohave, Piute and Pomo
> Chinese, Chicana and Japanese
> Filipina, Black and Latina
> Oklahoma refugees . . .[8]

© 1978 by Nancy Vogl

One ever-growing aspect of women's music has been the focus on music by women of color. Olivia Records has always had many women of color involved in their albums as session musicians and technicians, and has produced albums by Mary Watkins, Linda Tillery, and June Millington. Most recently, June Millington did a national tour in 1982 with an all-women-of-color band. These musicians have brought many stylistic changes to women's music, which at first was characterized by an acoustic, folk, solo-performer style. The introduction of electric instruments, intricate percussion sections, large brass sections, back-up singers, and high-energy dance music was brought about by the cultural expansion of women's music.

Music Produced by Women

Definition of the last category of women's music is quite controversial. Over the years, many albums released into the women's music market have had lyrics so vague that one is hard-pressed to categorize them as lesbian or specifically feminist in a rhetorical sense. They do express belief and support for women, and do not encourage heterosexuality. Their production has been by women-only companies and staff, and their primary audience has been the women's music circuit. Some argue that music produced by women must be essentially unique, although on many of these albums quite conventional musical styles, instrumentation, and lyrics give them a sound quite similar to the soft rock of the seventies mainstream. The content concerns primarily love, nature, and self-belief. Cris Williamson, June Millington, and Woody Simmons might be placed in this category. All three have been active in women's music production for many years, and both Williamson and Millington came to women's music after unhappy experiences in mainstream music, in which both had been featured on albums over which they had had little control. Wrote Williamson on her liner notes for her album *The Changer and the Changed:*

> I returned from the First National Women's Music Festival filled with such warmth in my soul, and I ran to my piano to capture the beautiful strength of women and its impact on me.[9]

Some performers who see themselves primarily as musicians have apparently found themselves quite uncomfortable with the expectations of the audience that they include succinct political statements in their music. A desire to reach wider audiences has also been given as a reason for softening the content. Said June Millington, "If performers are not deluding themselves inside, then they are not diluting their product. . . . If they feel really strong within themselves and in their identity and what they are doing, then there's no way anybody can touch them. The fact that people who aren't into them and their ideas are listening to the music should really be giving them energy. . . . There are born-again Christians, hopefully there will be born-again feminists, of both sexes."

Cris Williamson wrote what is probably the best-known and best-loved lyric in women's music:

> When you open up your life to the living,
> all things come spilling in on you
> And you're flowing like a river,

the Changer and the Changed
You've got to spill some over, spill some over. . . .
Filling up and spilling over, it's an endless waterfall
Filling up and spilling over, over all.[10]

© 1975 by Bird Ankles Music, Cris Williamson

The many controversies about the definition of women's music all add up to the fact that women's music cannot be clearly defined or described. Aside from the categories of music described above, all of which are heard on women-owned labels, there are many records by women performers on many other independent and mainstream labels. Many people consider these to be very much a part of women's music also. Even among those who insist that women's music must be produced only by women, the definition is not so clear-cut. A male-to-female transsexual engineered several Olivia albums, in addition to the presence of men in various technical roles on many albums. Some of the earliest women's music albums were produced largely by men because women-owned facilities and technicians were not available. The audiences for women's music have consisted largely of women, but many performers clearly want to expand to mixed audiences. And punk/New Wave music seems to be luring away women's audiences, plus attracting young lesbians who have come out so recently that they consider women's music to be old-fashioned and before their time. Despite the hopes for longevity by its founders, it is becoming clear that women's music is as subject to fads as any other type of popular music. But perhaps some compromise will be reached. One of the highlights of the 1982 Michigan festival was an open mike performer called Punk Mary. She sang, while in punk regalia, and in punk style, an angry, screaming piece called "I Hate Men."

Another aspect of women's music that must be mentioned is the support it has given to women moving into traditionally male roles in music. Classical musicians have put together women's symphony orchestras, with women conductors, performing works by women composers. The group Alive!, which has released two albums on women's labels and has done many national tours, is making a name for itself in traditional jazz circles. Robin Flower's band has helped carve a place for women instrumentalists in folk and bluegrass, a field where women have been singers, not players. While the feminist movement has given the theory and encouragement for women to move into traditionally male occupations, women's music, as a network or industry, has provided the real opportunity for women to work as performers, technicians, and producers in order to learn and practice the skills necessary for actually obtaining those jobs, whether they continue to work in all-women companies or take jobs in the mainstream. As the women of Olivia Records stated in 1975:

> Our purposes are to make high quality women's music available to the public, to give women musicians access to the recording industry, to offer training in the technical, musical and other fields related to the recording industry, and to provide jobs with decent pay in non-oppressive conditions. . . . The owners of this company are the women who work for it.[11]

Conclusion

How well has women's music succeeded in realizing the visions of its originators, the needs of the lesbian feminist community, and the expectations of its workers? This is quite a controversial topic. The quantitative success of women's music has been the establishment of an international network for performance and record distribution, plus the production of the many records. There are many women whose lives have been improved by the opportunity to work in women's music; and countless women have been affected by the messages of women's music. These are clearly the realizations of the dreams.

On the other hand, two recent articles in the feminist press reveal some disturbing developments. In the August 1982 issue of *Plexus,* a punk musician describes how she "humps" her guitar to give the audience a thrill, with no parody or political statement being intended. In the August 1982 issue of *Sojourner,*[12] a musician who is just beginning to perform for women discusses how she views the existing women's music scene as established and closed to newcomers. She claims that she doesn't resent the fact that there is no opportunity for her to break in, and she feels she will have to make her own way, even if it means setting up her own production and distribution network. Audiences, meanwhile, complain of high prices for concert tickets and records. Producers counter that they will no longer work for nothing, and take monetary risks to present newcomers or less popular performers. The owners of record companies talk of huge financial losses and the competition caused by so many albums attempting to reach a relatively small and economically poor market. It is very clear that in 1982 money is a primary factor in the existence of women's music. The unpaid volunteers who built up women's music are no longer available, for the idealism of the early years has turned to much more sophisticated attitudes.

What will women's music sound and look like in the future? Three groups of women will influence its direction: (1) The existing audience, which is sentimental and loyal to the women's music they have known and loved, and which is proving quite resistant to change. (2) The women who have been involved in the creation and production of women's music, who are struggling to satisfy personal artistic and political needs, the audience's expectations, and financial realities. (3) The future women's community, which includes both the women who will be coming out as lesbians, and the lesbians current and future who will decide to express and share their talents with the community.

This last group represents an unknown factor in the current delicate balance between consumers and producers of women's music. The extent to which they emulate or reject the ideals and experiences of their predecessors will play a powerful role in determining the future of women's music, and with it, probably, the direction of most of lesbian feminist culture. For women's music has proved, beyond a doubt, the immense power of music as an organizing tool in our community. It has brought together lesbian visions and realities, and challenged each of us to satisfy both.

Notes

1. Some of the unfootnoted quotes appearing in this article were first used in "Women's Music: Politics for Sale?" by Maida Tilchen, in *Gay Community News* (167 Tremont St., Boston, MA 02111), vol. 8, no. 45, June 6, 1981, GCN Music Supplement, pp. 1–5, 8, 12. Other unfootnoted quotes are taken from interviews that I have done as a lesbian journalist.

2. Lyrics from "Angry Atthis," © 1969, 1977 by Maxine Feldman. This song may not be reproduced in part or whole or be recorded by any means without written permission of the publisher, Atthis Music, 83 Dartmouth St., Boston, MA 02116.

3. Alix Dobkin, "Lavender Jane Loves Women," in Margaret Cruikshank, ed., *The Lesbian Path* (Monterey, Calif.: Angel Press, 1980), p. 204.

4. From "Olivia Records' 10th Anniversary Calls For An Encore" by Susan Wilson, in the *Boston Globe*, 29 November 1982, p. 22.

5. Lyrics from "Talking Lesbian" by Alix Dobkin on the album *Lavender Jane Loves Women*, 1975, from Ladyslipper Music, Box 3124, Durham, NC 27705.

6. Liner notes on the album *Mooncircles*, by Kay Gardner, 1974, Urana Records, available from Ladyslipper Music, Box 3124, Durham, NC 27705.

7. Lyrics from "You Bet," words by Holly Near, music by Meg Christian, © 1978 by Hereford Music/Thumbelina, from the album *Imagine My Surprise!*, Redwood Records. All rights reserved. Holly Near's albums and songbooks are available from Redwood Records, 476 W. MacArthur Blvd., Oakland, CA 94609. "B'lieve I'll Run On . . ." by Sweet Honey in the Rock is also available from Redwood Records.

8. Lyrics from "California" by Nancy Vogl on the album *Tryin' to Survive* by the

Berkeley Women's Music Collective, © 1978 by Nancy Vogl. Album distributed by Galaxia Records, Box 212, Woburn, MA 01801.

9. Liner notes from the album *The Changer and the Changed* by Cris Williamson, available from Olivia Records, 4400 Market Street, Oakland, CA 94608.

10. Lyrics from "Waterfall" by Cris Williamson on the album *The Changer and the Changed.* © 1975 by Bird Ankles Music and Cris Williamson.

11. Liner notes from *The Changer and the Changed.*

12. D. J. Adler, "Blazing Our Own Trails," *Sojourner,* August 1982: pp. 21, 30.

Glossary

amazon: Another term for lesbian.

butch-fem relationship: Lesbian relationships not intended to be replicas of heterosexual relationships. Joan Nestle has described the butch-fem relationship as "an erotic partnership, serving both as a conspicuous flag of rebellion and as an intimate exploration of women's sexuality."

coming out: Acknowledgment of lesbian or gay identity to one's self and others. Also may refer to first same-sex sexual experience.

dyke: Another term for lesbian. Usually considered as a positive term if used among lesbians but a negative term if used by outsiders.

gay: A term that can be used in reference to both lesbians and homosexual males. Although many lesbians consider *gay* a male term, it remains the most frequent general term for female and male homosexuals.

herstory: Women's history. Often used to refer to lesbian history.

heterosexism: The belief that everyone is or should be heterosexual.

homophile: Another term for homosexual, more commonly used prior to 1970.

homophobia: Fear of homosexuality in oneself or others. Doris Davenport has suggested the term *lesbophobia* to be applied more directly to the fear of lesbianism.

The Ladder: Considered by most lesbians to be the first important lesbian periodical in the United States, published monthly from October 1956 through September 1967 and every two months thereafter until it ceased publication in 1972.

lesbian community: A term that can refer to a group of lesbians living in one geographical area, such as lesbians living in Lincoln, Nebraska, or that can be used in reference to a political sense of solidarity and encompass vast geographical areas, such as the lesbian community in the United States, or the Canadian lesbian community.

Oedipus complex: The stage of psychosocial development, according to psychoanalysts, in which the child is said to have feelings of sexual desire toward one parent along with feelings of rivalry toward the other parent. Most commonly the term is used to describe the son's sexual desire for his mother as his first love object.

second wave of feminism: Political resurgence of feminism that began in the United States in the 1960s.

sexual identity: One's sense of one's sexuality; that which differentiates homosexuals from heterosexuals.

sexual orientation: Term suggesting that an individual is naturally inclined toward a particular sexual identity. Some sociologists and psychologists would say that orientations are set up in early childhood, while others would note that orientations may be quite open and flexible throughout the entire life cycle.

sexual preference: Term connoting that one is free to choose a particular sexual identity.

socialization: Lifelong learning process whereby one develops a self-identity.

women-identified women: Women who relate emotionally and/or sexually to other women. While this term technically can refer to feminist heterosexual women, it is used in this anthology to refer exclusively to lesbians.

women of color: Women of African, Asian, Latin American, or American Indian origin.

Selected Bibliography:
1972–1983

Abbott, Sidney, and Barbara Love. *Sappho Was a Right-On Woman: A Liberated View of Lesbianism.* New York: Stein & Day, 1972.

Adair, Nancy, and Casey Adair. *Word Is Out: Stories of Some of Our Lives.* New York: Dell, 1978.

Albro, Joyce, and Carol Tully. "A Study of Lesbian Lifestyles in the Homosexual Micro-Culture and the Heterosexual Macro-Culture." *Journal of Homosexuality* 4 (Summer 1979): 331–44.

Allen, Paula Gunn. *Coyote's Daylight Trip.* Albuquerque, N. Mex.: La Confluencia, 1978.

——— . *A Cannon Between My Knees.* New York: Strawberry Press, 1981.

Allison, Dorothy. "Confrontation Black White: Interview with Ginny Apuzzo and Betty Powell." *Quest* 3 (Spring 1977): 34–46.

Baetz, Ruth. *Lesbian Crossroads: Personal Stories of Lesbian Struggles and Triumphs.* New York: William Morrow, 1980.

Baracks, Barbara, and Kent Jarratt, eds. *Sage Writings From the Lesbian and Gay Men's Writing Workshop at Senior Action in a Gay Environment.* New York: Teachers and Writers Collaborative Publications, 1980.

Barnhart, Elizabeth. "Friends and Lovers in a Lesbian Counterculture Community." In *Old Family/New Family,* edited by Nona Glazer-Malbin, pp. 90–115. New York: Van Nostrand, 1975.

Bayer, Ronald. *Homosexuality and American Psychiatry: The Politics of Diagnosis.* New York: Basic Books, 1981.

Beck, Evelyn Torton. *Nice Jewish Girls: A Lesbian Anthology.* Watertown, Mass.: Persephone Press, 1982.

Bell, Alan P., and Martin S. Weinberg. *Homosexualities: A Study of Diversity Among Men and Women.* New York: Simon & Schuster, 1978.

Bell, Alan P., Martin S. Weinberg, and Sue Kiefer Hammersmith. *Sexual Preference: Its Development in Men and Women.* Bloomington, Ind.: Indiana University Press, 1981.

Bernikow, Louise. *The World Split Open: Four Centuries of Women Poets in England and America, 1552–1950.* New York: Random House, 1974.

Bethel, Lorraine, and Barbara Smith, eds. "The Black Women's Issue." *Conditions: Five* (Autumn 1979).

Birkby, Phyllis; Bertha Harris; Jill Johnston; Ester Newton; and Jane O'Wyatt, eds. *Amazon Expedition: A Lesbian Feminist Anthology.* New York: Times Change Press, 1973.

Bogus, SDiane. *Sapphire's Sampler: An Anthology of Poetry, Prose, and Drama.* College Corner, Ohio: WIM Publications, 1982.

Boxer, Marilyn. "For and About Women: The Theory and Practice of Women's Studies in the United States." *Signs: Journal of Women in Culture and Society* 7 (Spring 1982): 661–95.

Brady, Maureen, and Judith McDaniel. "Lesbians in the Mainstream: Images of Lesbians in Recent Commercial Fiction." *Conditions: Six* (Summer 1980): 82–105.

Broumas, Olga. *Beginning With O.* New Haven: Yale University Press, 1977.

Brown, Linda. "Dark Horse: A View of Writing and Publishing by Dark Lesbians." *Sinister Wisdom* 13 (Spring 1980): 42–50.

Brown, Rita Mae. *Rubyfruit Jungle.* New York: Bantam Books, 1973.

———. *A Plain Brown Rapper.* Oakland, Calif.: Diana Press, 1976.

———. *Six of One.* New York: Bantam Books, 1979.

Bulkin, Elly. "Racism and Writing: Some Implications for White Lesbian Critics." *Sinister Wisdom* 13 (Spring 1980): 3–22.

———. "Heterosexism and Women's Studies." *Radical Teacher* 17 (Winter 1981): 25–31.

Bulkin, Elly, and Joan Larkin, eds. *Lesbian Poetry: An Anthology.* Watertown, Mass.: Persephone Press, 1981.

Bunch, Charlotte. "Learning From Lesbian Separatism." In *Lavender Culture,* edited by Karla Jay and Allen Young, pp. 433–44. New York: Jove Publications, 1979.

Byrd, Stephanie. *25 Years of Malcontent.* Boston: Good Gay Poets Press, 1976.

Califia, Pat. *Sapphistry: The Book of Lesbian Sexuality.* Tallahassee, Fla.: Naiad Press, 1980.

Cliff, Michelle. "Notes on Speechlessness." *Sinister Wisdom* 5 (Spring 1978): 5–9.

———. *Claiming an Identity They Taught Me to Despise.* Watertown, Mass.: Persephone Press, 1980.

Cook, Blanche Wiesen. "Female Support Networks and Political Activism: Lillian Wald, Crystal Eastman, Emma Goldman." *Chrysalis* 3 (1977), pp. 43–61.

———. "Women Alone Stir My Imagination: Lesbianism in the Cultural Tradition." *Signs: Journal of Women in Culture and Society* 4 (Summer 1979): 718–39.

Cornwell, Anita. "To a Bamboozled Soul Sister." *Sinister Wisdom* 3 (Spring 1977): 46–48.

Covina, Gina, and Laurel Galena, eds. *The Lesbian Reader.* Oakland, Calif.: Amazon Press, 1977.

Cruikshank, Margaret, ed. *The Lesbian Path.* Monterey, Calif.: Angel Press, 1980.

Cruikshank, Margaret, ed. *Lesbian Studies: Present and Future.* Old Westbury, N.Y.: Feminist Press, 1982.

de Monteflores, Carmen, and Stephen Schultz. "Coming Out: Similarities and Differences for Lesbians and Gay Men." *Journal of Social Issues* 34 (Summer 1978): 59–72.

Deming, Barbara. *We Cannot Live Without Our Lives.* New York: Viking, 1974.

Dobkin, Alix. *Alix Dobkin's Adventures in Women's Music.* Preston Hollow, N.Y.: Tomato Publications, 1979.

Escamilla-Mondanaro, Josette. "Lesbians and Therapy." In *Psychotherapy for Women: Treatment Toward Equality,* edited by Edna Rawlings and Dianne Carter, pp. 256–65. Springfield, Ill.: Charles C. Thomas, 1977.

Ettore, E. M. *Lesbians, Women and Society.* London: Routledge & Kegan Paul, 1980.

Faderman, Lillian. *Surpassing the Love of Men: Romantic Friendship and Love Between Women from the Renaissance to the Present.* New York: William Morrow, 1981.

Fairchild, Betty, and Nancy Hayward. *Now That You Know: What Every Parent Should Know About Homosexuality.* New York: Harcourt Brace Jovanovich, 1979.

Falk, Ruth. *Women Loving.* New York: Random House, 1975.

Gagnon, John; Suzanne Keller; Ronald Lawson; Patricia Miller; William Simon; and Joan Huber. "Report of the American Sociological Association's Task Group on Homosexuality." *American Sociologist* 17 (August 1982): 164–80.

Gearhart, Sally Miller. *The Wanderground.* Watertown, Mass.: Persephone Press, 1979.

Gibbs, Joan, and Sara Bennett, eds. *Top Ranking: A Collection of Articles on Racism and Classism in the Lesbian Community.* Brooklyn, N.Y.: February 3rd Press, 1980.

Grahn, Judy. *The Work of a Common Woman: The Collected Poetry of Judy Grahn, 1964–1977.* Oakland, Calif.: Diana Press, 1978.

Grier, Barbara, and Coletta Reid, eds. *The Lavender Herring: Lesbian Essays From The Ladder.* Baltimore, Md.: Diana Press, 1976.

Grier, Barbara, and Coletta Reid, eds. *The Lesbians' Home Journal: Stories From The Ladder.* Oakland, Calif.: Diana Press, 1976.

Grier, Barbara, Jan Watson, and Robin Jordan, eds. *The Lesbian in Literature: A Bibliography.* Tallahassee, Fla.: Naiad Press, 1981.

Hart, John, and Diane Richardson, eds. *The Theory and Practice of Homosexuality.* London: Routledge & Kegan Paul, 1981.

Heyward, Carter. "Coming Out: Journey Without Maps." *Christianity and Crisis,* 11 June 1979, pp. 153–56.

Hidalgo, Hilda, and Elia Hidalgo-Christensen. "The Puerto Rican Lesbian and the Puerto Rican Community." *Journal of Homosexuality* 2 (Winter 1976): 109–21.

Hitchens, Donna. "Social Attitudes, Legal Standards, and Personal Trauma in Child Custody Cases." *Journal of Homosexuality* 5 (Fall–Winter 1979/80): 89–96.

Hodges, Beth. "Interview with Joan and Deborah of the Lesbian Herstory Archives." *Sinister Wisdom* 11 (Fall 1979): 3–13. Part 2, *Sinister Wisdom* 13 (Spring 1980): 101–5.

Humphreys, Laud. *Out of the Closets: The Sociology of Homosexual Liberation.* Englewood Cliffs, N.J.: Prentice-Hall, 1972.

Jay, Karla, and Allen Young. *The Gay Report: Lesbians and Gay Men Speak Out About Sexual Experiences and Lifestyles.* New York: Summit Books, 1979.

Jay, Karla, and Allen Young, eds. *After You're Out.* New York: Pyramid Publications, 1977.

Jay, Karla, and Allen Young, eds. *Out of the Closets: Voices of Gay Liberation.* New York: Jove Publications, 1977.

Jay, Karla, and Allen Young, eds. *Lavender Culture.* New York: Jove Publications, 1979.

Johnson, Susan R.; Susan Guenther; Douglas W. Laube; and William Keettel. "Factors Influencing Lesbian Gynecologic Care: A Preliminary Study." *American Journal of Obstetrics and Gynecology* 140 (1 May 1981): 20–28.

Johnston, Jill. *Lesbian Nation: The Feminist Solution.* New York: Simon & Schuster, 1973.

Jumpcut 24/25 (March 1981). Special section on Lesbians and Film.

Katz, Jonathan. *Gay American History: Lesbians and Gay Men in the U.S.A.* New York: Thomas Y. Crowell, 1976.

Kaye, Melanie. *We Speak in Code.* Pittsburgh: Motheroot Publications, 1980.

Klaich, Dolores. *Woman Plus Woman: Attitudes Toward Lesbianism.* New York: William Morrow, 1974.

Koedt, Anne, Ellen Levine, and Anita Rapone, eds. *Radical Feminism.* New York: Quadrangle Books, 1973.

Krestan, Jo-Ann, and Claudia Bepko. "The Problem of Fusion in the Lesbian Relationship." *Family Process* 19 (1980): 277–89.

Krieger, Susan. "Lesbian Identity and Community: Recent Social Science Literature." *Signs: Journal of Women in Culture and Society* 8 (Autumn 1982): 91–108.

———. *The Mirror Dance: Identity in a Women's Community.* Philadelphia: Temple University Press, 1983.

Lewis, Sasha Gregory. *Sunday's Women: A Report on Lesbian Life Today.* Boston: Beacon Press, 1979.

Lorde, Audre. "Scratching the Surface: Some Notes on Barriers to Women and Loving." *The Black Scholar* 9 (April 1978): 31–35.

———. *The Black Unicorn.* New York: W. W. Norton, 1978.

———. "I've Been Standing on This Street Corner a Hell of a Long Time!" In *Our Right to Love: A Lesbian Resource Book,* edited by Ginny Vida, pp. 222–25. Englewood Cliffs, N.J.: Prentice-Hall, 1978.

———. "Man Child: A Black Lesbian Feminist's Response." *Conditions: Four* (Winter 1979): 30–36.

———. "Breast Cancer: A Black Lesbian Feminist Experience." *Sinister Wisdom* 10 (Summer 1979): 44–61.

———. *The Cancer Journals.* Argyle, N.Y.: Spinsters Ink, 1980.

Martin, Del, and Phyllis Lyon. *Lesbian/Woman.* San Francisco: Glide Publications, 1972.

McDaniel, Judith, et al. "We Were Fired: Lesbian Experiences in Academe." *Sinister Wisdom* 20 (Spring 1982): 30–43.

Moraga, Cherríe, and Gloria Anzaldúa, eds. *This Bridge Called My Back: Writings by Radical Women of Color.* Watertown, Mass.: Persephone Press, 1981.

Morin, Stephen. "Heterosexual Bias in Psychological Research on Lesbianism and Male Homosexuality." *American Psychologist* 32 (1977): 629–37.

Moses, Alice E. *Identity Management in Lesbian Women.* New York: Praeger, 1978.

Moses, A. Elfin, and Robert O. Hawkins, Jr. *Counseling Lesbian Women and Gay Men: A Life-Issues Approach.* St. Louis: C. V. Mosby, 1982.

Myron, Nancy, and Charlotte Bunch, eds. *Lesbianism and the Women's Movement.* Oakland, Calif.: Diana Press, 1975.

Nardi, Peter M. "Alcohol Treatment and the Non-Traditional Family Structures of Gays and Lesbians." *Journal of Alcohol and Drug Education* 27 (Winter 1982): 83–89.

———. "Alcoholism and Homosexuality: A Theoretical Perspective." *Journal of Homosexuality* 7 (Summer 1982): 9–25.

Nestle, Joan. "I Didn't Go Back There Anymore: Mabel Hampton Talks About the South." *Feminary* 10 (1977): 6–16.

———. "Surviving and More: Interview with Mabel Hampton." *Sinister Wisdom* 10 (Summer 1979): 19–24.

———. "Butch-Fem Relationships: Sexual Courage in the 1950's." *Heresies* 3 (1981): 21–24.

Nomadic Sisters. *Loving Women.* 2d ed. Sonora, Calif.: The Nomadic Sisters, 1976.

Oberstone, Andrea, and Harriet Sukoneck. "Psychological Adjustment and Life Style of Single Lesbians and Single Heterosexual Women." *Psychology of Women Quarterly* 2 (Winter 1976): 172–88.

O'Donnell, Mary. "Lesbian Health Care: Issues and Literature." *Science for the People,* May/June 1978, pp. 8–19.

O'Donnell, Mary; Kater Pollock; Val Leoffler; and Ziesel Saunders. *Lesbian Health Matters!* Santa Cruz, Calif.: Santa Cruz Women's Health Collective, 1979.

Pagelow, Mildred. "Heterosexual and Lesbian Single Mothers: A Comparison of Problems, Coping, and Solutions." *Journal of Homosexuality* 5 (September 1980): 189–204.

Painter, Dorothy S. "Lesbian Humor as a Normalization Device." In *Communication, Language, and Sex: Proceedings from the First Annual Conference,* edited by Virginia A. Eman and Cynthia L. Berryman, pp. 132–48. Rowley, Mass.: Newbury, 1980.

Parker, Pat. *Movement in Black: The Collected Poetry of Pat Parker, 1961–1978.* Oakland, Calif.: Diana Press, 1978.

Paul, William; James D. Weinrich; John C. Gonsiorek; and Mary E. Hotvedt, eds. *Homosexuality: Social, Psychological, and Biological Issues.* Beverly Hills, Calif.: Sage Publications, 1982.

Peplau, Letitia Anne; Susan Cochran; Karen Rook; and Christine Padesky. "Loving Women: Attachment and Autonomy in Lesbian Relationships." *Journal of Social Issues* 34 (Summer 1978): 7–27.

Peplau, Letitia Anne, and Steven L. Gordon. "The Intimate Relationships of Lesbians and Gay Men." In *Changing Boundaries: Gender Roles and Sexual Behavior,* edited by Elizabeth Rice Allgeier and Naomi B. McCormick, pp. 226–44. Palo Alto, Calif.: Mayfield, 1983.

Plummer, Kenneth. *Sexual Stigma: An Interactionist Account.* London: Routledge & Kegan Paul, 1975.

Ponse, Barbara. *Identities in the Lesbian World: The Social Construction of Self.* Westport, Conn.: Greenwood Press, 1978.

Potter, Sandra, and Trudy Darty. "Social Work and the Invisible Minority: An Exploration of Lesbianism." *Social Work* 26 (May 1981): 187–92.

Pratt, Minnie Bruce. *The Sound of One Fork: Poems.* Durham, N.C.: Night Heron Press, 1981.

Radicalesbians. "The Woman-Identified Woman." In *Radical Feminism,* edited by Anne Koedt, Ellen Levine, and Anita Rapone, pp. 240–45. New York: Quadrangle Books, 1973.

Rich, Adrienne. *Poems: Selected and New, 1950–1974.* New York: W. W. Norton, 1974.

———. *Of Woman Born.* New York: W. W. Norton, 1976.

———. *The Dream of a Common Language: Poems, 1974–1977.* New York: W. W. Norton, 1978.

———. *On Lies, Secrets, and Silence: Selected Prose, 1966–1978.* New York: W. W. Norton, 1979.

———. *A Wild Patience Has Taken Me This Far: Poems 1978–1981.* New York: W. W. Norton, 1981.

Riddle, Dorothy, and Barbara Sang. "Psychotherapy With Lesbians." *Journal of Social Issues* 34 (Summer 1978): 34–100.

Roberts, J. R. *Black Lesbians: An Annotated Bibliography.* Tallahassee, Fla.: Naiad Press, 1981.

Rule, Jane. *Lesbian Images.* Garden City: Doubleday, 1975.

Sang, Barbara. "Psychotherapy with Lesbians: Some Observations and Tentative Generalizations." In *Psychotherapy for Women: Treatment Toward Equality,* edited by Edna Rawlings and Dianne Carter, pp. 266–75. Springfield, Ill.: Charles C. Thomas, 1977.

Schneider, Beth. "Consciousness About Sexual Harassment Among Heterosexual and Lesbian Women Workers." *Journal of Social Issues* 38 (December 1982): 75–95.

Schwarz, Judith. "Researching Lesbian History." *Sinister Wisdom* 5 (Spring 1978): 55–59.

———. "On Being Physically Different." *Sinister Wisdom* 7 (Fall 1978): 41–50.

———. "Yellow Clover: Katharine Lee Bates and Katharine Coman." *Frontiers* 4 (Spring 1979): 59–67.

———. "Lesbian Photography." In *Eye to Eye: Portraits of Lesbians,* photographs by JEB, pp. 7–11. Washington, D.C.: Glad Hag Books, 1979.

———. *Radical Feminists of Heterodoxy.* Lebanon, N.H.: New Victoria Publishers, 1982.

Schwarz, Judith, special consulting editor. "Lesbian History Issue." *Frontiers: A Journal of Women Studies* 4 (Fall 1979).

Shockley, Ann. *Loving Her.* New York: Avon Books, 1974.

———. *The Black and White of It.* Tallahassee, Fla.: Naiad Press, 1980.

———. *Say Jesus and Come to Me.* New York: Avon Books, 1982.

Simpson, Ruth. *From the Closets to the Courts.* New York: Viking Press, 1976.

Sisley, Emily L. "Notes on Lesbian Theatre." *The Drama Review* 25 (March 1981): 47–56.

Sisley, Emily L., and Bertha Harris. *The Joy of Lesbian Sex.* New York: Crown Books, 1977.

Smith, Barbara, ed. *Home Girls: A Black Feminist Anthology.* Watertown, Mass.: Persephone Press, 1983.

Smith, Barbara, and Beverly Smith. "I Am Not Meant To Be Alone Without You Who Understands: Letters from Black Feminists, 1972–1978." *Conditions: Four* (Winter 1979): 62–77.

Smith-Rosenberg, Carroll. "The Female World of Love and Ritual: Relations Between Women in Nineteenth-Century America." *Signs: A Journal of Women in Culture and Society* 1 (Fall 1975): 1–29.

Stanley, Julia Penelope, and Susan J. Wolfe, eds. *The Coming Out Stories.* Watertown, Mass.: Persephone Press, 1980.

Sternburg, Janet, ed. *The Writer on Her Work.* New York: W. W. Norton, 1980.

Tanner, Donna. *The Lesbian Couple.* Lexington, Mass.: Lexington Books, 1978.

Task Force on the Status of Lesbian and Gay Male Psychologists. *Removing the Stigma: Final Report of the Board of Social and Ethical Responsibility.* Washington, D.C.: American Psychological Association, 1979.

Vida, Ginny, ed. *Our Right to Love: A Lesbian Resource Book.* Englewood Cliffs, N.J.: Prentice-Hall, 1978.

Whyte, John, and Lisa Capaldini. "Treating the Lesbian or Gay Patient." *Delaware Medical Journal* 52 (May 1980): 271–80.

Wirth, Scott. "Coming Out Close to Home: Principles for Psychotherapy with Families of Lesbians and Gay Men." *Catalyst: A Socialist Journal of the Social Services* 1 (1979): 6–23.

Wittig, Monique. *The Lesbian Body.* New York: William Morrow, 1975.

Wittig, Monique, and Sande Zeig. *Lesbian People: Material for a Dictionary.* New York: Avon Books, 1979.

Wolf, Deborah Goleman. *The Lesbian Community.* Berkeley: University of California Press, 1979.

Woodman, Natalie J., and Harry R. Lenna. *Counseling With Gay Men and Women: A Guide for Facilitating Positive Life-Styles.* San Francisco: Jossey-Bass, 1980.

Zimmerman, Bonnie. "Lesbianism 101." *Radical Teacher* 17 (Spring 1981): 20–24.

———. "What Has Never Been: An Overview of Lesbian Feminist Literary Criticism." *Feminist Studies* 7 (Fall 1981): 451–76.

Selected List of Lesbian Periodicals

Compiled by
DEBORAH EDEL AND
CLARE POTTER

Atlanta (earlier *ALFA Newsletter*). First issue, September 1973; monthly. Atlanta Lesbian Feminist Alliance, P.O. Box 5502, Atlanta, GA 30307.

Azalea: A Magazine for Third World Lesbians. First issue, Winter 1977/78; quarterly. C/o Linda Brown, 314 East 91st St., Apt. 5E, New York, NY 10028; or 306 Lafayette Avenue, Brooklyn, NY 11238.

Big Apple Dyke News. First issue, March 1981; monthly. B.A.D. News, 192 Spring Street #15, New York, NY 10012.

Common Lives/Lesbian Lives. First issue, August 1981; quarterly. P.O. Box 1553, Iowa City, IA 52244.

Conditions: A Magazine of Writing by Women with an Emphasis on Writing by Lesbians. First issue, 1977; quarterly. P.O. Box 56, Van Brunt Station, Brooklyn, NY 11215.

Feminary: Lesbian Feminist Journal for the South. First issue with a lesbian focus, October 1978; semiannually. P.O. Box 954, Chapel Hill, NC 27514.

Focus: A Journal for Lesbians (earlier *Maiden Voyage*). First issue, December 1969; bimonthly. Boston Daughters of Bilitis, 1151 Massachusetts Avenue, Cambridge, MA 02138.

In the Life: Newsletter of West Coast Lesbian Collections. First issue, Fall 1982; irregular publication. P.O. Box 23753, Oakland, CA 94623.

Lavender Prairie News. First issue, December 1976; monthly. P.O. Box 2096, Station A, Champaign, IL 61820.

Lesbe'informed. First issue, 1974; monthly. C/o Lesbian Resource Center, 2708 E. Lake Street, Suite 229/230, Minneapolis, MN 55406.

Lesbian Connection. First issue, November 1974; bimonthly. Helen Diner Memorial Women's Center/Ambitious Amazons, P.O. Box 811, East Lansing, MI 48823.

Lesbian Herstory Archives Newsletter. First issue, June 1975; monthly. P.O. Box 1258, New York, NY 10116.

The Lesbian Insider/Insighter/Inciter. First issue, 1980; monthly. P.O. Box 7038, Powderhorn Station, Minneapolis, MN 55407.

Lunatic Fringe: A Newsletter for Separatist, Anarchist, and Radical Feminist Lesbians in

Chicago. First issue, July 1980; bimonthly. C/o Sidney Spinster, 5201 S. Blackstone, 3W, Chicago, IL 60615.

Maine Lesbian Feminist Newsletter. First issue, 1979; monthly. P.O. Box 125, Belfast, ME 04915.

Matrices: A Lesbian Feminist Research Newsletter. First issue, Fall/Winter 1977/1978; thrice yearly. Julia Penelope (Stanley), University of Nebraska, Dept. of English, Lincoln, NE 68588.

Mom's Apple Pie: Lesbian Mother's National Defense Fund. First issue, November 1974; quarterly. 2446 Lorentz Place West, Seattle, WA 98109.

New Hampshire Lambda Newsletter. First issue, 1979; monthly. P.O. Box 1043, Concord, NH 03301.

Otherviews/Innerviews. First issue, December 1978; monthly. C/o Aradia, Inc., P.O. Box 7516, Grand Rapids, MI 49410.

Out and About: Seattle Lesbian/Feminist Newsletter. First issue, May 1976; monthly. 4535 Thackeray NE, Seattle, WA 98105.

Sinister Wisdom. First issue, July 1976; quarterly. P.O. Box 1023, Rockland, MA 04841.

Telewoman. First issue, 1978; monthly. C/o Anne, P.O. Box 2306, Pleasant Hill, CA 94523.